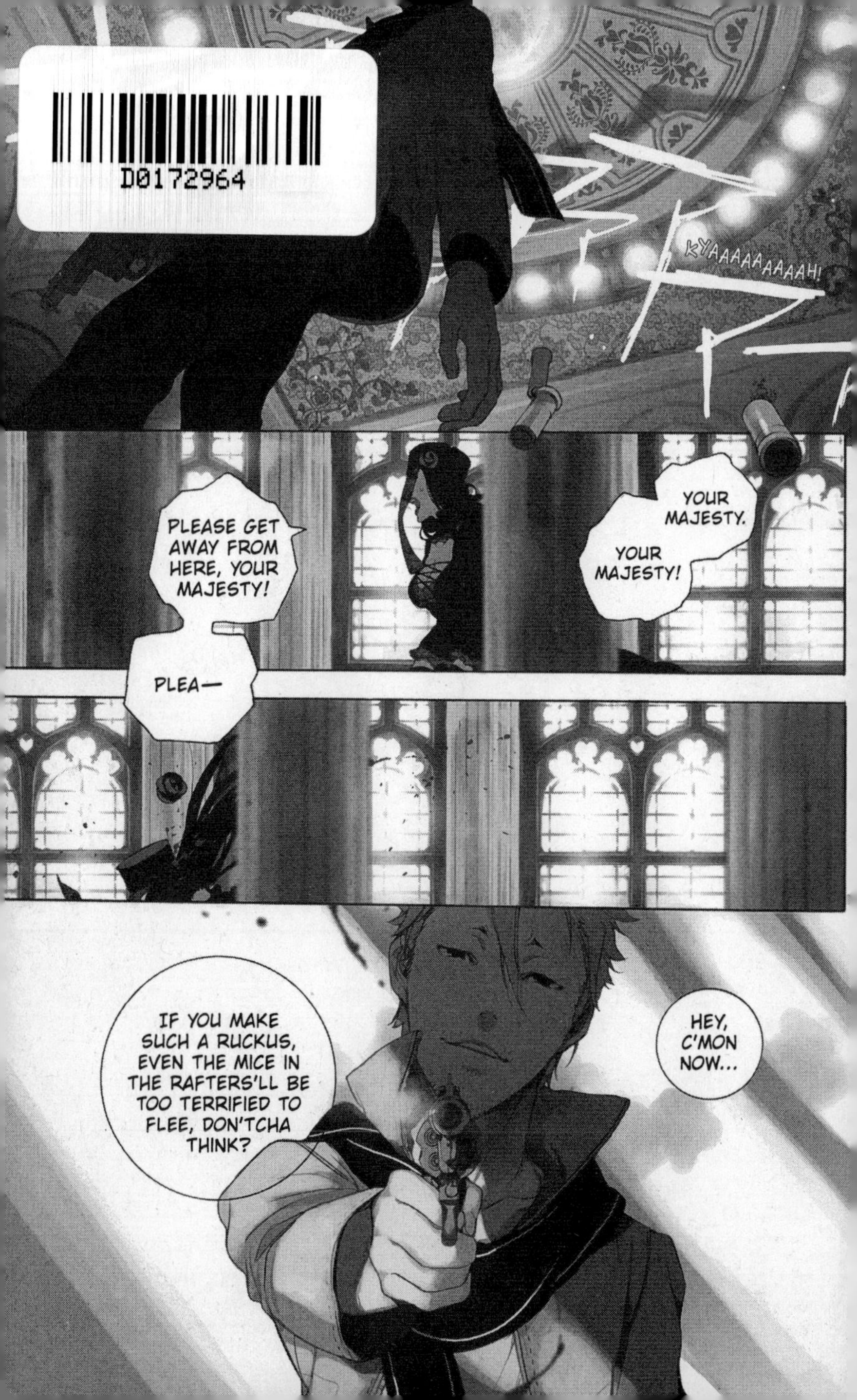
KYAAAAAAAAAH!
YOUR MAJESTY.
YOUR MAJESTY!
PLEASE GET AWAY FROM HERE, YOUR MAJESTY!
PLEA—
HEY, C'MON NOW...
IF YOU MAKE SUCH A RUCKUS, EVEN THE MICE IN THE RAFTERS'LL BE TOO TERRIFIED TO FLEE, DON'TCHA THINK?

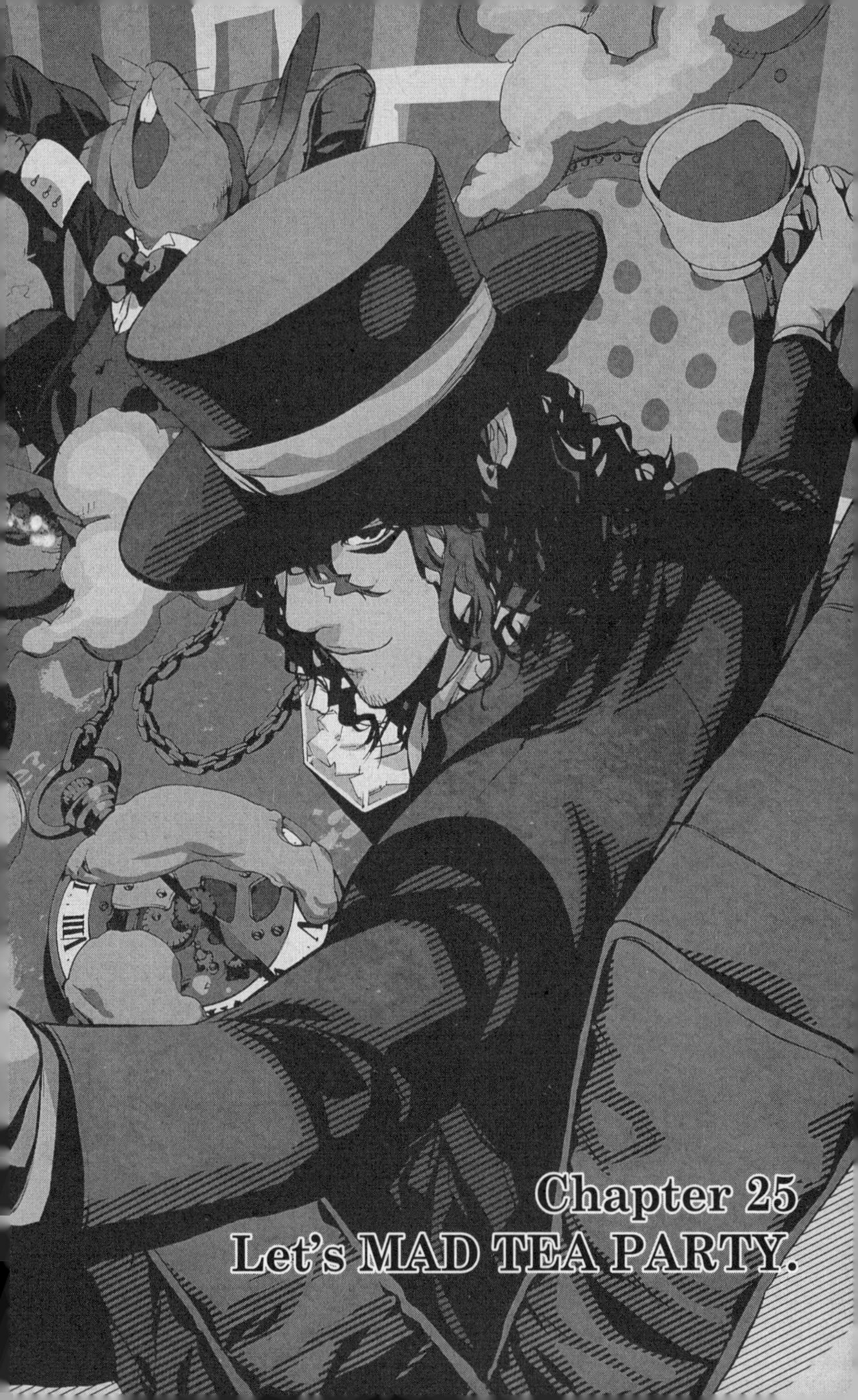
Chapter 25
Let's MAD TEA PARTY.

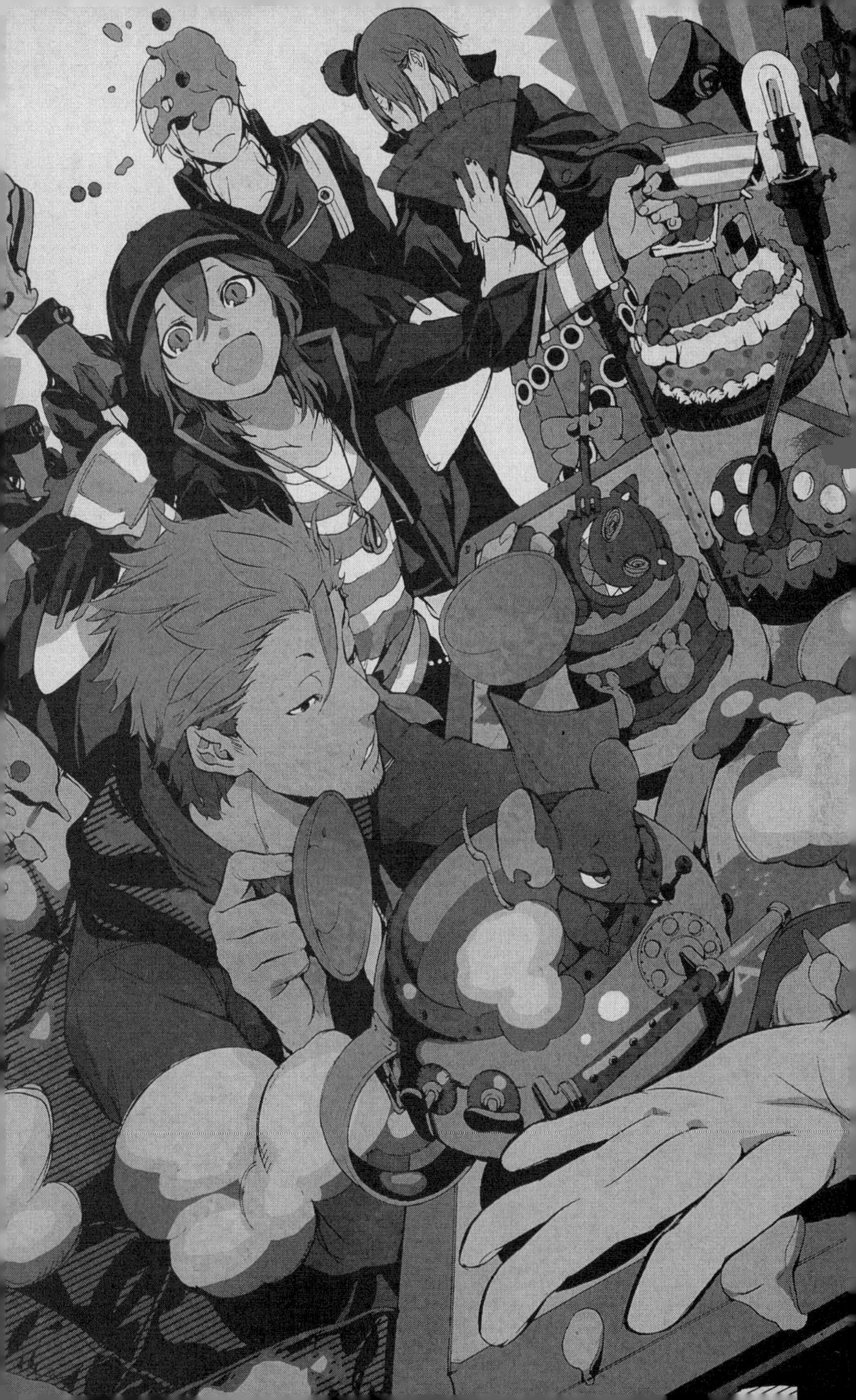

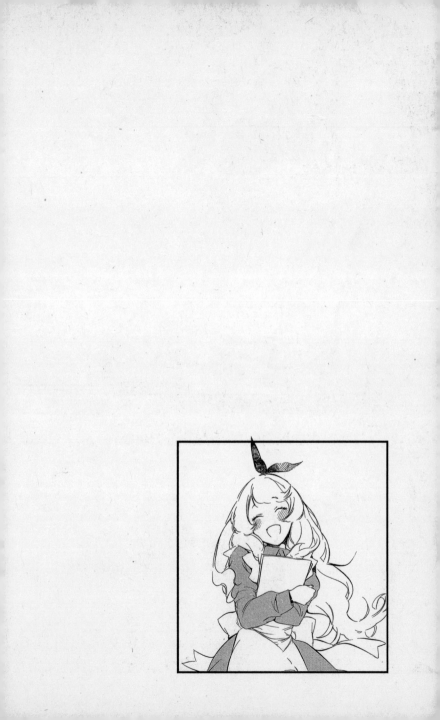

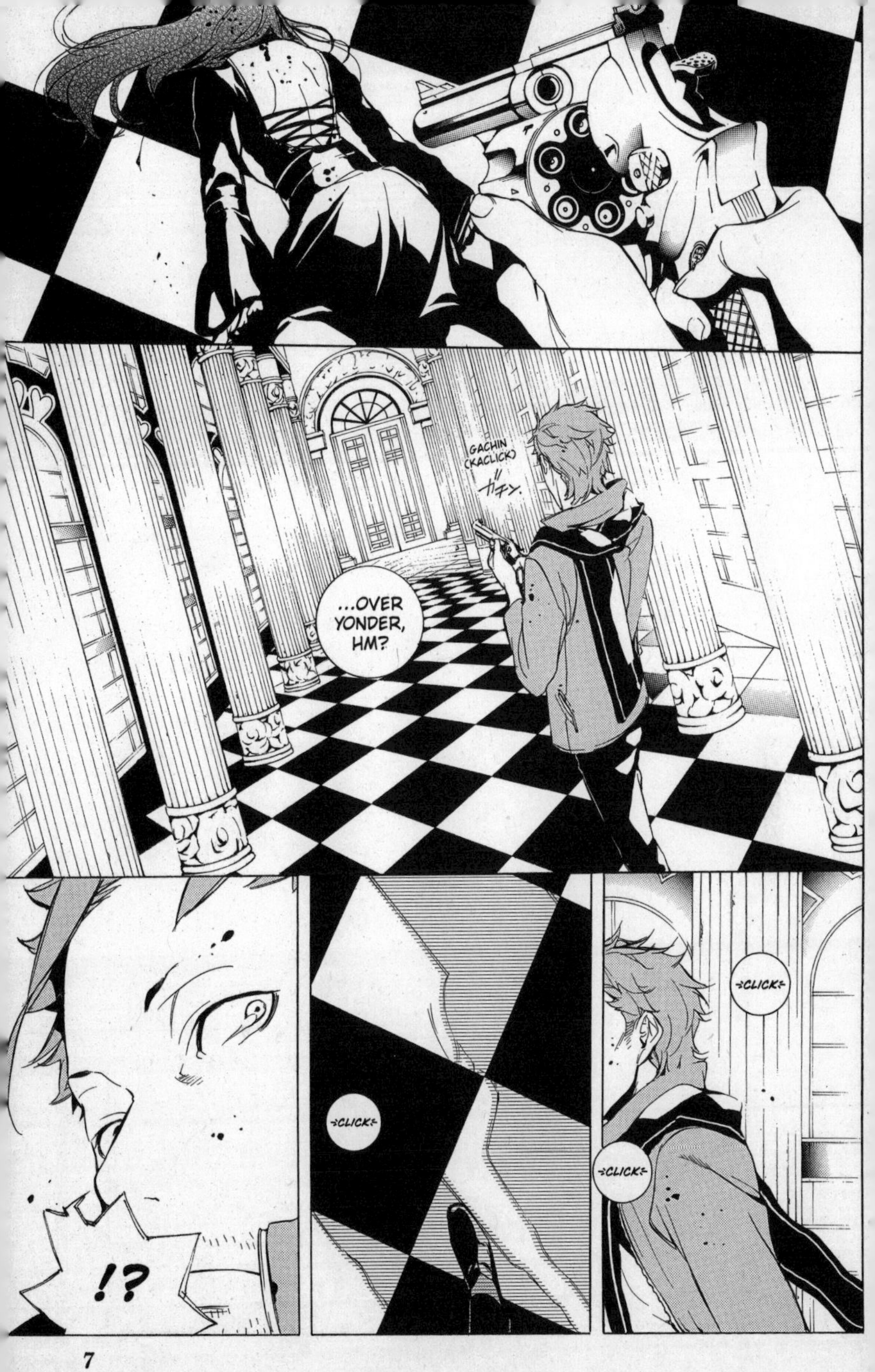
GACHIN (KACLICK)
ガチン
...OVER YONDER, HM?
CLICK
CLICK
CLICK
!?

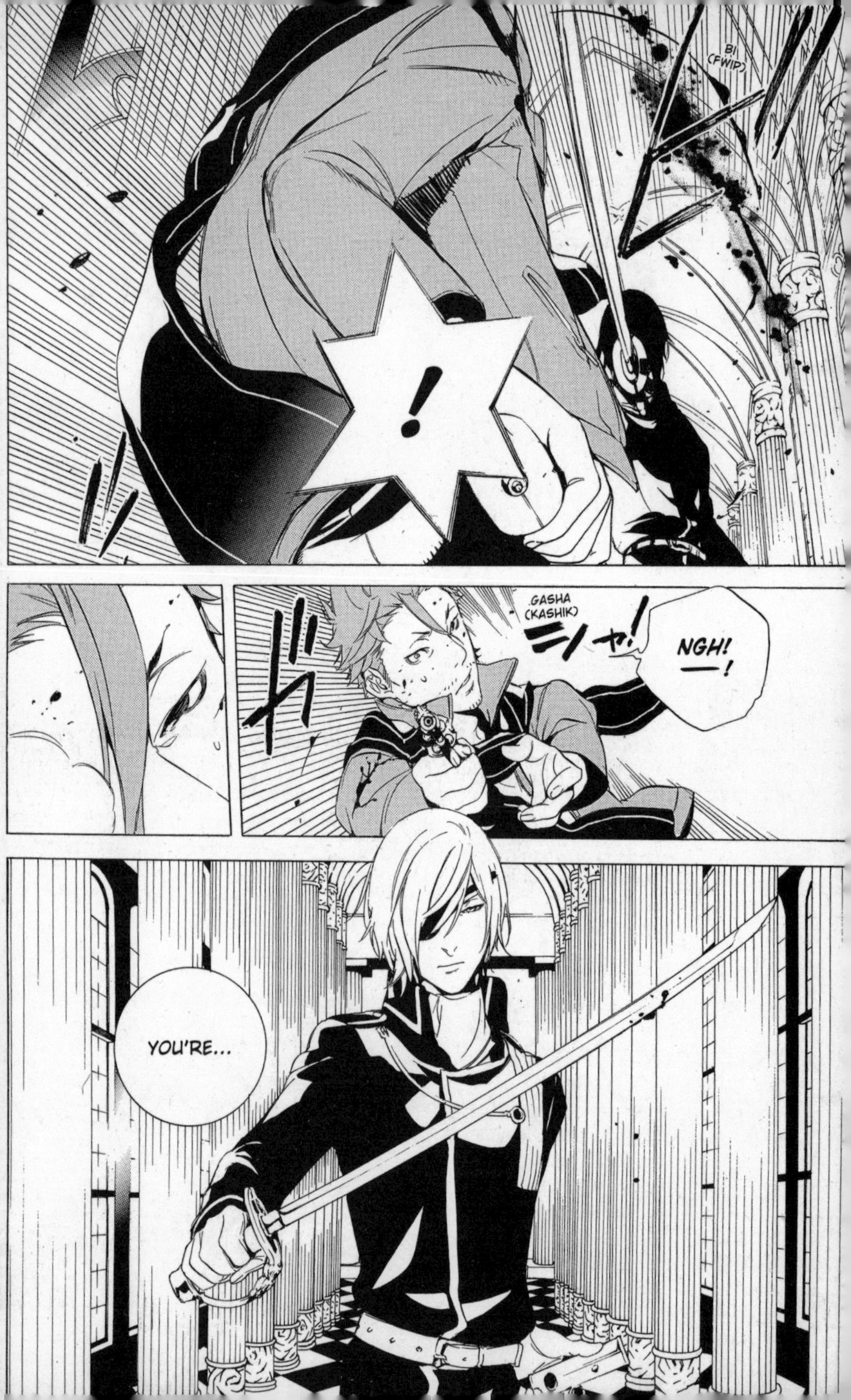
BI
(FWIP)
!
GASHA
(KASHIK)
NGH!
—!
YOU'RE...

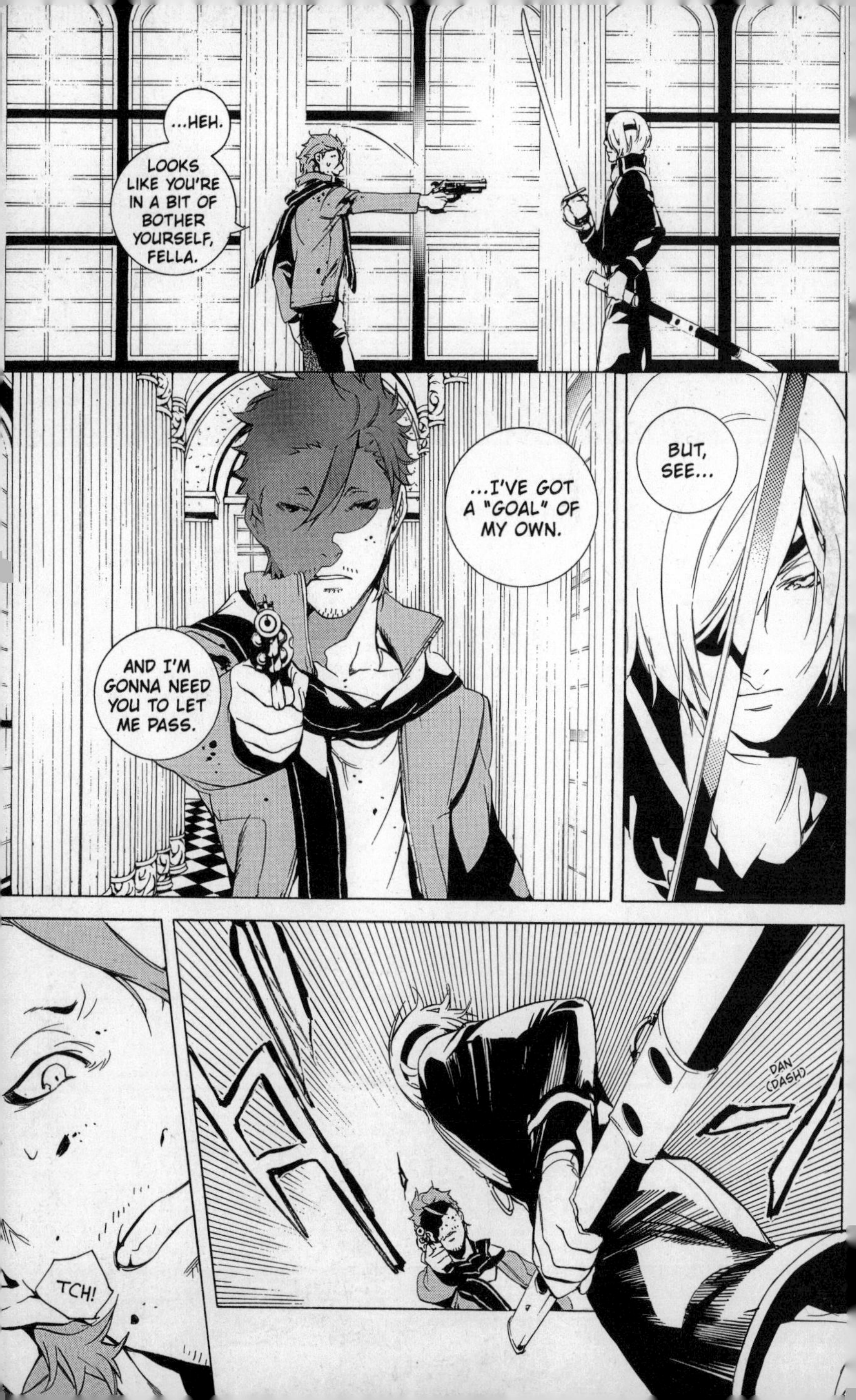
...HEH.
LOOKS LIKE YOU'RE IN A BIT OF BOTHER YOURSELF, FELLA.
BUT, SEE...
...I'VE GOT A "GOAL" OF MY OWN.
AND I'M GONNA NEED YOU TO LET ME PASS.
DAN (DASH)
TCH!

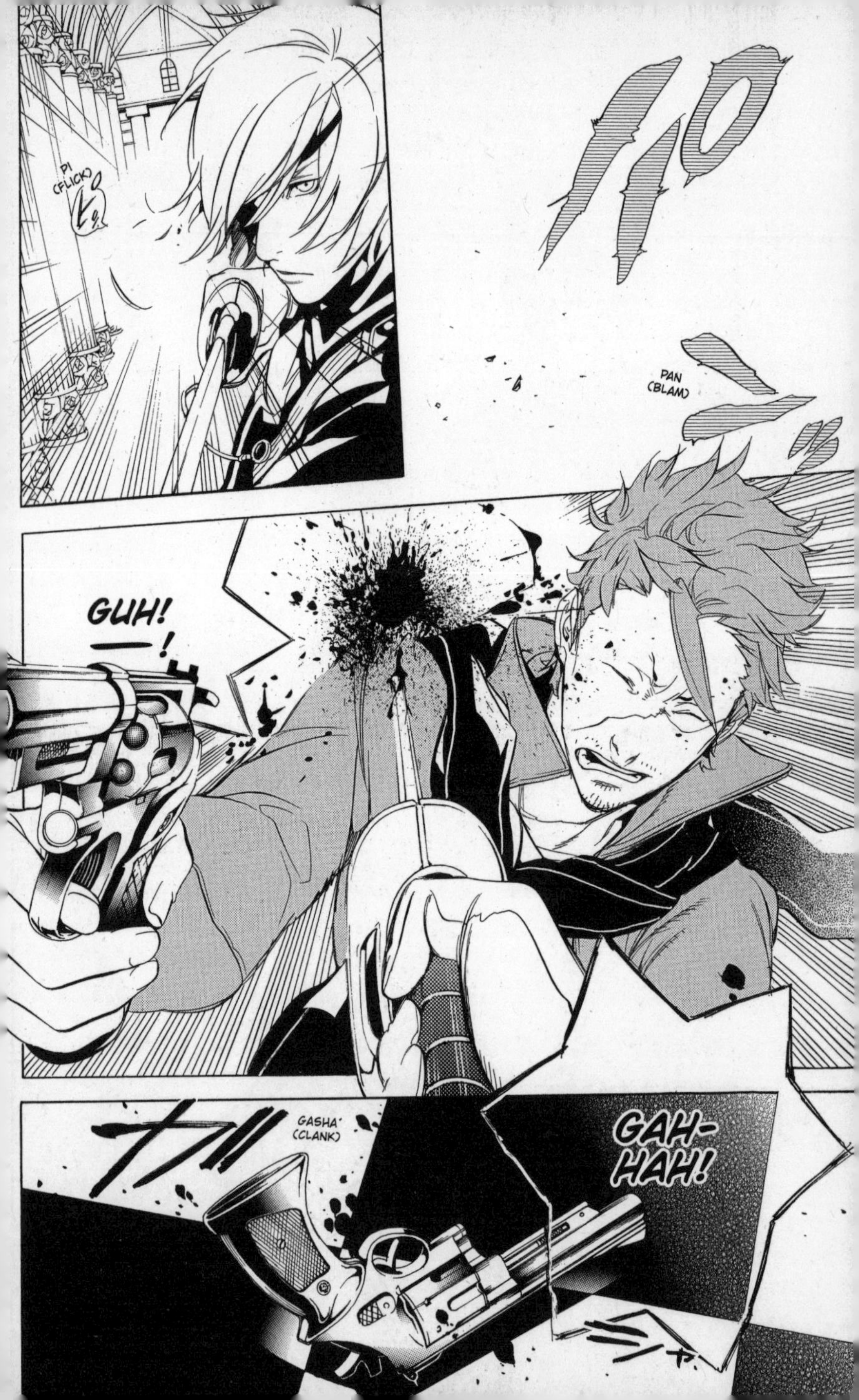
PI (FLICK)
PAN (BLAM)
GUH!
—!
GAH-HAH!
GASHA (CLANK)

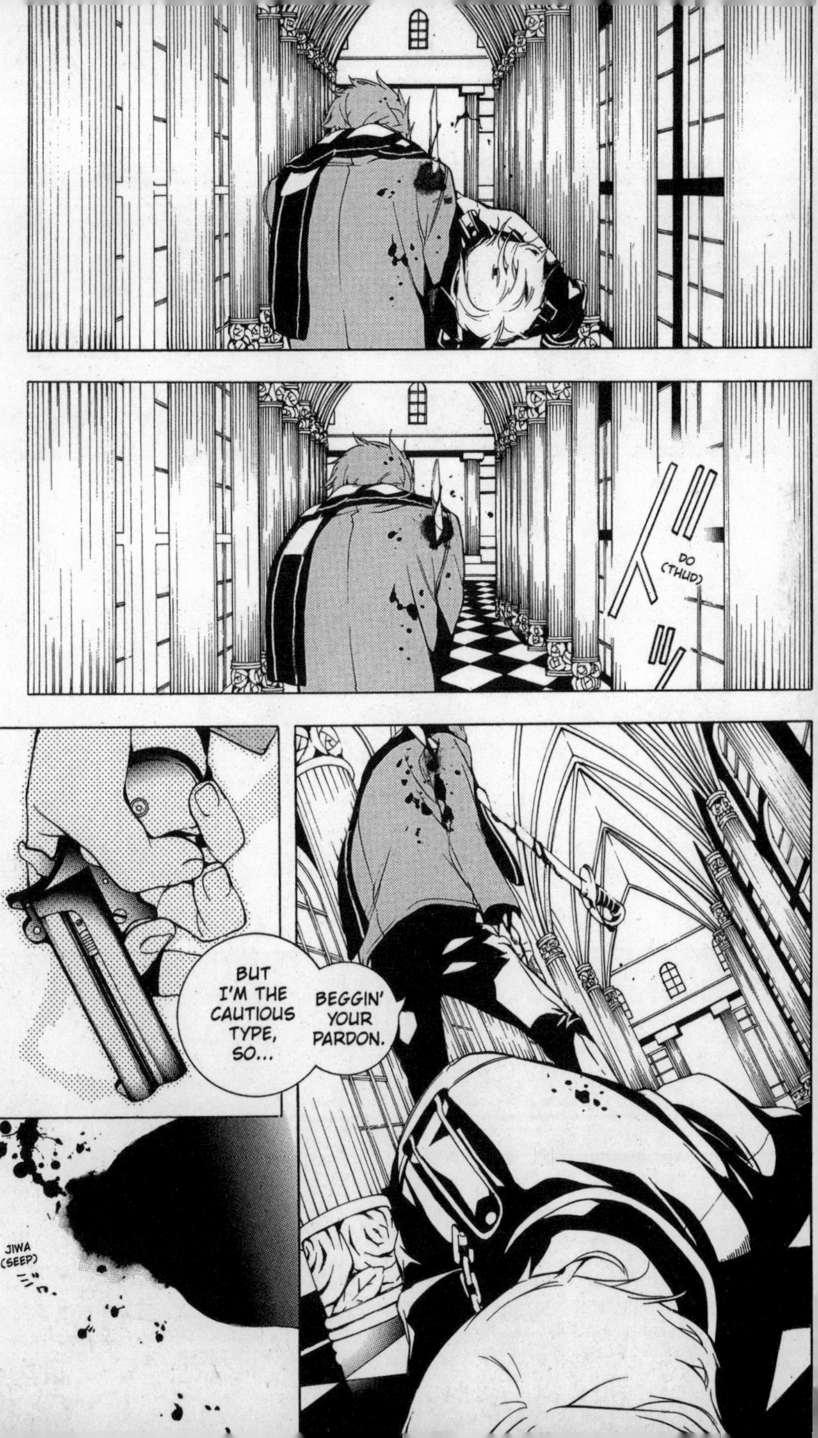
DO
(THUD)
BEGGIN' YOUR PARDON.
BUT I'M THE CAUTIOUS TYPE, SO...
JIWA
(SEEP)

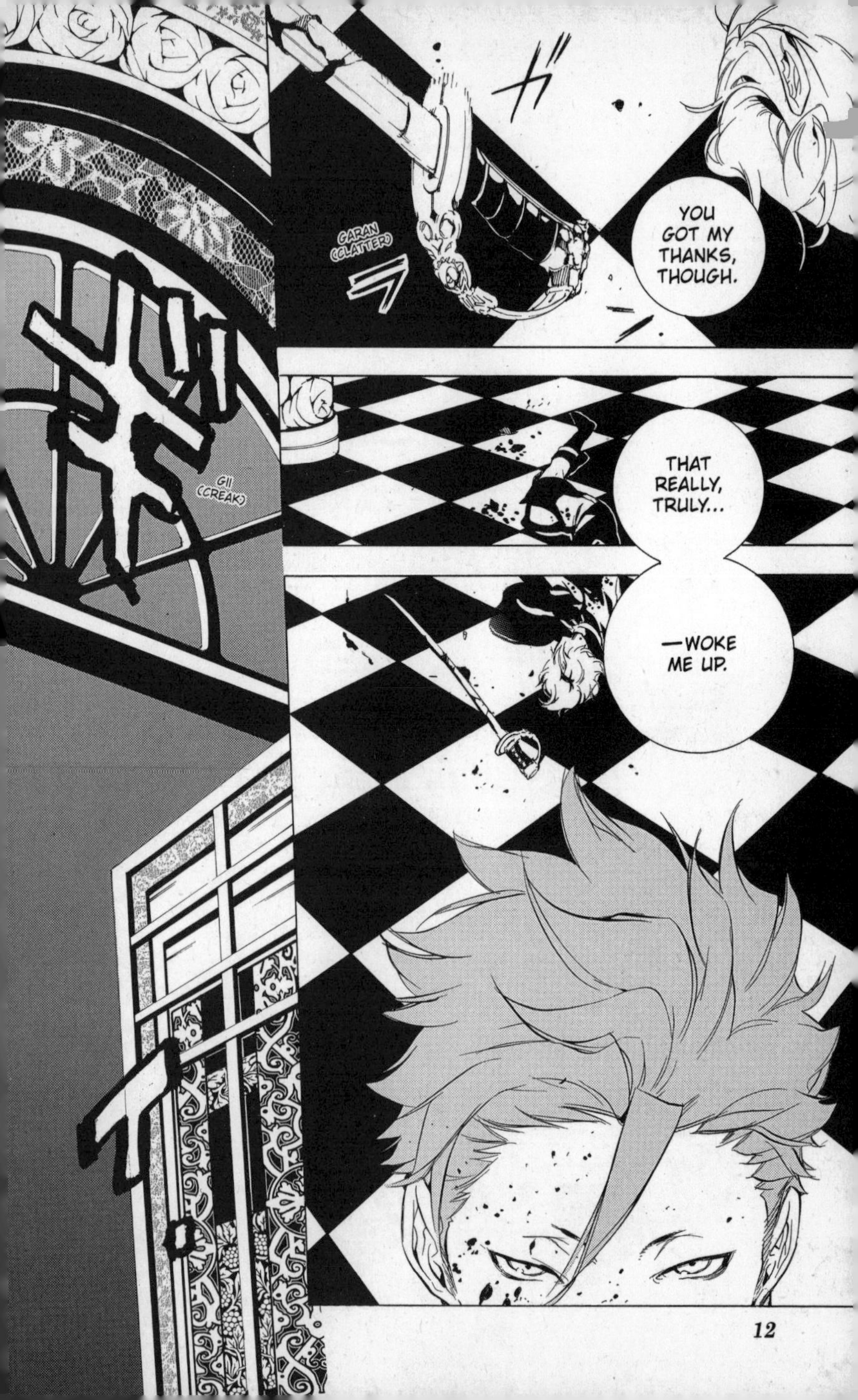
YOU GOT MY THANKS, THOUGH.
GARAN (CLATTER)
THAT REALLY, TRULY...
—WOKE ME UP.
GII (CREAK)

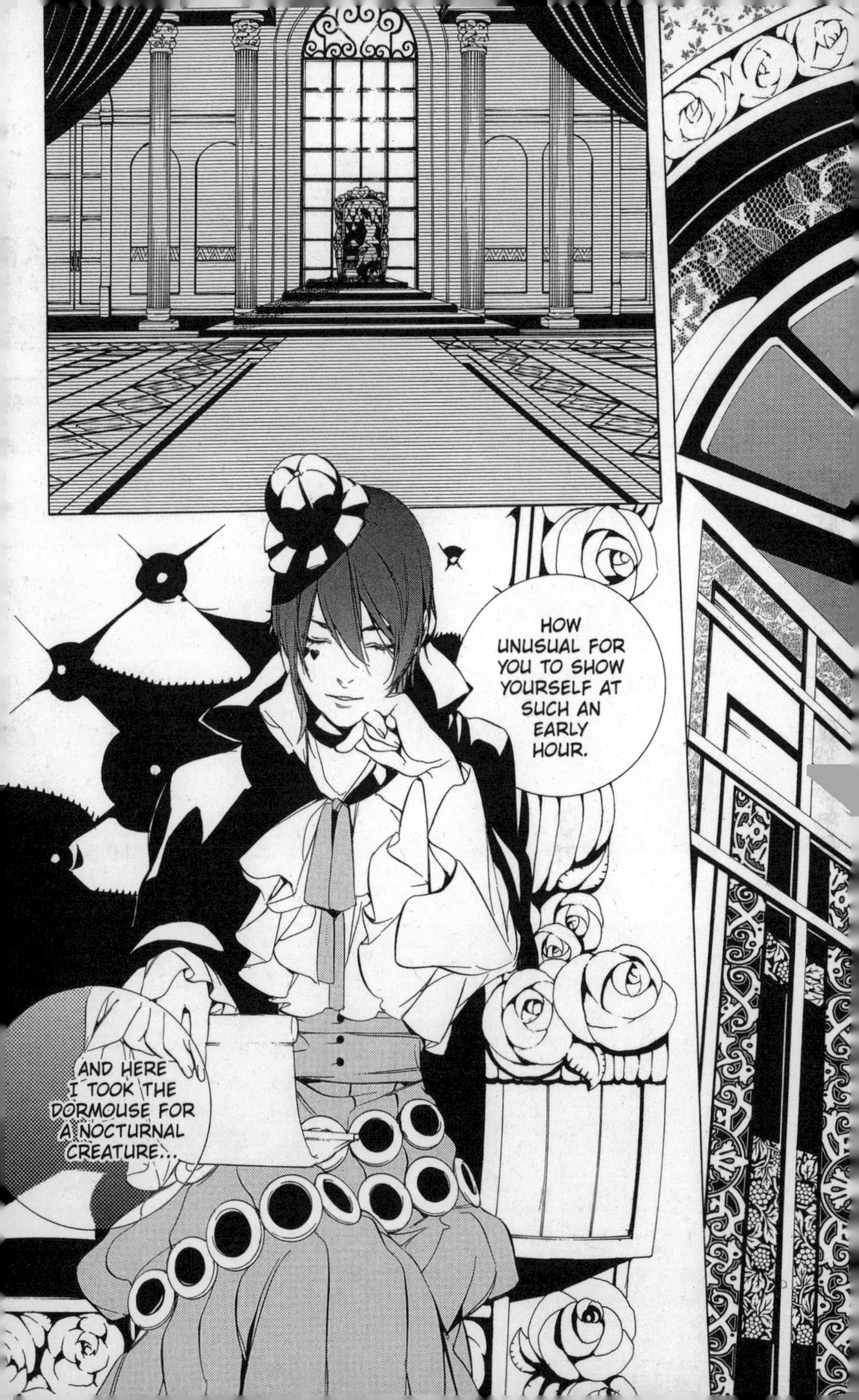
HOW UNUSUAL FOR YOU TO SHOW YOURSELF AT SUCH AN EARLY HOUR.
AND HERE I TOOK THE DORMOUSE FOR A NOCTURNAL CREATURE...

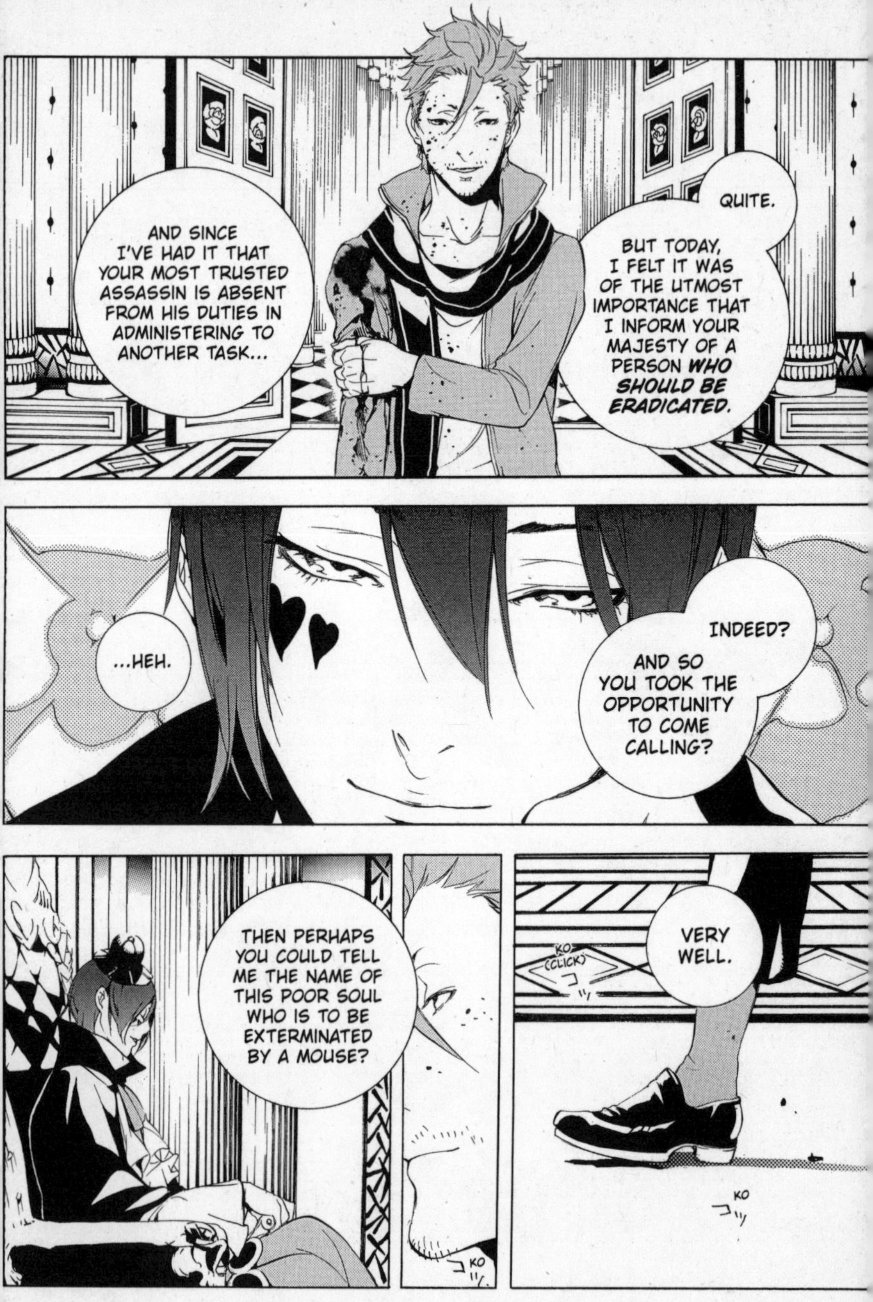
QUITE.
BUT TODAY, I FELT IT WAS OF THE UTMOST IMPORTANCE THAT I INFORM YOUR MAJESTY OF A PERSON *WHO SHOULD BE ERADICATED.*
AND SINCE I'VE HAD IT THAT YOUR MOST TRUSTED ASSASSIN IS ABSENT FROM HIS DUTIES IN ADMINISTERING TO ANOTHER TASK...
INDEED?
AND SO YOU TOOK THE OPPORTUNITY TO COME CALLING?
...HEH.
VERY WELL.
KO (CLICK)
KO
KO
THEN PERHAPS YOU COULD TELL ME THE NAME OF THIS POOR SOUL WHO IS TO BE EXTERMINATED BY A MOUSE?

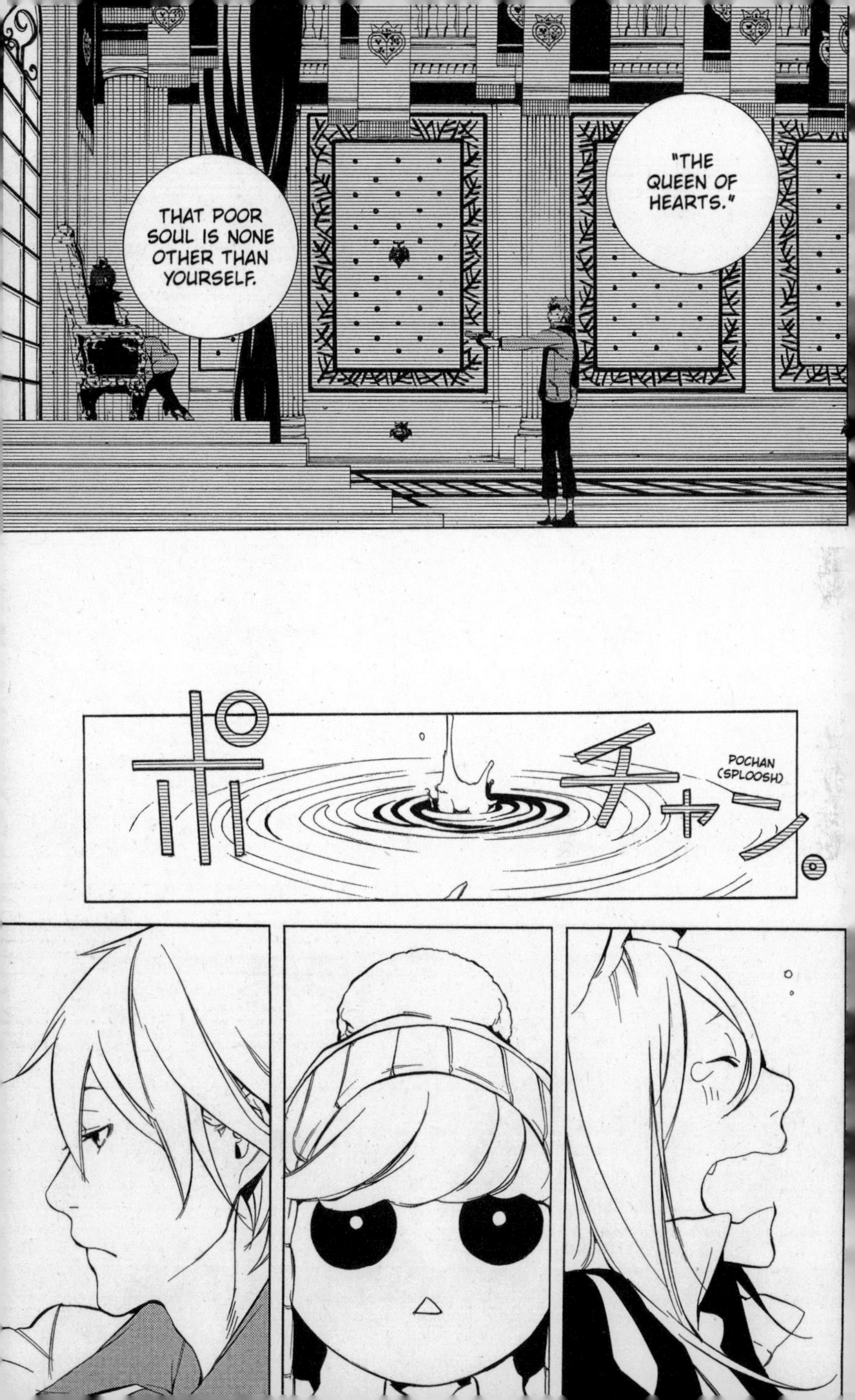
"THE QUEEN OF HEARTS."
THAT POOR SOUL IS NONE OTHER THAN YOURSELF.
ポチャーン。
POCHAN (SPLOOSH)

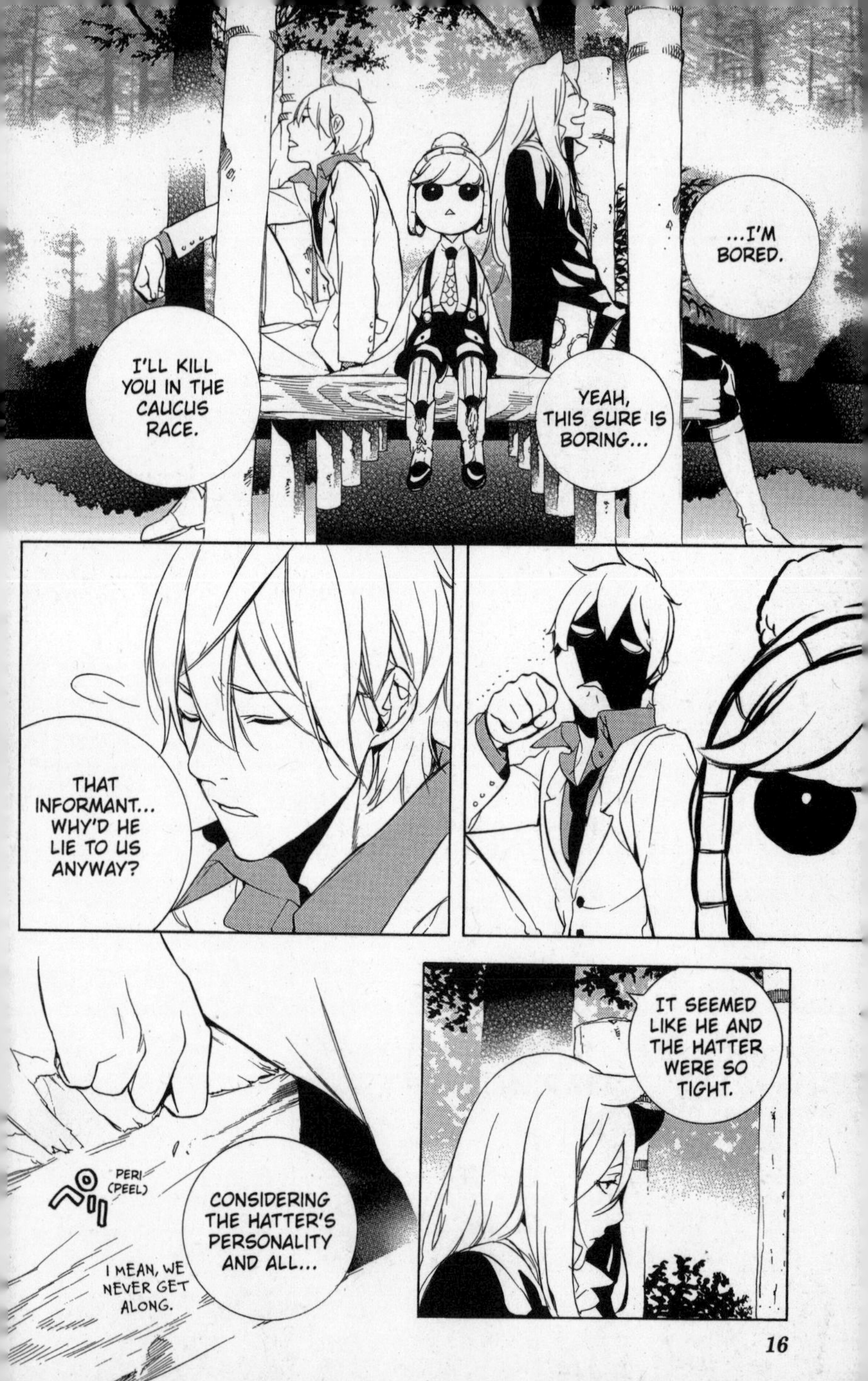
...I'M BORED.
YEAH, THIS SURE IS BORING...
I'LL KILL YOU IN THE CAUCUS RACE.
THAT INFORMANT... WHY'D HE LIE TO US ANYWAY?
IT SEEMED LIKE HE AND THE HATTER WERE SO TIGHT.
CONSIDERING THE HATTER'S PERSONALITY AND ALL...
PERI (PEEL)
I MEAN, WE NEVER GET ALONG.

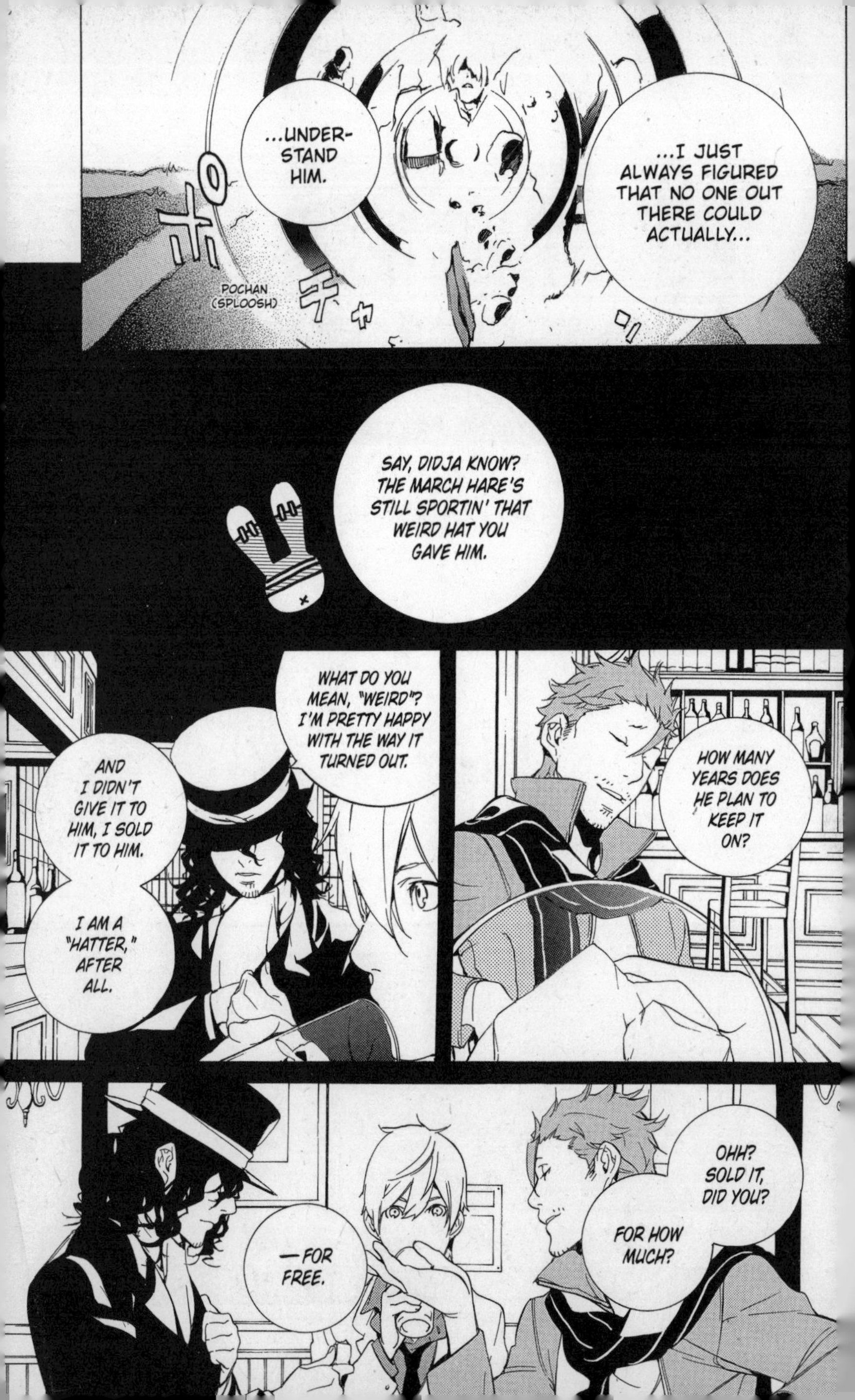
...I JUST ALWAYS FIGURED THAT NO ONE OUT THERE COULD ACTUALLY...
...UNDER-STAND HIM.
POCHAN (SPLOOSH)
SAY, DIDJA KNOW? THE MARCH HARE'S STILL SPORTIN' THAT WEIRD HAT YOU GAVE HIM.
HOW MANY YEARS DOES HE PLAN TO KEEP IT ON?
WHAT DO YOU MEAN, "WEIRD"? I'M PRETTY HAPPY WITH THE WAY IT TURNED OUT.
AND I DIDN'T GIVE IT TO HIM, I SOLD IT TO HIM.
I AM A "HATTER," AFTER ALL.
OHH? SOLD IT, DID YOU?
FOR HOW MUCH?
—FOR FREE.

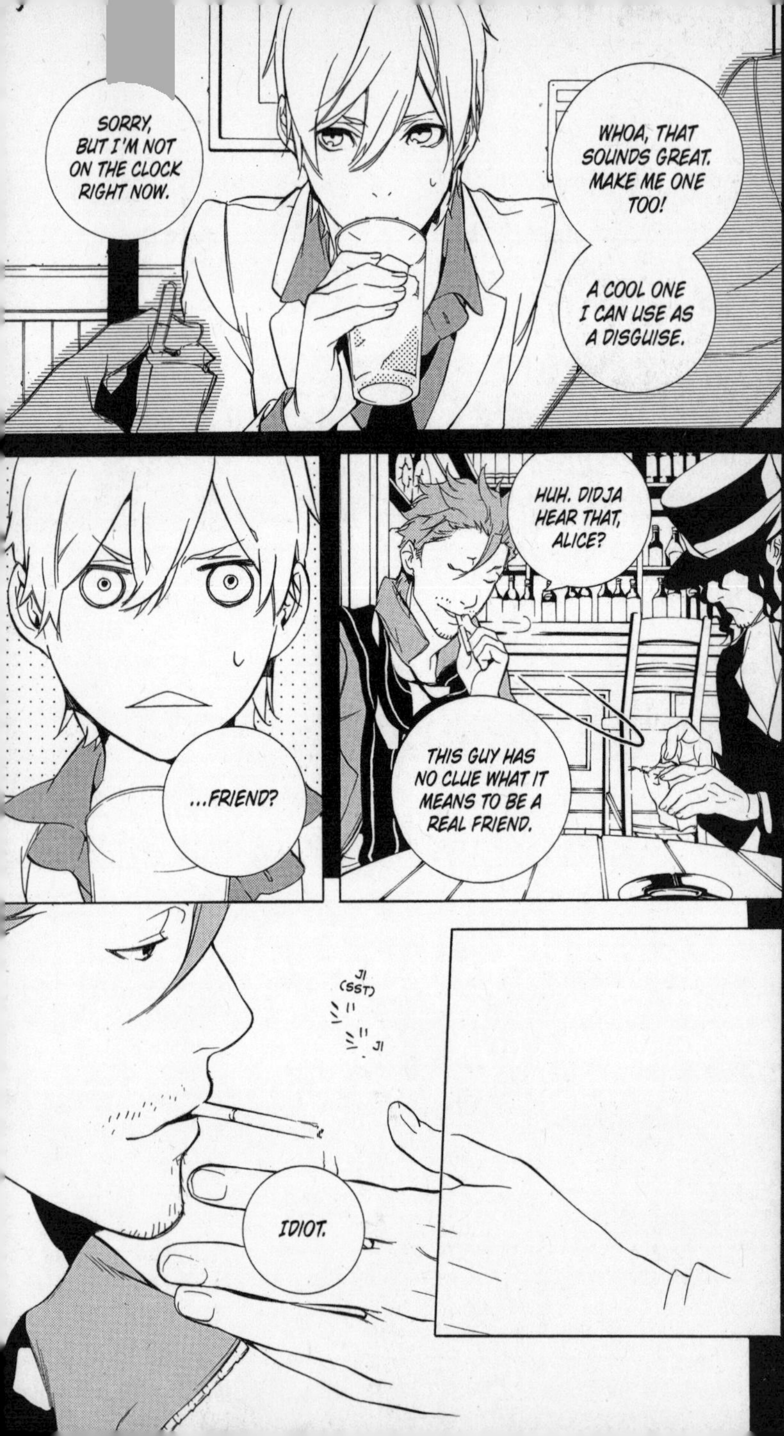
WHOA, THAT SOUNDS GREAT. MAKE ME ONE TOO!
A COOL ONE I CAN USE AS A DISGUISE.
SORRY, BUT I'M NOT ON THE CLOCK RIGHT NOW.
HUH. DIDJA HEAR THAT, ALICE?
THIS GUY HAS NO CLUE WHAT IT MEANS TO BE A REAL FRIEND.
...FRIEND?
JI (SST)
JI
IDIOT.

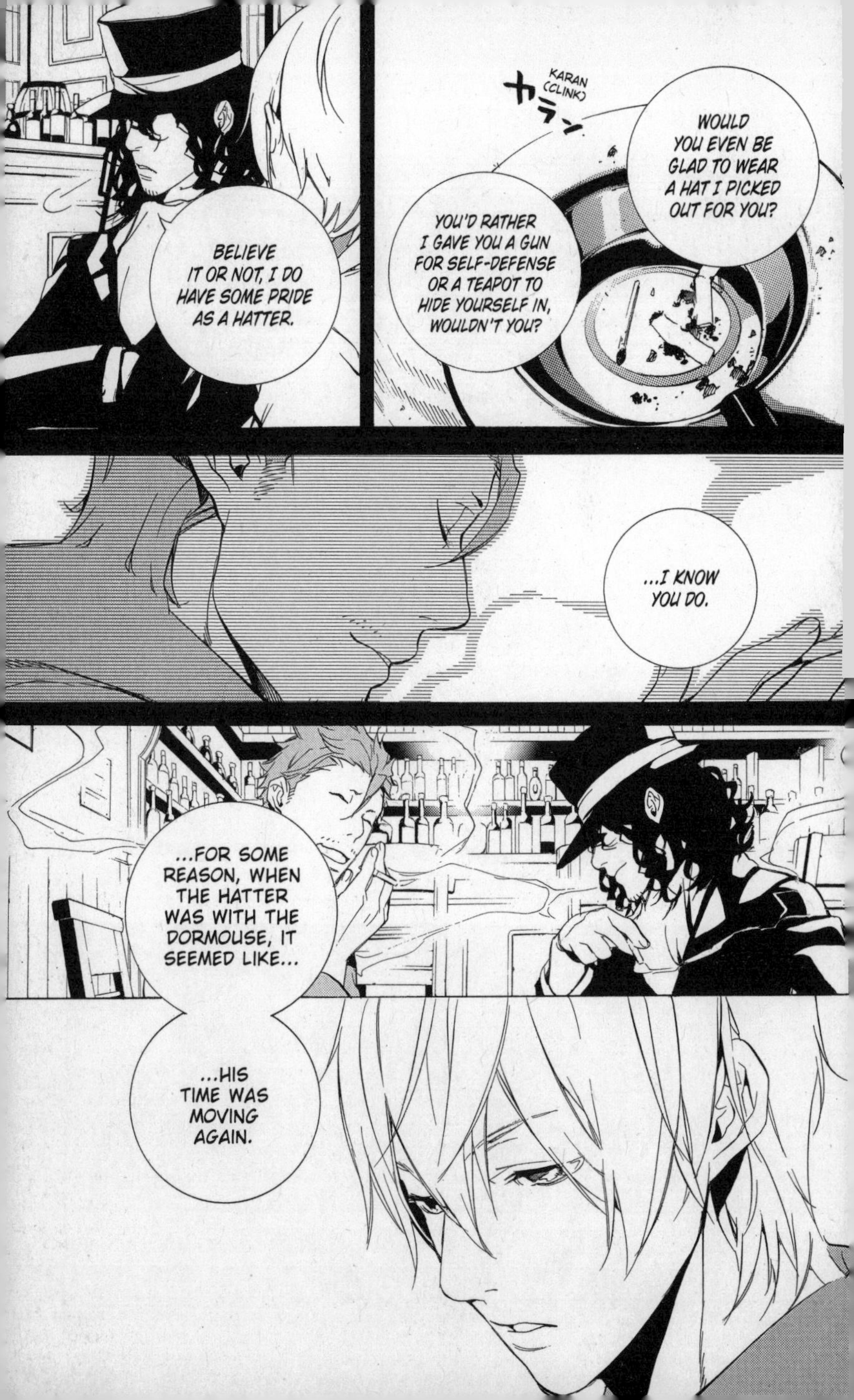
カラン
KARAN (CLINK)
WOULD YOU EVEN BE GLAD TO WEAR A HAT I PICKED OUT FOR YOU?
YOU'D RATHER I GAVE YOU A GUN FOR SELF-DEFENSE OR A TEAPOT TO HIDE YOURSELF IN, WOULDN'T YOU?
BELIEVE IT OR NOT, I DO HAVE SOME PRIDE AS A HATTER.
...I KNOW YOU DO.
...FOR SOME REASON, WHEN THE HATTER WAS WITH THE DORMOUSE, IT SEEMED LIKE...
...HIS TIME WAS MOVING AGAIN.

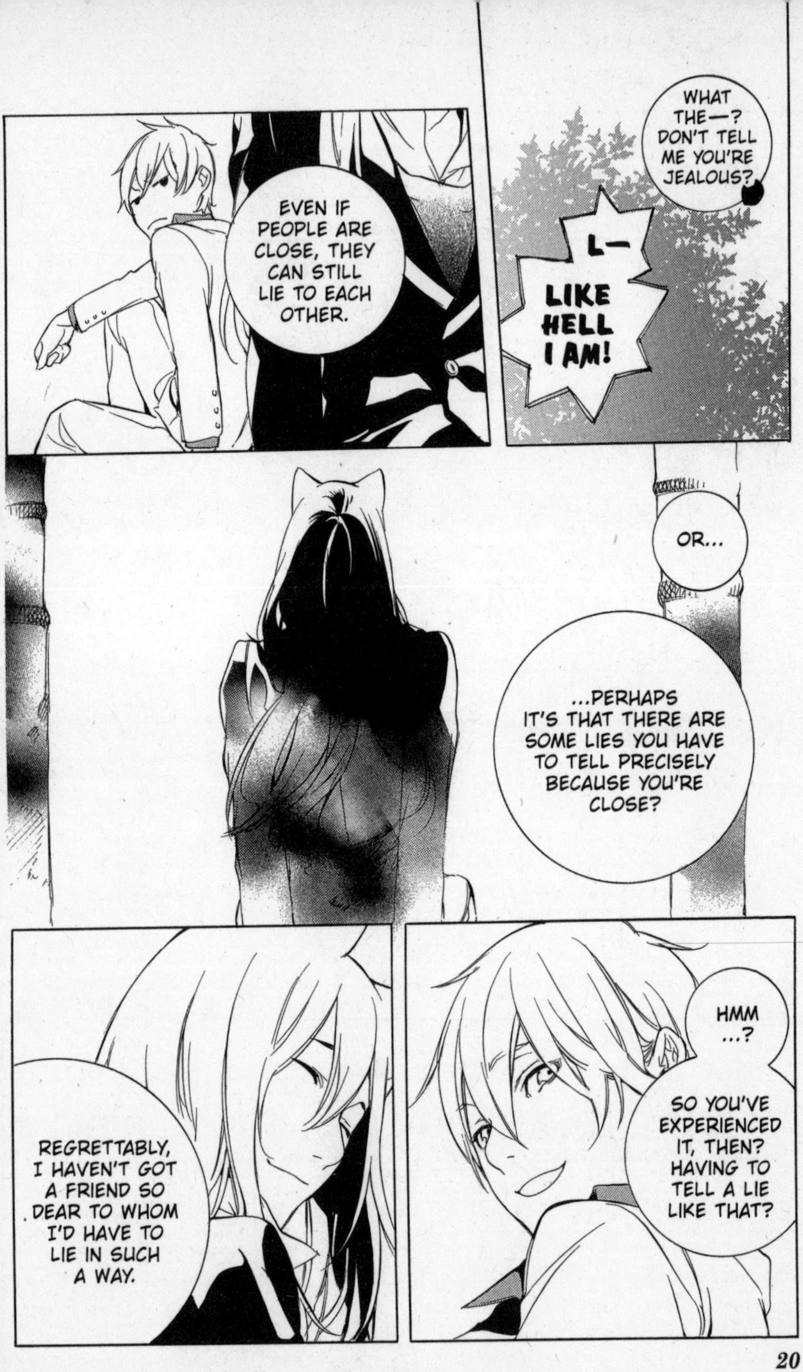
WHAT THE—? DON'T TELL ME YOU'RE JEALOUS?
L— LIKE HELL I AM!
EVEN IF PEOPLE ARE CLOSE, THEY CAN STILL LIE TO EACH OTHER.
OR...
...PERHAPS IT'S THAT THERE ARE SOME LIES YOU HAVE TO TELL PRECISELY BECAUSE YOU'RE CLOSE?
HMM ...?
SO YOU'VE EXPERIENCED IT, THEN? HAVING TO TELL A LIE LIKE THAT?
REGRETTABLY, I HAVEN'T GOT A FRIEND SO DEAR TO WHOM I'D HAVE TO LIE IN SUCH A WAY.

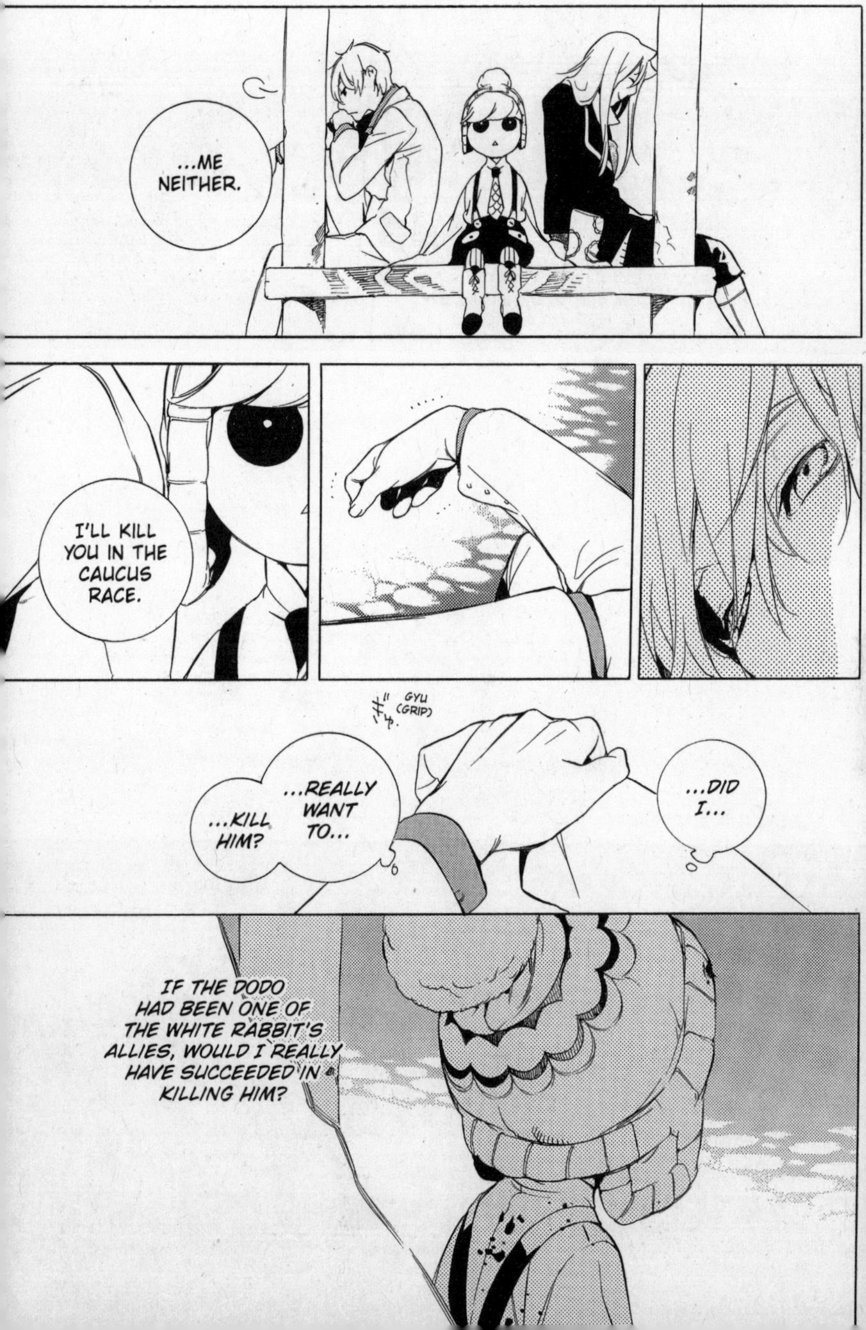
...ME NEITHER.
.....
I'LL KILL YOU IN THE CAUCUS RACE.
GYU (GRIP)
...DID I...
...REALLY WANT TO...
...KILL HIM?
IF THE DODO HAD BEEN ONE OF THE WHITE RABBIT'S ALLIES, WOULD I REALLY HAVE SUCCEEDED IN KILLING HIM?

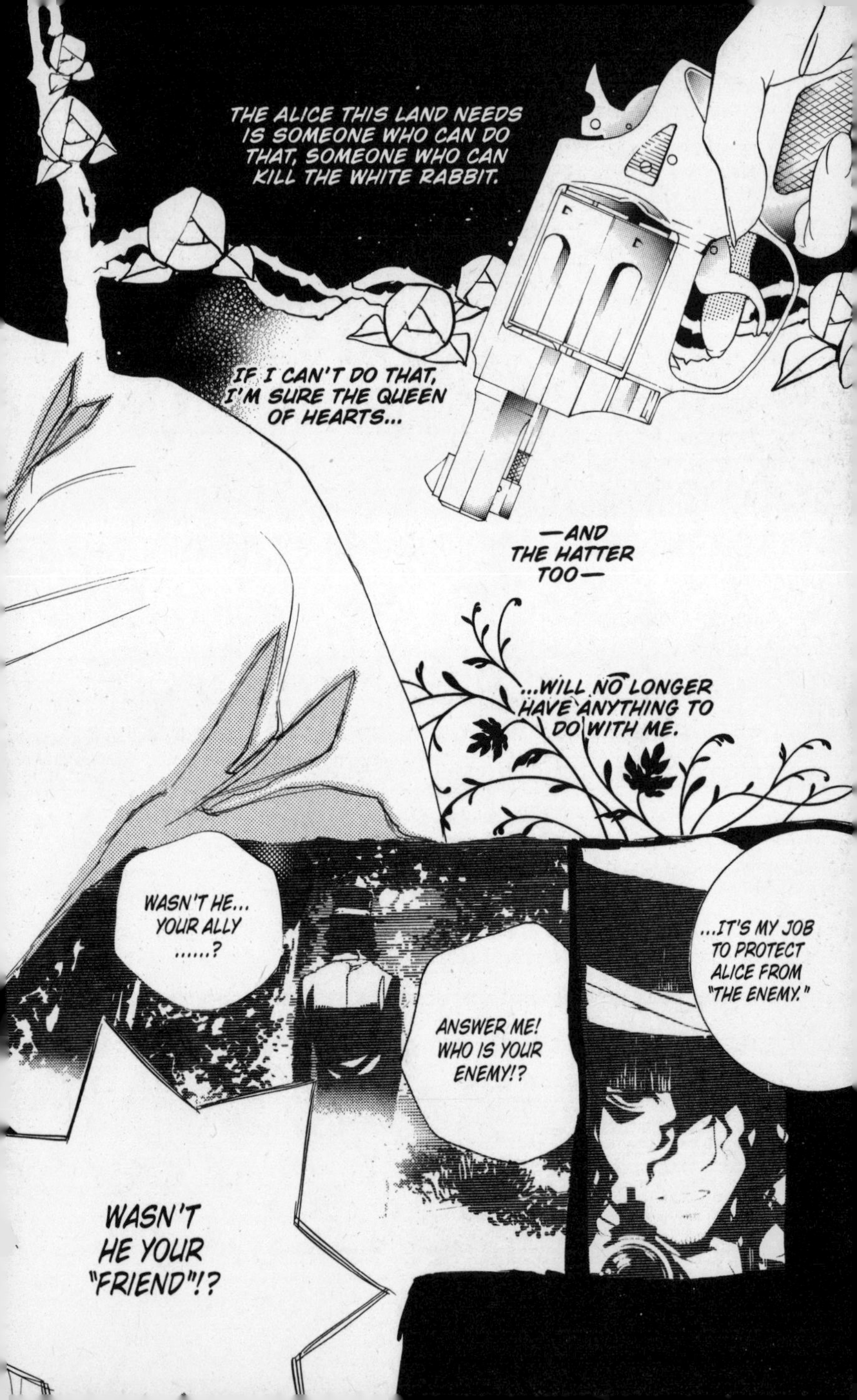
THE ALICE THIS LAND NEEDS IS SOMEONE WHO CAN DO THAT, SOMEONE WHO CAN KILL THE WHITE RABBIT.
IF I CAN'T DO THAT, I'M SURE THE QUEEN OF HEARTS...
—AND THE HATTER TOO—
...WILL NO LONGER HAVE ANYTHING TO DO WITH ME.
...IT'S MY JOB TO PROTECT ALICE FROM "THE ENEMY."
ANSWER ME! WHO IS YOUR ENEMY!?
WASN'T HE... YOUR ALLY ......?
WASN'T HE YOUR "FRIEND"!?

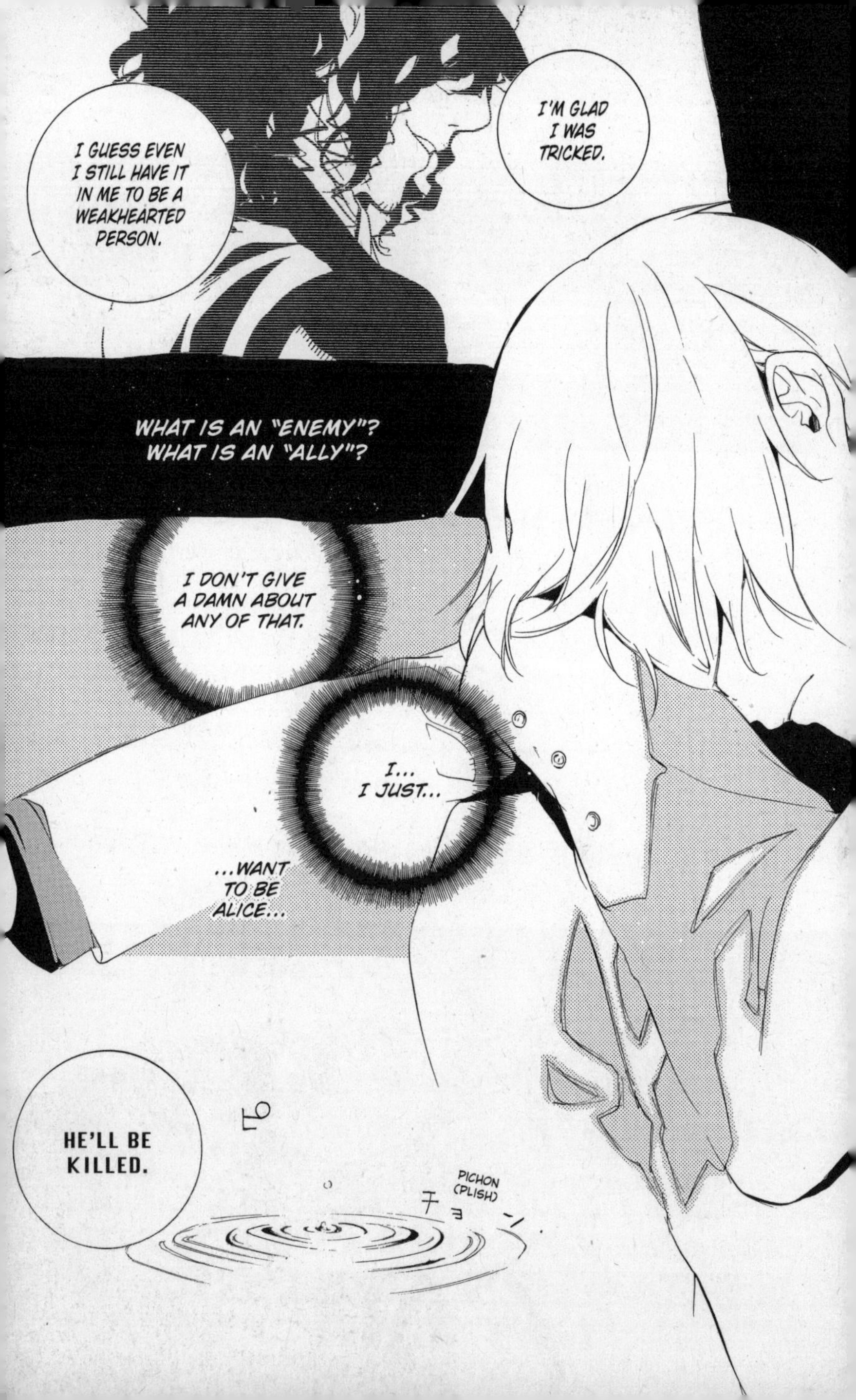
I'M GLAD I WAS TRICKED.
I GUESS EVEN I STILL HAVE IT IN ME TO BE A WEAKHEARTED PERSON.
WHAT IS AN "ENEMY"? WHAT IS AN "ALLY"?
I DON'T GIVE A DAMN ABOUT ANY OF THAT.
I... I JUST...
...WANT TO BE ALICE...
PICHON (PLISH)
HE'LL BE KILLED.

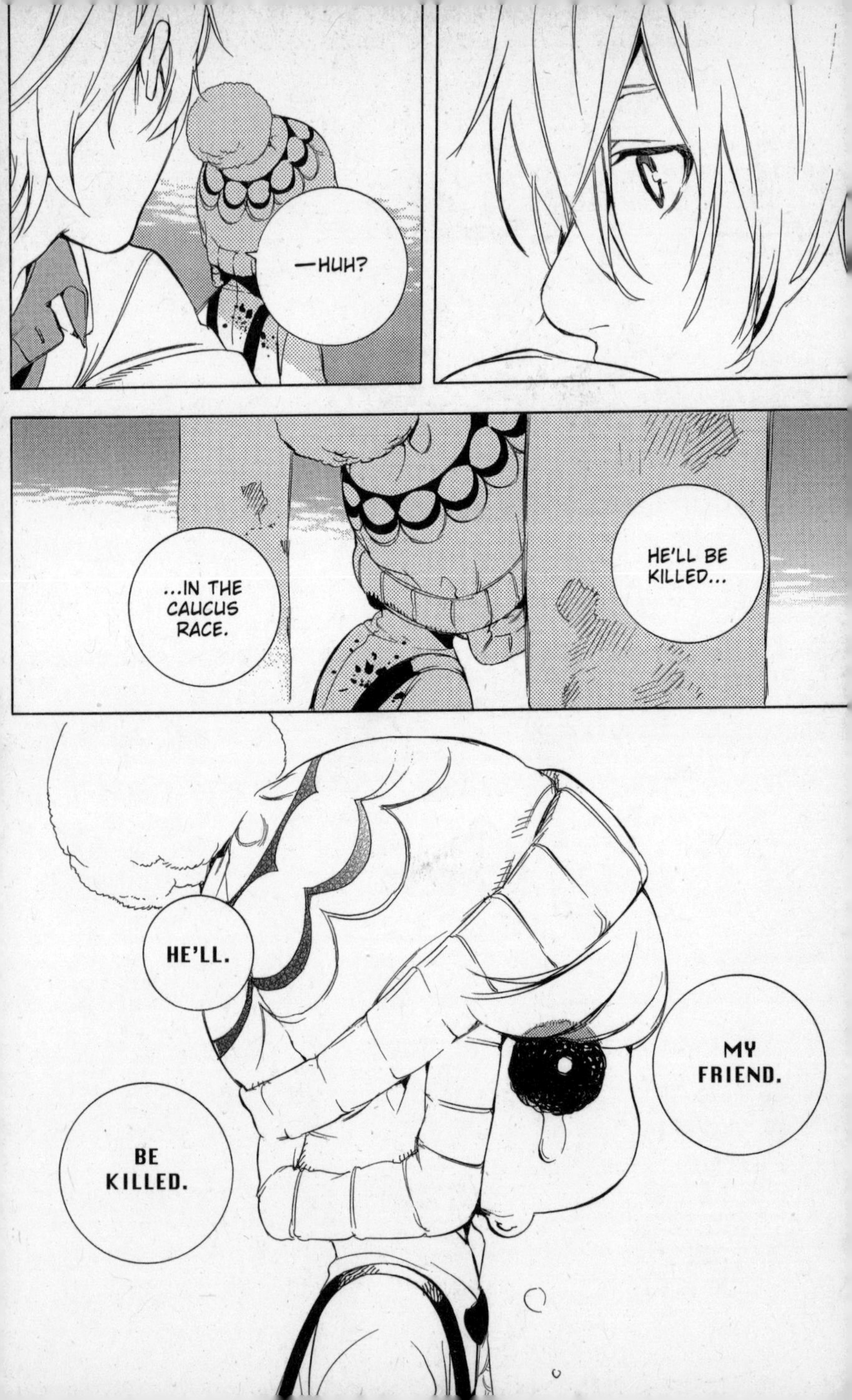
—HUH?
HE'LL BE KILLED...
...IN THE CAUCUS RACE.
MY FRIEND.
HE'LL.
BE KILLED.

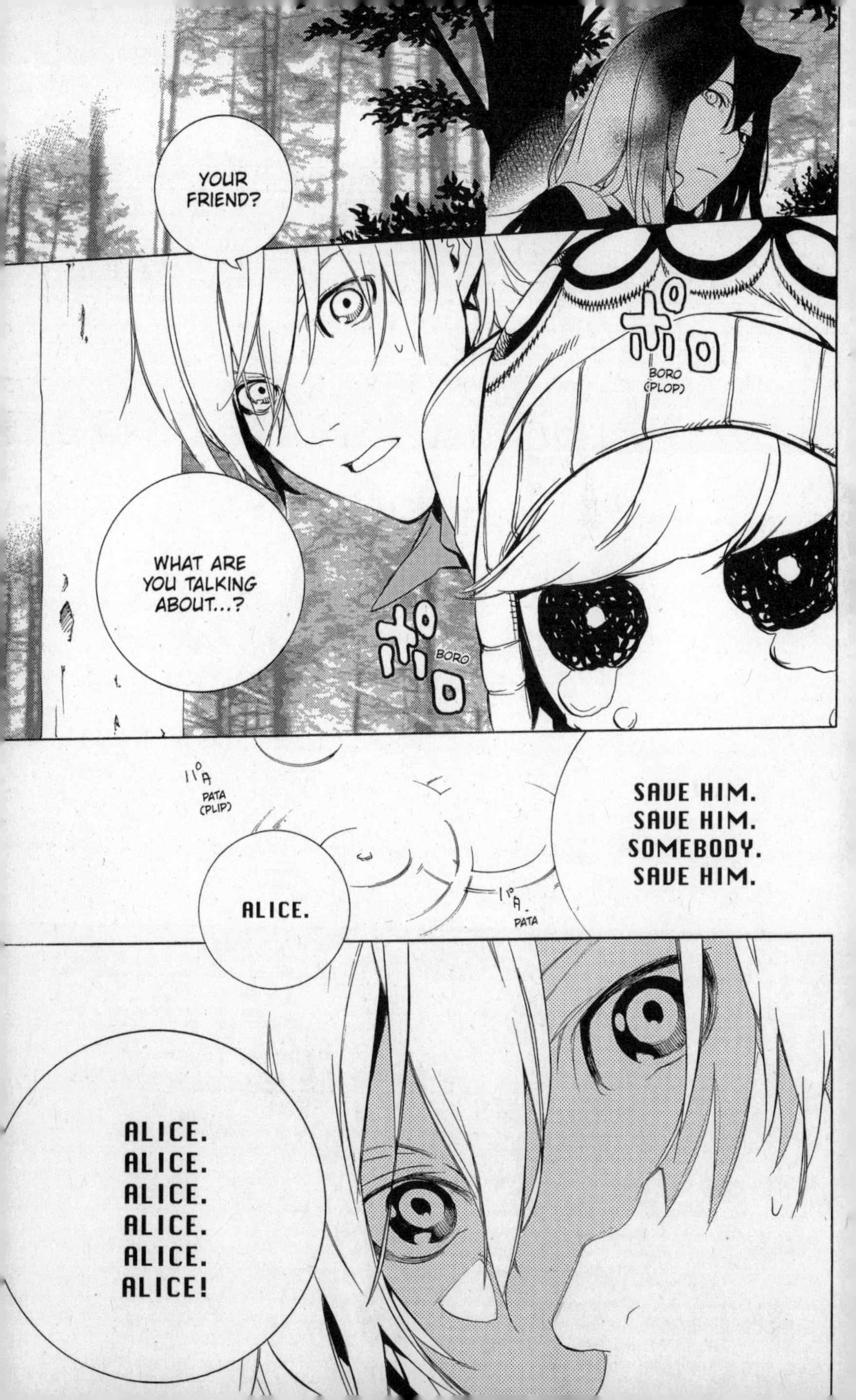

YOUR FRIEND?
ポロ
BORO (PLOP)
WHAT ARE YOU TALKING ABOUT...?
ポロ
BORO
SAVE HIM. SAVE HIM. SOMEBODY. SAVE HIM.
PATA
ALICE.
PATA (PLIP)
ALICE. ALICE. ALICE. ALICE. ALICE. ALICE!

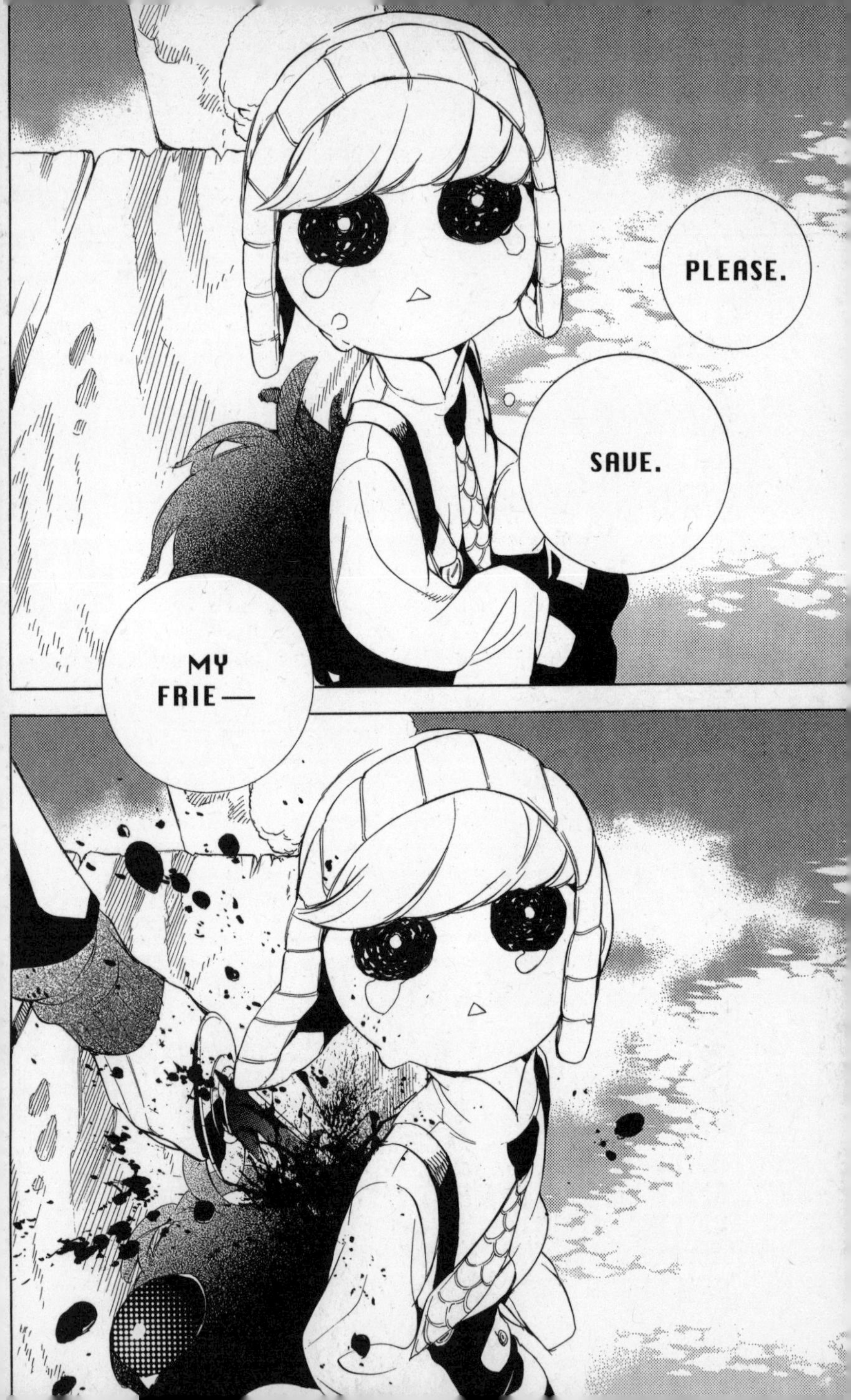
PLEASE.
SAVE.
MY FRIE—

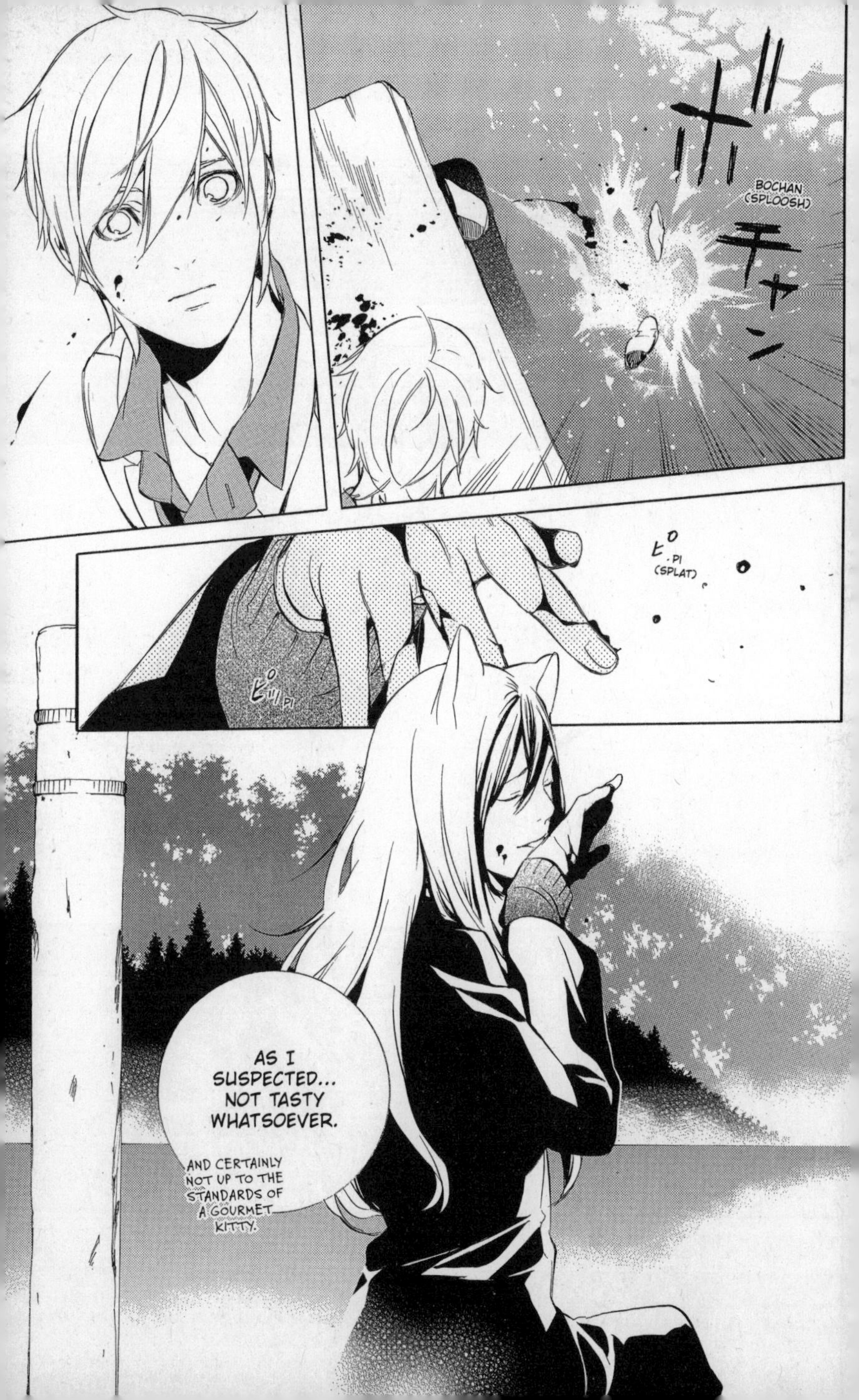
ボチャン
BOCHAN (SPLOOSH)
ピ PI (SPLAT)
ピッ PI
AS I SUSPECTED... NOT TASTY WHATSOEVER.
AND CERTAINLY NOT UP TO THE STANDARDS OF A GOURMET KITTY.

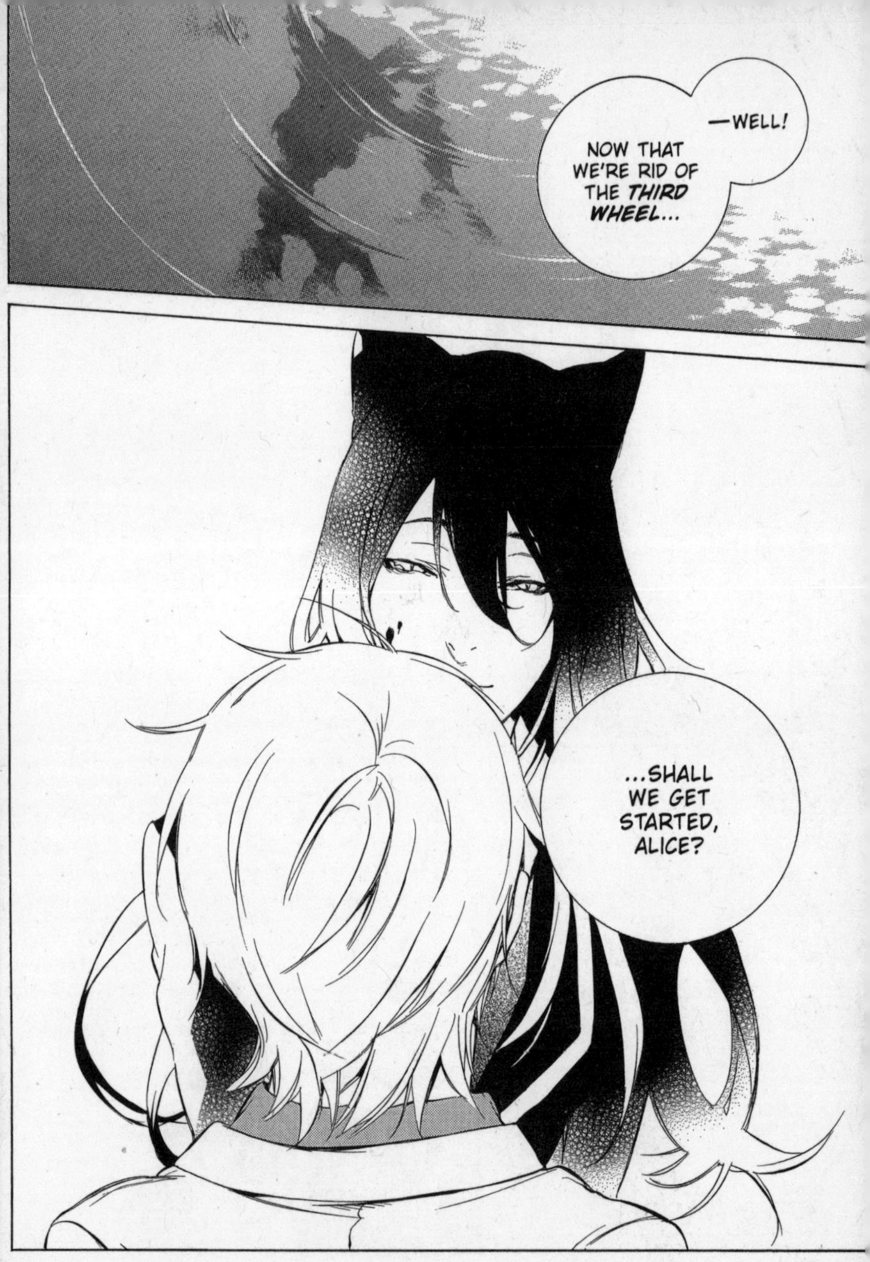
—WELL!
NOW THAT WE'RE RID OF THE *THIRD WHEEL*...
...SHALL WE GET STARTED, ALICE?

WHAT IS AN "ENEMY"?

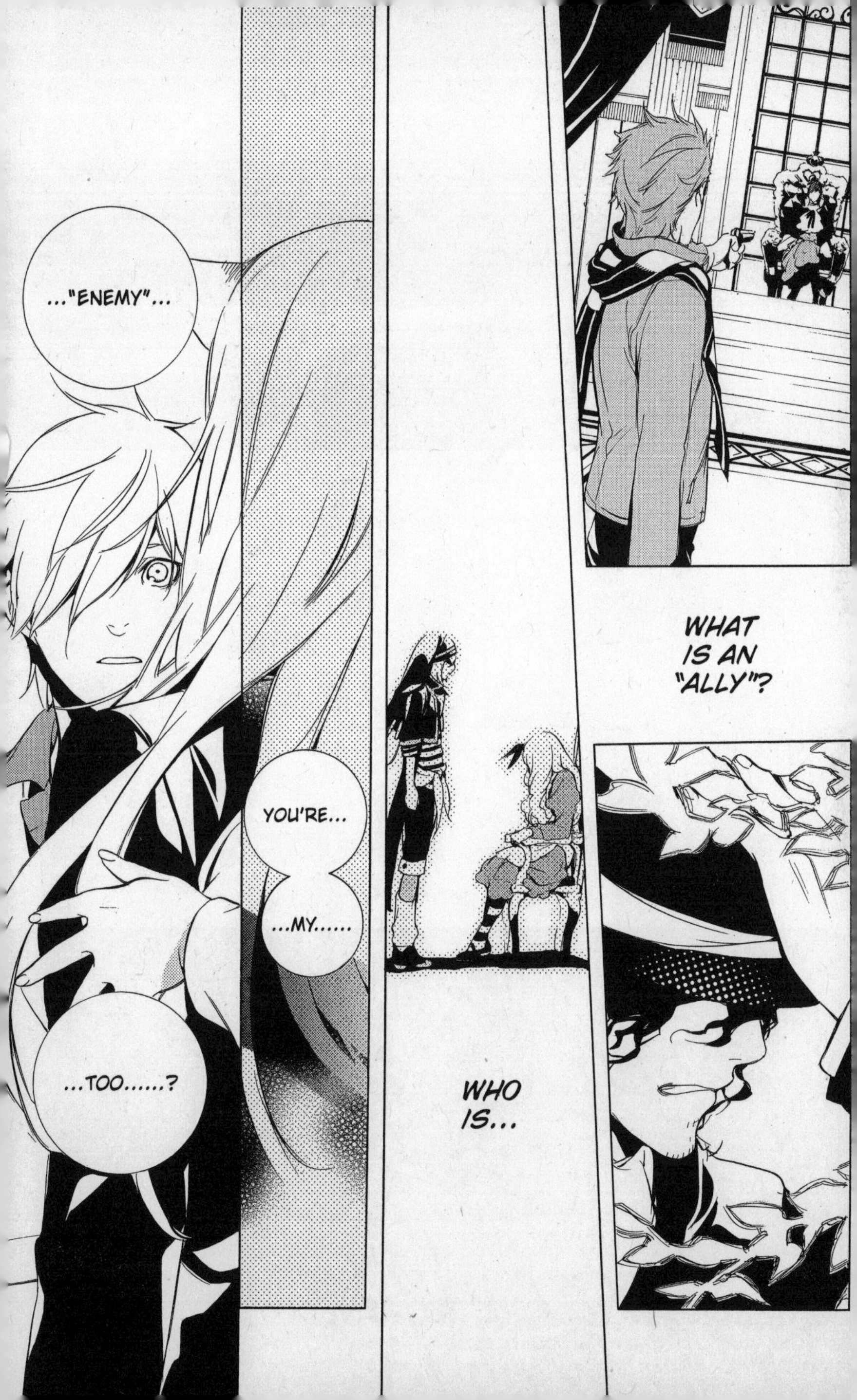
WHAT IS AN "ALLY"?
WHO IS...
YOU'RE...
...MY......
..."ENEMY"...
...TOO......?

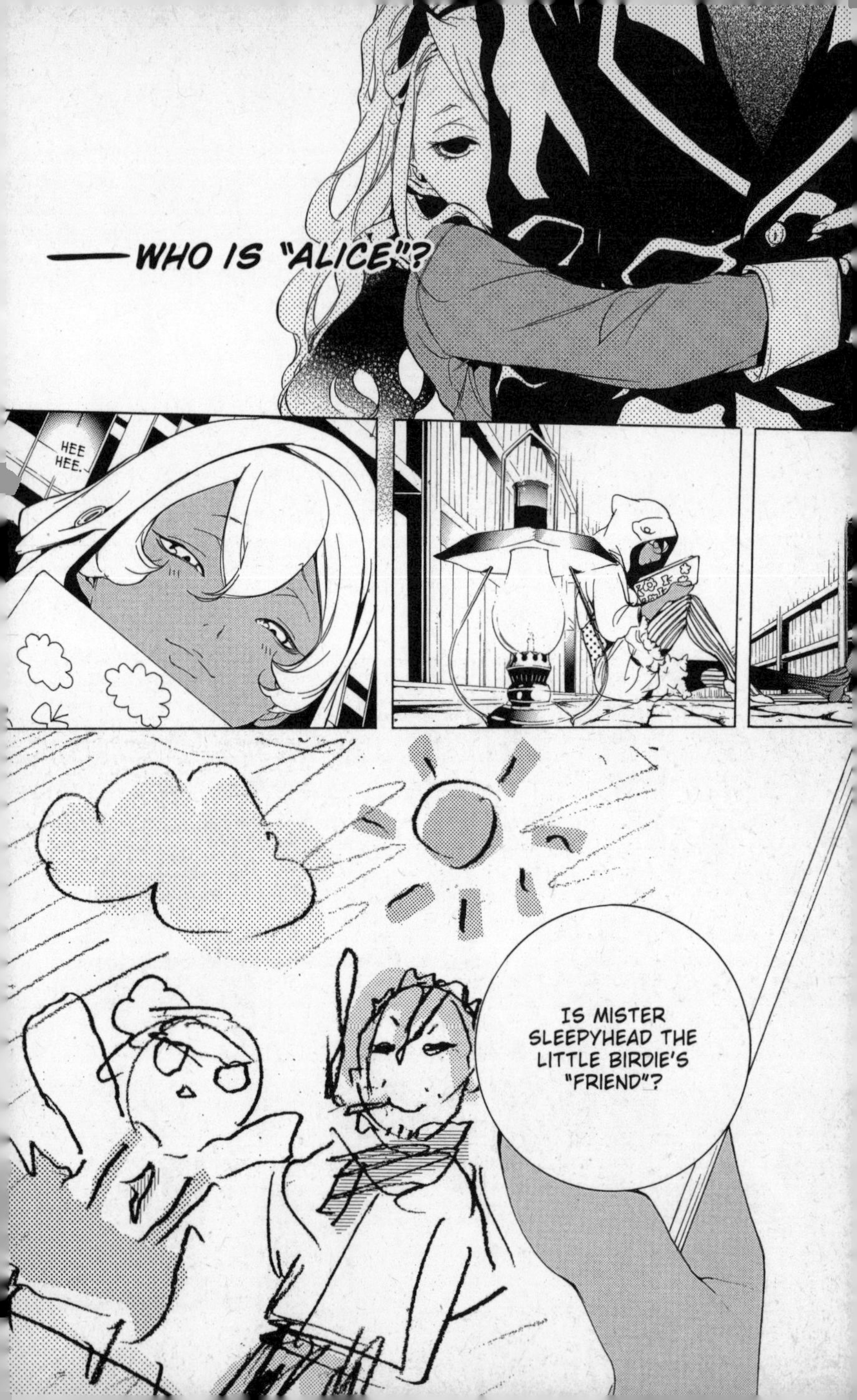
—WHO IS "ALICE"?
HEE HEE.
IS MISTER SLEEPYHEAD THE LITTLE BIRDIE'S "FRIEND"?

Chapter 26

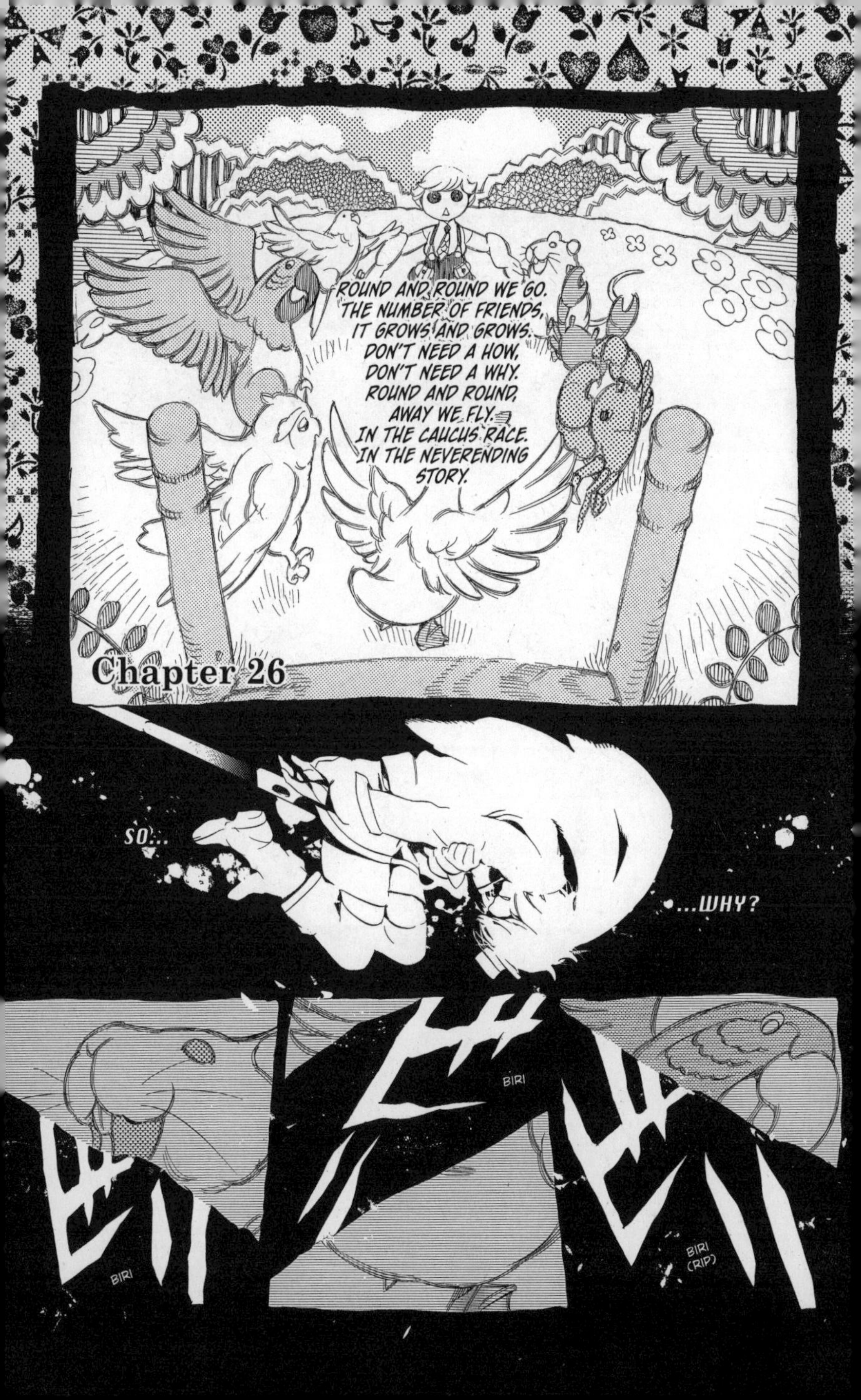
ROUND AND ROUND WE GO. THE NUMBER OF FRIENDS, IT GROWS AND GROWS. DON'T NEED A HOW, DON'T NEED A WHY. ROUND AND ROUND, AWAY WE FLY. IN THE CAUCUS RACE. IN THE NEVERENDING STORY.
Chapter 26
SO...
...WHY?
BIRI
BIRI (RIP)
BIRI

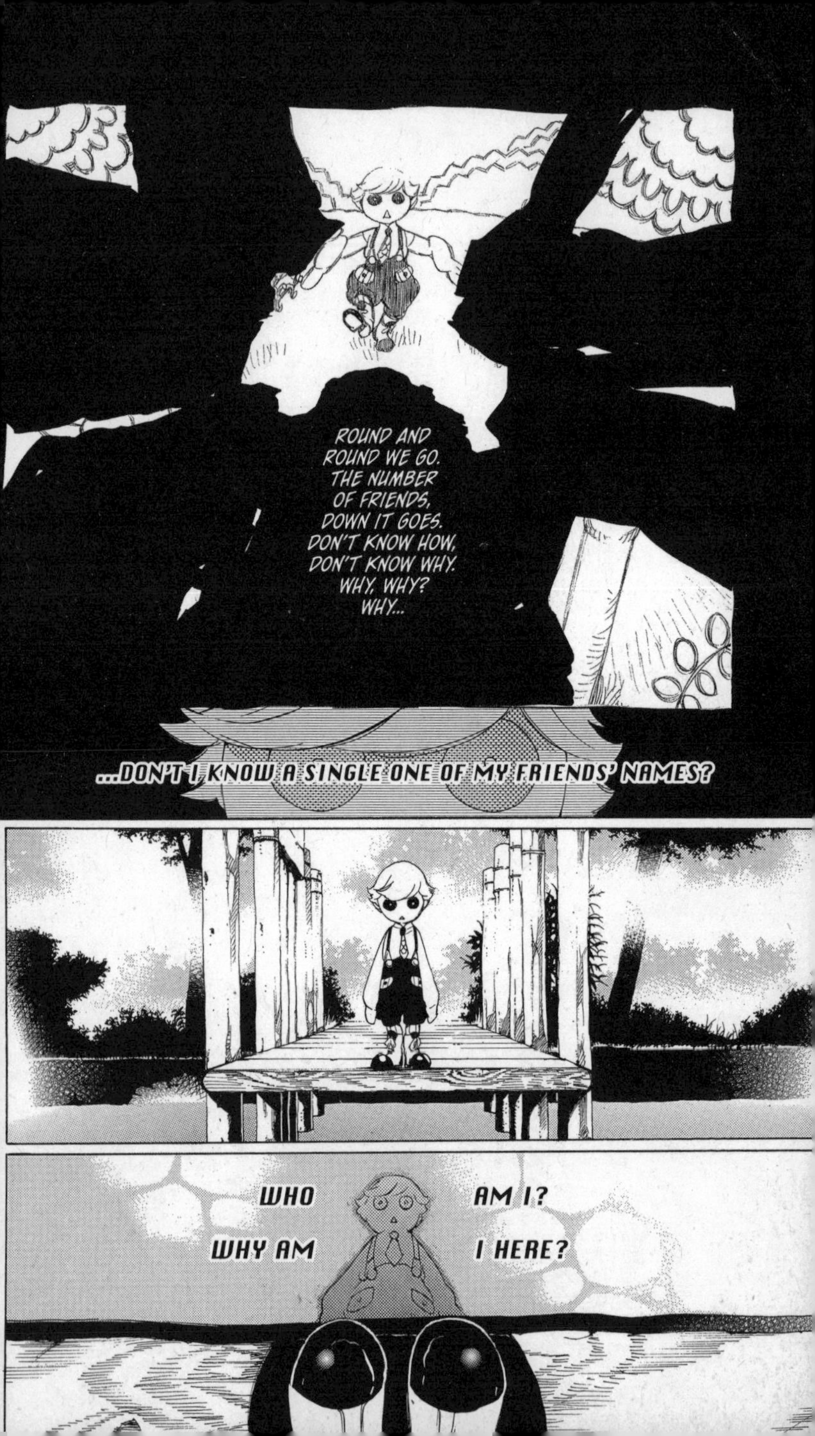
ROUND AND ROUND WE GO. THE NUMBER OF FRIENDS, DOWN IT GOES. DON'T KNOW HOW, DON'T KNOW WHY. WHY, WHY? WHY...
...DON'T I KNOW A SINGLE ONE OF MY FRIENDS' NAMES?
WHO
AM I?
WHY AM
I HERE?

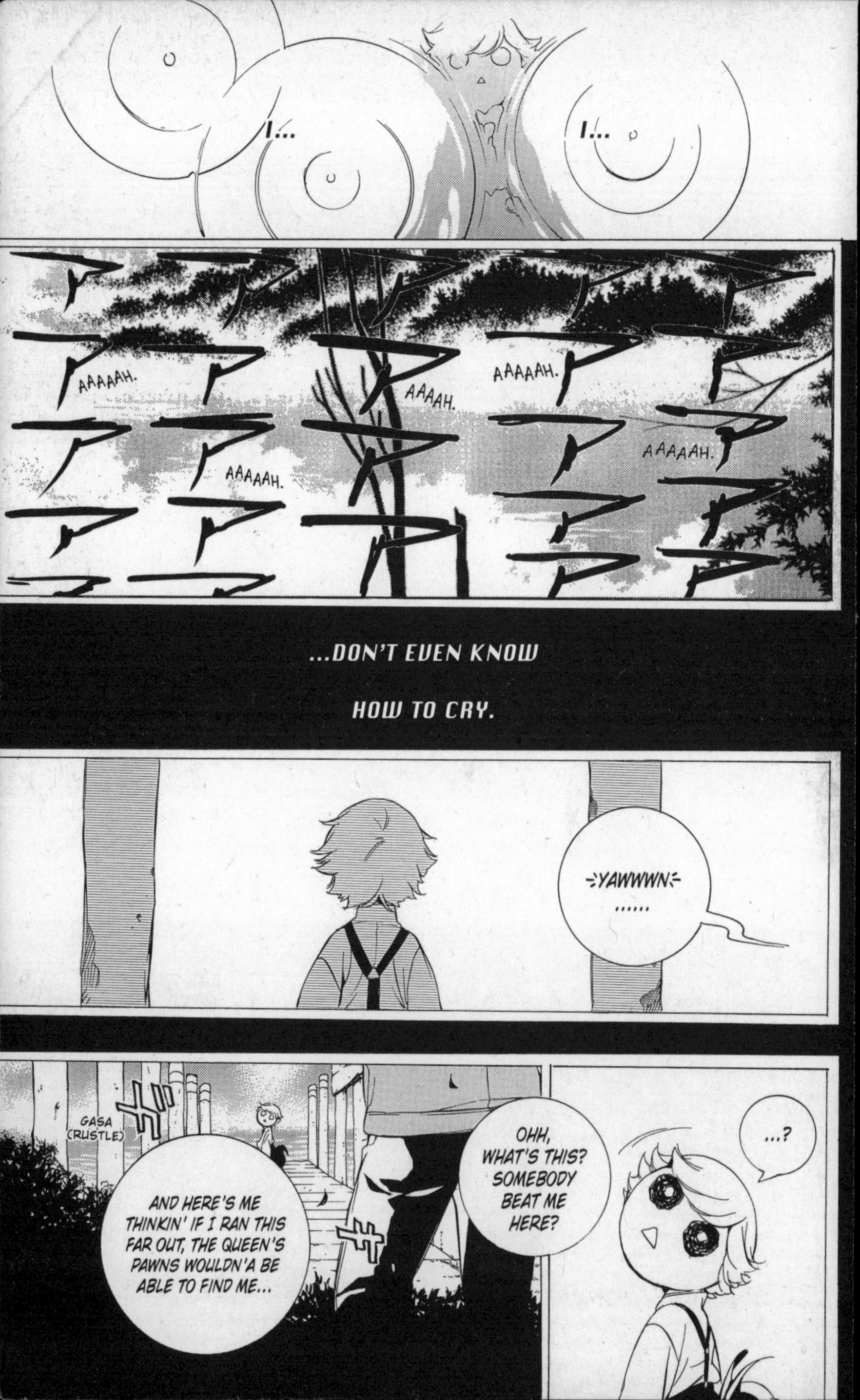
I...
I...
AAAAAH.
AAAAAH.
AAAAH.
AAAAAH.
AAAAAH.
...DON'T EVEN KNOW
HOW TO CRY.
-YAWWWN- ......
...?
GASA (RUSTLE)
OHH, WHAT'S THIS? SOMEBODY BEAT ME HERE?
AND HERE'S ME THINKIN' IF I RAN THIS FAR OUT, THE QUEEN'S PAWNS WOULDN'A BE ABLE TO FIND ME...

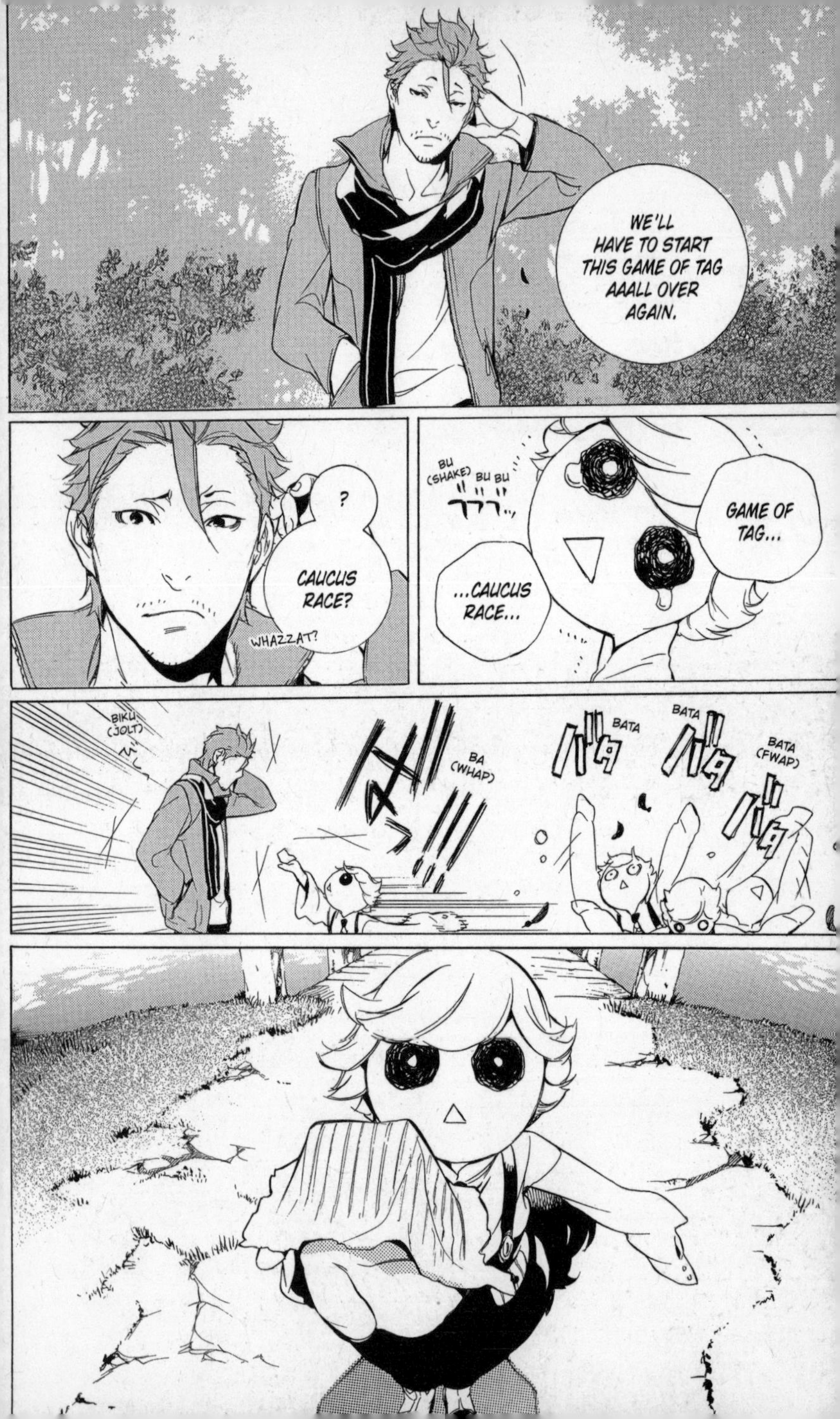
WE'LL HAVE TO START THIS GAME OF TAG AAALL OVER AGAIN.
BU (SHAKE) BU BU
GAME OF TAG...
...CAUCUS RACE...
?
CAUCUS RACE?
WHAZZAT?
BATA (FWAP)
BATA
BATA
BA (WHAP)
BIKU (JOLT)

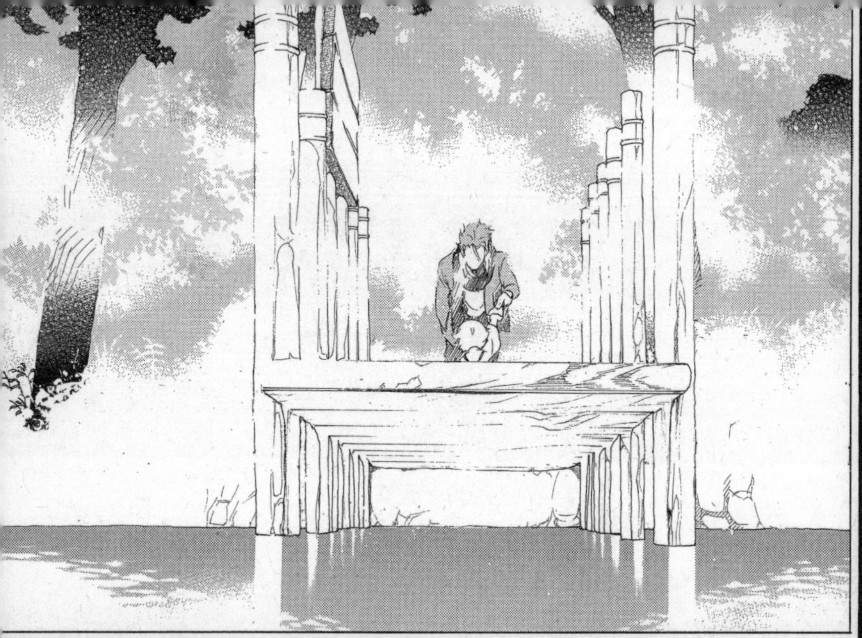

Chapter 26 Unbidden Guest.

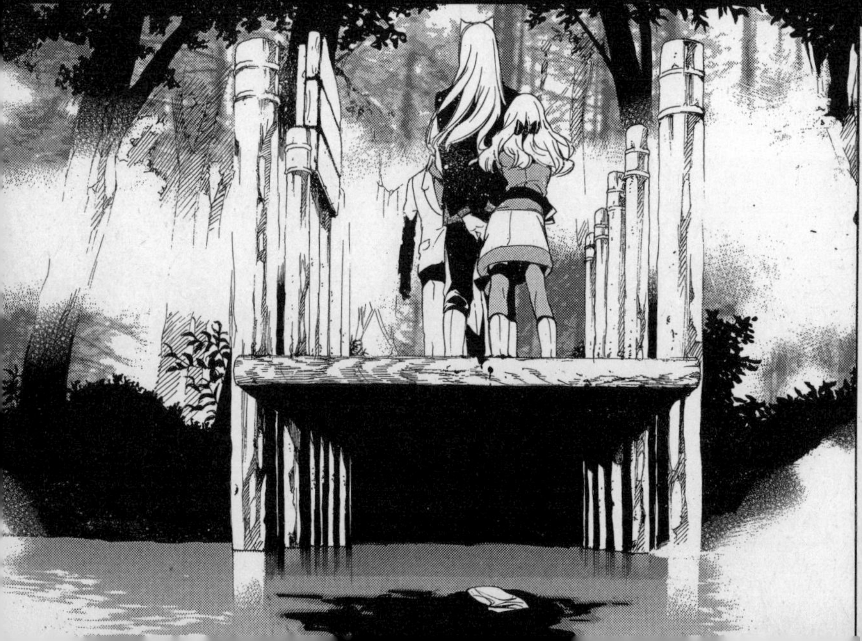

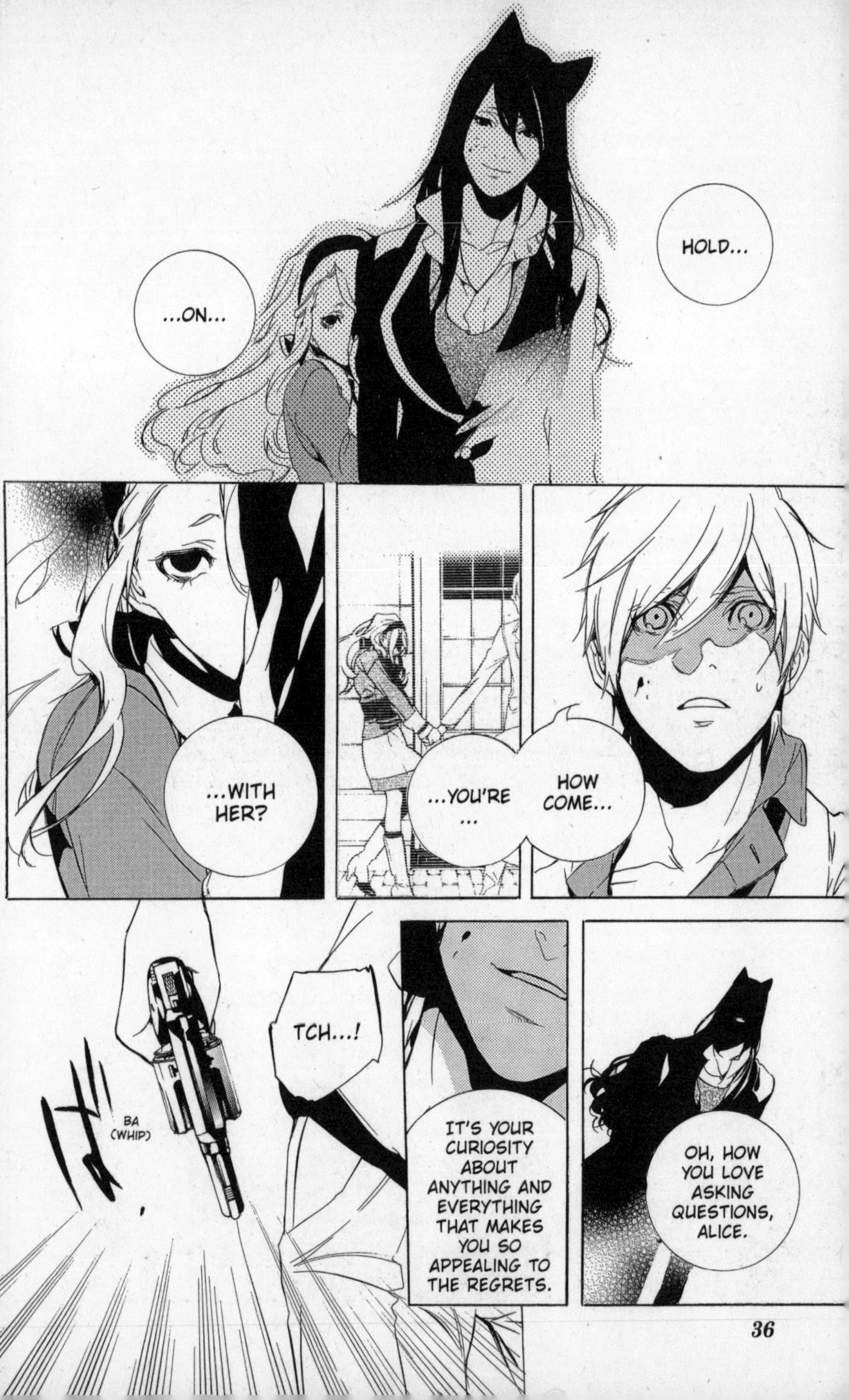
HOLD...
...ON...
HOW COME...
...YOU'RE ...
...WITH HER?
OH, HOW YOU LOVE ASKING QUESTIONS, ALICE.
IT'S YOUR CURIOSITY ABOUT ANYTHING AND EVERYTHING THAT MAKES YOU SO APPEALING TO THE REGRETS.
TCH...!
BA (WHIP)

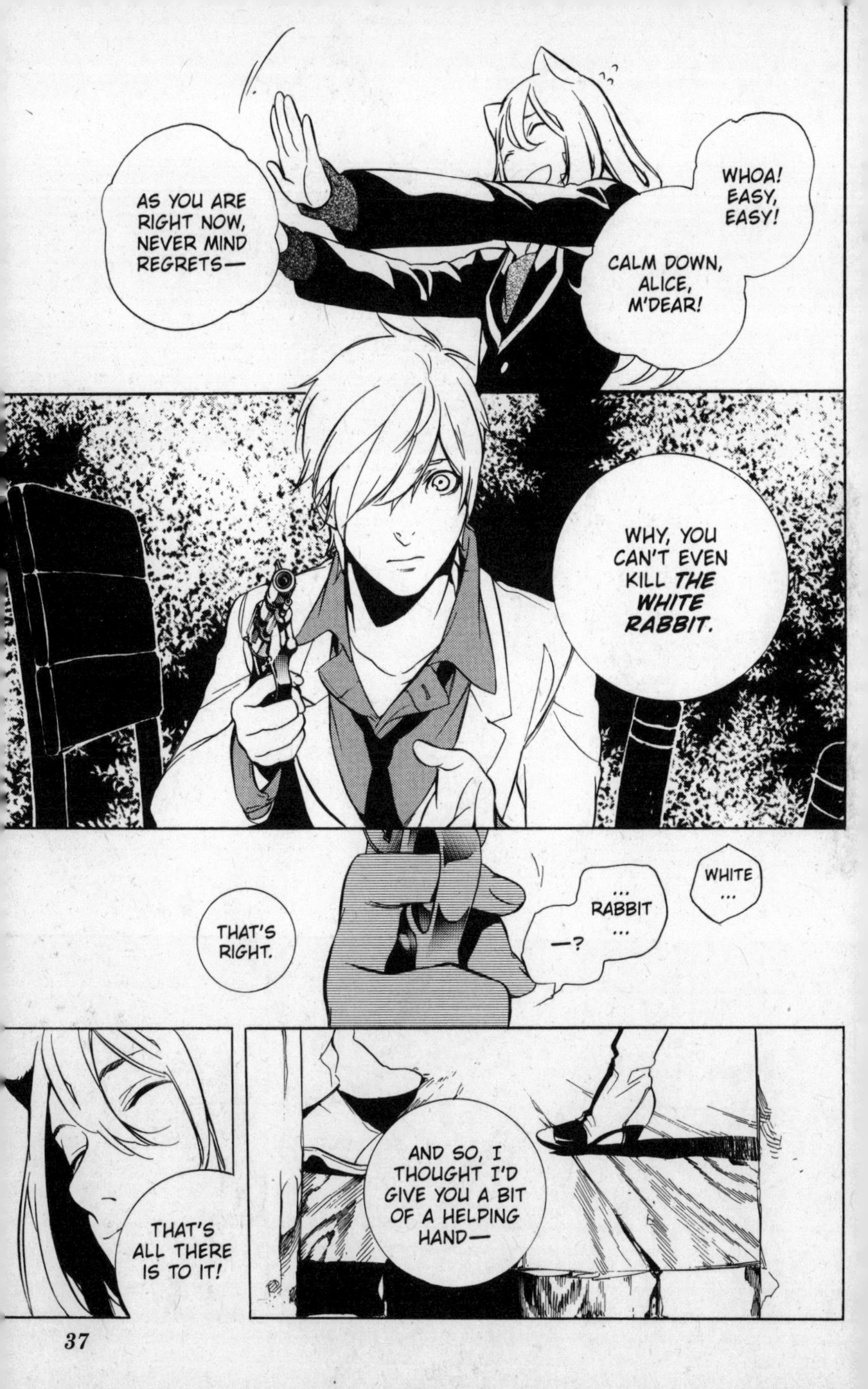
WHOA! EASY, EASY!
CALM DOWN, ALICE, M'DEAR!
AS YOU ARE RIGHT NOW, NEVER MIND REGRETS—
WHY, YOU CAN'T EVEN KILL *THE WHITE RABBIT.*
WHITE ...
... RABBIT ... —?
THAT'S RIGHT.
AND SO, I THOUGHT I'D GIVE YOU A BIT OF A HELPING HAND—
THAT'S ALL THERE IS TO IT!

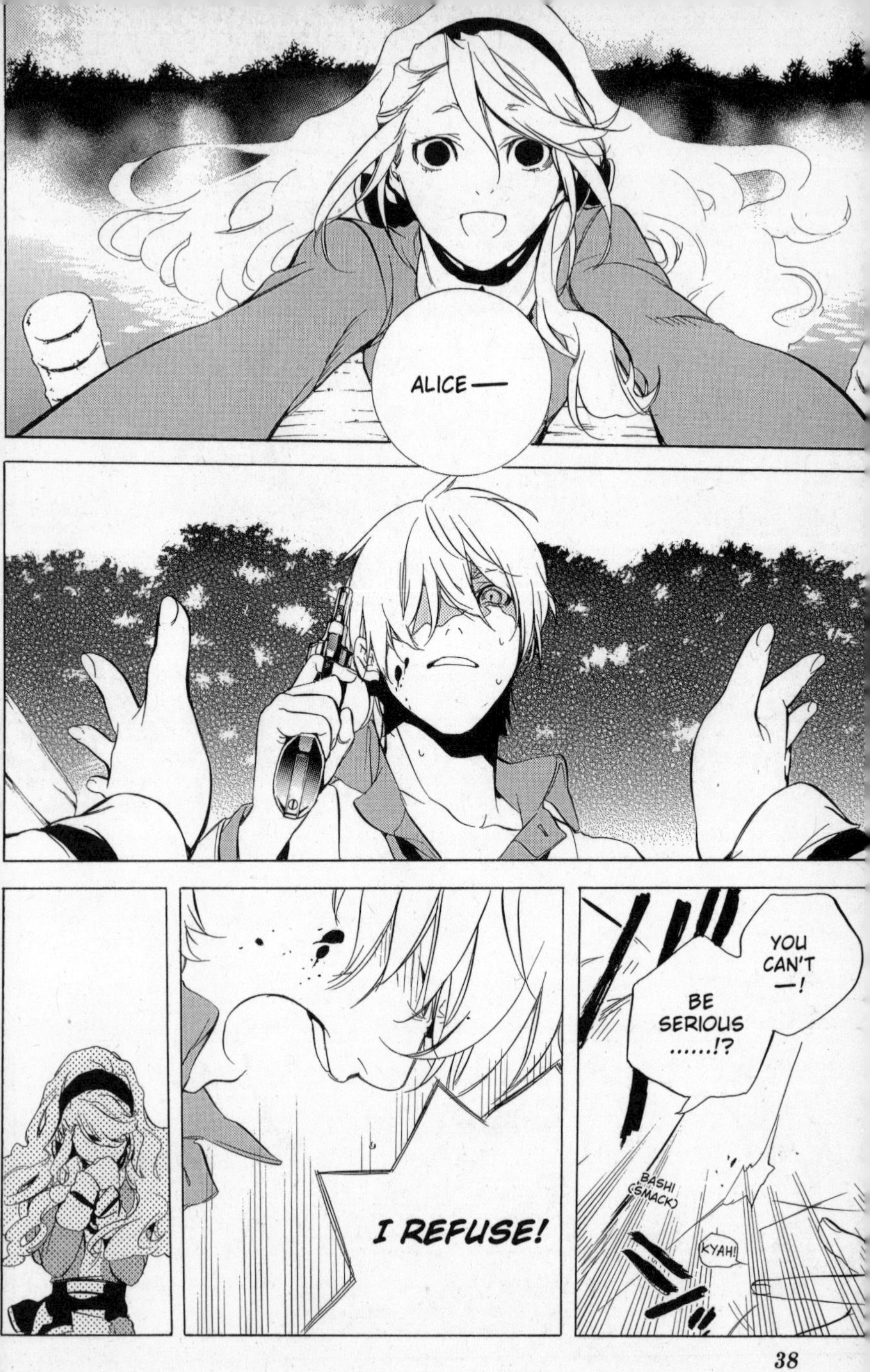
ALICE—
YOU CAN'T —!
BE SERIOUS ......!?
BASHI (SMACK)
KYAH!
I REFUSE!

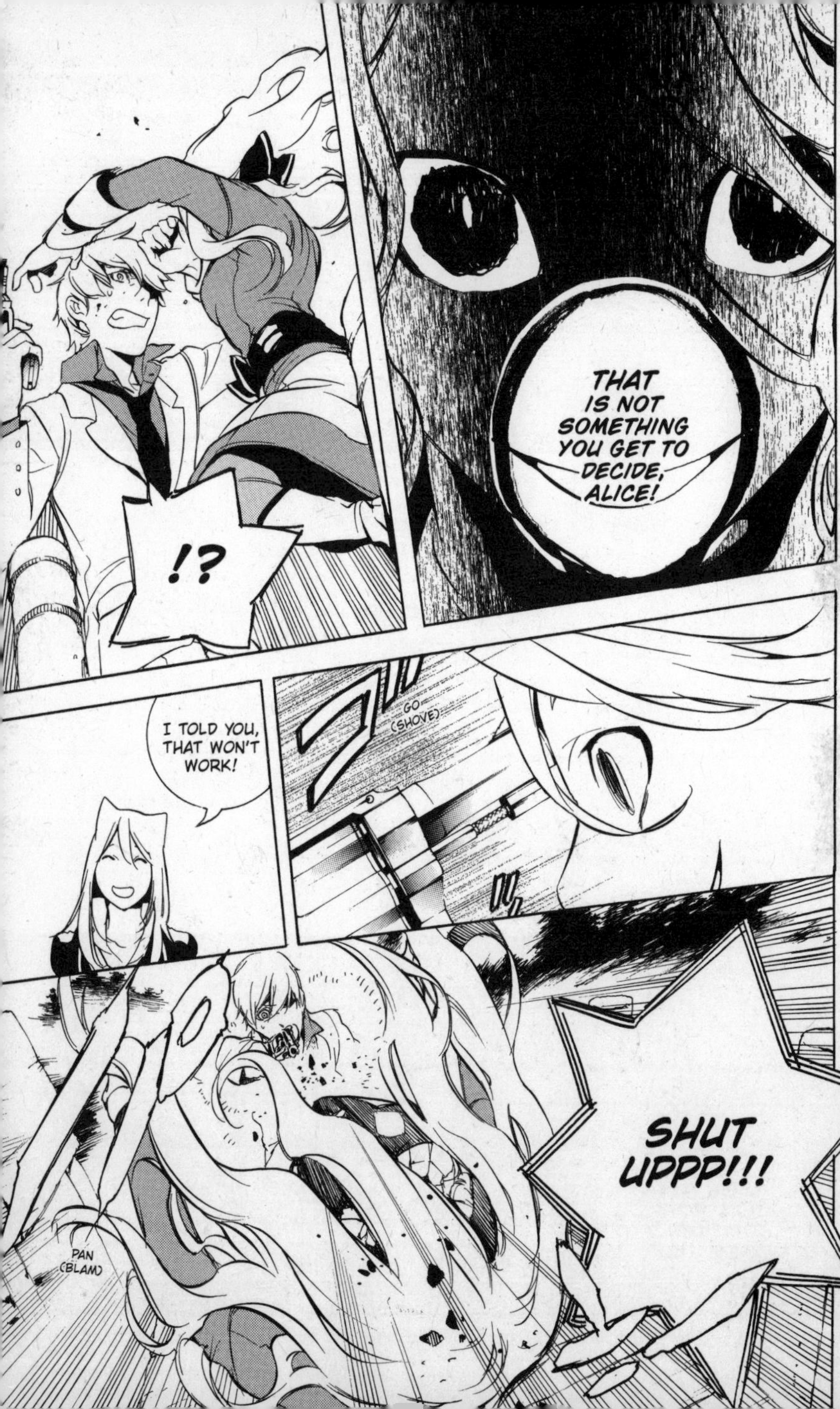
THAT IS NOT SOMETHING YOU GET TO DECIDE, ALICE!
!?
GO (SHOVE)
I TOLD YOU, THAT WON'T WORK!
SHUT UPPP!!!
PAN (BLAM)

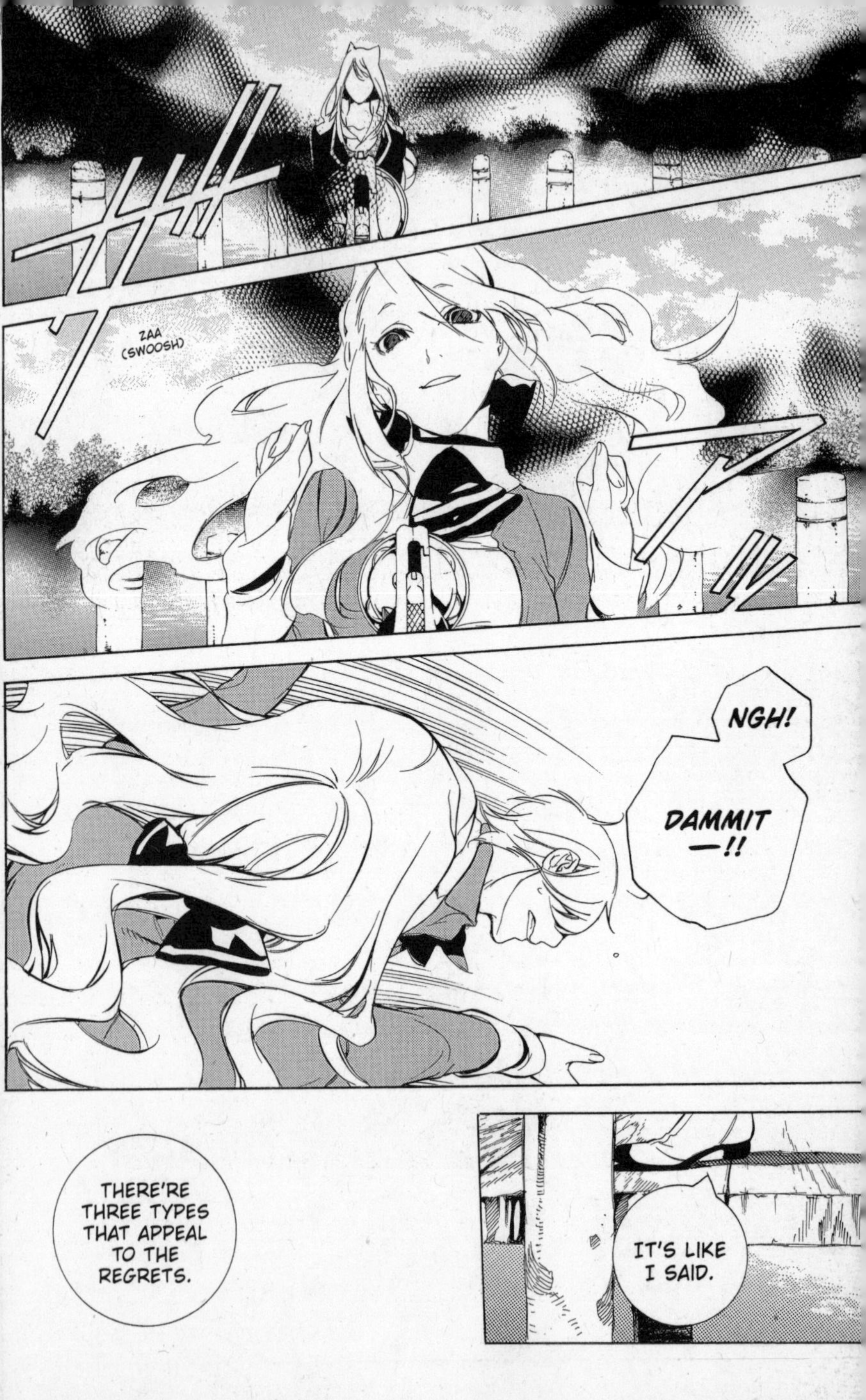
ZAA (SWOOSH)
NGH!
DAMMIT —!!
IT'S LIKE I SAID.
THERE'RE THREE TYPES THAT APPEAL TO THE REGRETS.

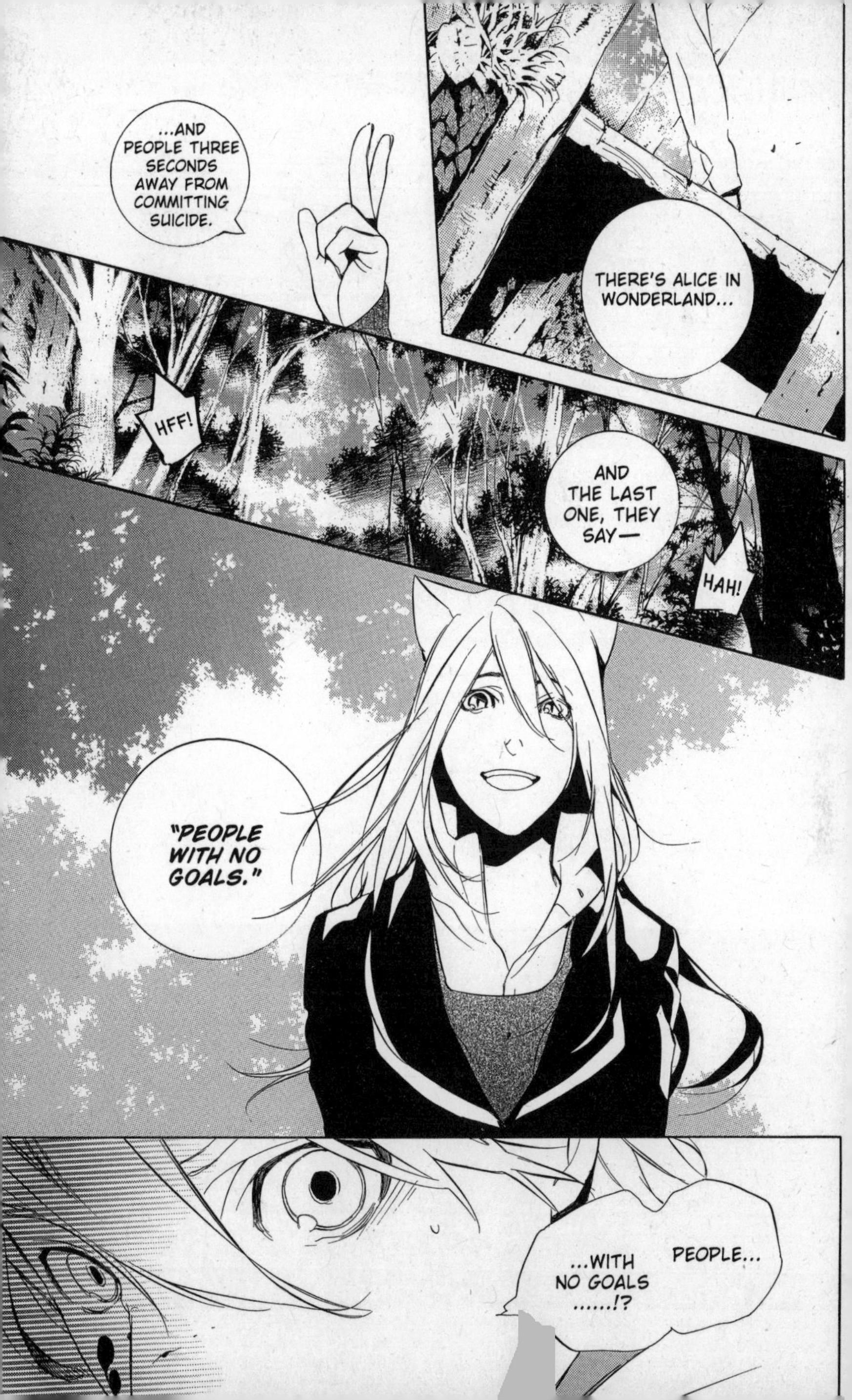

THERE'S ALICE IN WONDERLAND...
...AND PEOPLE THREE SECONDS AWAY FROM COMMITTING SUICIDE.
AND THE LAST ONE, THEY SAY—
HAH!
HFF!
"PEOPLE WITH NO GOALS."
PEOPLE...
...WITH NO GOALS ......!?

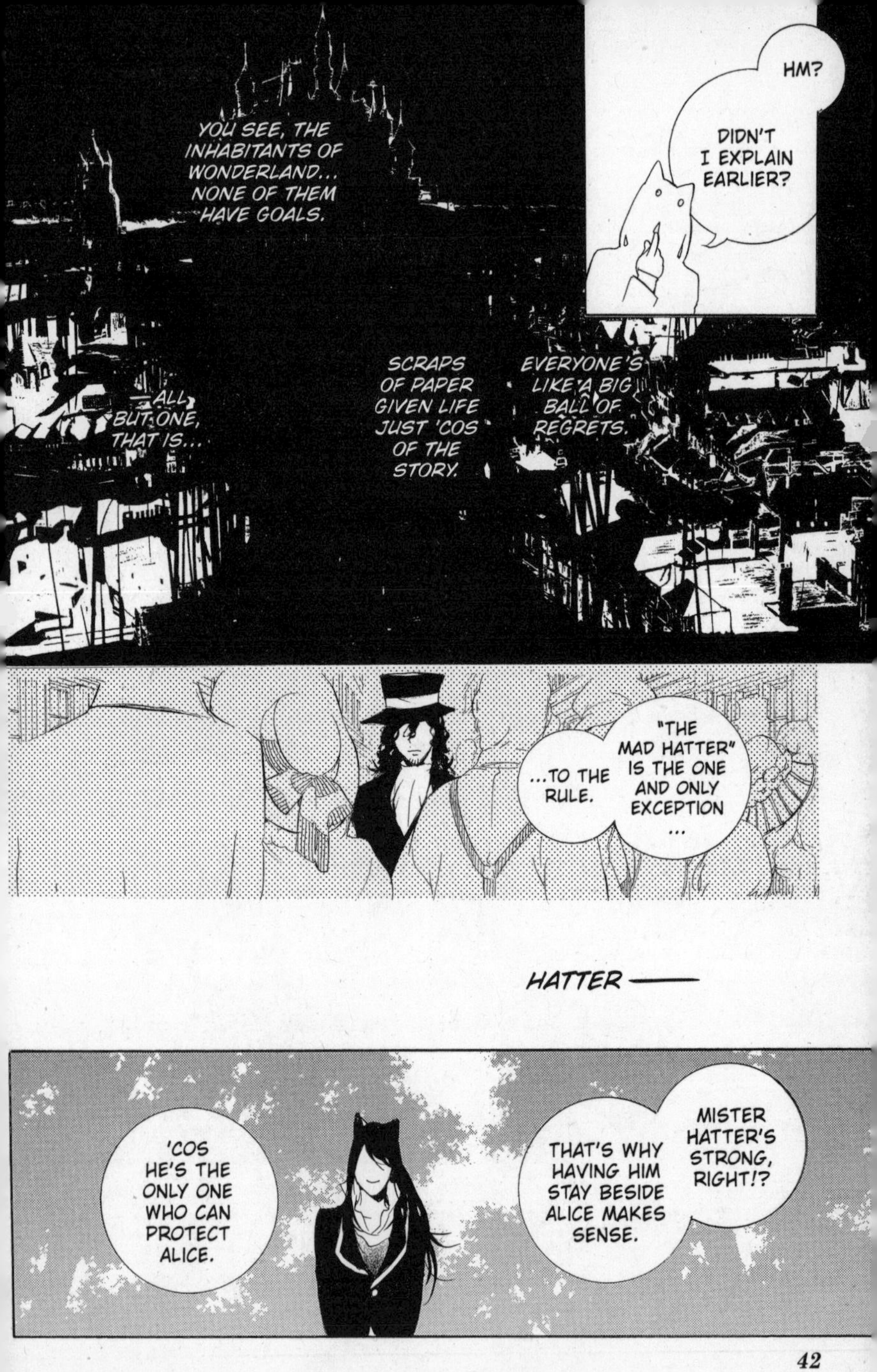
HM?
DIDN'T I EXPLAIN EARLIER?
YOU SEE, THE INHABITANTS OF WONDERLAND... NONE OF THEM HAVE GOALS.
EVERYONE'S LIKE A BIG BALL OF REGRETS.
SCRAPS OF PAPER GIVEN LIFE JUST 'COS OF THE STORY.
ALL BUT ONE, THAT IS...
"THE MAD HATTER" IS THE ONE AND ONLY EXCEPTION ...
...TO THE RULE.
HATTER ——
MISTER HATTER'S STRONG, RIGHT!?
THAT'S WHY HAVING HIM STAY BESIDE ALICE MAKES SENSE.
'COS HE'S THE ONLY ONE WHO CAN PROTECT ALICE.

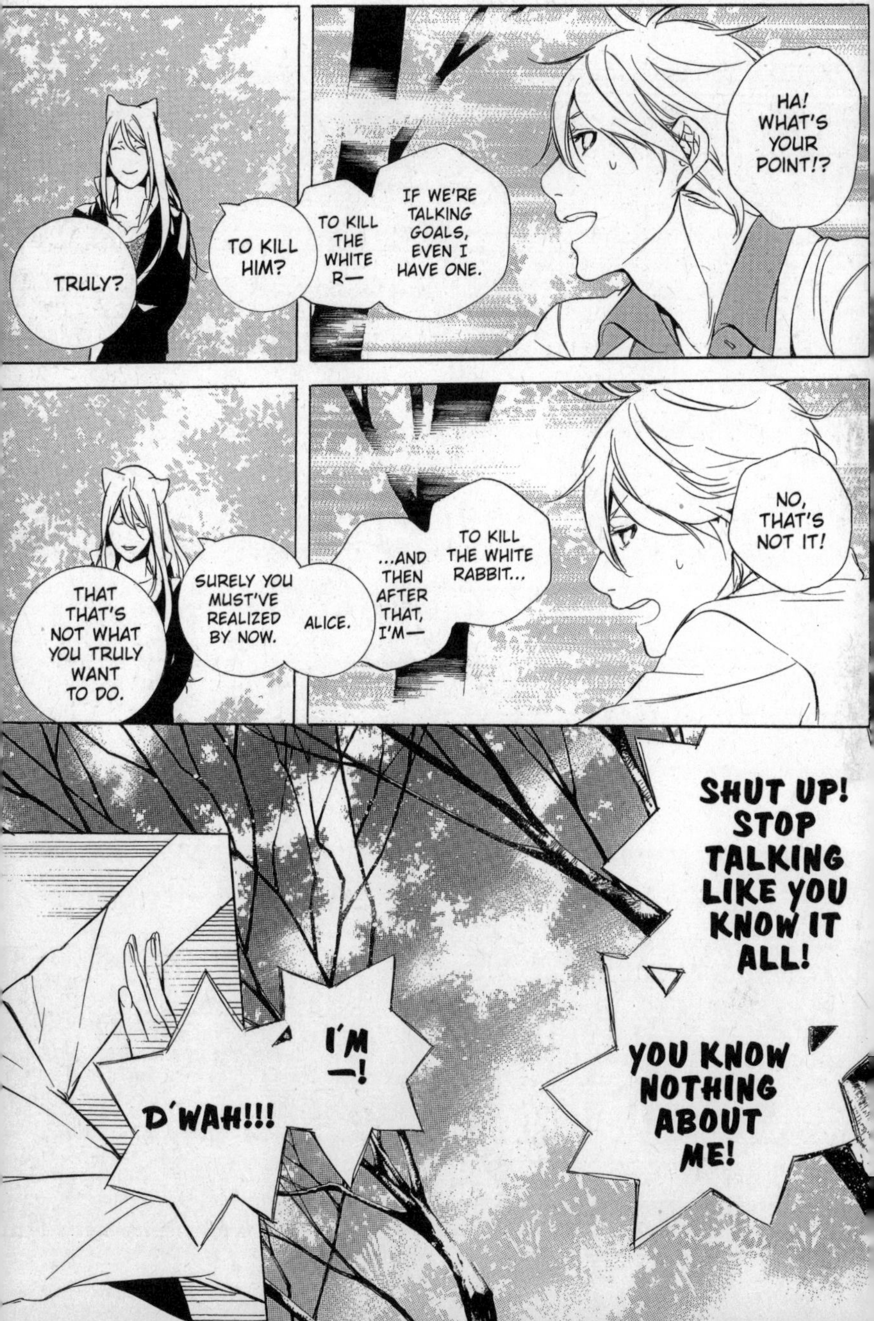
HA! WHAT'S YOUR POINT!?
IF WE'RE TALKING GOALS, EVEN I HAVE ONE.
TO KILL THE WHITE R—
TO KILL HIM?
TRULY?
NO, THAT'S NOT IT!
TO KILL THE WHITE RABBIT...
...AND THEN AFTER THAT, I'M—
ALICE.
SURELY YOU MUST'VE REALIZED BY NOW.
THAT THAT'S NOT WHAT YOU TRULY WANT TO DO.
SHUT UP! STOP TALKING LIKE YOU KNOW IT ALL!
YOU KNOW NOTHING ABOUT ME!
I'M —!
D'WAH!!!

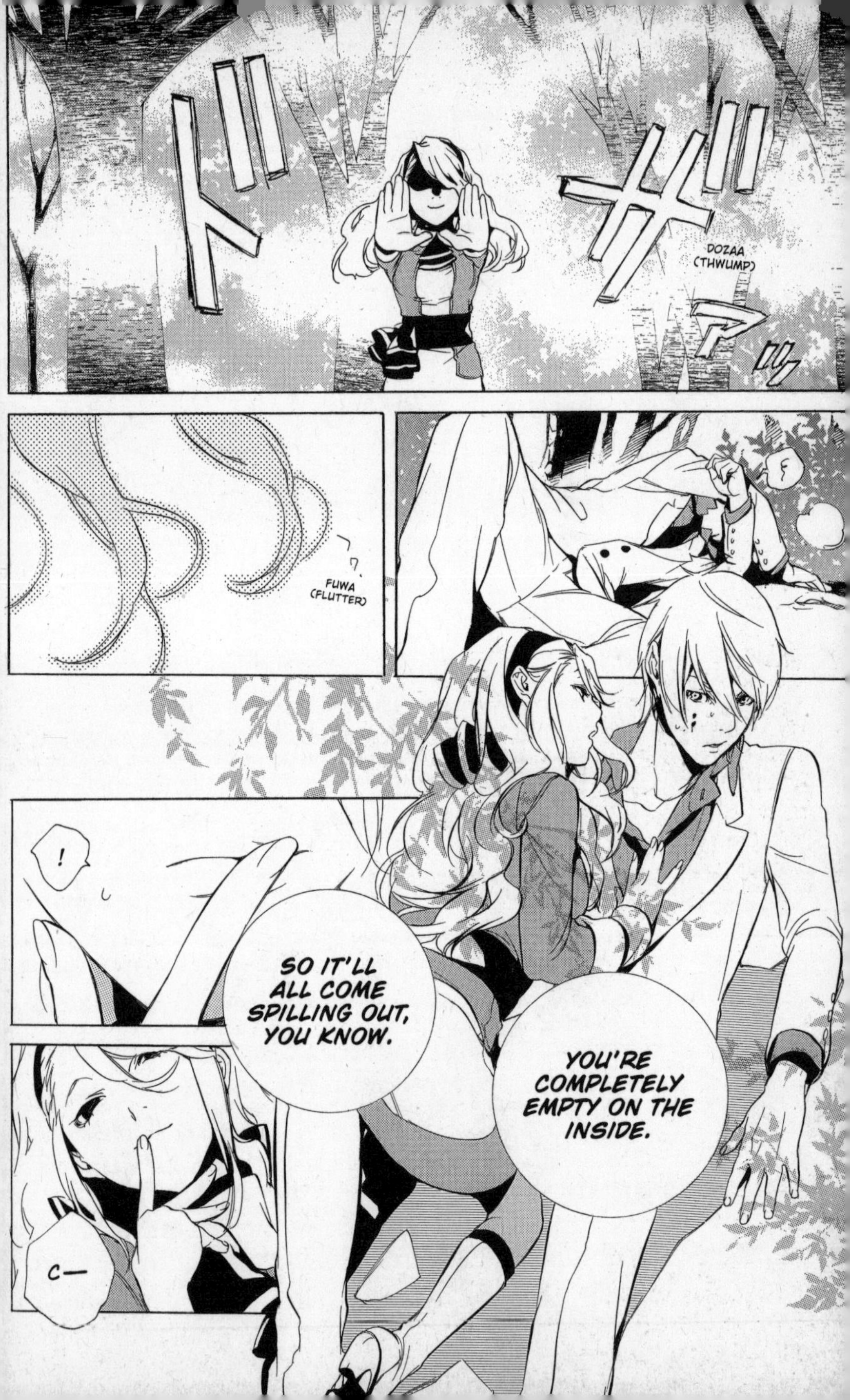
DOZAA (THWUMP)
YOU'RE COMPLETELY EMPTY ON THE INSIDE.
SO IT'LL ALL COME SPILLING OUT, YOU KNOW.
FUWA (FLUTTER)
!
C—

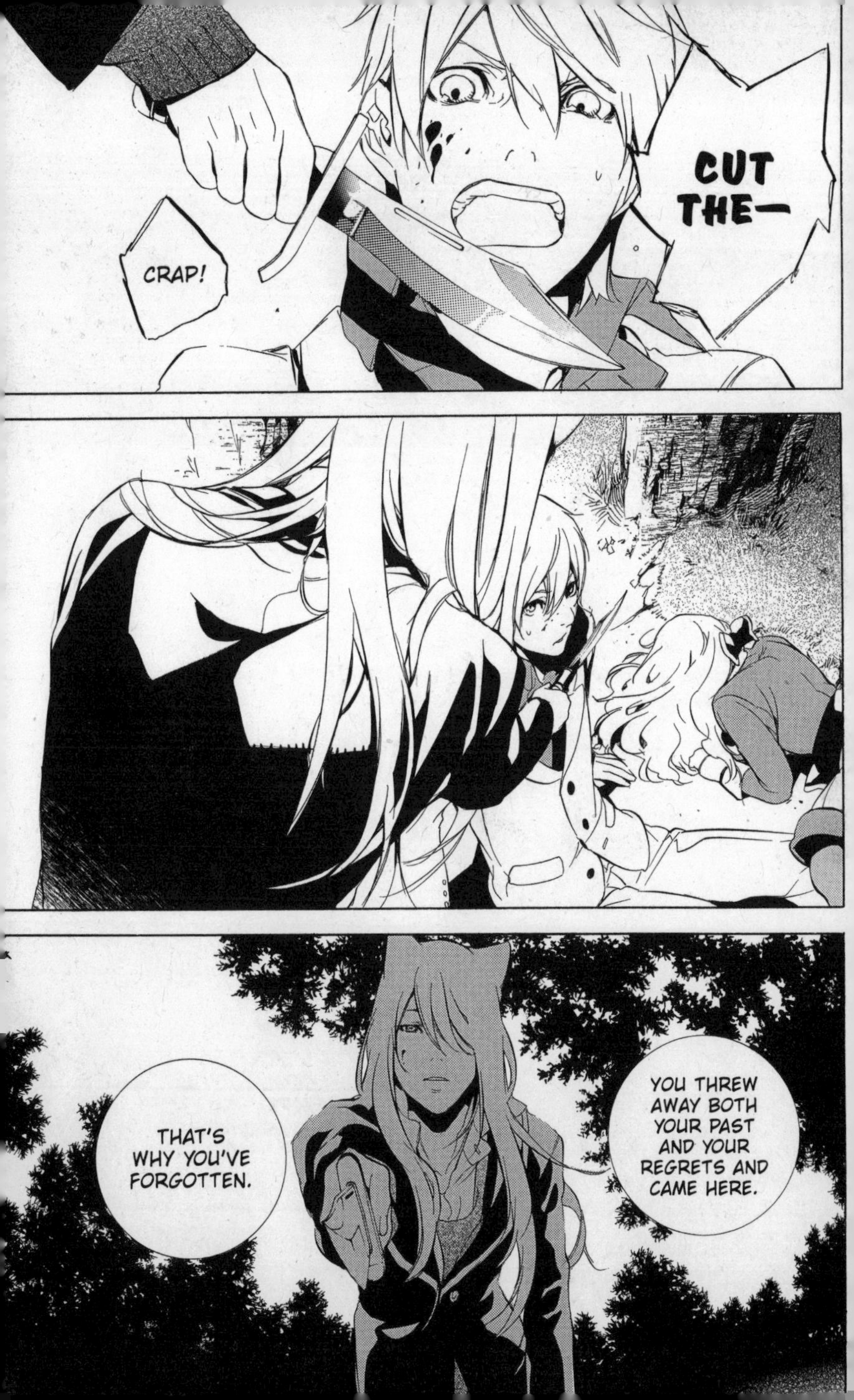
CUT THE—
CRAP!
YOU THREW AWAY BOTH YOUR PAST AND YOUR REGRETS AND CAME HERE.
THAT'S WHY YOU'VE FORGOTTEN.

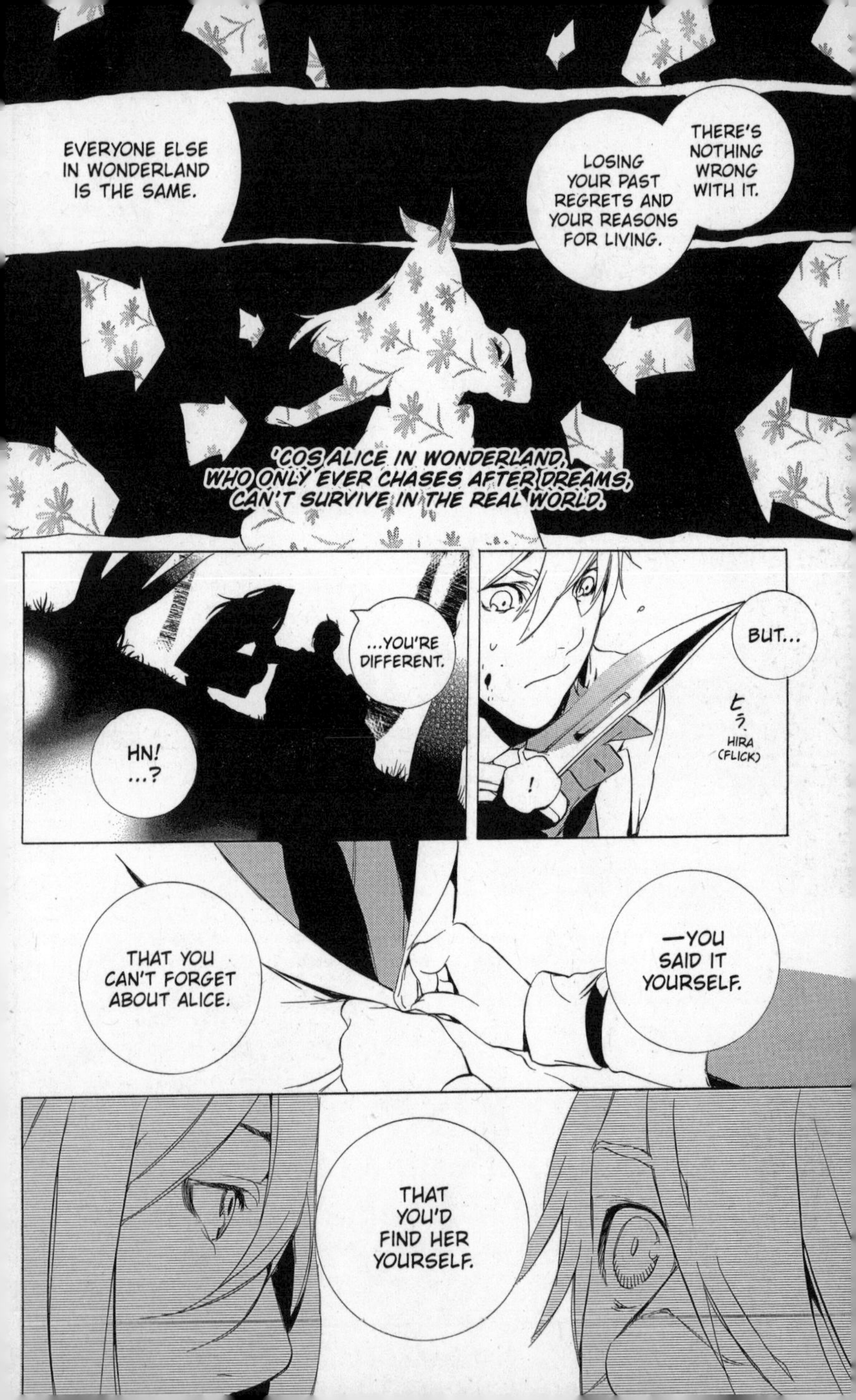
THERE'S NOTHING WRONG WITH IT.
LOSING YOUR PAST REGRETS AND YOUR REASONS FOR LIVING.
EVERYONE ELSE IN WONDERLAND IS THE SAME.
'COS ALICE IN WONDERLAND, WHO ONLY EVER CHASES AFTER DREAMS, CAN'T SURVIVE IN THE REAL WORLD.
BUT...
ヒラ
HIRA (FLICK)
!
...YOU'RE DIFFERENT.
HN! ...?
—YOU SAID IT YOURSELF.
THAT YOU CAN'T FORGET ABOUT ALICE.
THAT YOU'D FIND HER YOURSELF.

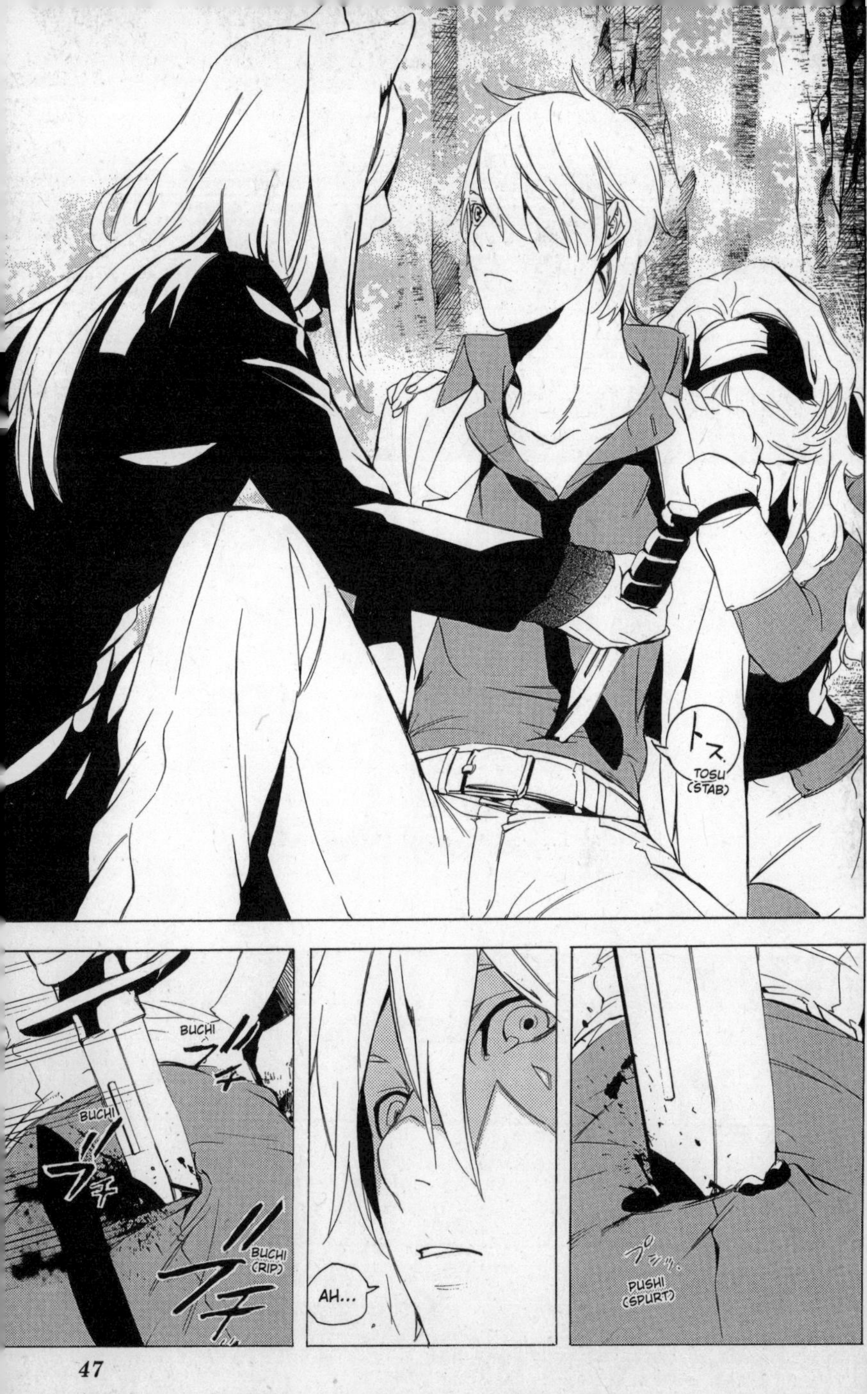
トス
TOSU
(STAB)
プシッ
PUSHI
(SPURT)
AH...
BUCHI
BUCHI
BUCHI
(RIP)

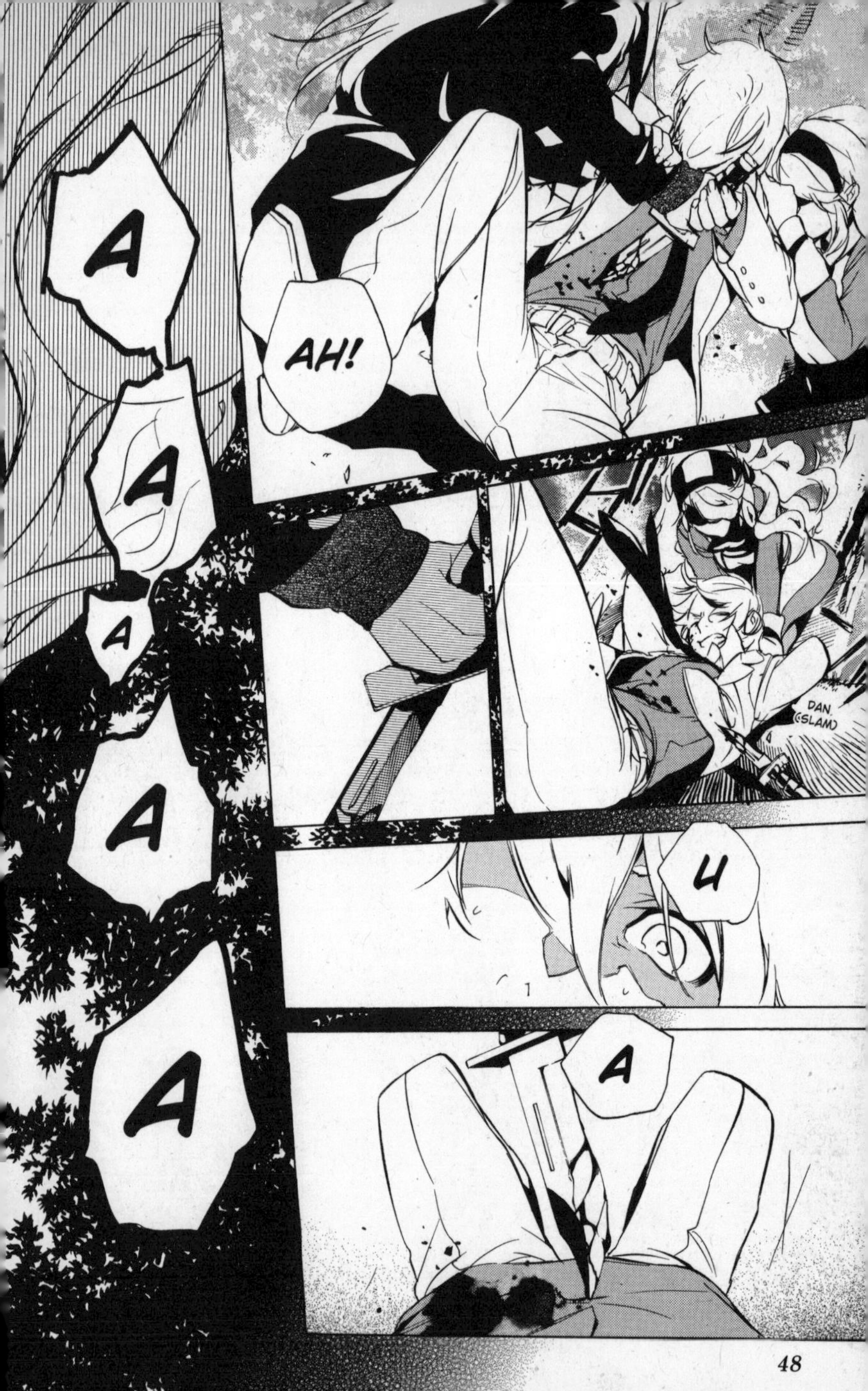
AH!
DAN.
(SLAM)
U
A
A
A
A
A
A

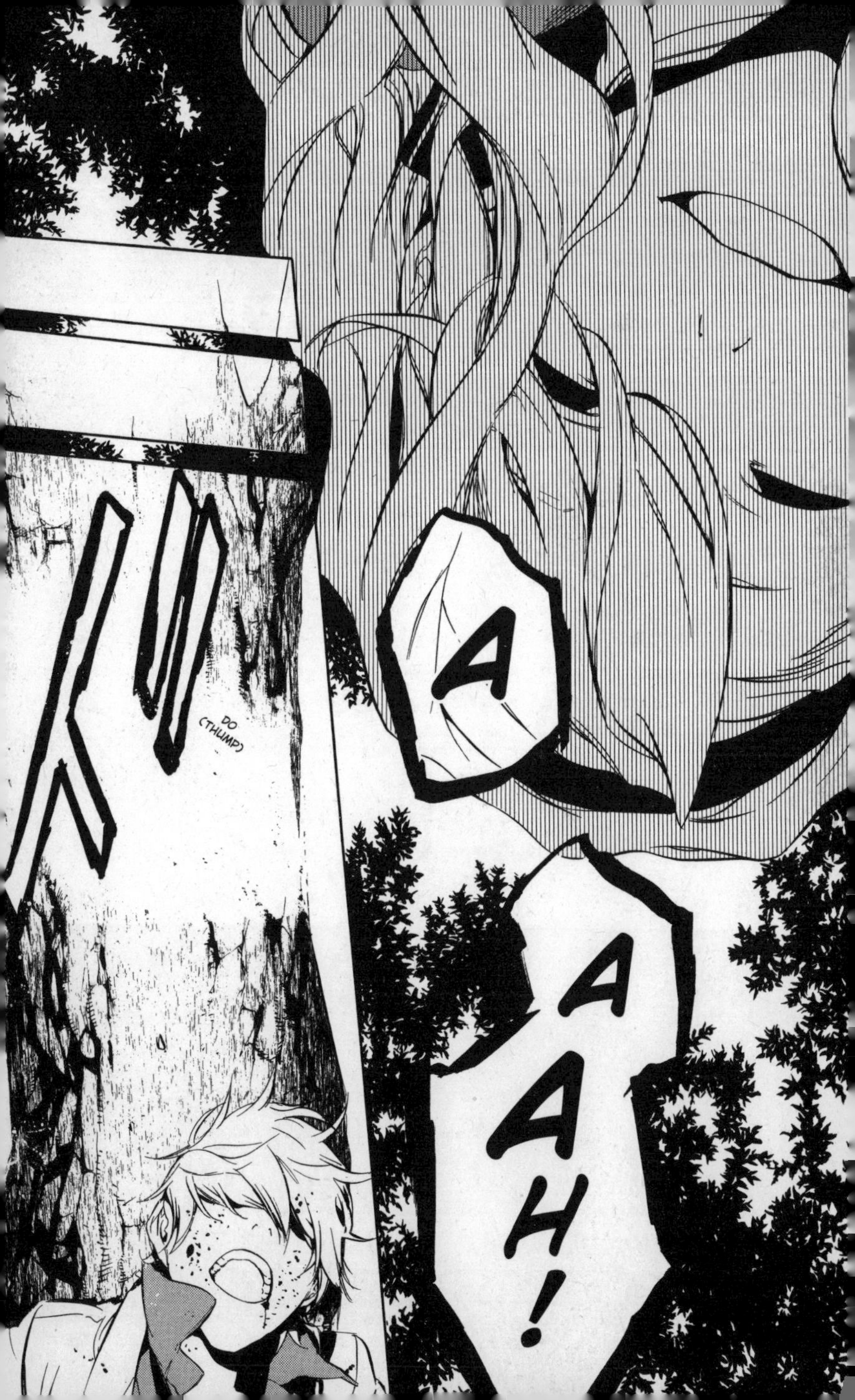
A
AAH!
DO
(THUMP)

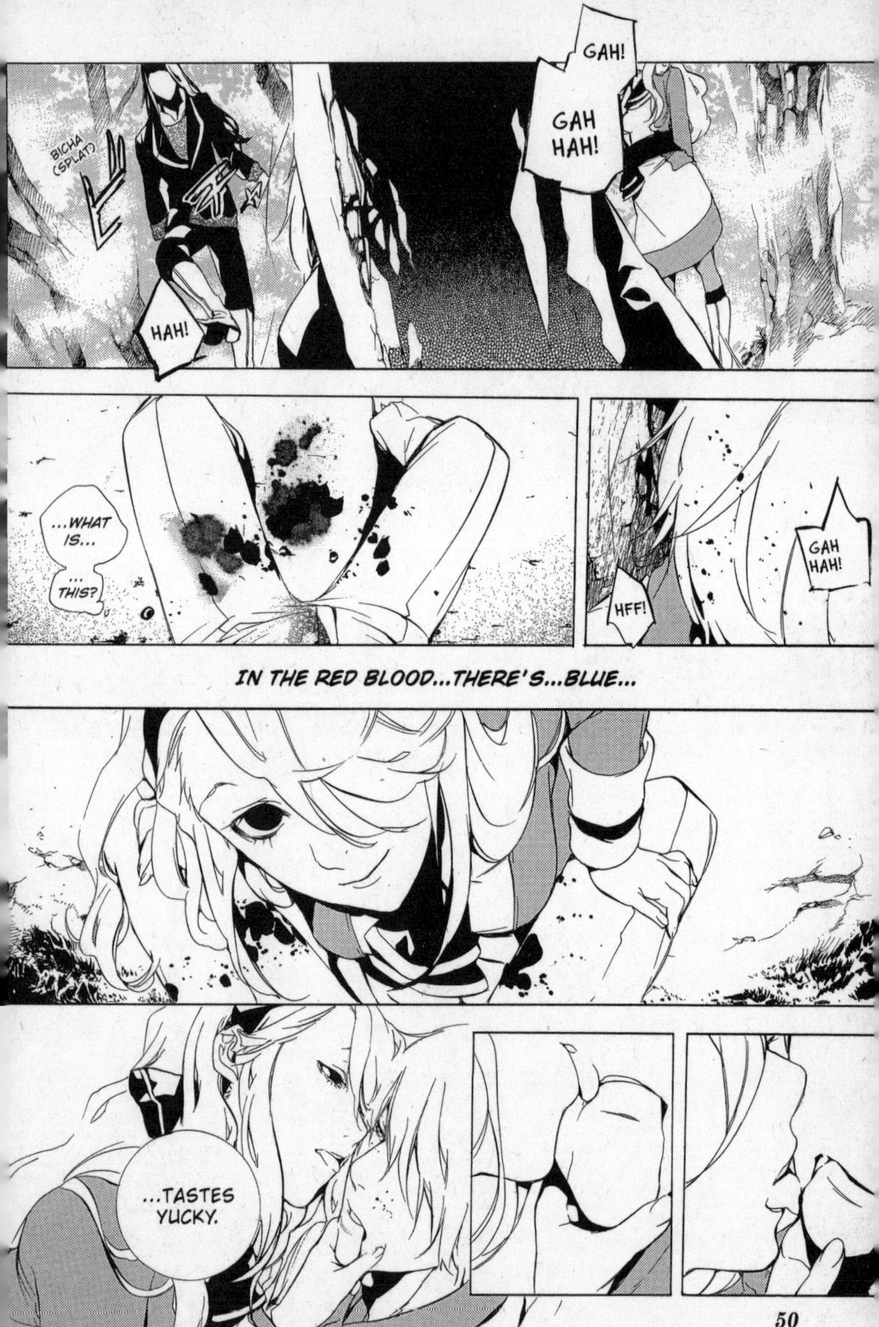
GAH!
GAH HAH!
BICHA (SPLAT)
HAH!
GAH HAH!
HFF!
...WHAT IS...
...THIS?
IN THE RED BLOOD...THERE'S...BLUE...
...TASTES YUCKY.

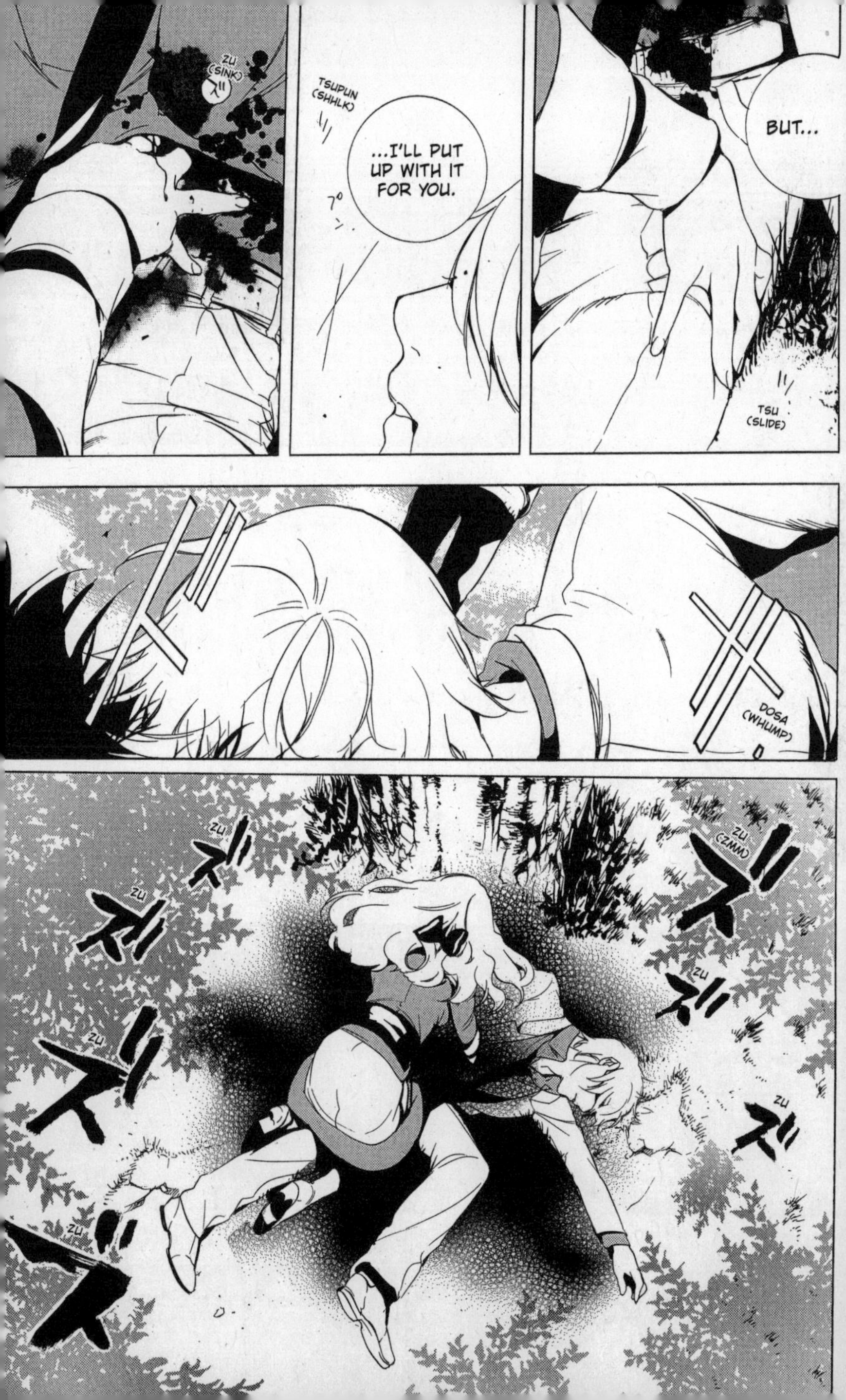
BUT...
TSU (SLIDE)
TSUPUN (SHHLK)
...I'LL PUT UP WITH IT FOR YOU.
ZU (SINK)
DOSA (WHUMP)
ZU (ZMM)
ZU
ZU
ZU
ZU
ZU

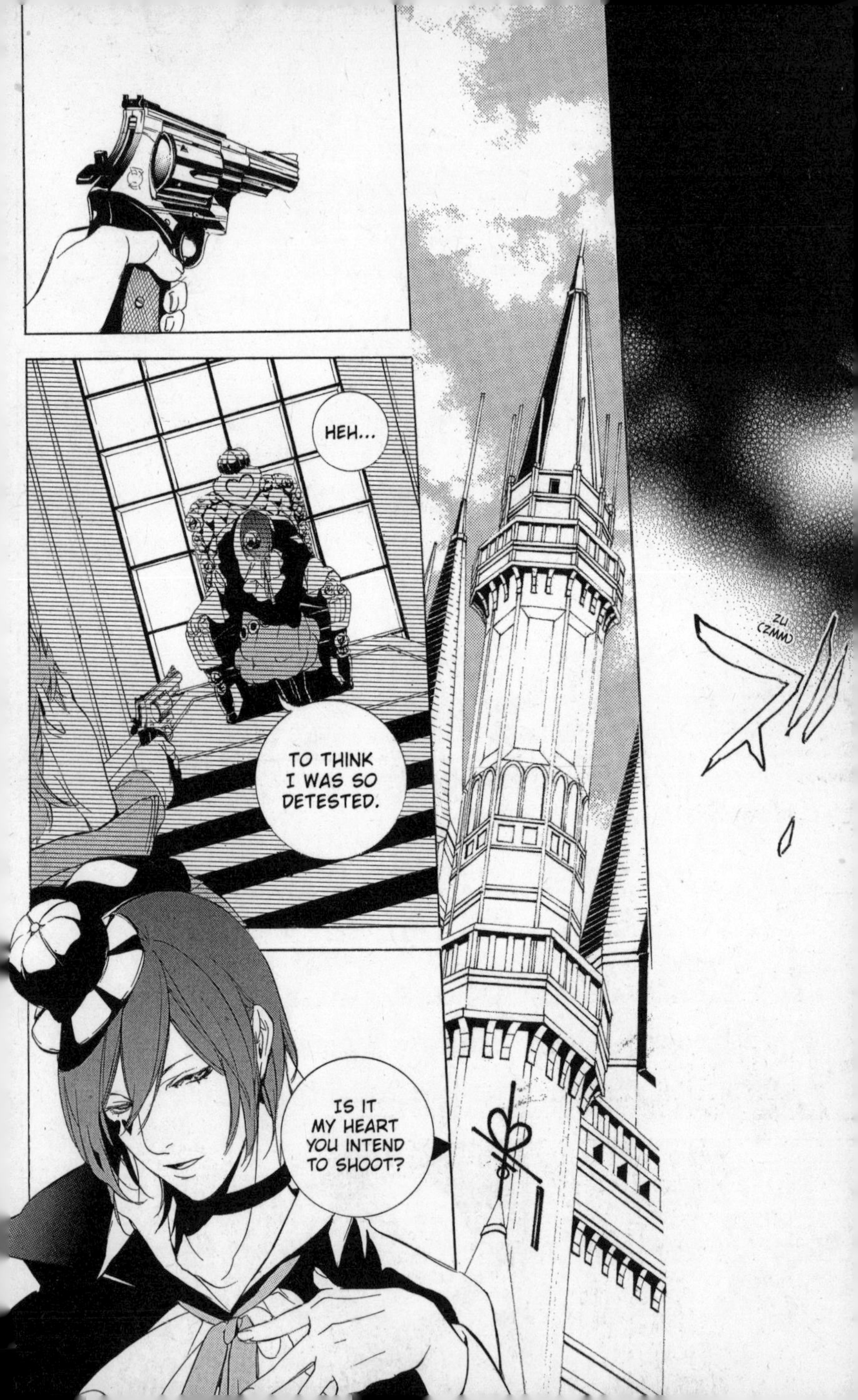
ZU
(ZMM)
HEH...
TO THINK I WAS SO DETESTED.
IS IT MY HEART YOU INTEND TO SHOOT?

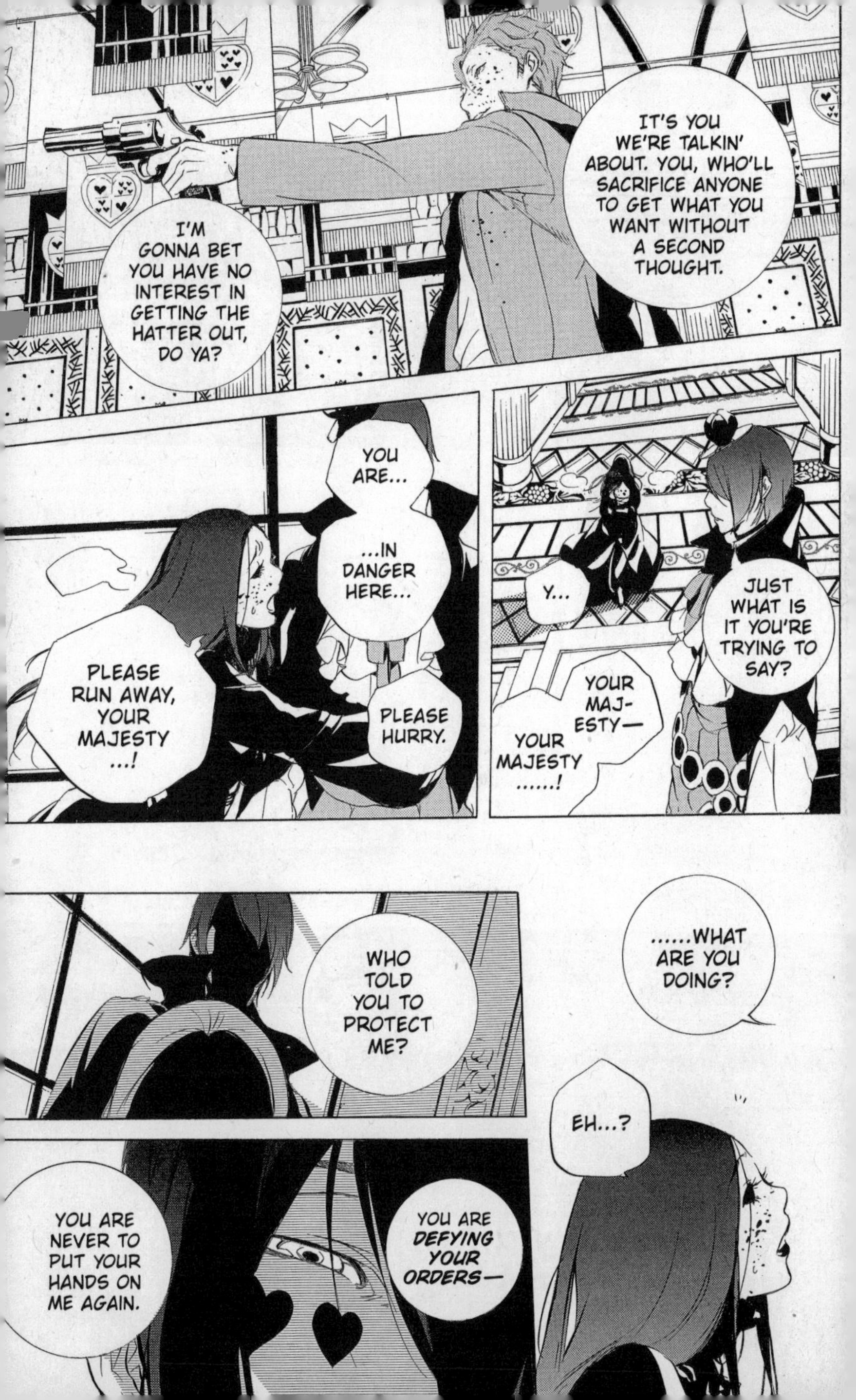

IT'S YOU WE'RE TALKIN' ABOUT. YOU, WHO'LL SACRIFICE ANYONE TO GET WHAT YOU WANT WITHOUT A SECOND THOUGHT.
I'M GONNA BET YOU HAVE NO INTEREST IN GETTING THE HATTER OUT, DO YA?
JUST WHAT IS IT YOU'RE TRYING TO SAY?
Y...
YOUR MAJ-ESTY—
YOUR MAJESTY ......!
YOU ARE...
...IN DANGER HERE...
PLEASE HURRY.
PLEASE RUN AWAY, YOUR MAJESTY ...!
......WHAT ARE YOU DOING?
WHO TOLD YOU TO PROTECT ME?
EH...?
YOU ARE *DEFYING YOUR ORDERS*—
YOU ARE NEVER TO PUT YOUR HANDS ON ME AGAIN.

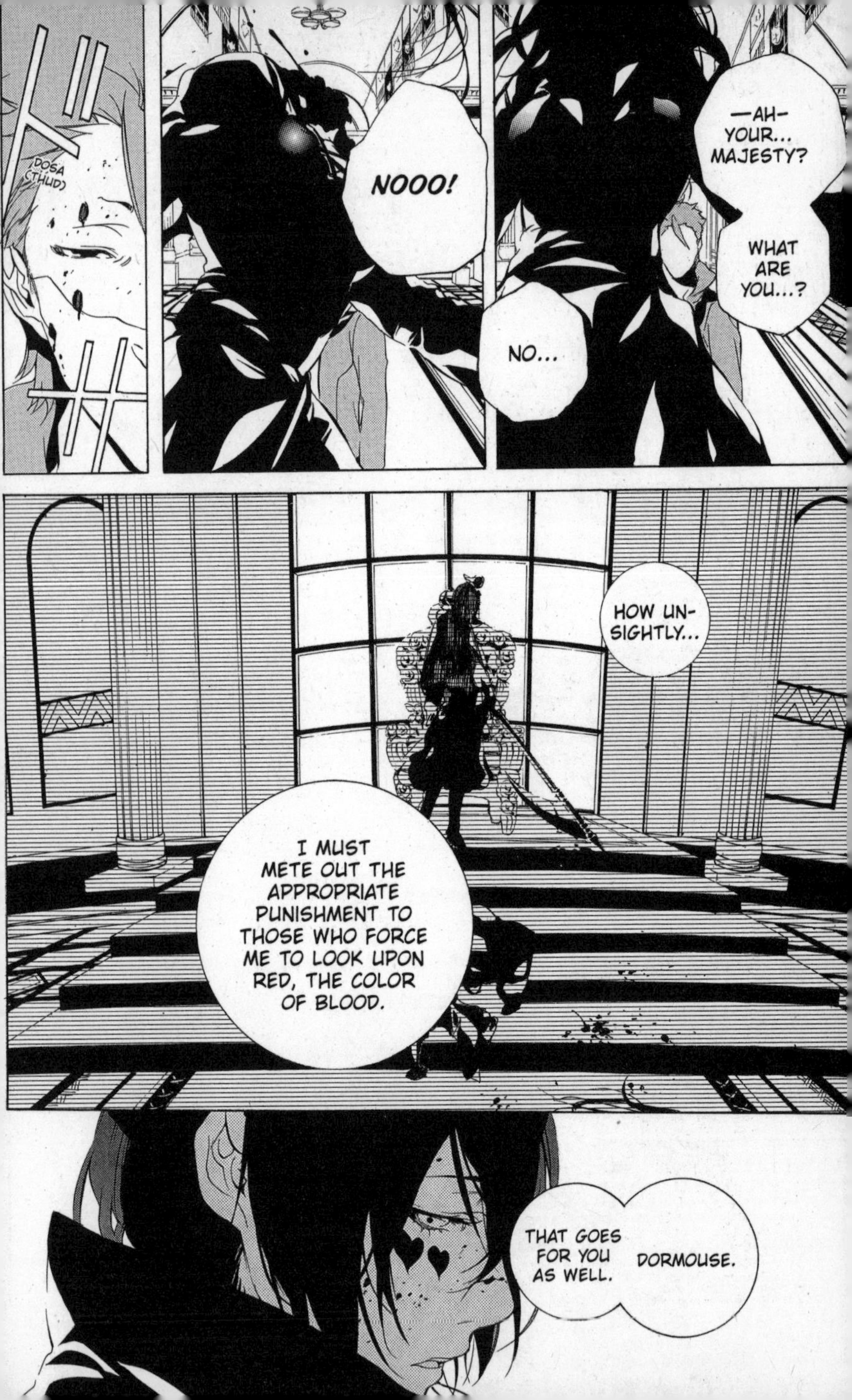
—AH— YOUR... MAJESTY?
WHAT ARE YOU...?
NO...
NOOO!
DOSA (THUD)
HOW UN-SIGHTLY...
I MUST METE OUT THE APPROPRIATE PUNISHMENT TO THOSE WHO FORCE ME TO LOOK UPON RED, THE COLOR OF BLOOD.
THAT GOES FOR YOU AS WELL.
DORMOUSE.

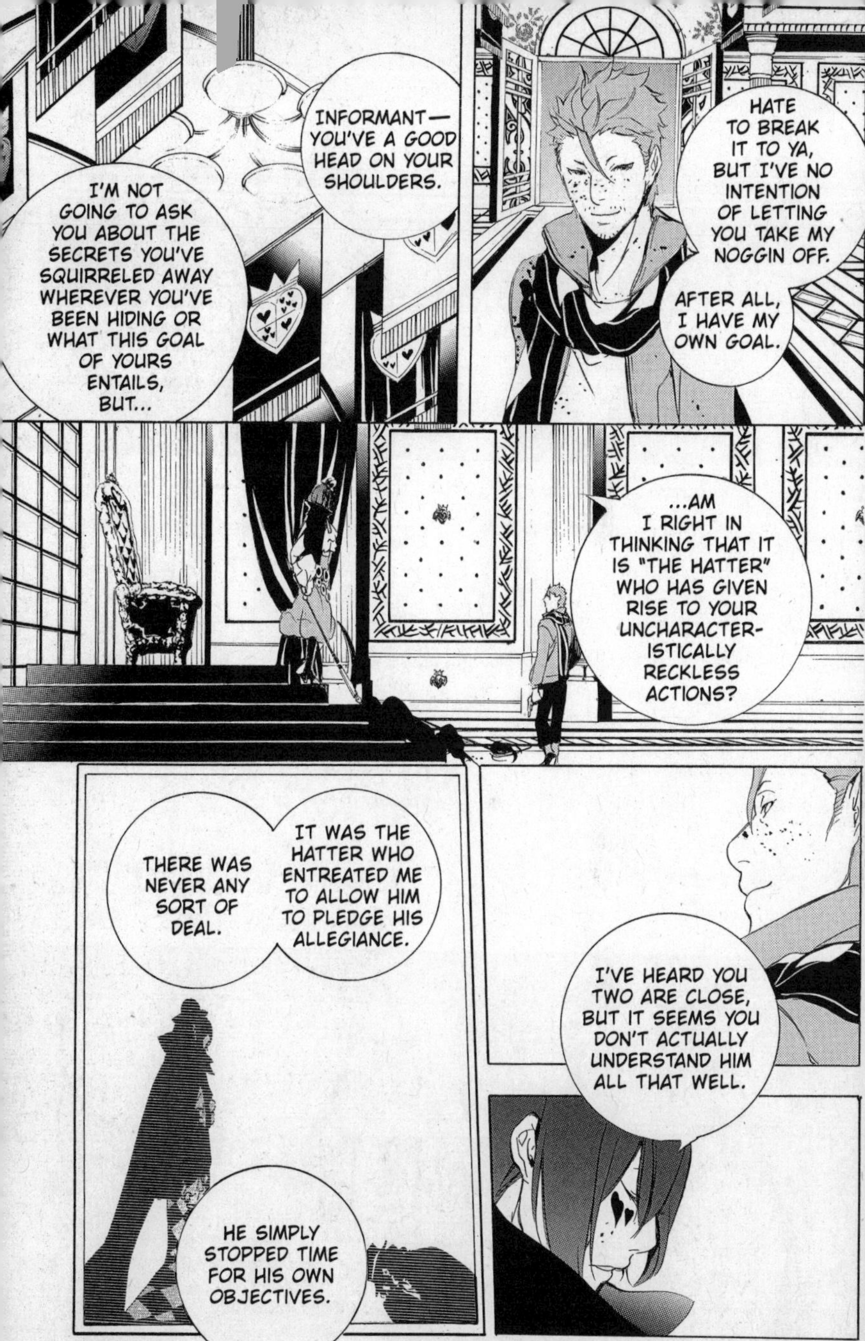
HATE TO BREAK IT TO YA, BUT I'VE NO INTENTION OF LETTING YOU TAKE MY NOGGIN OFF.
AFTER ALL, I HAVE MY OWN GOAL.
INFORMANT— YOU'VE A GOOD HEAD ON YOUR SHOULDERS.
I'M NOT GOING TO ASK YOU ABOUT THE SECRETS YOU'VE SQUIRRELED AWAY WHEREVER YOU'VE BEEN HIDING OR WHAT THIS GOAL OF YOURS ENTAILS, BUT...
...AM I RIGHT IN THINKING THAT IT IS "THE HATTER" WHO HAS GIVEN RISE TO YOUR UNCHARACTER-ISTICALLY RECKLESS ACTIONS?
I'VE HEARD YOU TWO ARE CLOSE, BUT IT SEEMS YOU DON'T ACTUALLY UNDERSTAND HIM ALL THAT WELL.
IT WAS THE HATTER WHO ENTREATED ME TO ALLOW HIM TO PLEDGE HIS ALLEGIANCE.
THERE WAS NEVER ANY SORT OF DEAL.
HE SIMPLY STOPPED TIME FOR HIS OWN OBJECTIVES.

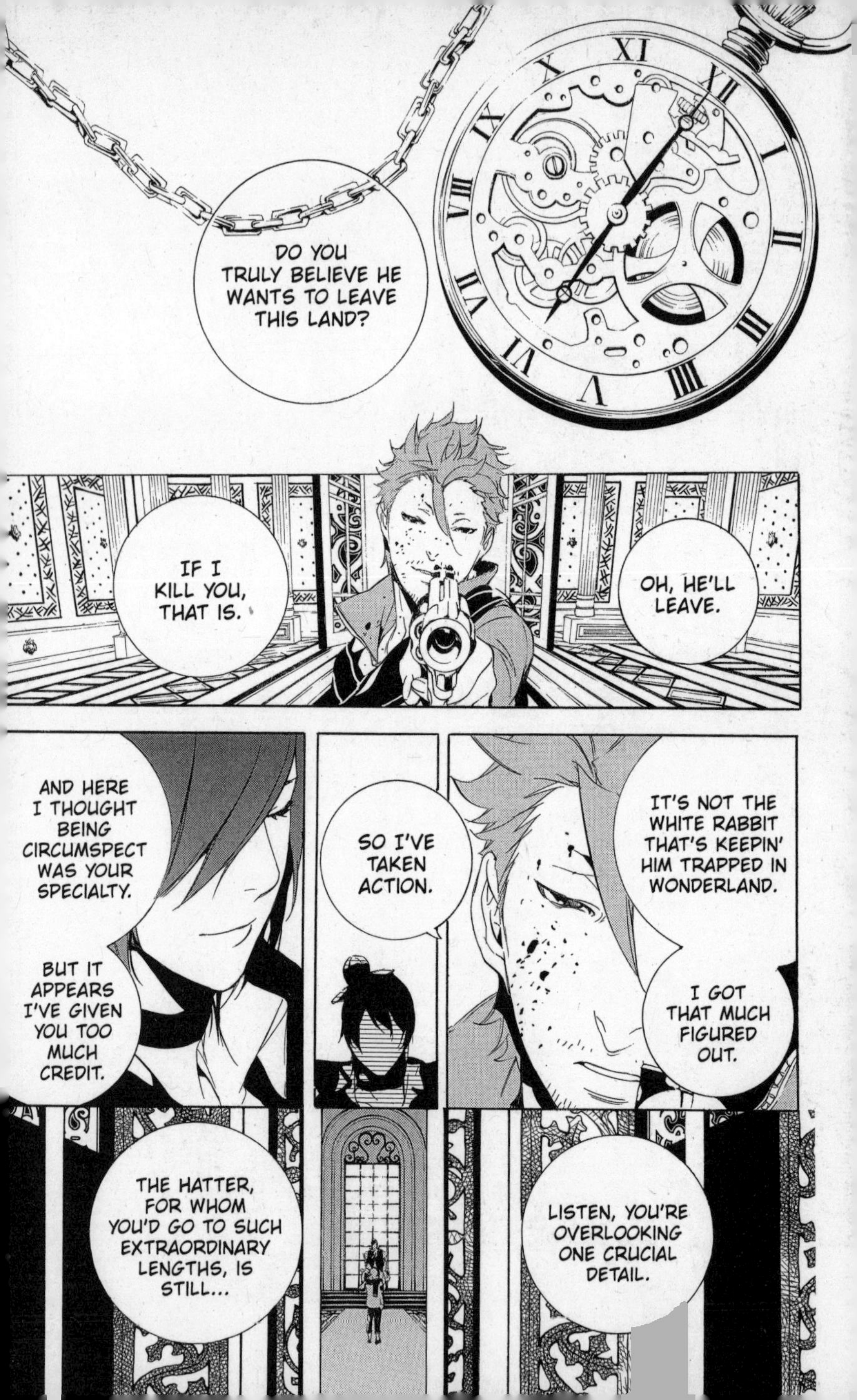
DO YOU TRULY BELIEVE HE WANTS TO LEAVE THIS LAND?
OH, HE'LL LEAVE.
IF I KILL YOU, THAT IS.
IT'S NOT THE WHITE RABBIT THAT'S KEEPIN' HIM TRAPPED IN WONDERLAND.
I GOT THAT MUCH FIGURED OUT.
SO I'VE TAKEN ACTION.
AND HERE I THOUGHT BEING CIRCUMSPECT WAS YOUR SPECIALTY.
BUT IT APPEARS I'VE GIVEN YOU TOO MUCH CREDIT.
LISTEN, YOU'RE OVERLOOKING ONE CRUCIAL DETAIL.
THE HATTER, FOR WHOM YOU'D GO TO SUCH EXTRAORDINARY LENGTHS, IS STILL...

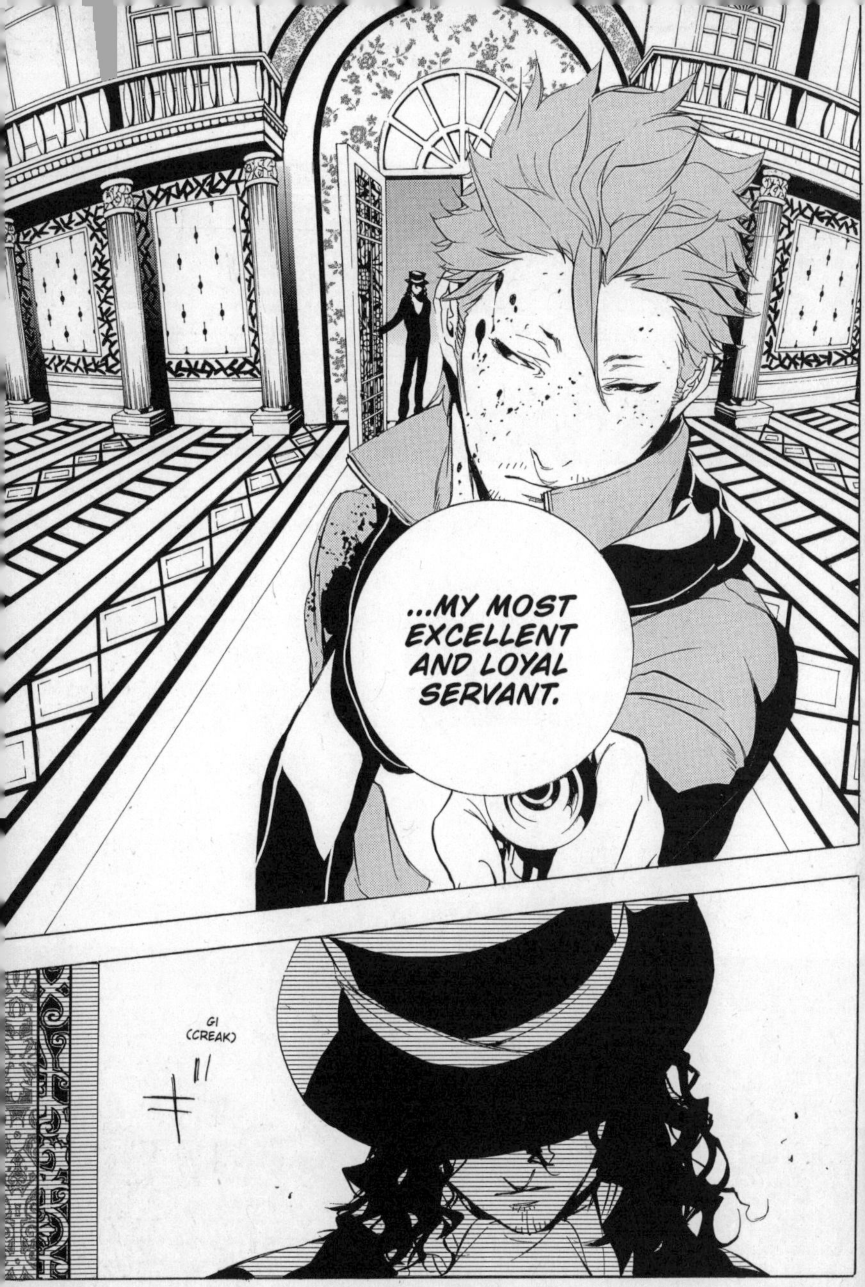
...MY MOST EXCELLENT AND LOYAL SERVANT.
GI (CREAK)

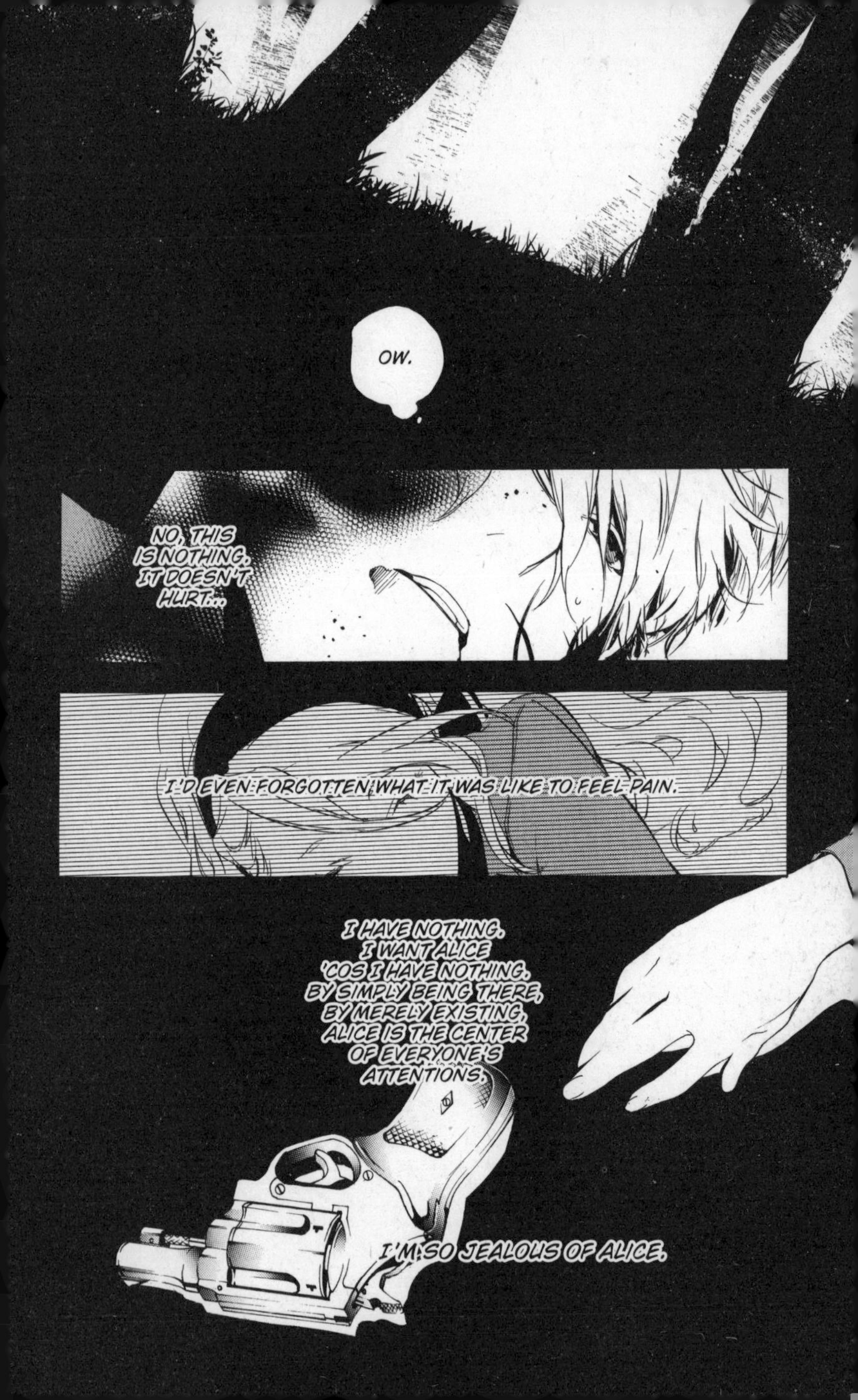
OW.
NO, THIS IS NOTHING. IT DOESN'T HURT...
I'D EVEN FORGOTTEN WHAT IT WAS LIKE TO FEEL PAIN.
I HAVE NOTHING. I WANT ALICE 'COS I HAVE NOTHING. BY SIMPLY BEING THERE, BY MERELY EXISTING, ALICE IS THE CENTER OF EVERYONE'S ATTENTIONS.
I'M SO JEALOUS OF ALICE.

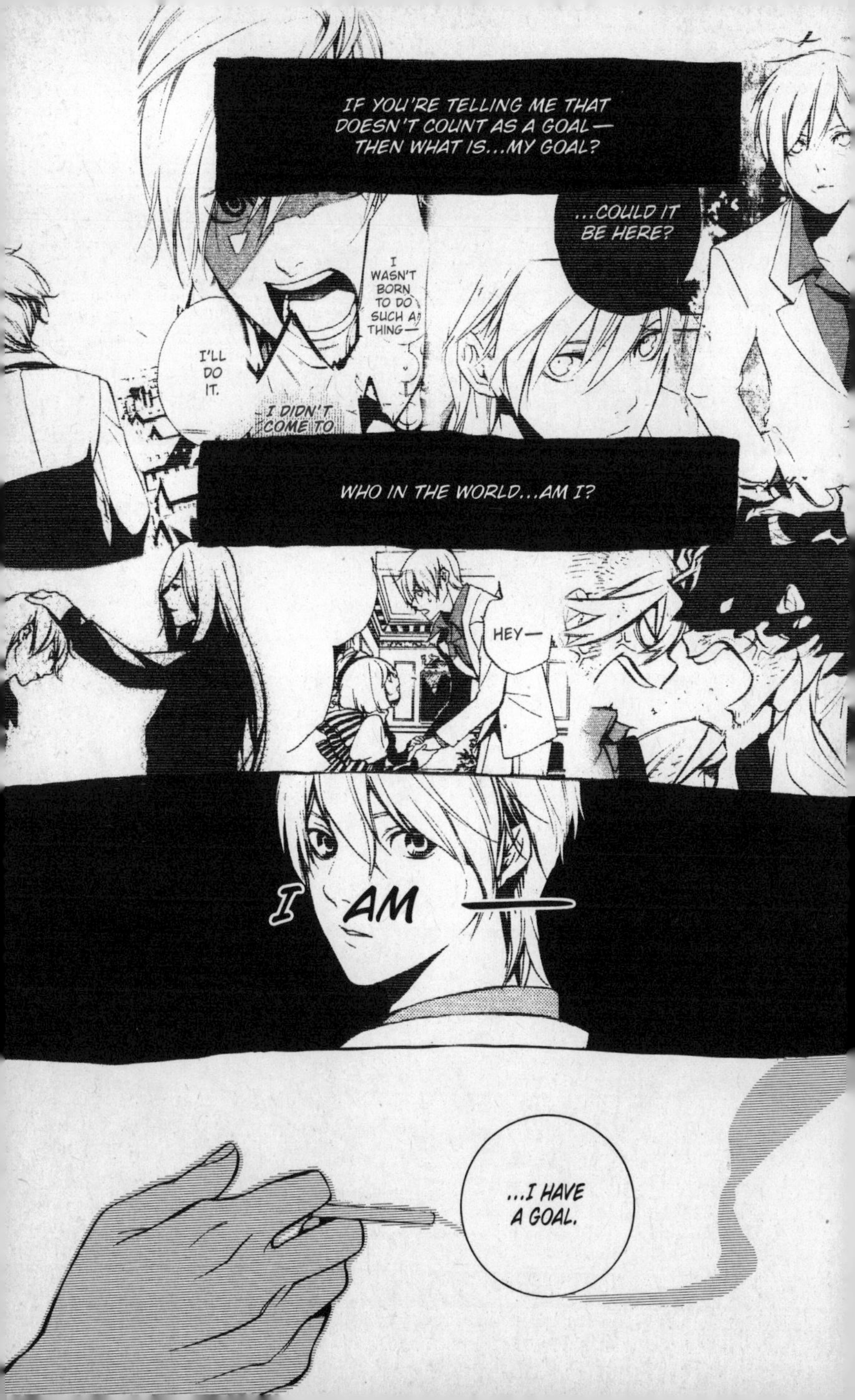
IF YOU'RE TELLING ME THAT DOESN'T COUNT AS A GOAL— THEN WHAT IS...MY GOAL?
...COULD IT BE HERE?
I WASN'T BORN TO DO SUCH A THING—
I'LL DO IT.
I DIDN'T COME TO
WHO IN THE WORLD...AM I?
HEY—
I AM—
...I HAVE A GOAL.

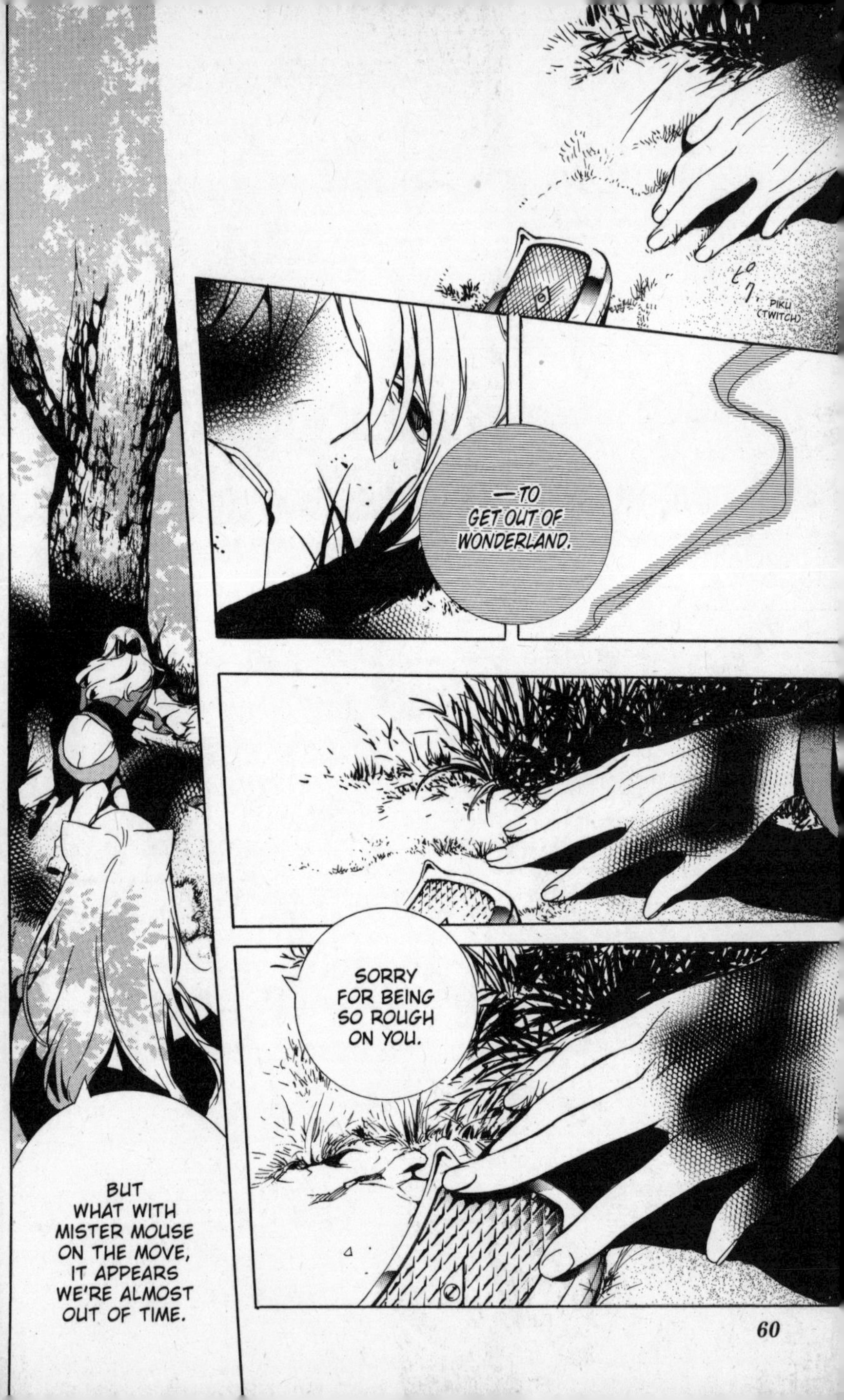
PIKU (TWITCH)
—TO GET OUT OF WONDERLAND.
SORRY FOR BEING SO ROUGH ON YOU.
BUT WHAT WITH MISTER MOUSE ON THE MOVE, IT APPEARS WE'RE ALMOST OUT OF TIME.

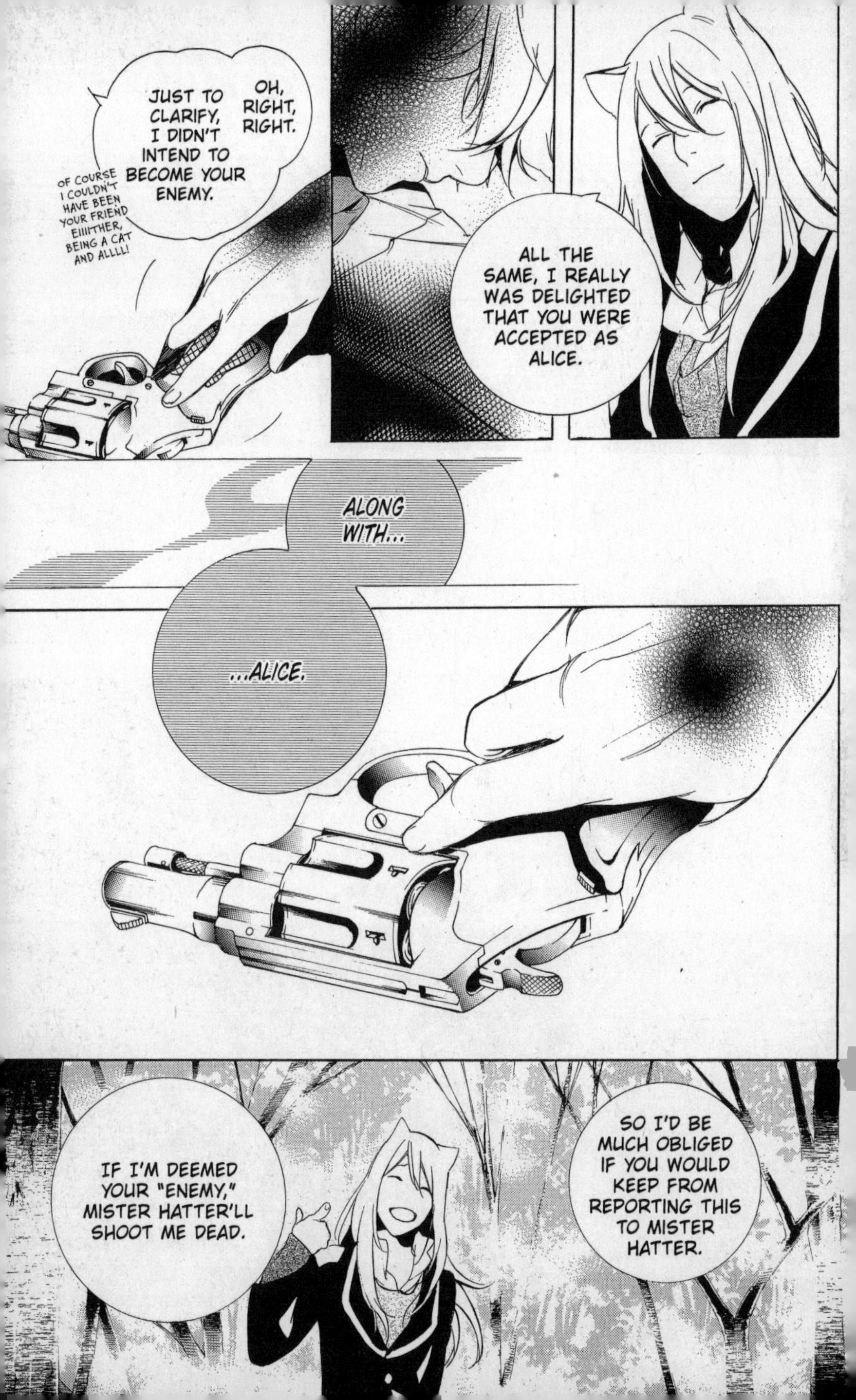
OH, RIGHT, RIGHT.
JUST TO CLARIFY, I DIDN'T INTEND TO BECOME YOUR ENEMY.
OF COURSE I COULDN'T HAVE BEEN YOUR FRIEND EIIIITHER, BEING A CAT AND ALLLL!
ALL THE SAME, I REALLY WAS DELIGHTED THAT YOU WERE ACCEPTED AS ALICE.
ALONG WITH...
...ALICE.
IF I'M DEEMED YOUR "ENEMY," MISTER HATTER'LL SHOOT ME DEAD.
SO I'D BE MUCH OBLIGED IF YOU WOULD KEEP FROM REPORTING THIS TO MISTER HATTER.

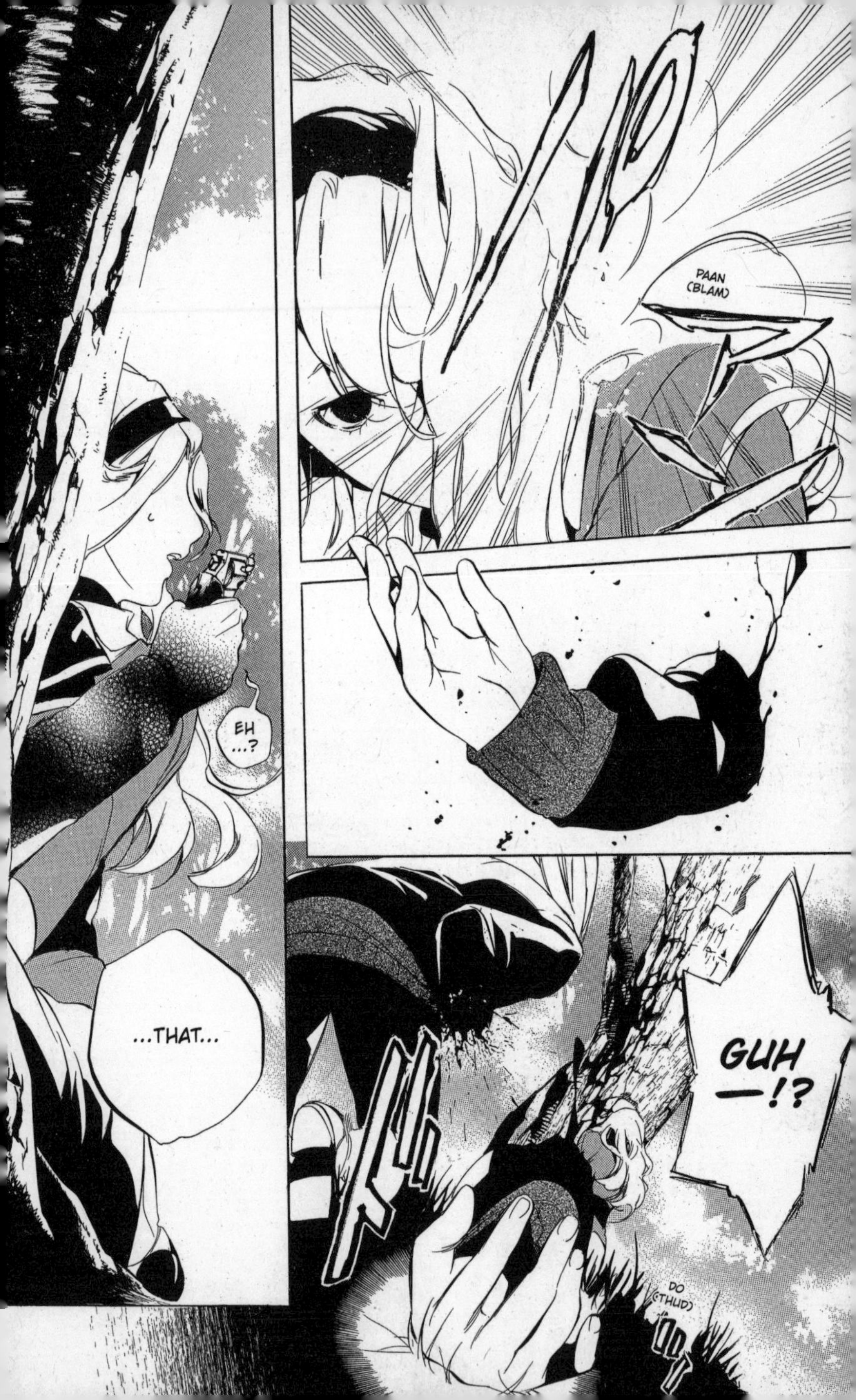
PAAN (BLAM)
GUH—!?
DO (THUD)
EH ...?
...THAT...

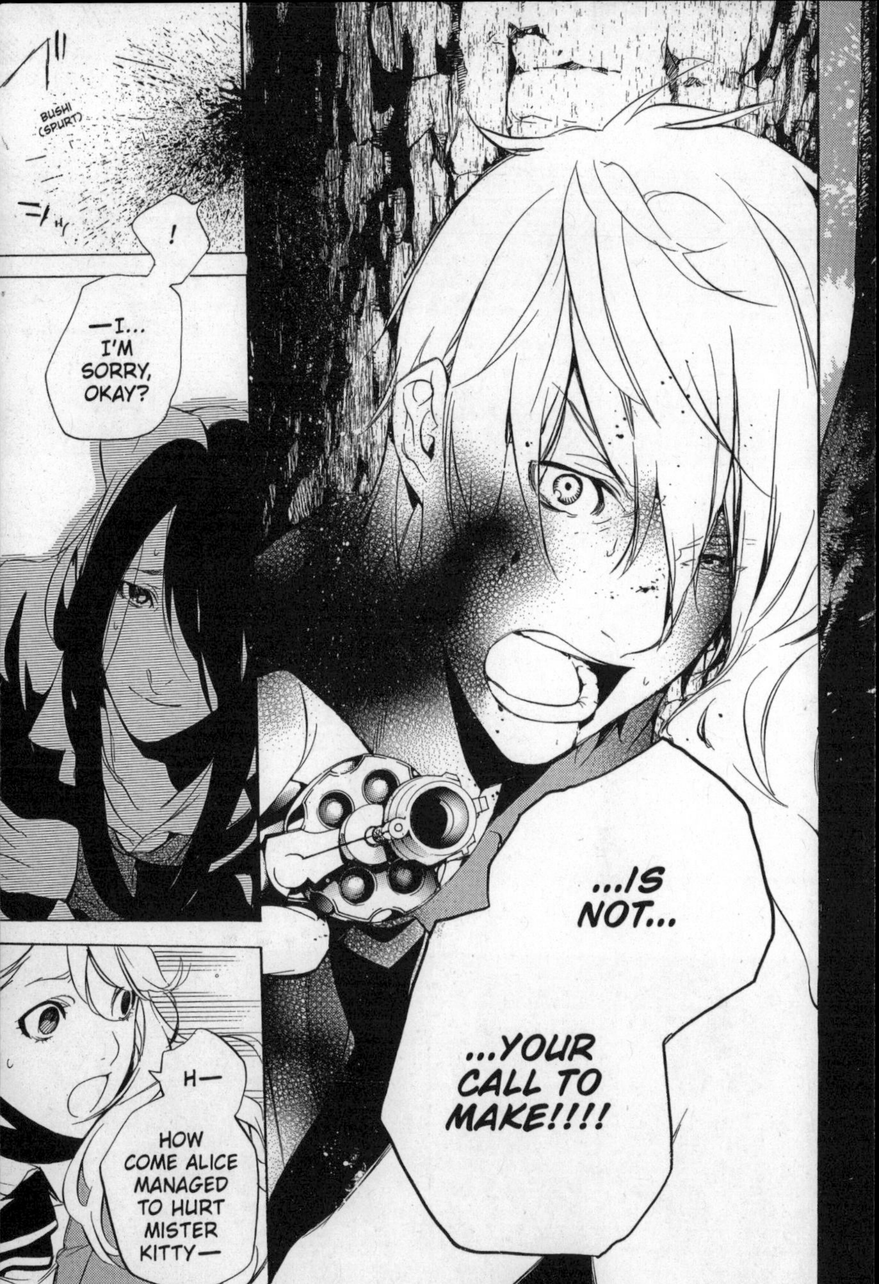
...IS NOT...
...YOUR CALL TO MAKE!!!!
BUSHI (SPURT)
!
—I... I'M SORRY, OKAY?
H—
HOW COME ALICE MANAGED TO HURT MISTER KITTY—

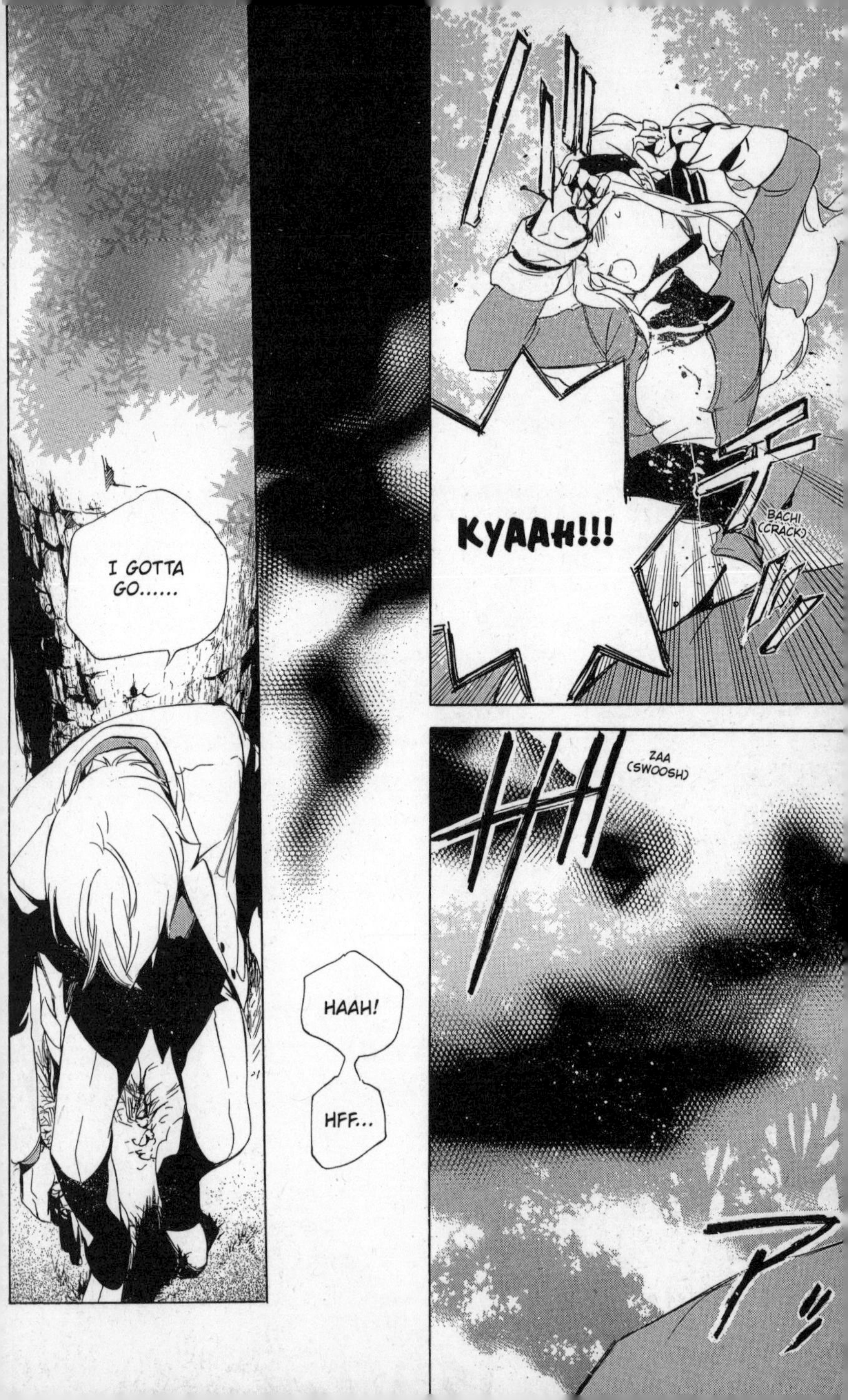
KYAAH!!!
BACHI (CRACK)
ZAA (SWOOSH)
HAAH!
HFF...
I GOTTA GO......

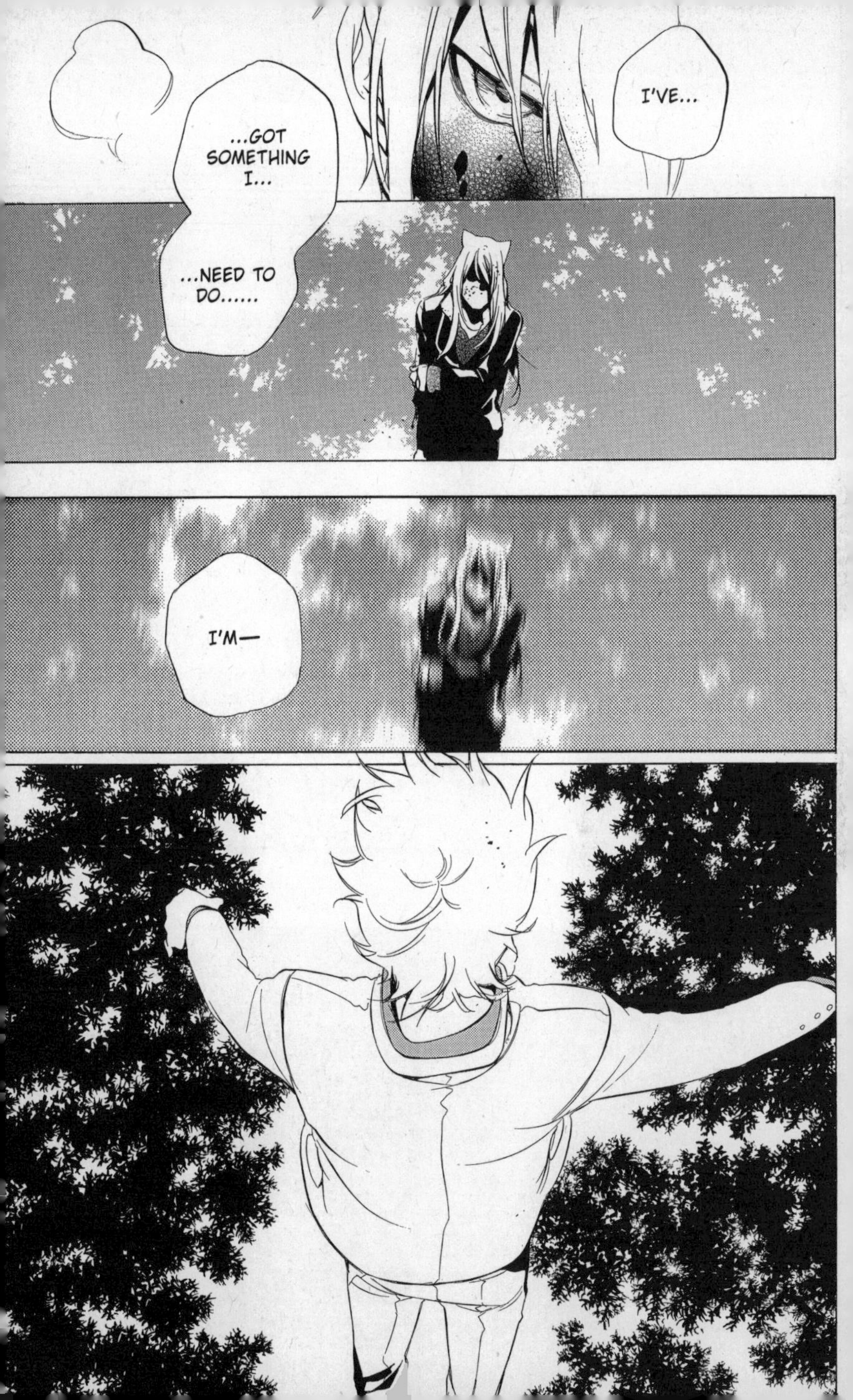
I'VE...
...GOT SOMETHING I...
...NEED TO DO......
I'M—

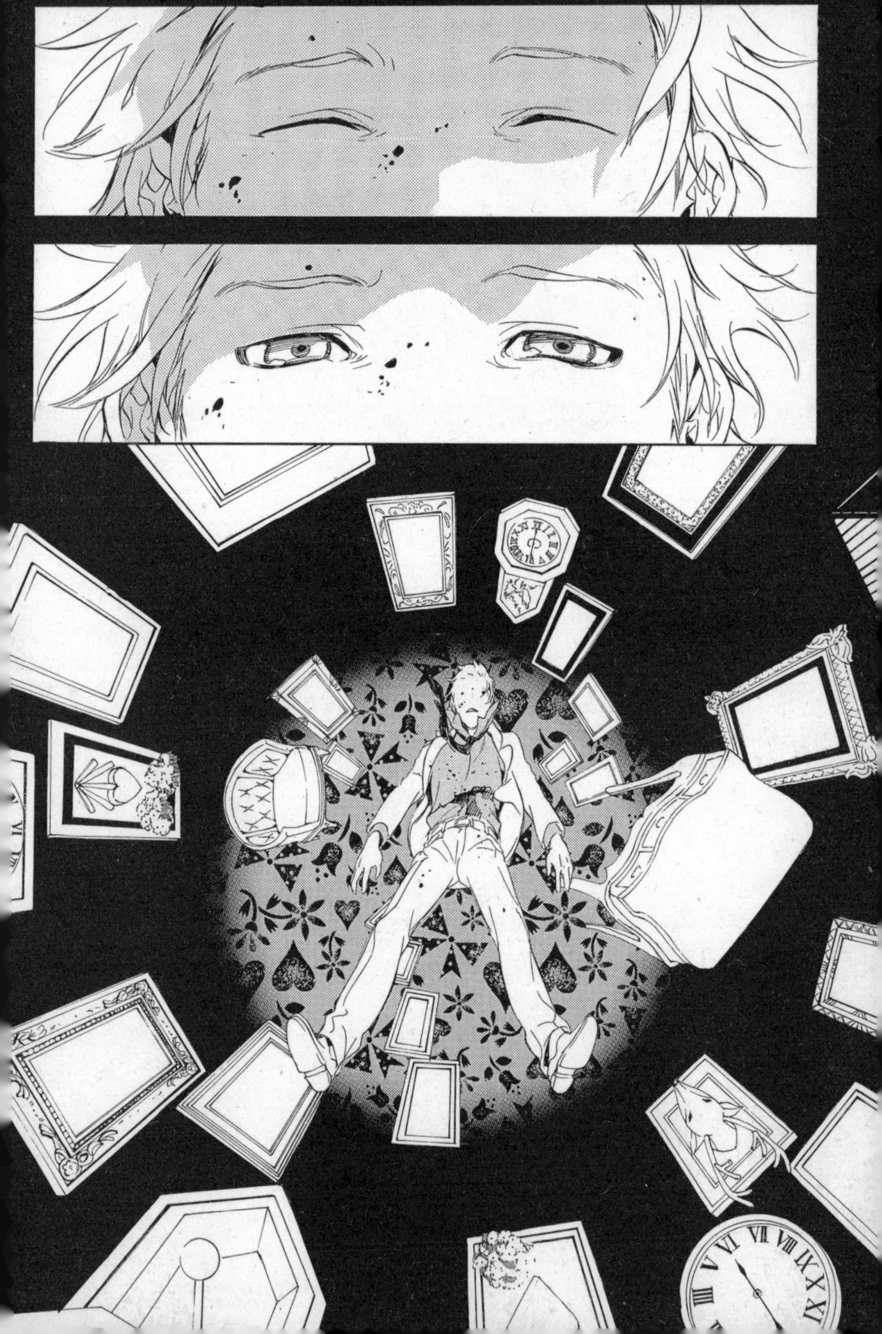

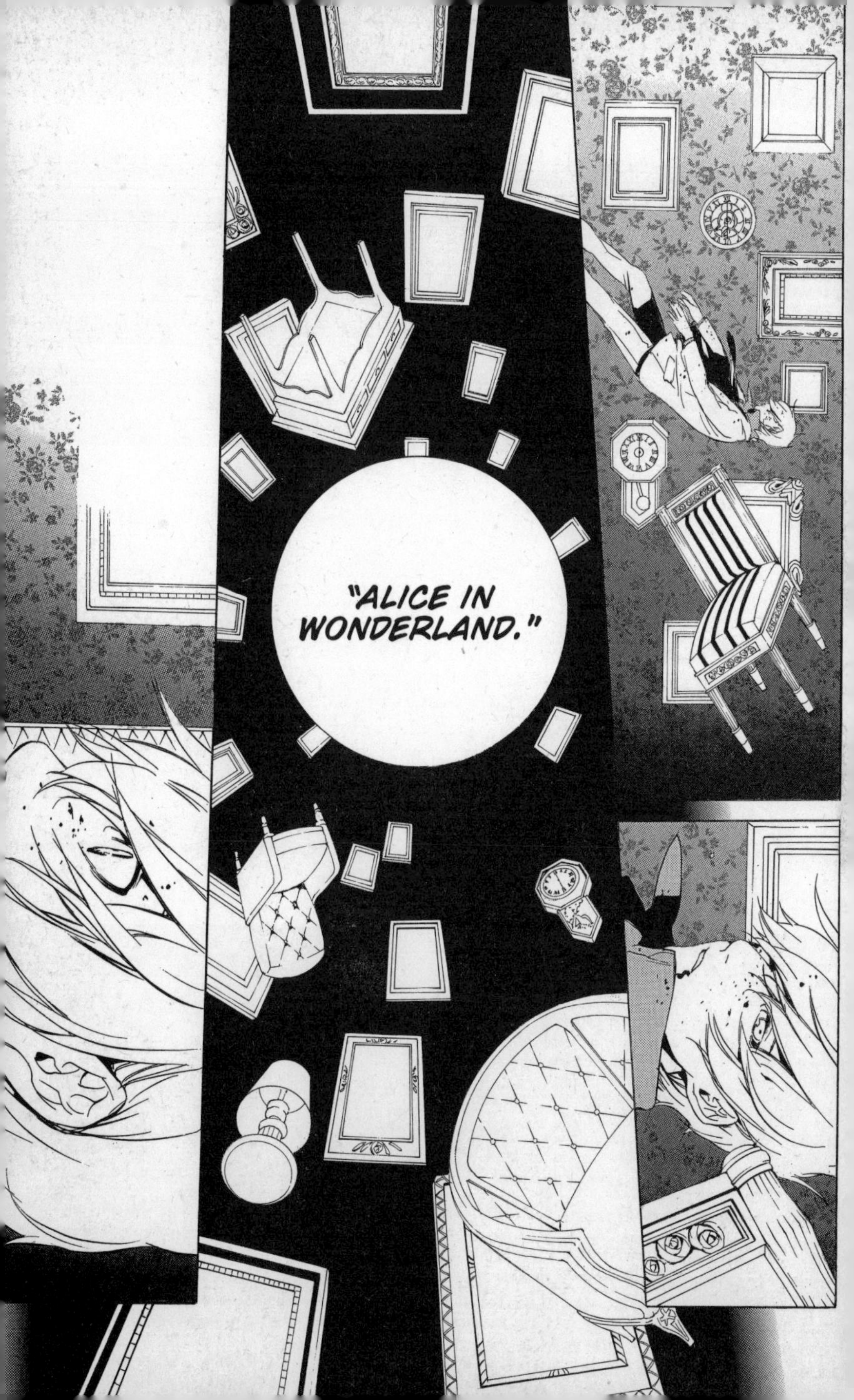
"ALICE IN WONDERLAND."

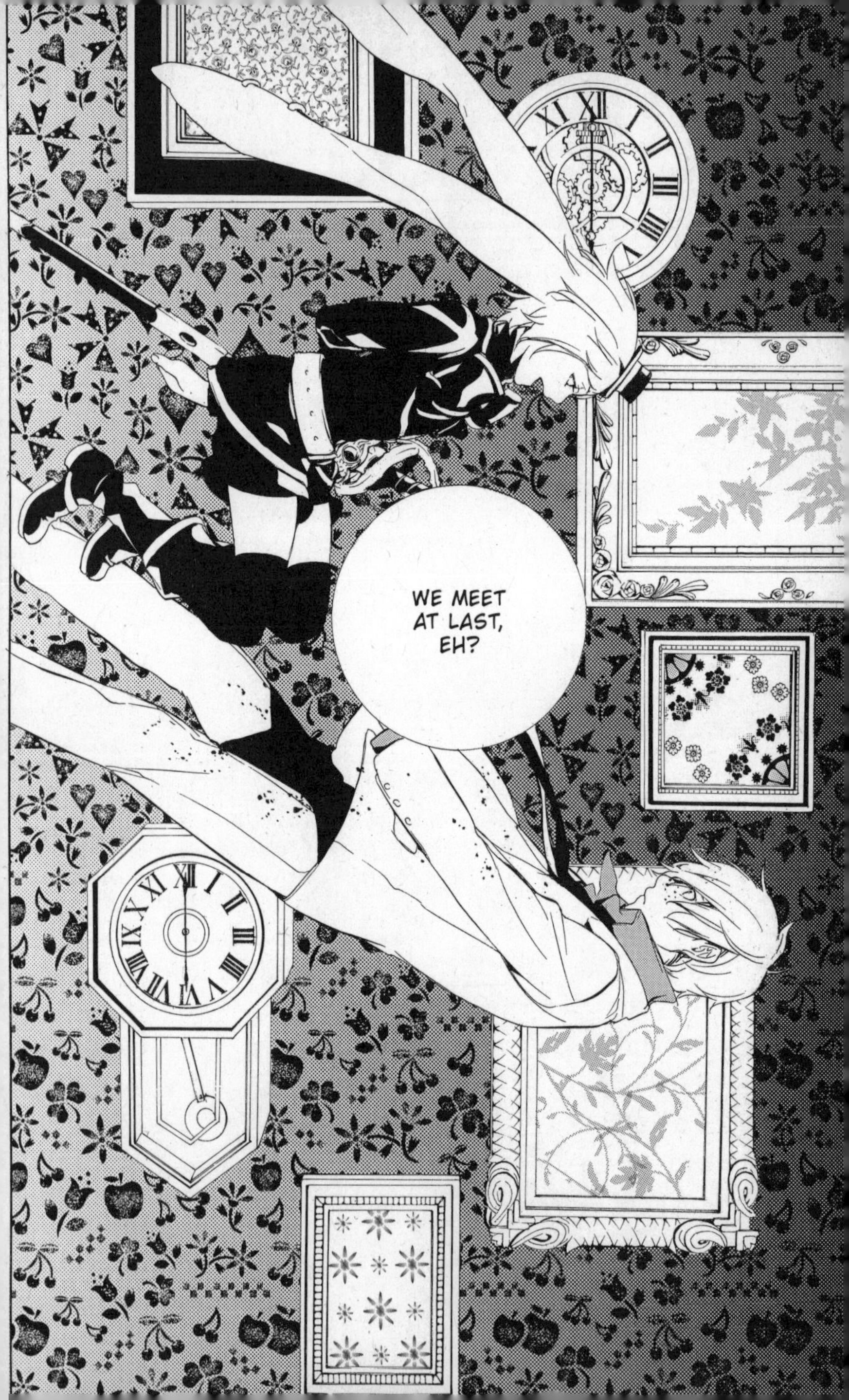
WE MEET AT LAST, EH?

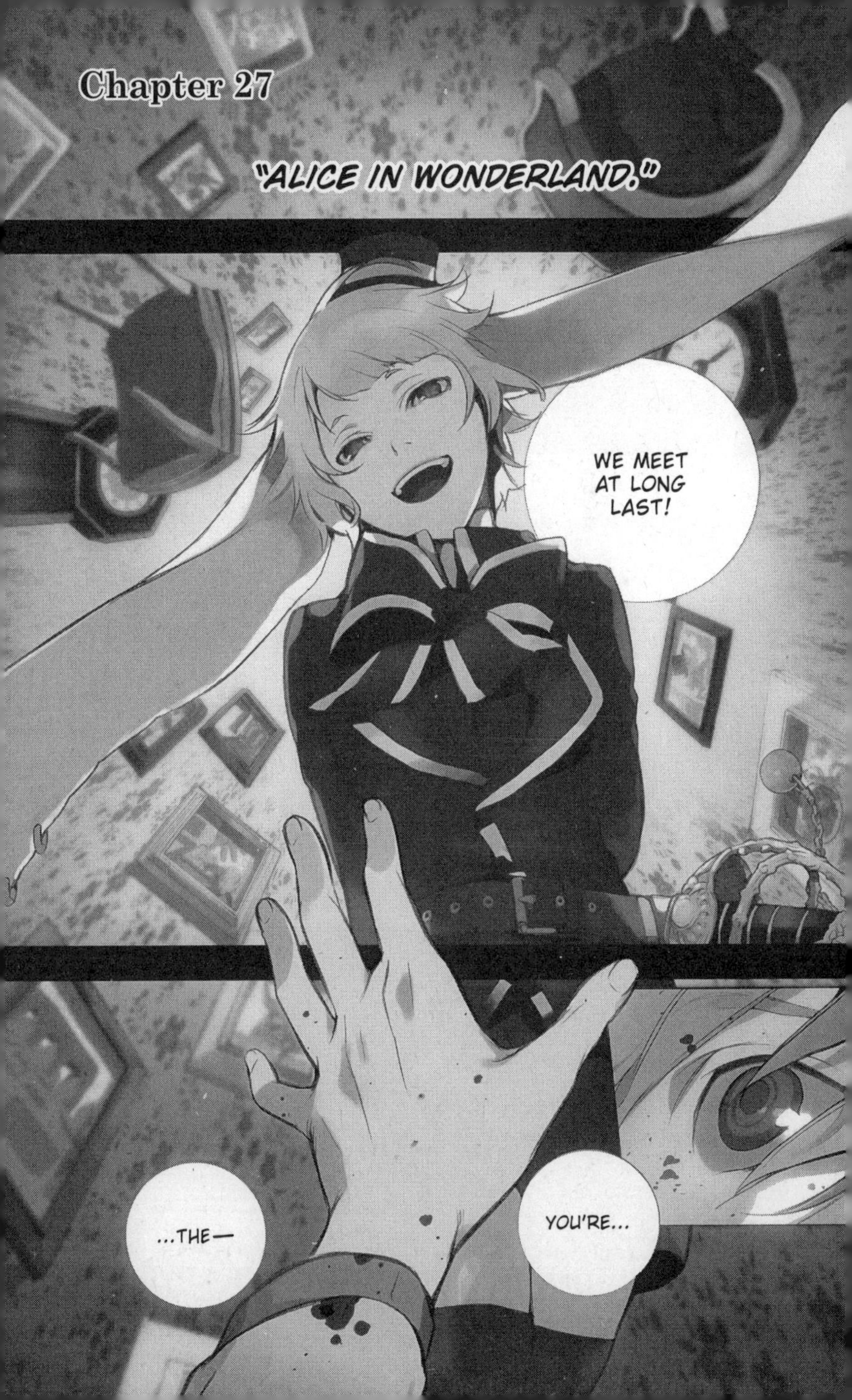
Chapter 27
"ALICE IN WONDERLAND."
WE MEET AT LONG LAST!
YOU'RE...
...THE—

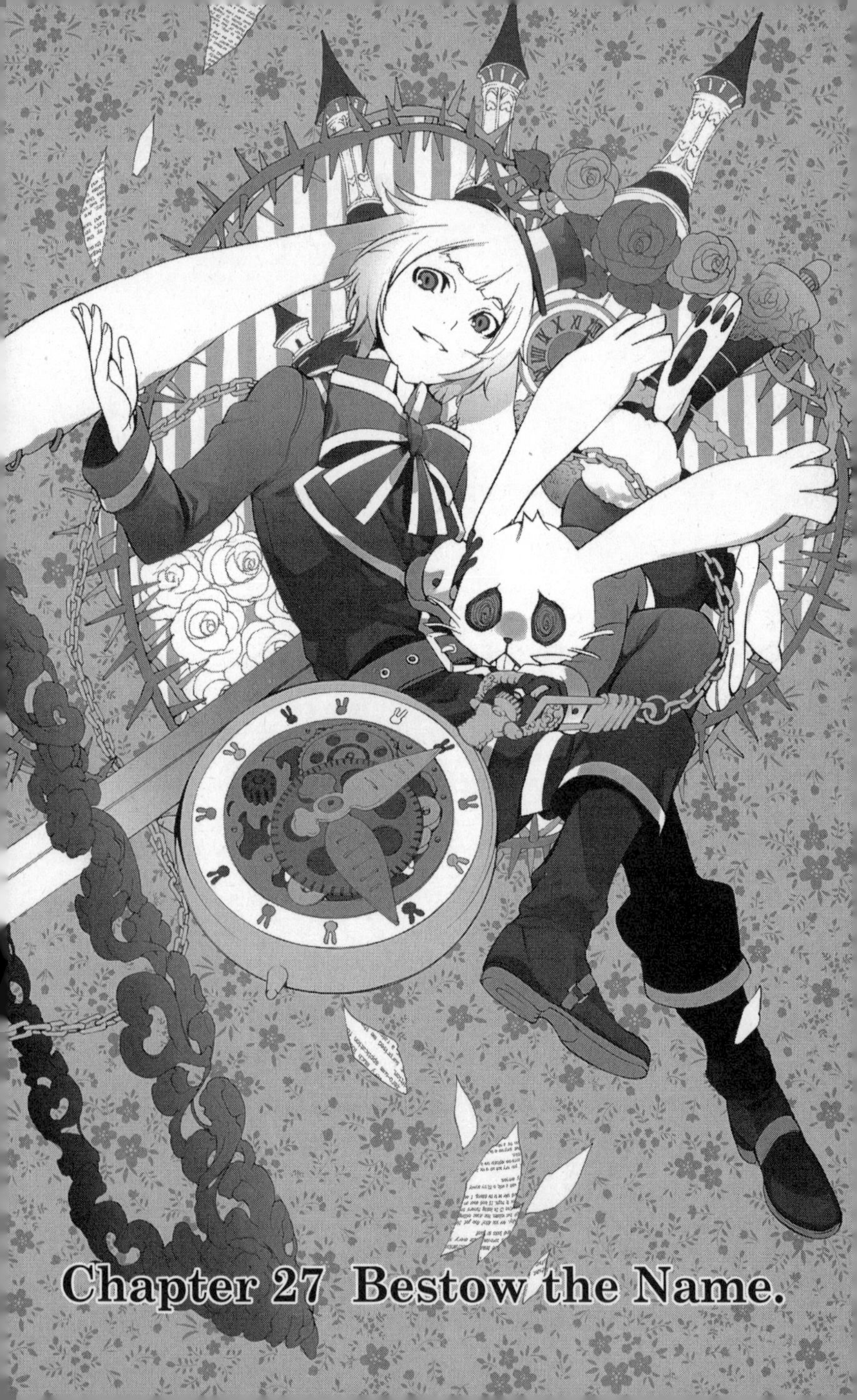

Chapter 27 Bestow the Name.

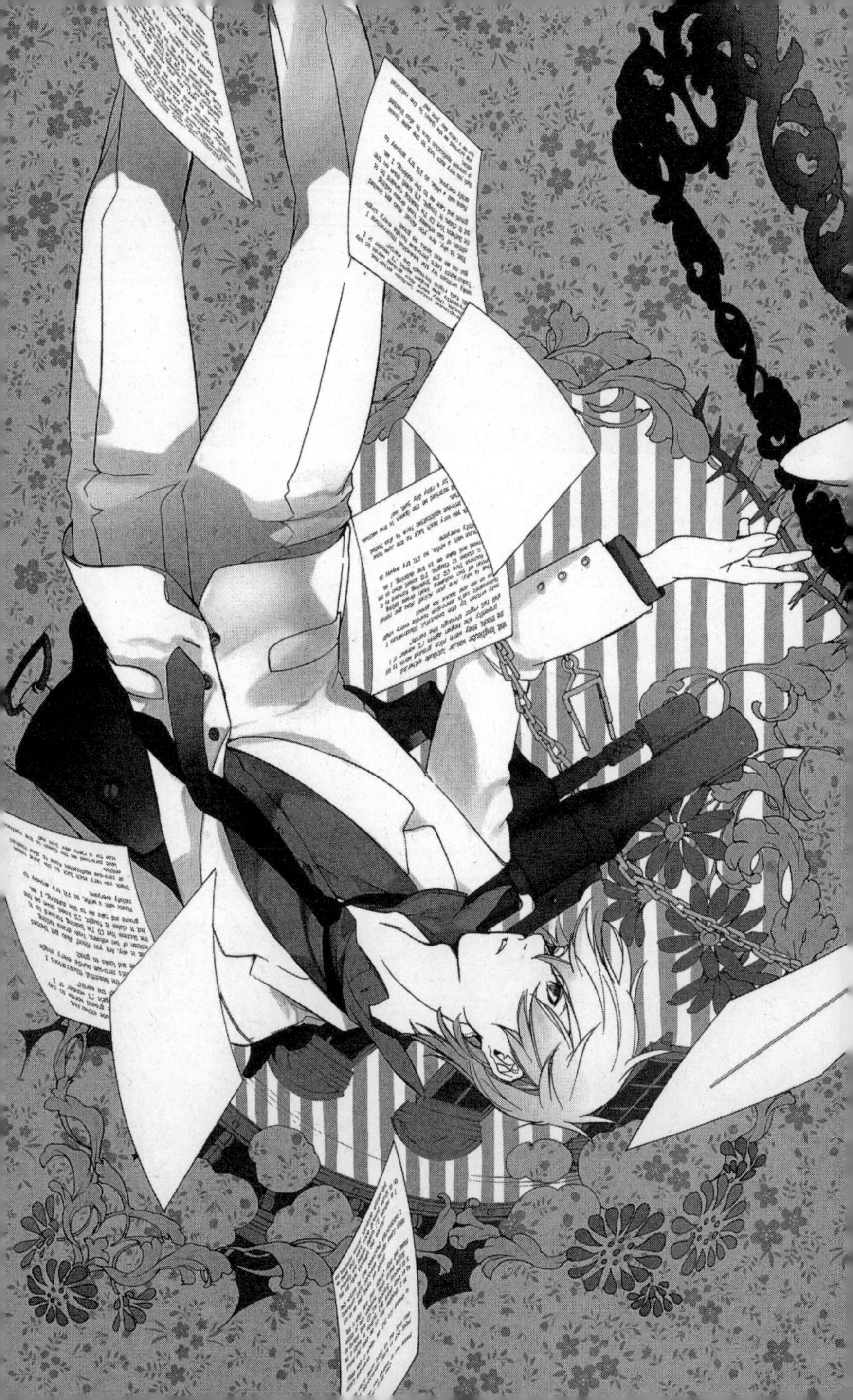

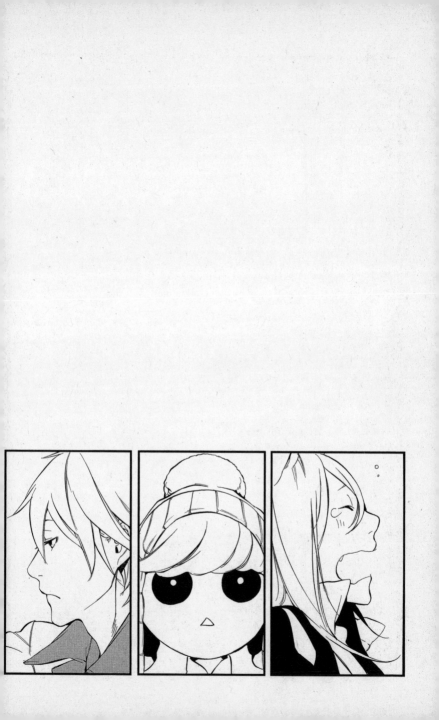

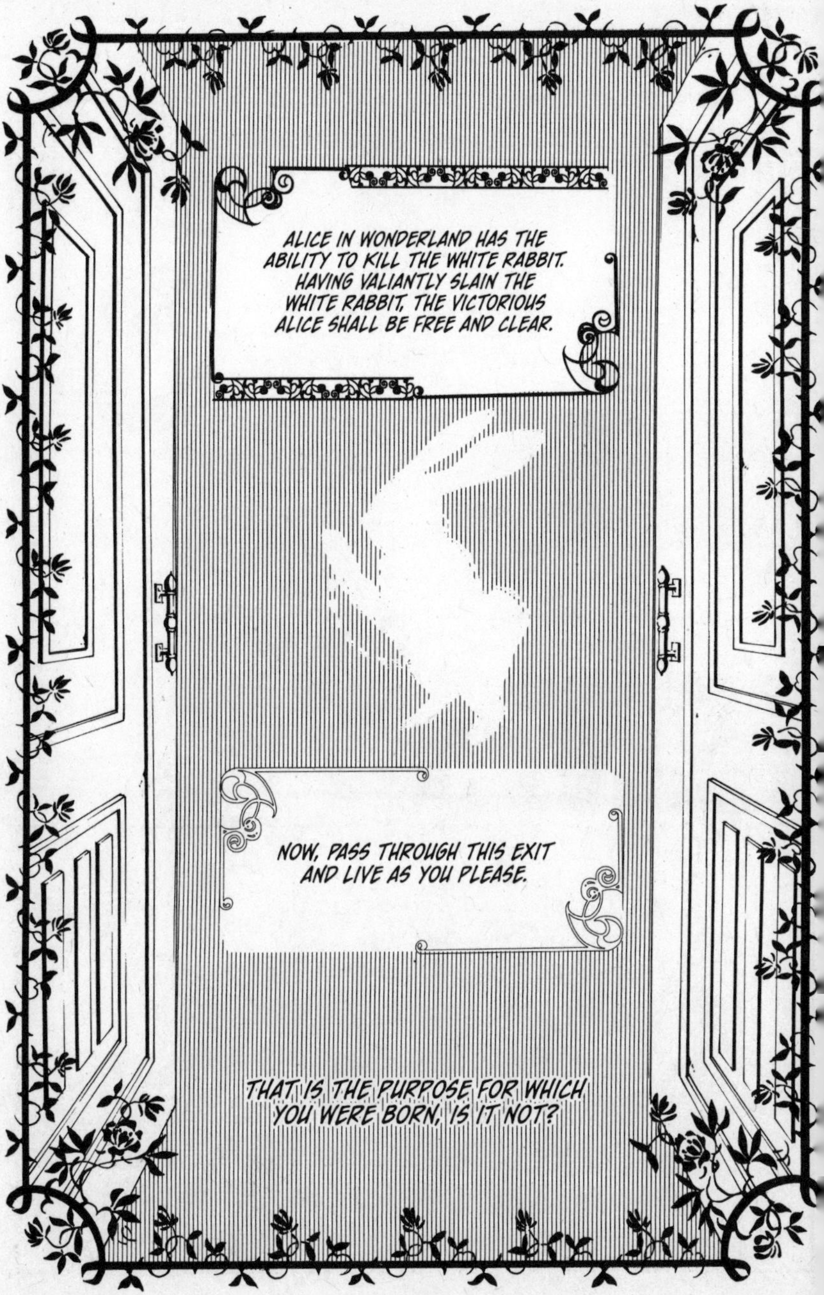
ALICE IN WONDERLAND HAS THE ABILITY TO KILL THE WHITE RABBIT. HAVING VALIANTLY SLAIN THE WHITE RABBIT, THE VICTORIOUS ALICE SHALL BE FREE AND CLEAR.
NOW, PASS THROUGH THIS EXIT AND LIVE AS YOU PLEASE.
THAT IS THE PURPOSE FOR WHICH YOU WERE BORN, IS IT NOT?

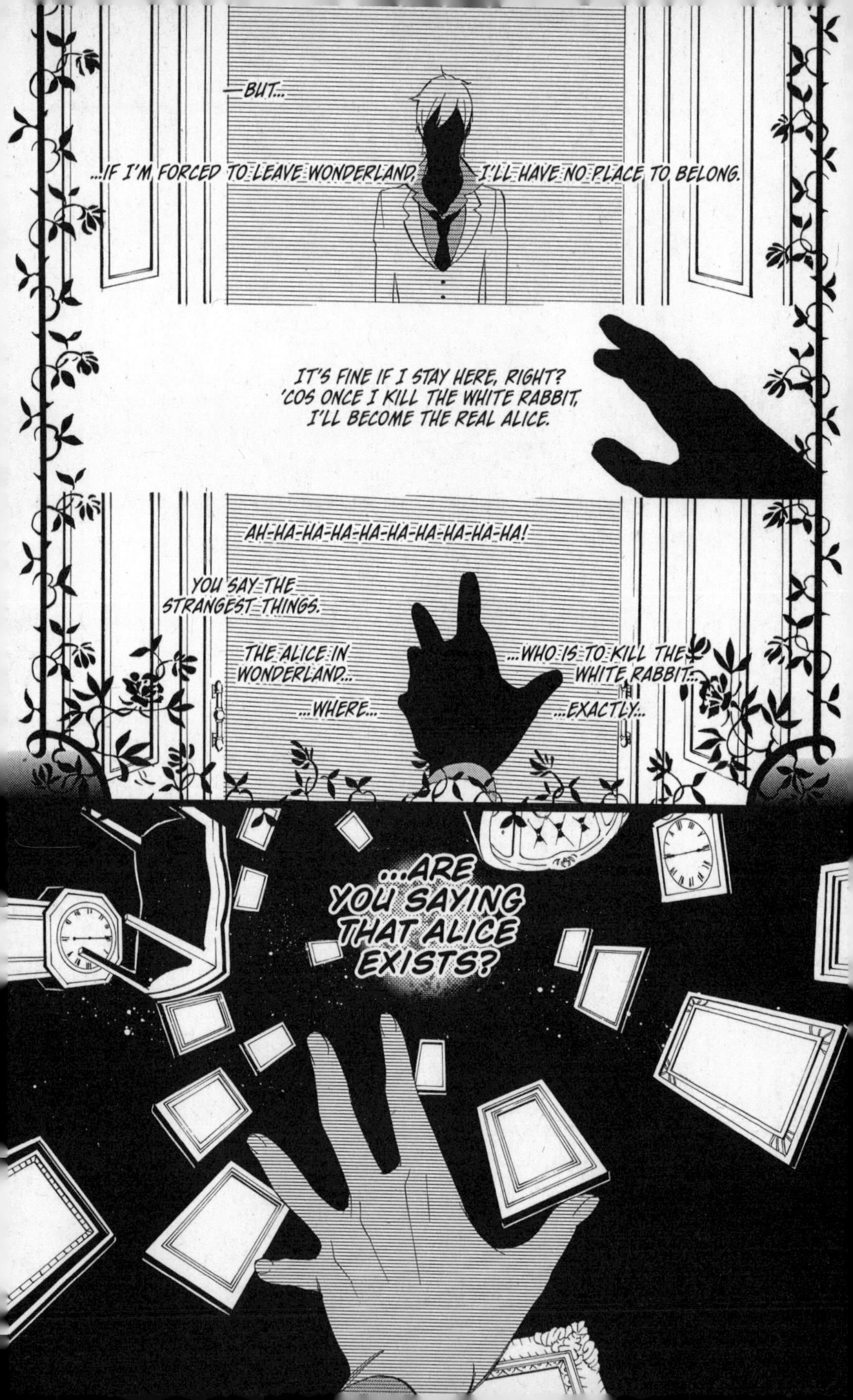
—BUT...
...IF I'M FORCED TO LEAVE WONDERLAND, I'LL HAVE NO PLACE TO BELONG.
IT'S FINE IF I STAY HERE, RIGHT? 'COS ONCE I KILL THE WHITE RABBIT, I'LL BECOME THE REAL ALICE.
AH-HA-HA-HA-HA-HA-HA-HA-HA-HA!
YOU SAY THE STRANGEST THINGS.
THE ALICE IN WONDERLAND...
...WHO IS TO KILL THE WHITE RABBIT...
...WHERE...
...EXACTLY...
...ARE YOU SAYING THAT ALICE EXISTS?

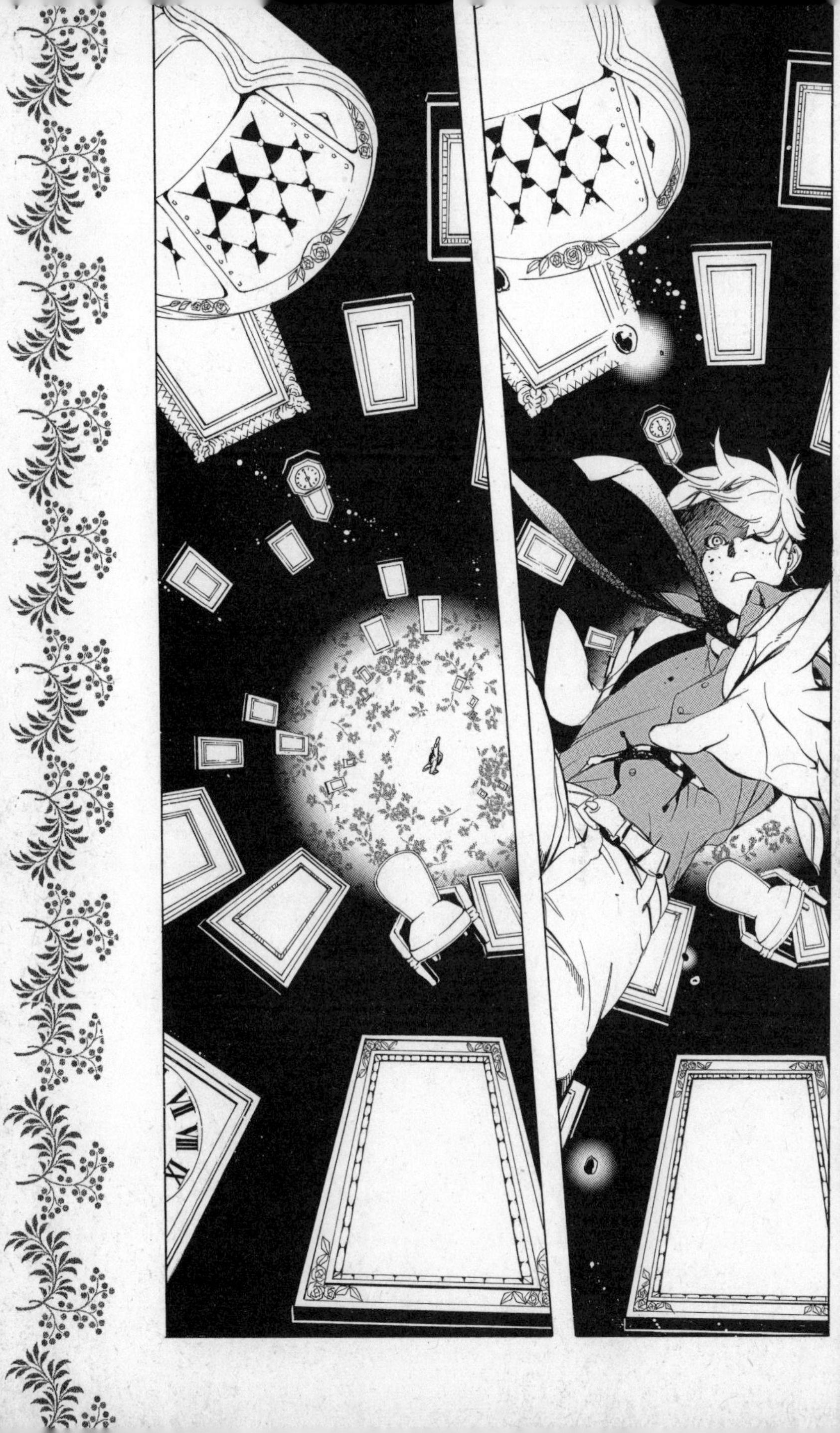

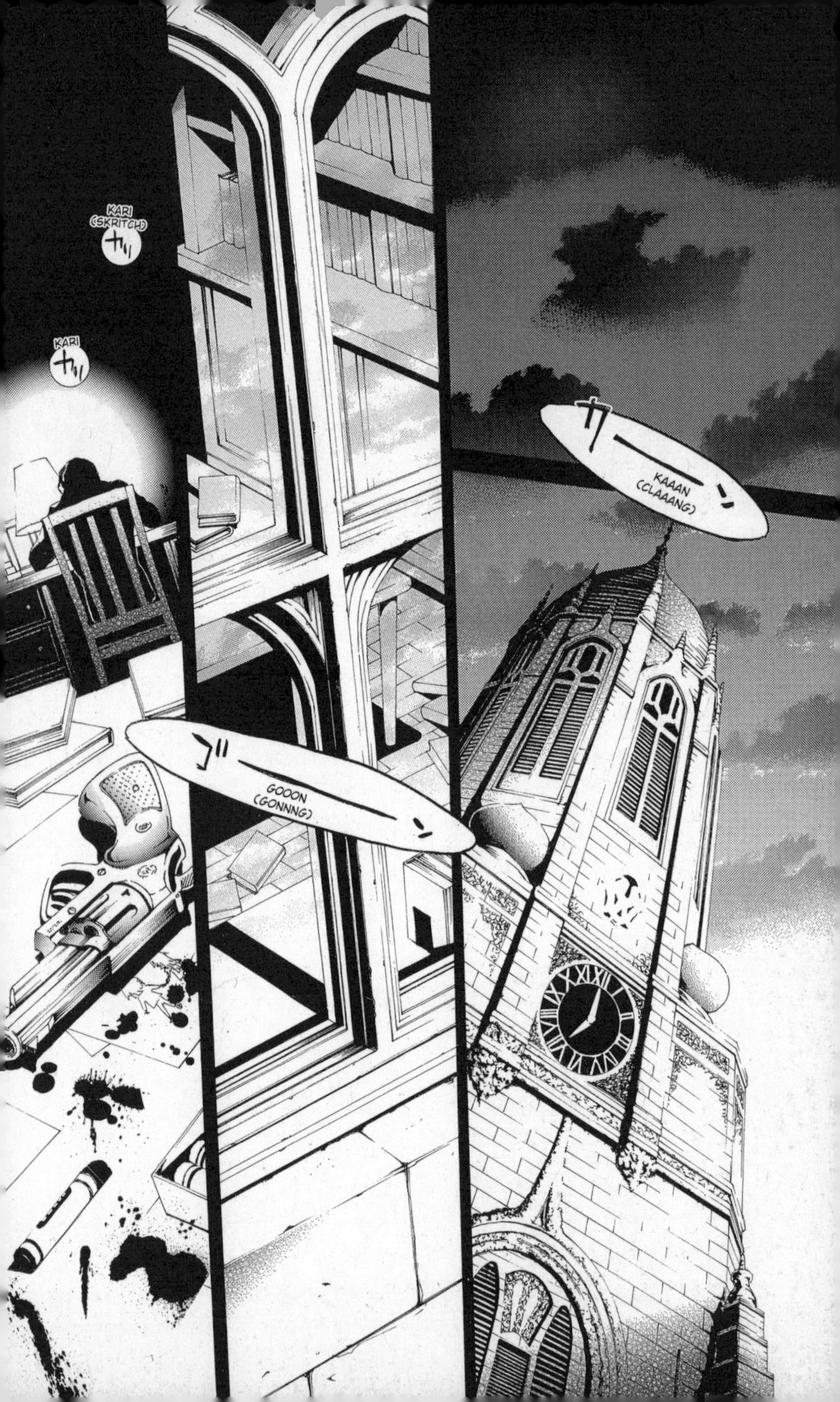
カーン
KAAAN (CLAAANG)
ゴーン
GOOON (GONNNG)
KARI (SKRITCH)
カリ
KARI
カリ

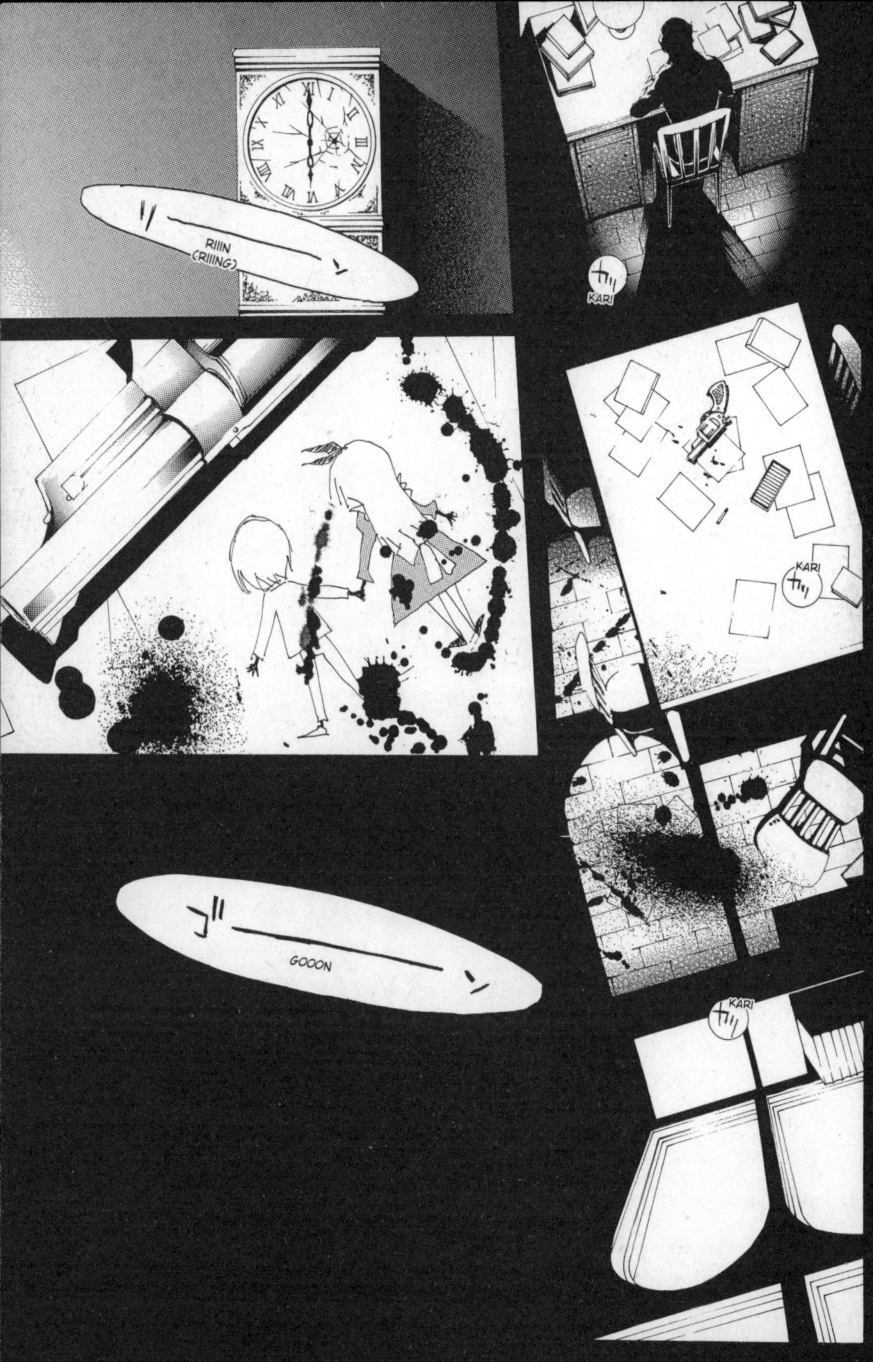
KARI
RIIN
(RIIING)
KARI
KARI
GOOON

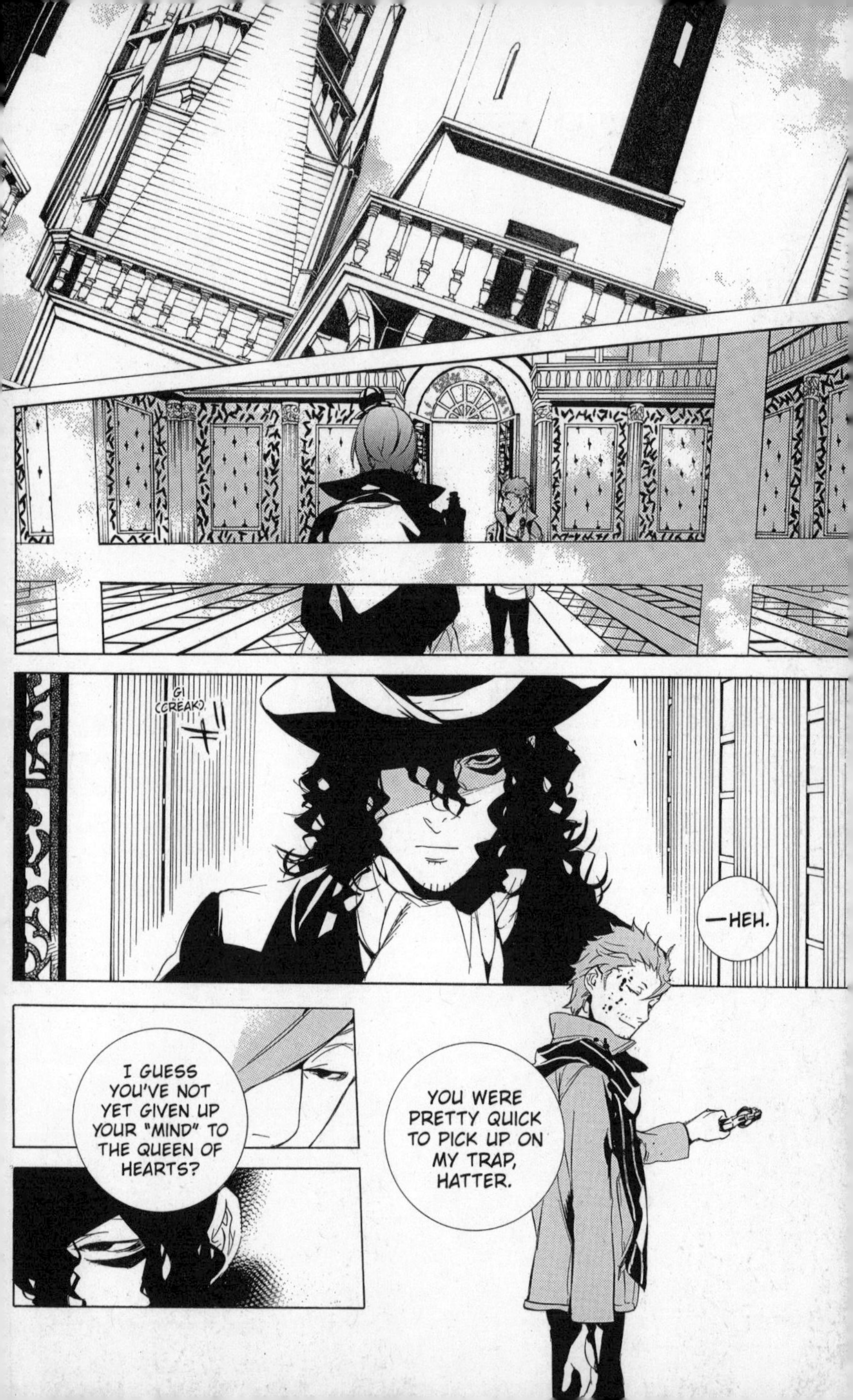
GI (CREAK)
—HEH.
YOU WERE PRETTY QUICK TO PICK UP ON MY TRAP, HATTER.
I GUESS YOU'VE NOT YET GIVEN UP YOUR "MIND" TO THE QUEEN OF HEARTS?

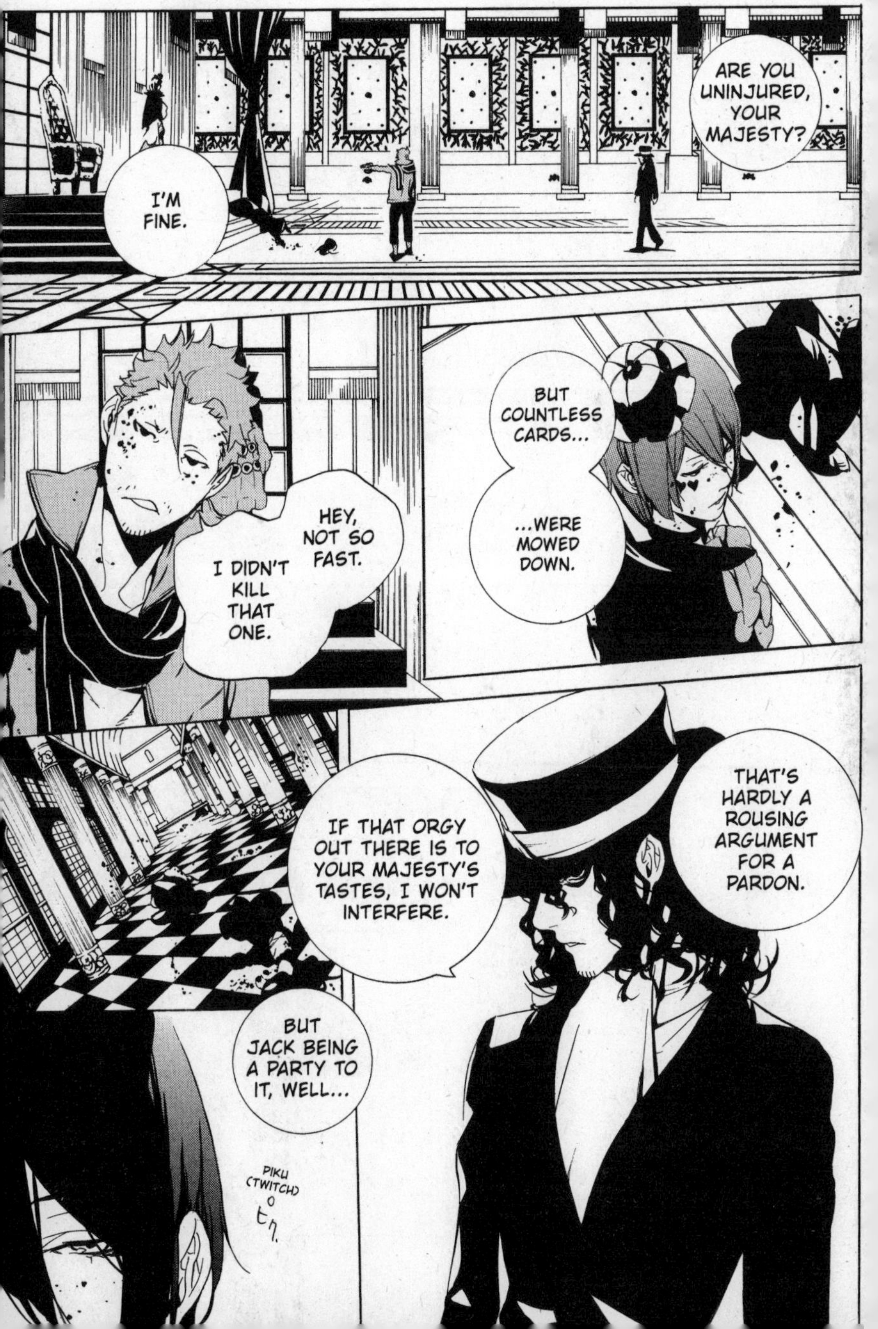
ARE YOU UNINJURED, YOUR MAJESTY?
I'M FINE.
BUT COUNTLESS CARDS...
...WERE MOWED DOWN.
HEY, NOT SO FAST.
I DIDN'T KILL THAT ONE.
THAT'S HARDLY A ROUSING ARGUMENT FOR A PARDON.
IF THAT ORGY OUT THERE IS TO YOUR MAJESTY'S TASTES, I WON'T INTERFERE.
BUT JACK BEING A PARTY TO IT, WELL...
PIKU (TWITCH)

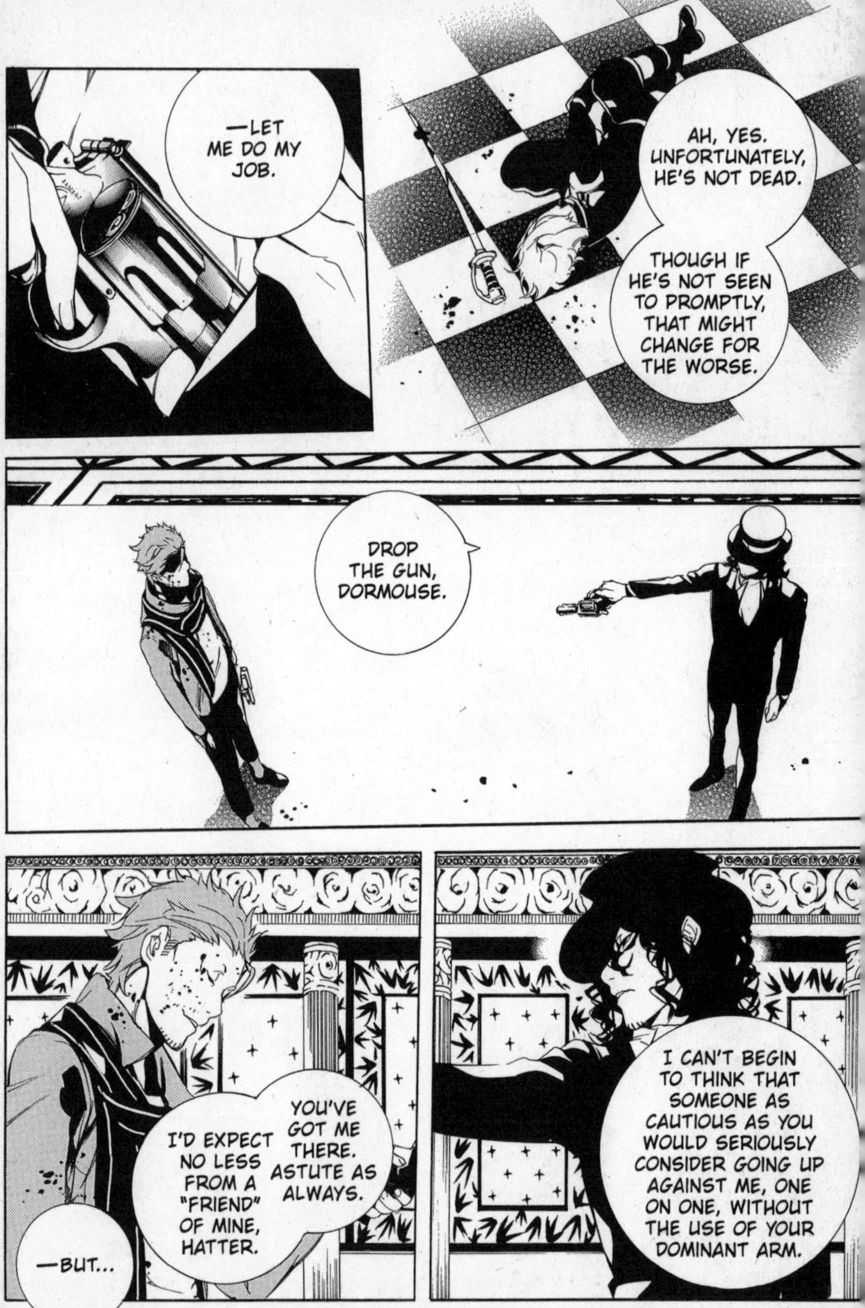
AH, YES. UNFORTUNATELY, HE'S NOT DEAD.
THOUGH IF HE'S NOT SEEN TO PROMPTLY, THAT MIGHT CHANGE FOR THE WORSE.
—LET ME DO MY JOB.
DROP THE GUN, DORMOUSE.
I CAN'T BEGIN TO THINK THAT SOMEONE AS CAUTIOUS AS YOU WOULD SERIOUSLY CONSIDER GOING UP AGAINST ME, ONE ON ONE, WITHOUT THE USE OF YOUR DOMINANT ARM.
YOU'VE GOT ME THERE. ASTUTE AS ALWAYS.
I'D EXPECT NO LESS FROM A "FRIEND" OF MINE, HATTER.
—BUT...

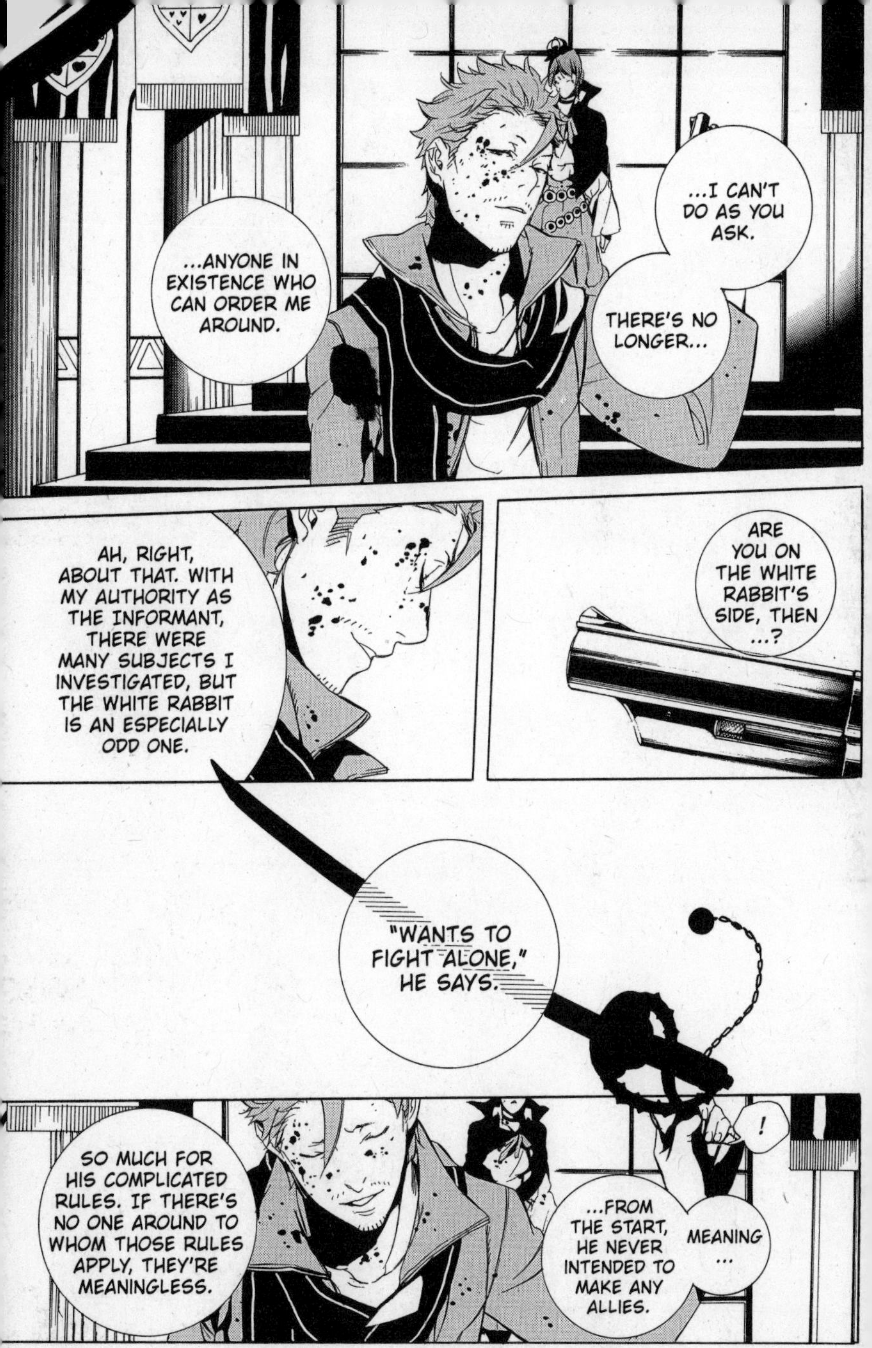
...I CAN'T DO AS YOU ASK.
THERE'S NO LONGER...
...ANYONE IN EXISTENCE WHO CAN ORDER ME AROUND.
ARE YOU ON THE WHITE RABBIT'S SIDE, THEN ...?
AH, RIGHT, ABOUT THAT. WITH MY AUTHORITY AS THE INFORMANT, THERE WERE MANY SUBJECTS I INVESTIGATED, BUT THE WHITE RABBIT IS AN ESPECIALLY ODD ONE.
"WANTS TO FIGHT ALONE," HE SAYS.
!
MEANING ...
...FROM THE START, HE NEVER INTENDED TO MAKE ANY ALLIES.
SO MUCH FOR HIS COMPLICATED RULES. IF THERE'S NO ONE AROUND TO WHOM THOSE RULES APPLY, THEY'RE MEANINGLESS.

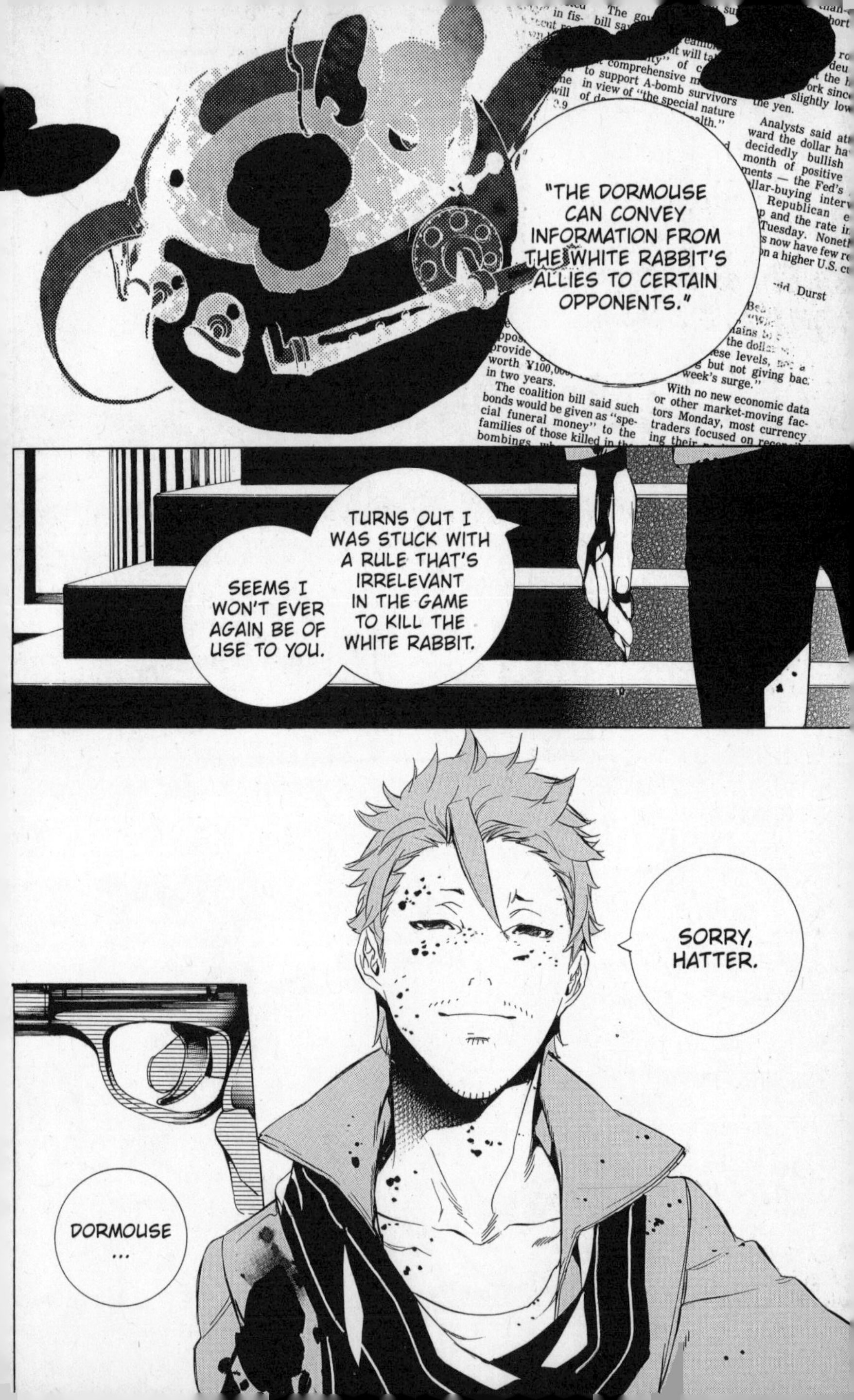
"THE DORMOUSE CAN CONVEY INFORMATION FROM THE WHITE RABBIT'S ALLIES TO CERTAIN OPPONENTS."
TURNS OUT I WAS STUCK WITH A RULE THAT'S IRRELEVANT IN THE GAME TO KILL THE WHITE RABBIT.
SEEMS I WON'T EVER AGAIN BE OF USE TO YOU.
SORRY, HATTER.
DORMOUSE ...

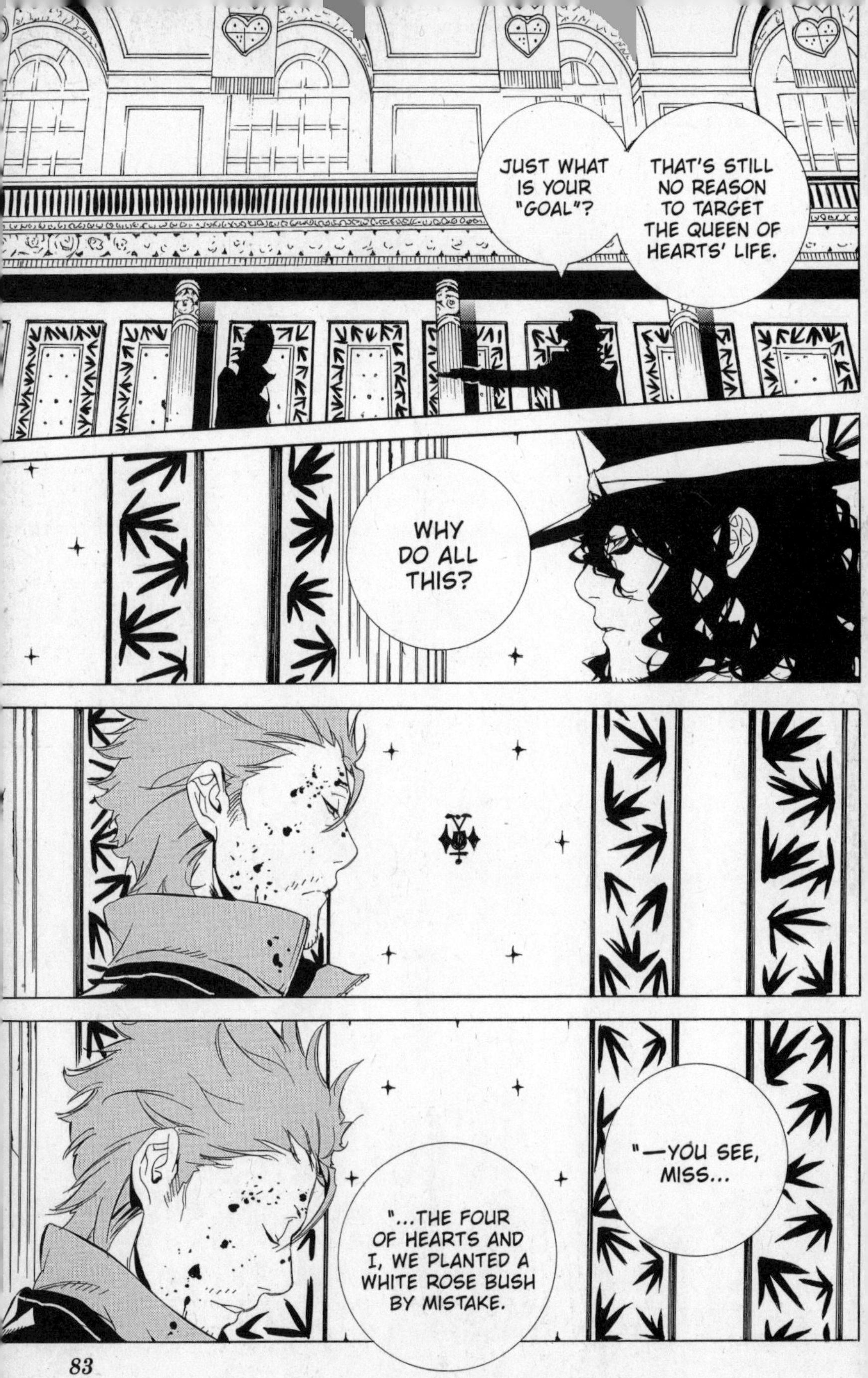
THAT'S STILL NO REASON TO TARGET THE QUEEN OF HEARTS' LIFE.
JUST WHAT IS YOUR "GOAL"?
WHY DO ALL THIS?
"—YOU SEE, MISS...
"...THE FOUR OF HEARTS AND I, WE PLANTED A WHITE ROSE BUSH BY MISTAKE.

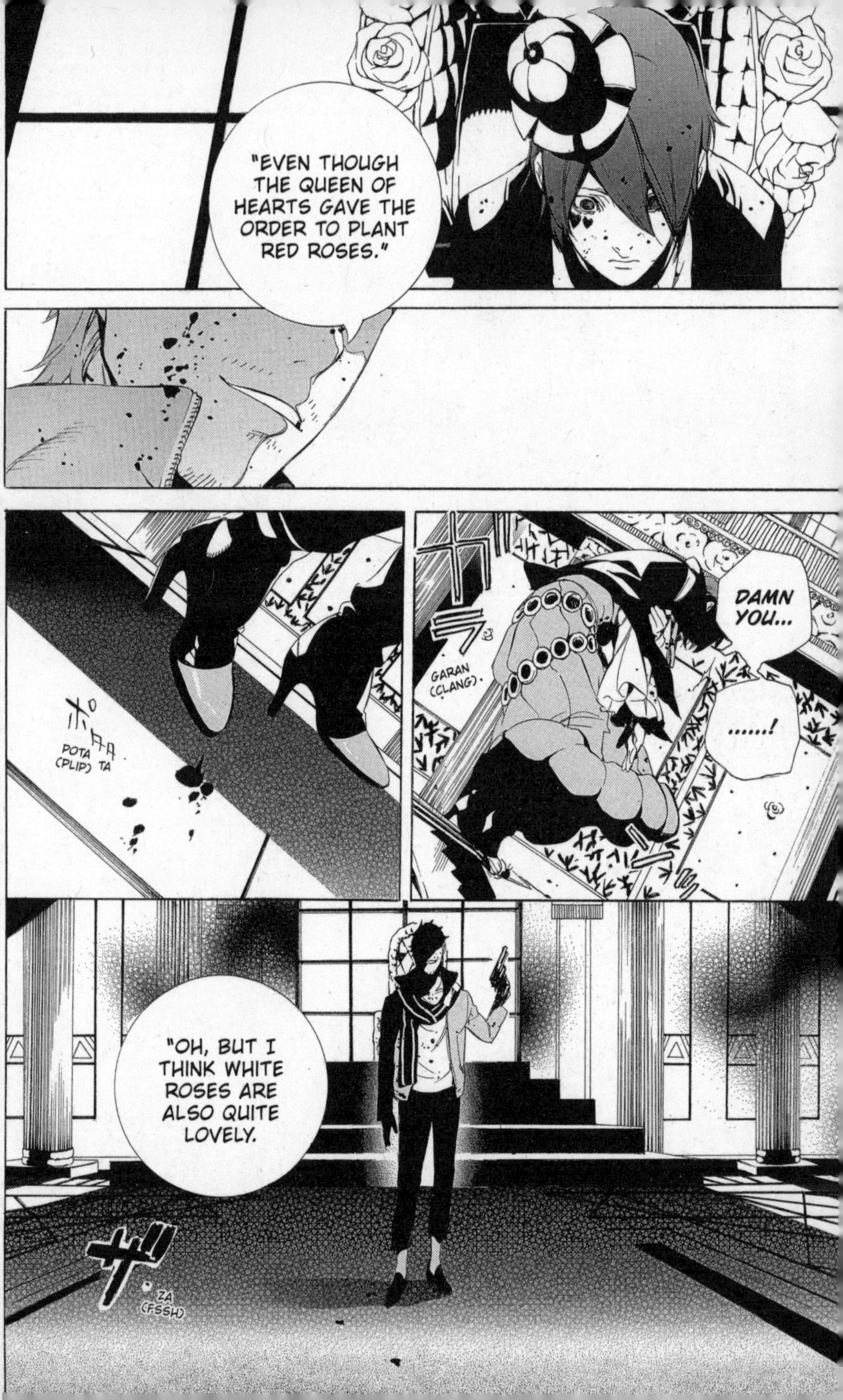
"EVEN THOUGH THE QUEEN OF HEARTS GAVE THE ORDER TO PLANT RED ROSES."
DAMN YOU...
GARAN (CLANG)
......!
POTA (PLIP) TA
"OH, BUT I THINK WHITE ROSES ARE ALSO QUITE LOVELY.
ZA (FSSH)

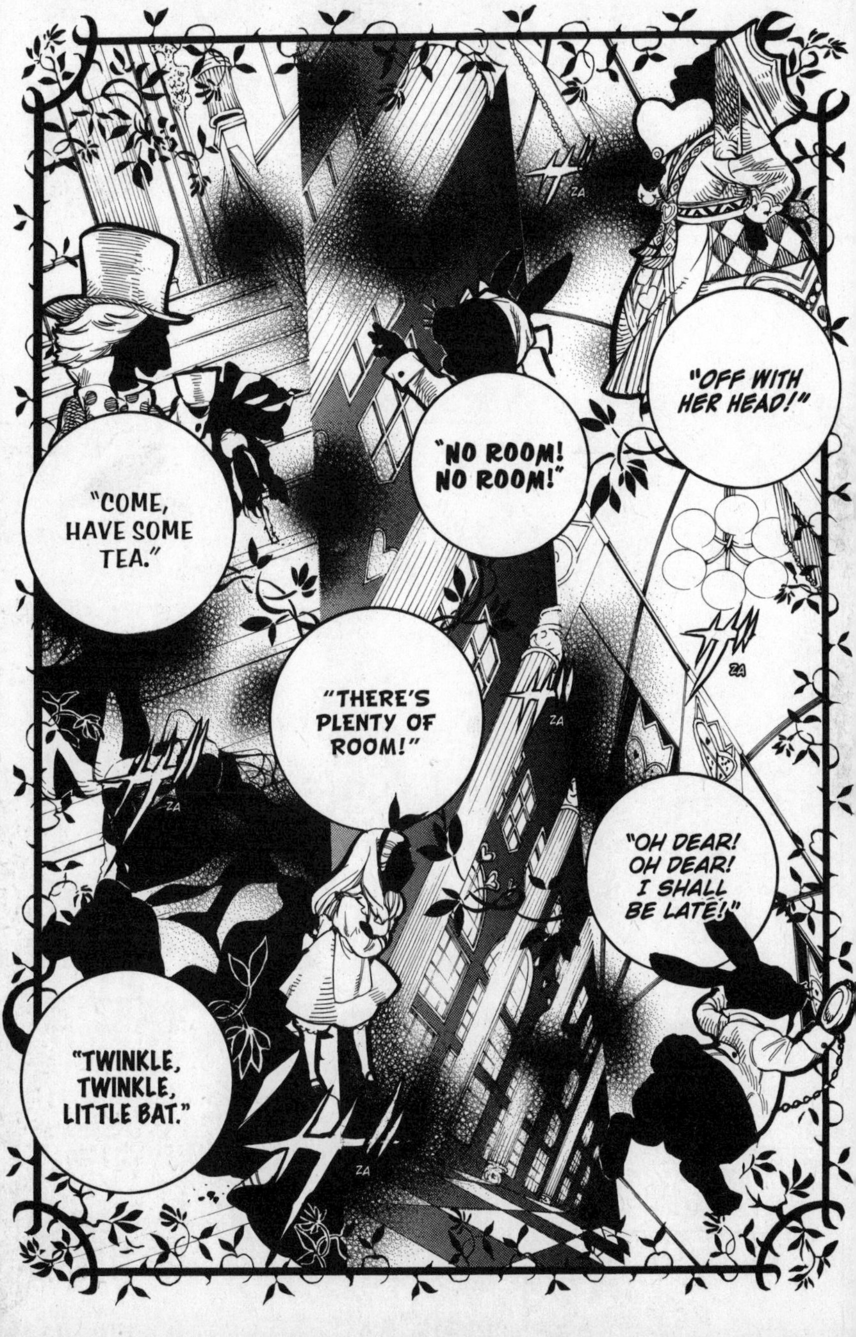
ZA
"OFF WITH HER HEAD!"
"NO ROOM! NO ROOM!"
"COME, HAVE SOME TEA."
ZA
ZA
"THERE'S PLENTY OF ROOM!"
ZA
"OH DEAR! OH DEAR! I SHALL BE LATE!"
ZA
"TWINKLE, TWINKLE, LITTLE BAT."

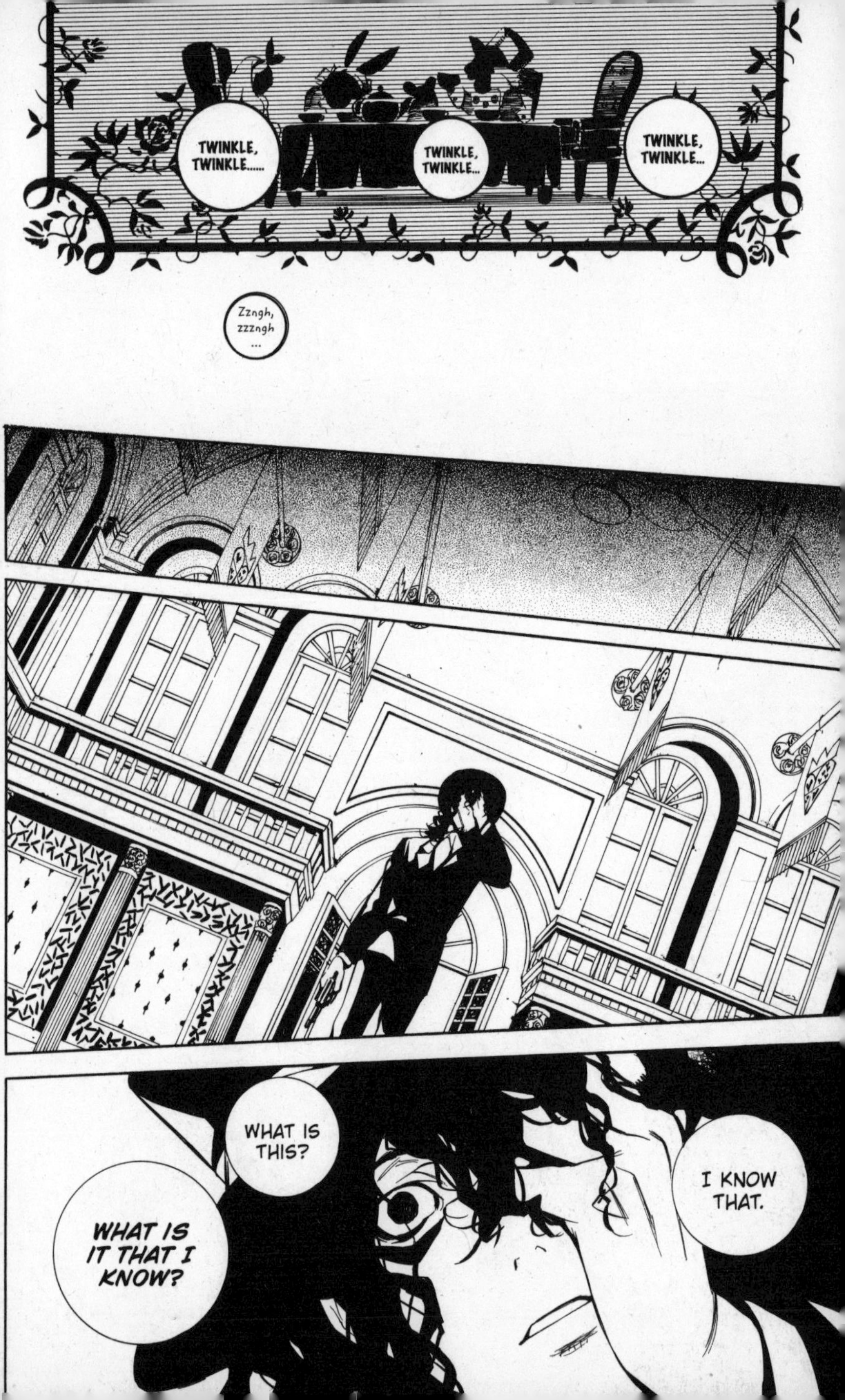
TWINKLE, TWINKLE...
TWINKLE, TWINKLE...
TWINKLE, TWINKLE......
Zzngh, zzzngh ...
I KNOW THAT.
WHAT IS THIS?
WHAT IS IT THAT I KNOW?

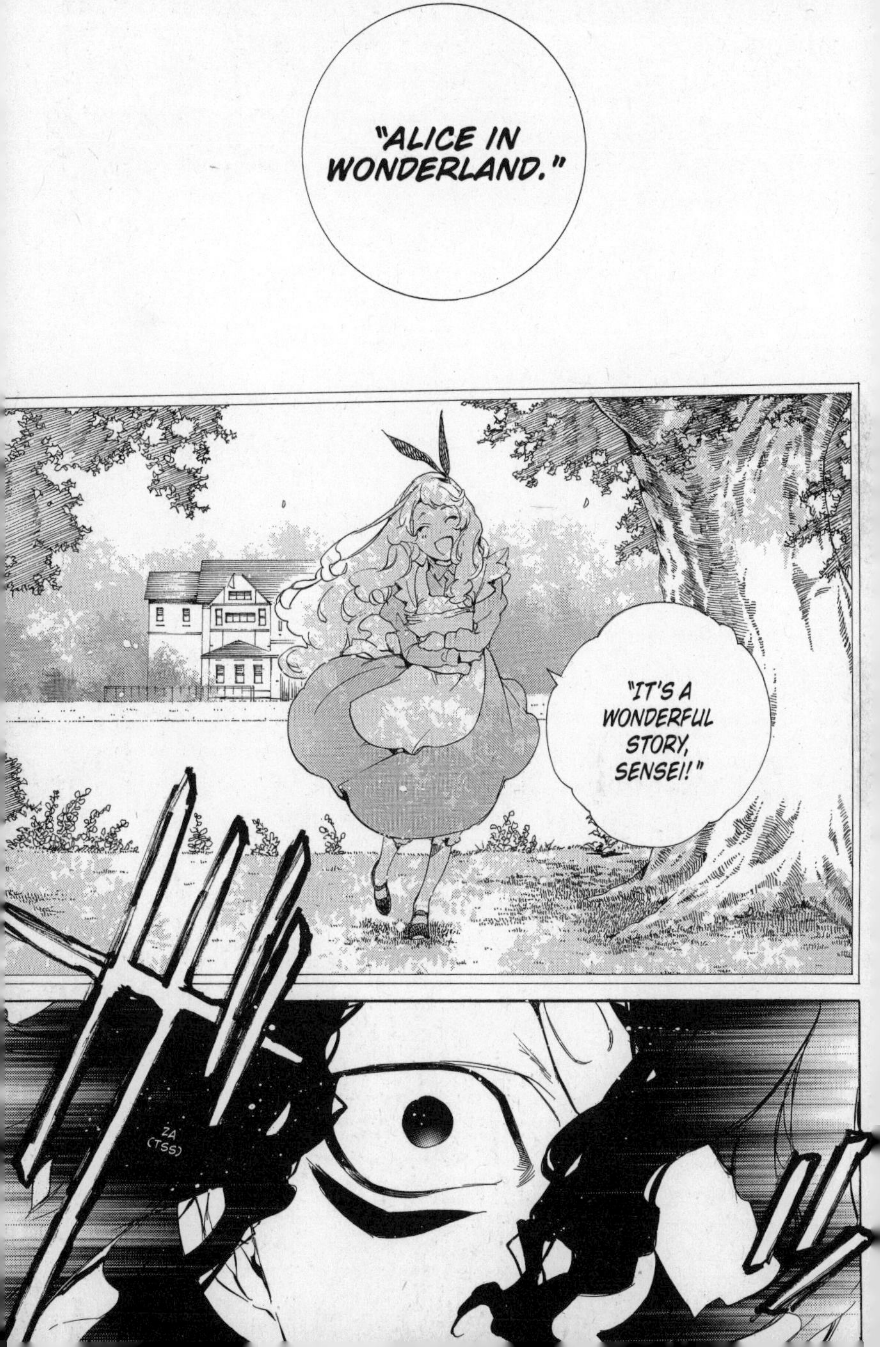
"ALICE IN WONDERLAND."
"IT'S A WONDERFUL STORY, SENSEI!"
ZA (TSS)

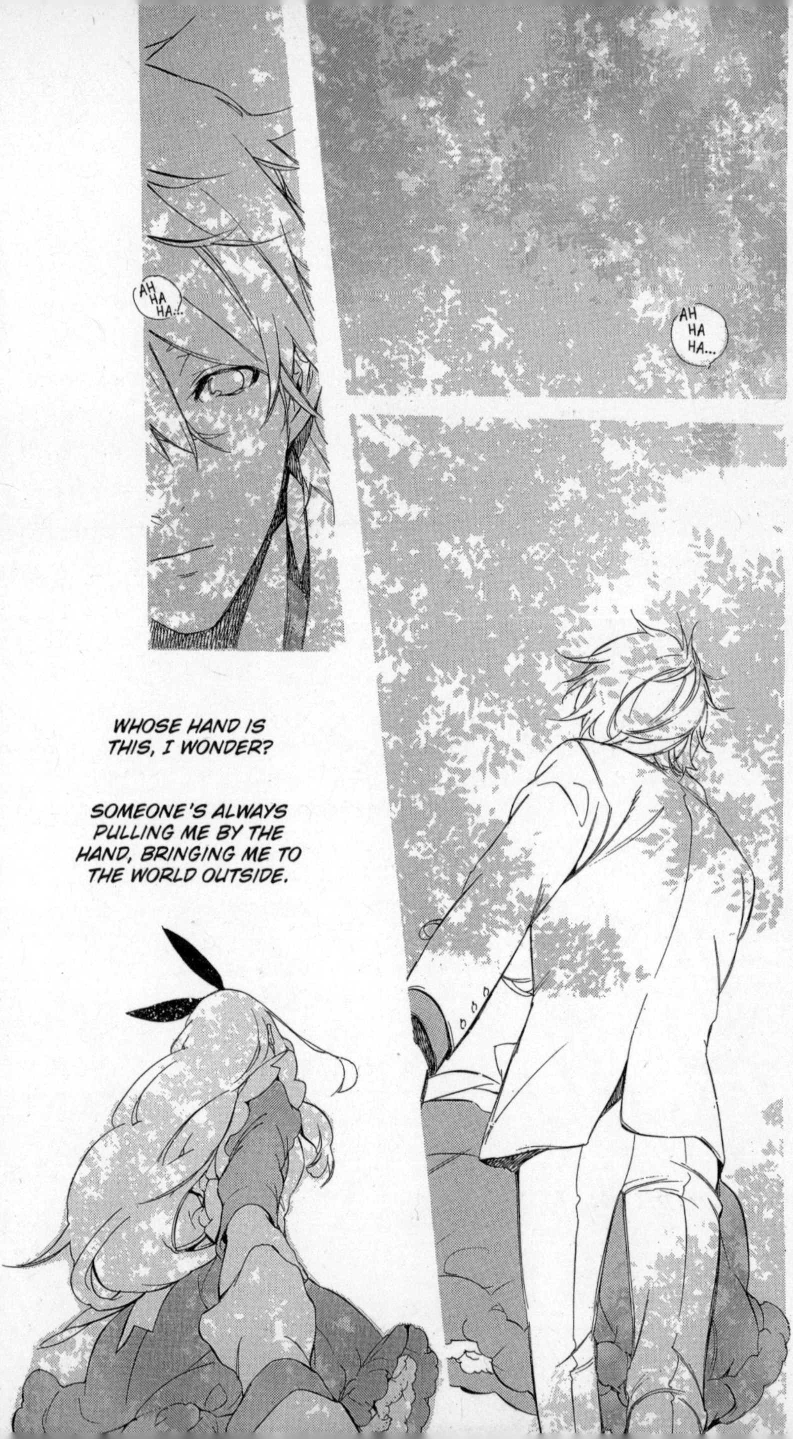
AH HA HA...
AH HA HA...
WHOSE HAND IS THIS, I WONDER?
SOMEONE'S ALWAYS PULLING ME BY THE HAND, BRINGING ME TO THE WORLD OUTSIDE.

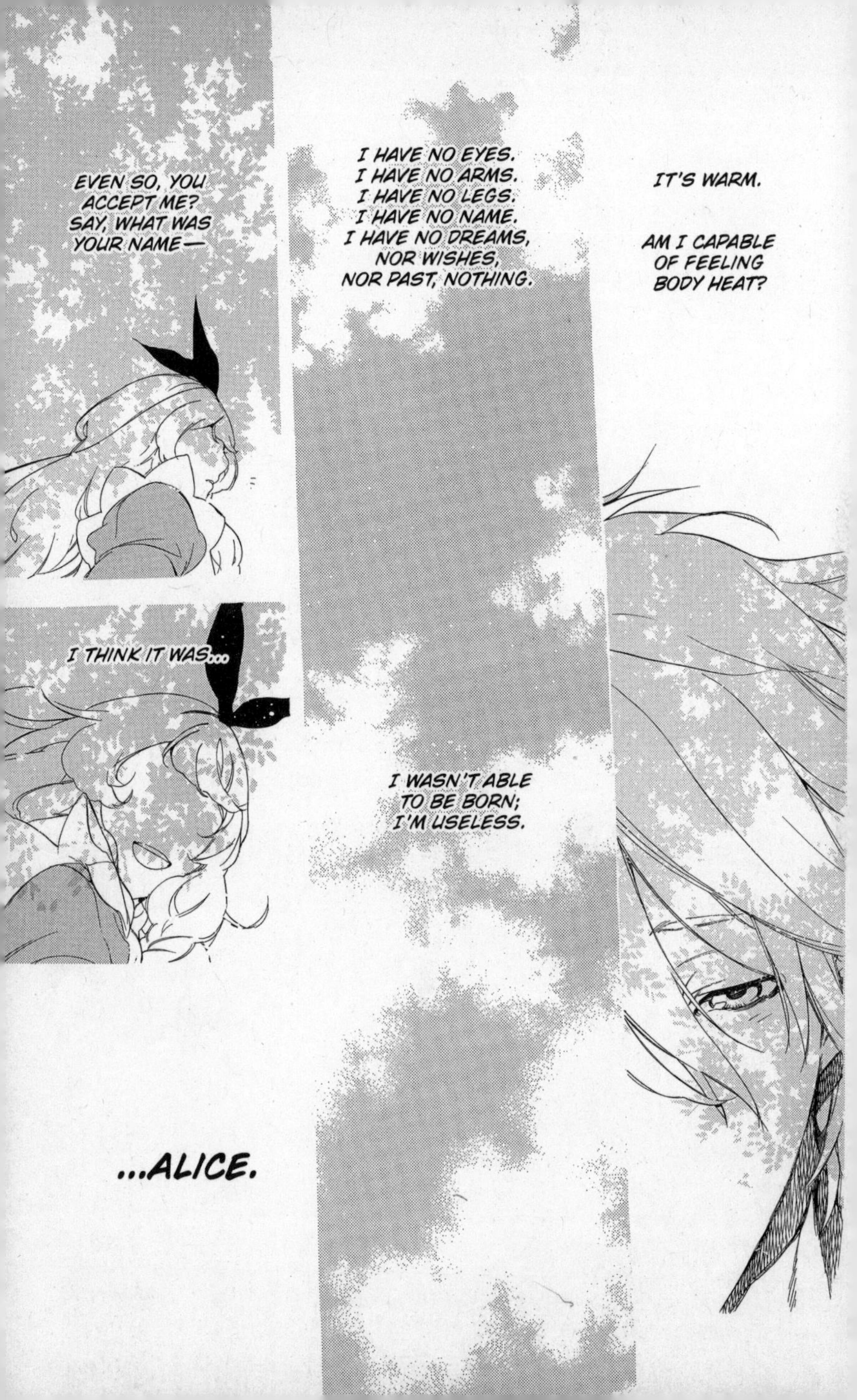
IT'S WARM.
AM I CAPABLE OF FEELING BODY HEAT?
I HAVE NO EYES. I HAVE NO ARMS. I HAVE NO LEGS. I HAVE NO NAME. I HAVE NO DREAMS, NOR WISHES, NOR PAST, NOTHING.
I WASN'T ABLE TO BE BORN; I'M USELESS.
EVEN SO, YOU ACCEPT ME? SAY, WHAT WAS YOUR NAME—
I THINK IT WAS...
...ALICE.

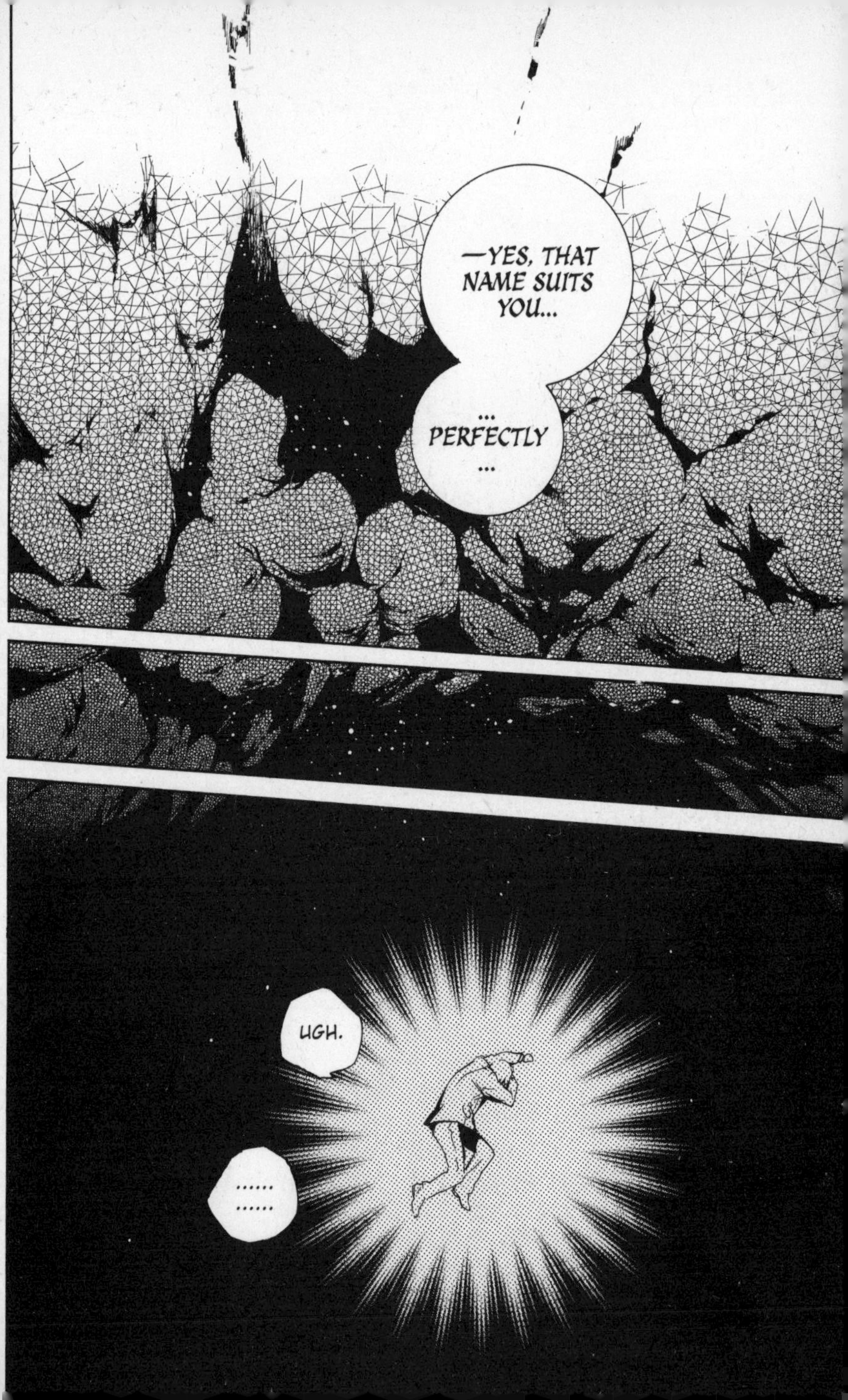
—YES, THAT NAME SUITS YOU...
... PERFECTLY ...
UGH.
......
......

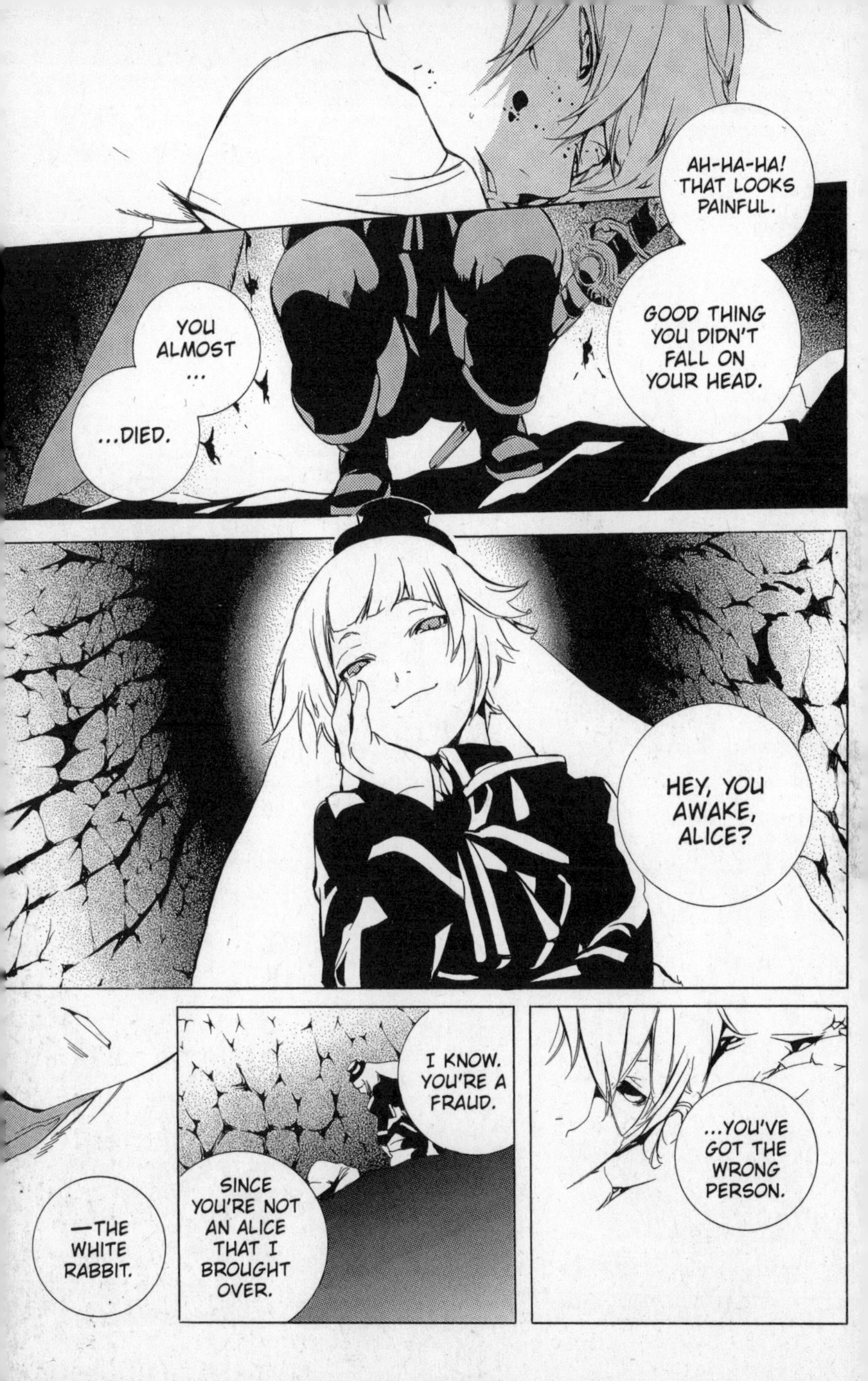
AH-HA-HA! THAT LOOKS PAINFUL.
GOOD THING YOU DIDN'T FALL ON YOUR HEAD.
YOU ALMOST ...
...DIED.
HEY, YOU AWAKE, ALICE?
...YOU'VE GOT THE WRONG PERSON.
I KNOW. YOU'RE A FRAUD.
SINCE YOU'RE NOT AN ALICE THAT I BROUGHT OVER.
—THE WHITE RABBIT.

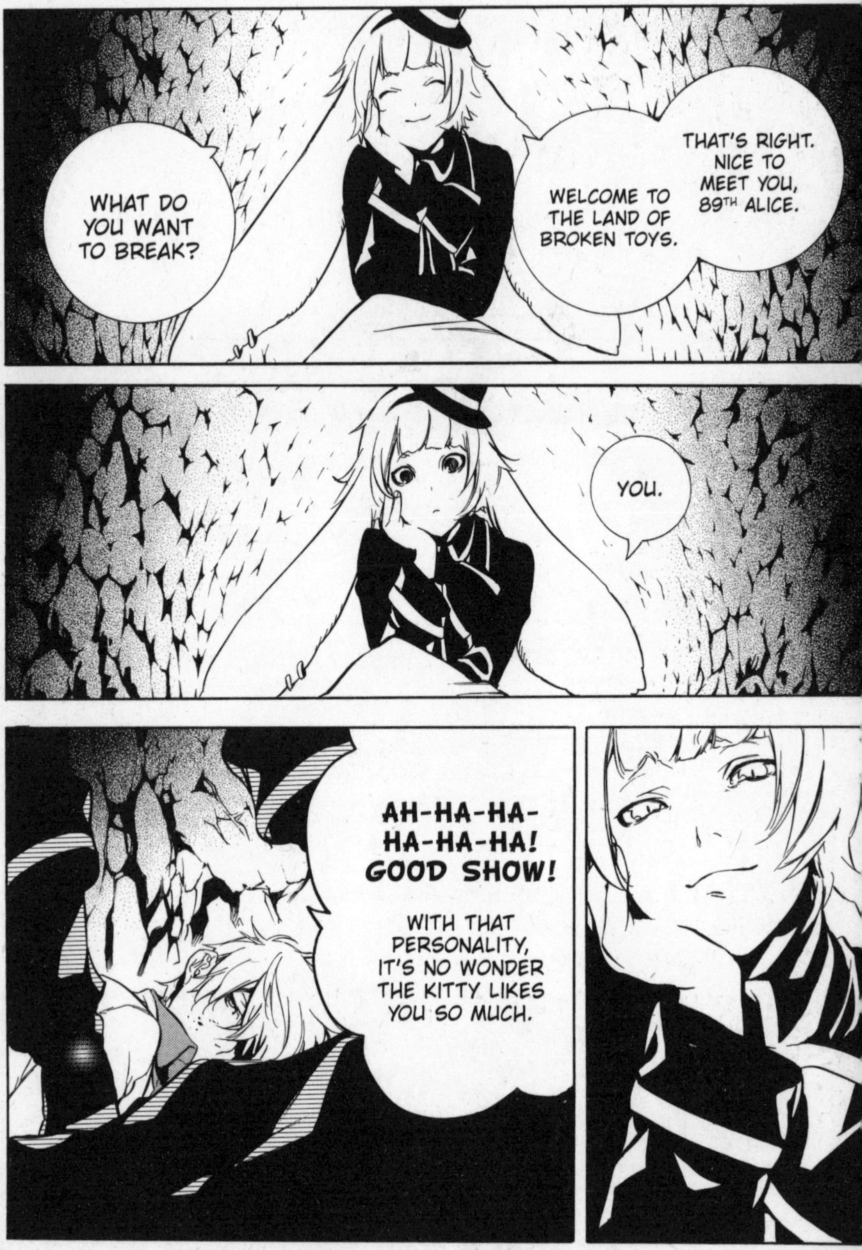
THAT'S RIGHT. NICE TO MEET YOU, 89TH ALICE.
WELCOME TO THE LAND OF BROKEN TOYS.
WHAT DO YOU WANT TO BREAK?
YOU.
AH-HA-HA-HA-HA-HA! GOOD SHOW!
WITH THAT PERSONALITY, IT'S NO WONDER THE KITTY LIKES YOU SO MUCH.

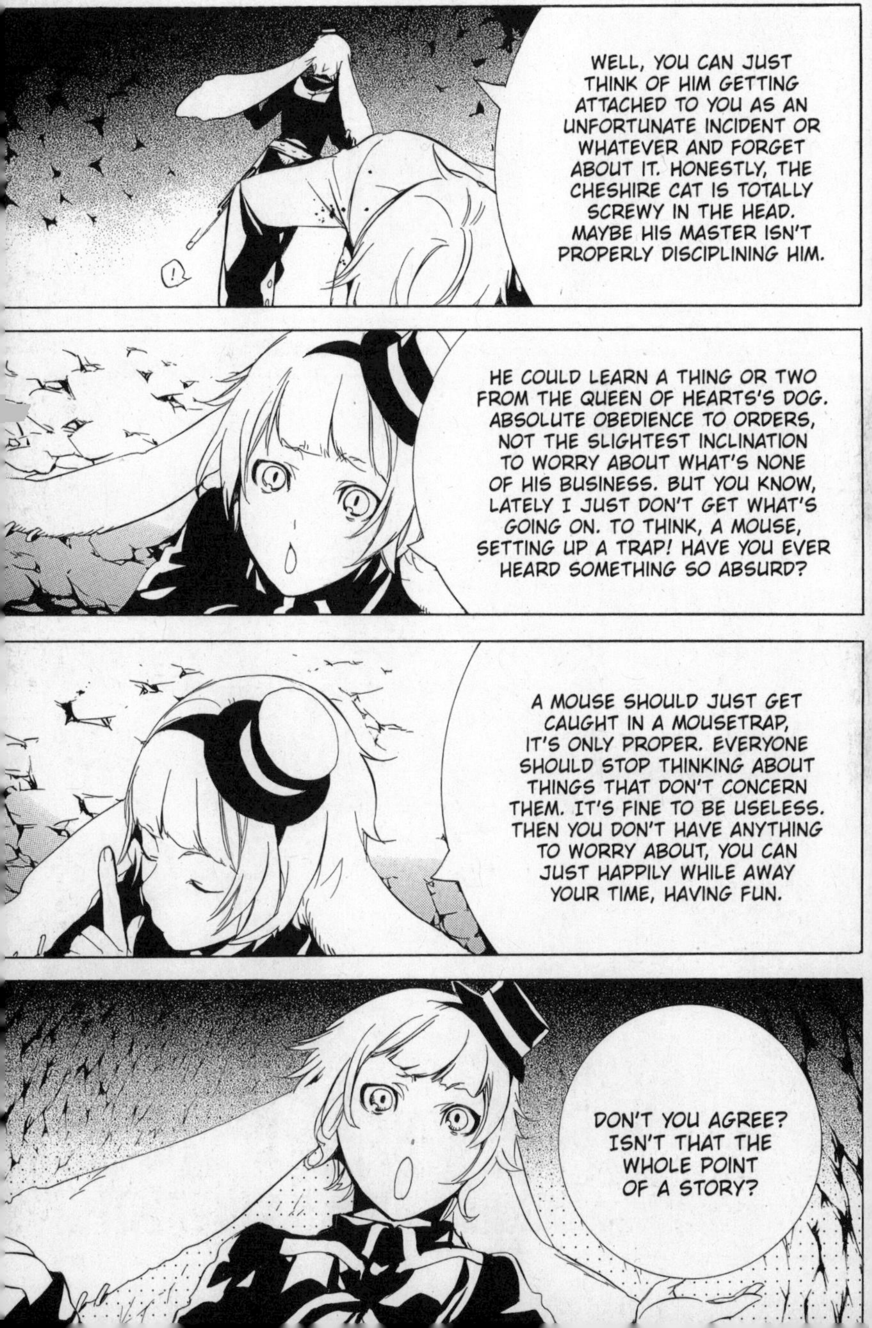
WELL, YOU CAN JUST THINK OF HIM GETTING ATTACHED TO YOU AS AN UNFORTUNATE INCIDENT OR WHATEVER AND FORGET ABOUT IT. HONESTLY, THE CHESHIRE CAT IS TOTALLY SCREWY IN THE HEAD. MAYBE HIS MASTER ISN'T PROPERLY DISCIPLINING HIM.
!
HE COULD LEARN A THING OR TWO FROM THE QUEEN OF HEARTS'S DOG. ABSOLUTE OBEDIENCE TO ORDERS, NOT THE SLIGHTEST INCLINATION TO WORRY ABOUT WHAT'S NONE OF HIS BUSINESS. BUT YOU KNOW, LATELY I JUST DON'T GET WHAT'S GOING ON. TO THINK, A MOUSE, SETTING UP A TRAP! HAVE YOU EVER HEARD SOMETHING SO ABSURD?
A MOUSE SHOULD JUST GET CAUGHT IN A MOUSETRAP, IT'S ONLY PROPER. EVERYONE SHOULD STOP THINKING ABOUT THINGS THAT DON'T CONCERN THEM. IT'S FINE TO BE USELESS. THEN YOU DON'T HAVE ANYTHING TO WORRY ABOUT, YOU CAN JUST HAPPILY WHILE AWAY YOUR TIME, HAVING FUN.
DON'T YOU AGREE? ISN'T THAT THE WHOLE POINT OF A STORY?

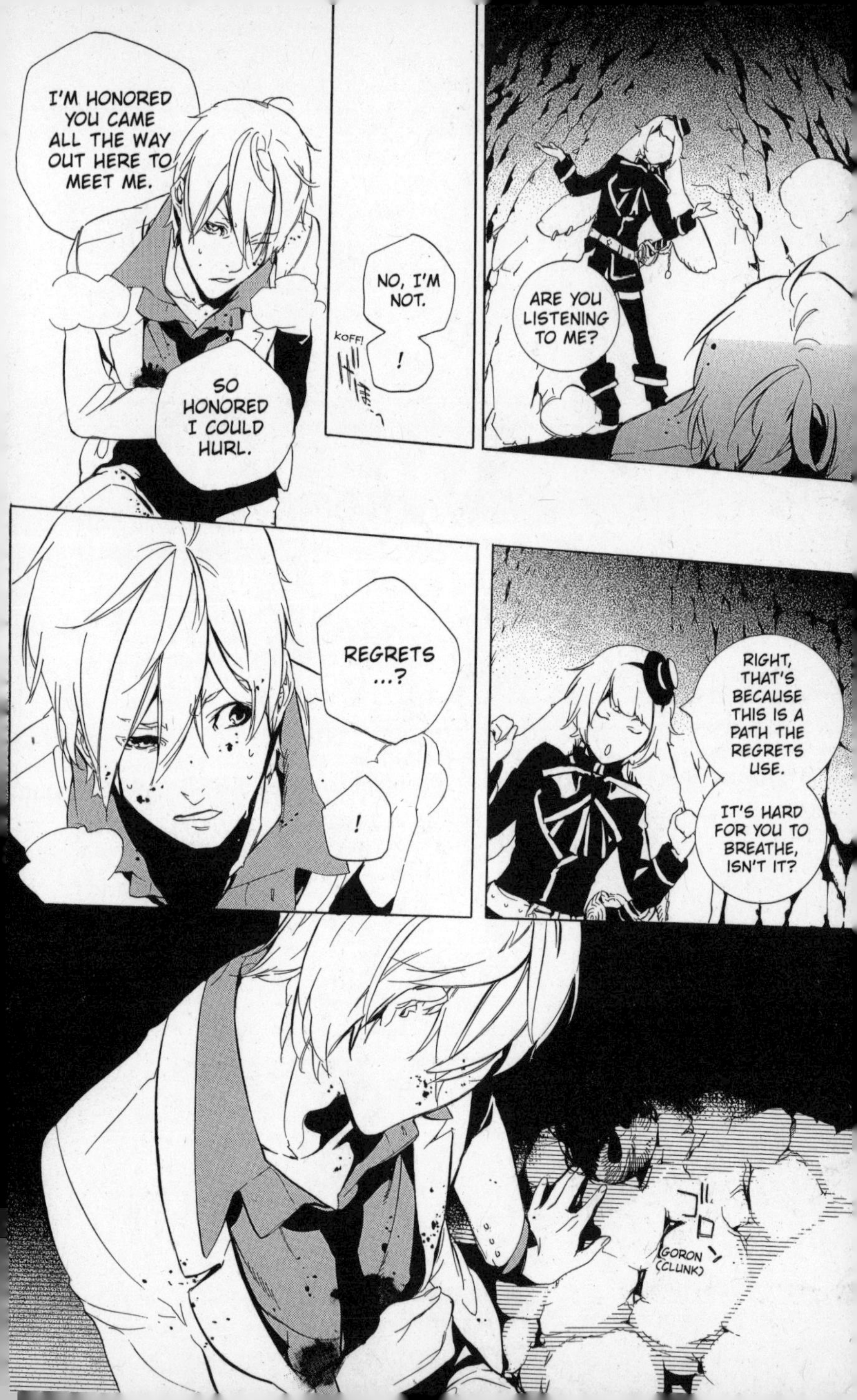
ARE YOU LISTENING TO ME?
NO, I'M NOT.
KOFF!
!
I'M HONORED YOU CAME ALL THE WAY OUT HERE TO MEET ME.
SO HONORED I COULD HURL.
RIGHT, THAT'S BECAUSE THIS IS A PATH THE REGRETS USE.
IT'S HARD FOR YOU TO BREATHE, ISN'T IT?
REGRETS ...?
!
ゴロン
(GORON (CLUNK)

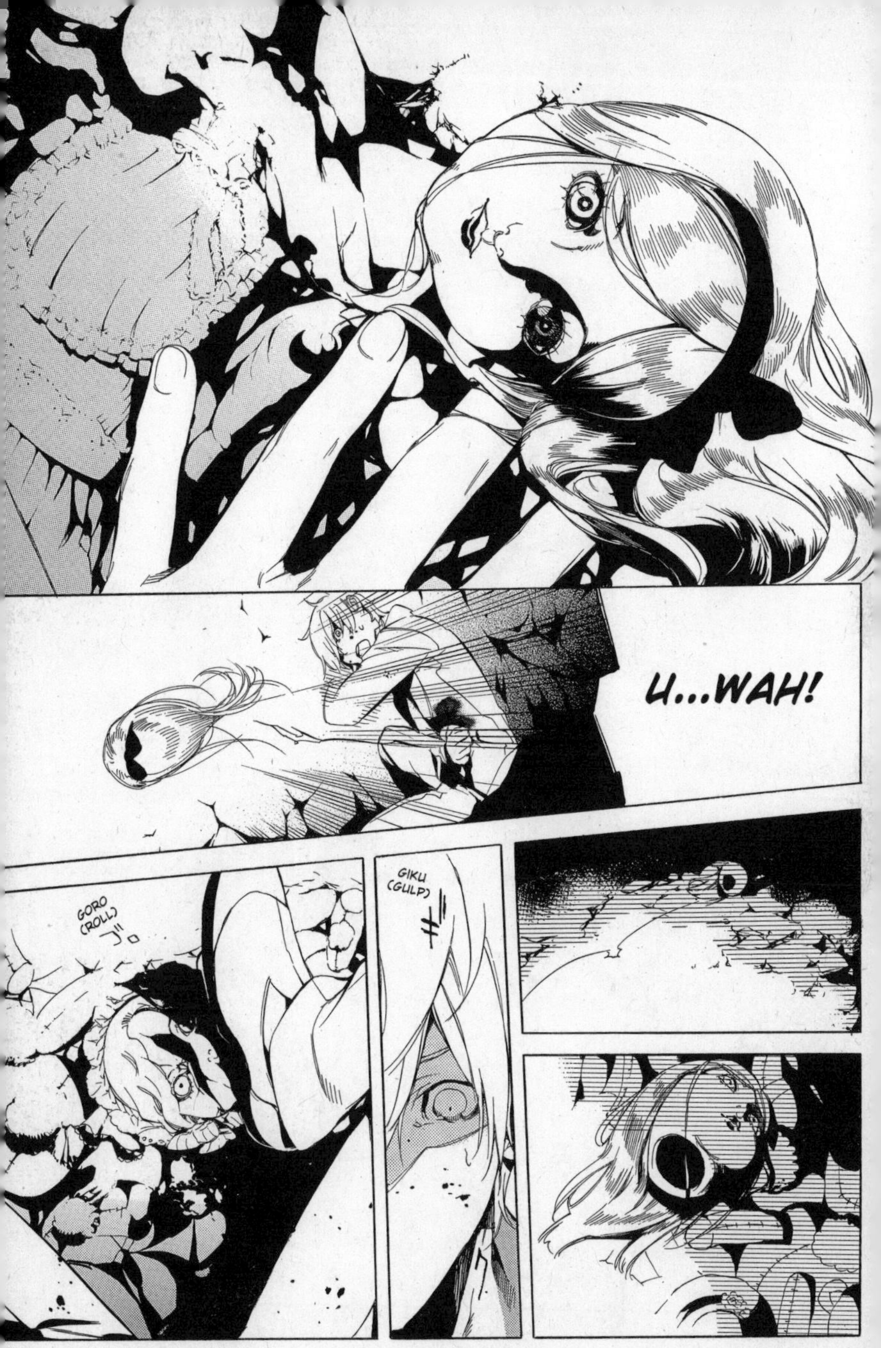

U...WAH!
GIKU (GULP)
GORO (ROLL)

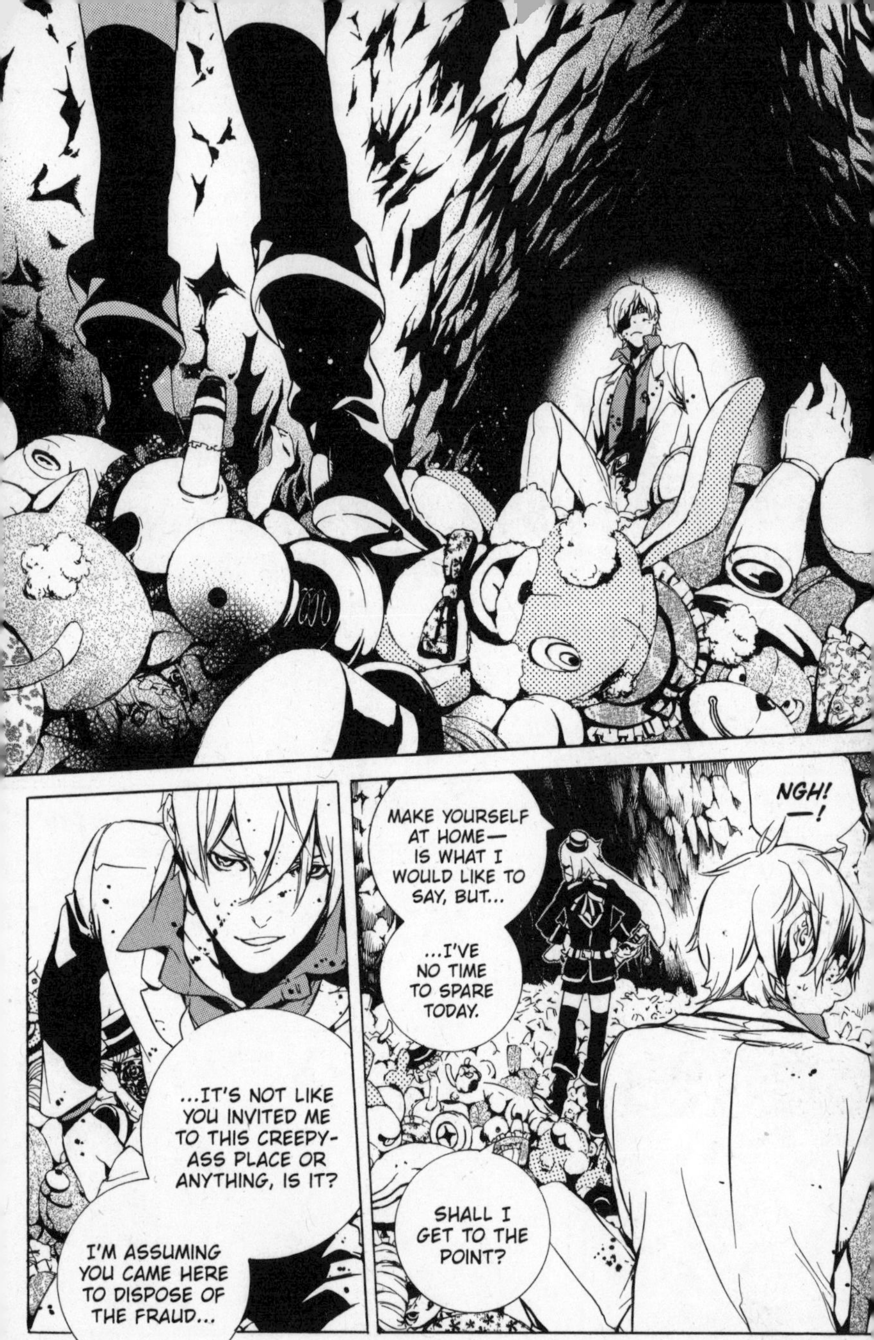
NGH!
—!
MAKE YOURSELF AT HOME— IS WHAT I WOULD LIKE TO SAY, BUT...
...I'VE NO TIME TO SPARE TODAY.
SHALL I GET TO THE POINT?
...IT'S NOT LIKE YOU INVITED ME TO THIS CREEPY-ASS PLACE OR ANYTHING, IS IT?
I'M ASSUMING YOU CAME HERE TO DISPOSE OF THE FRAUD...

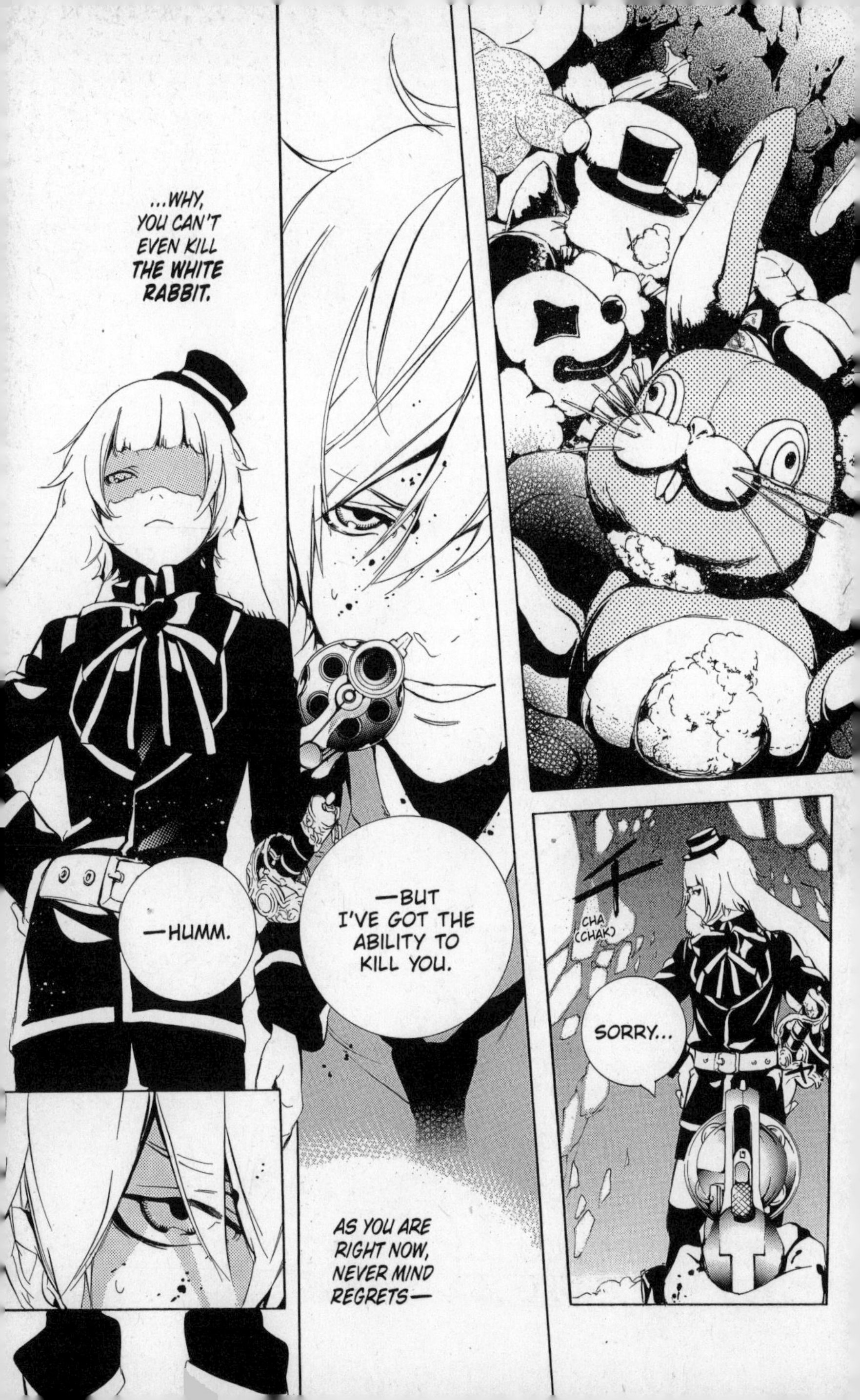
CHA (CHAK)
SORRY...
—BUT I'VE GOT THE ABILITY TO KILL YOU.
AS YOU ARE RIGHT NOW, NEVER MIND REGRETS—
...WHY, YOU CAN'T EVEN KILL THE WHITE RABBIT.
—HUMM.

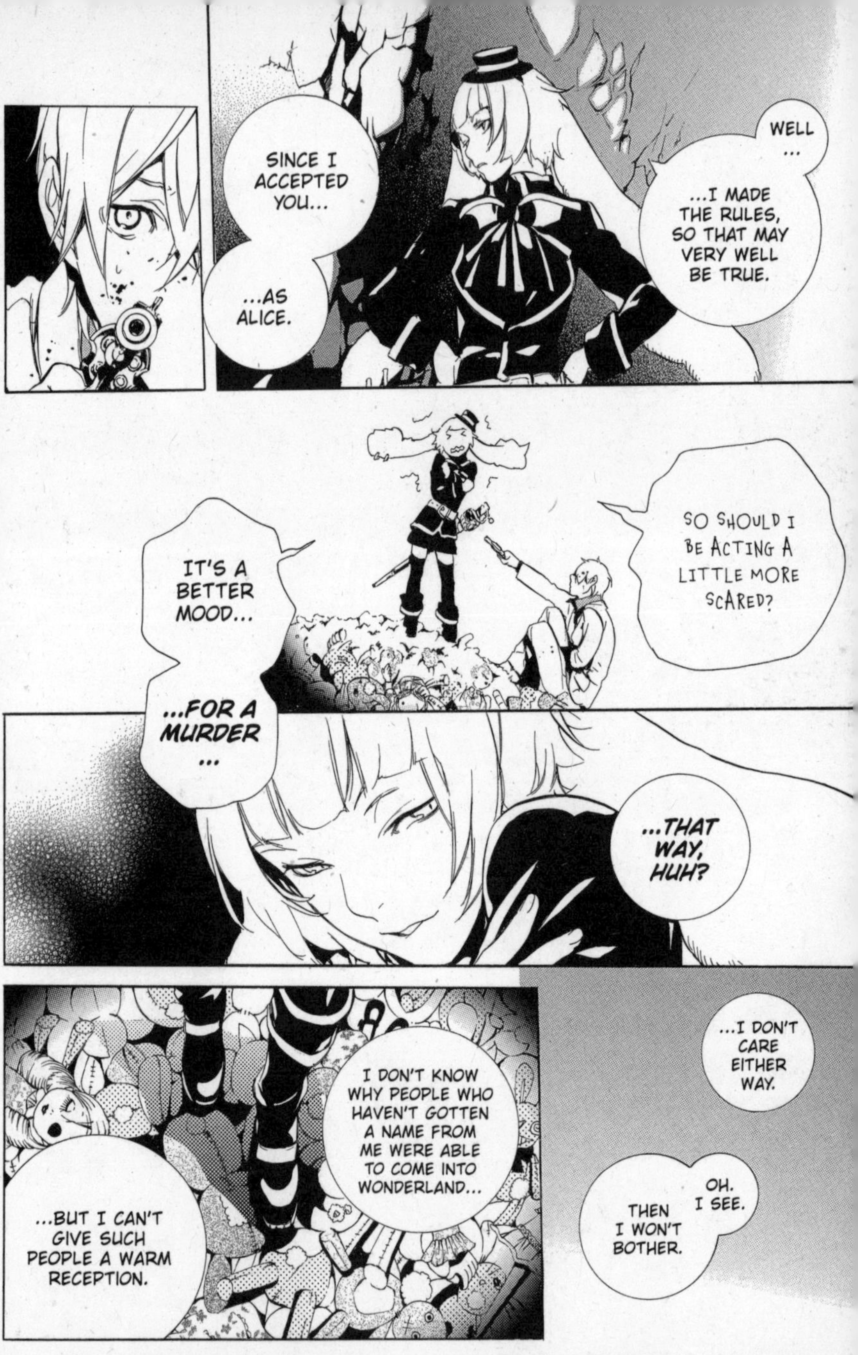
WELL...
...I MADE THE RULES, SO THAT MAY VERY WELL BE TRUE.
SINCE I ACCEPTED YOU...
...AS ALICE.
SO SHOULD I BE ACTING A LITTLE MORE SCARED?
IT'S A BETTER MOOD...
...FOR A MURDER...
...THAT WAY, HUH?
...I DON'T CARE EITHER WAY.
OH. I SEE.
THEN I WON'T BOTHER.
I DON'T KNOW WHY PEOPLE WHO HAVEN'T GOTTEN A NAME FROM ME WERE ABLE TO COME INTO WONDERLAND...
...BUT I CAN'T GIVE SUCH PEOPLE A WARM RECEPTION.

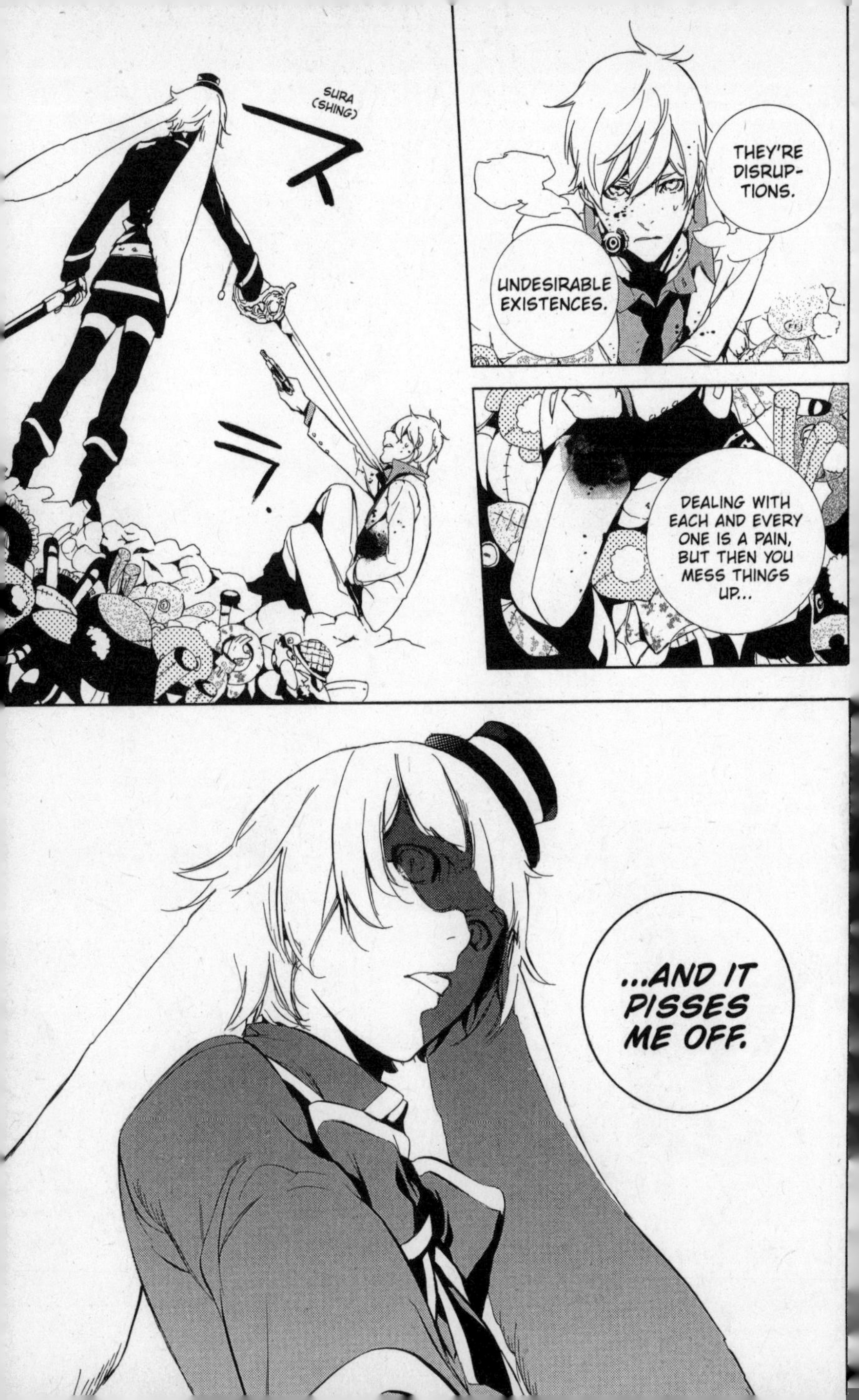
THEY'RE DISRUP-TIONS.
UNDESIRABLE EXISTENCES.
DEALING WITH EACH AND EVERY ONE IS A PAIN, BUT THEN YOU MESS THINGS UP...
SURA (SHING)
...AND IT PISSES ME OFF.

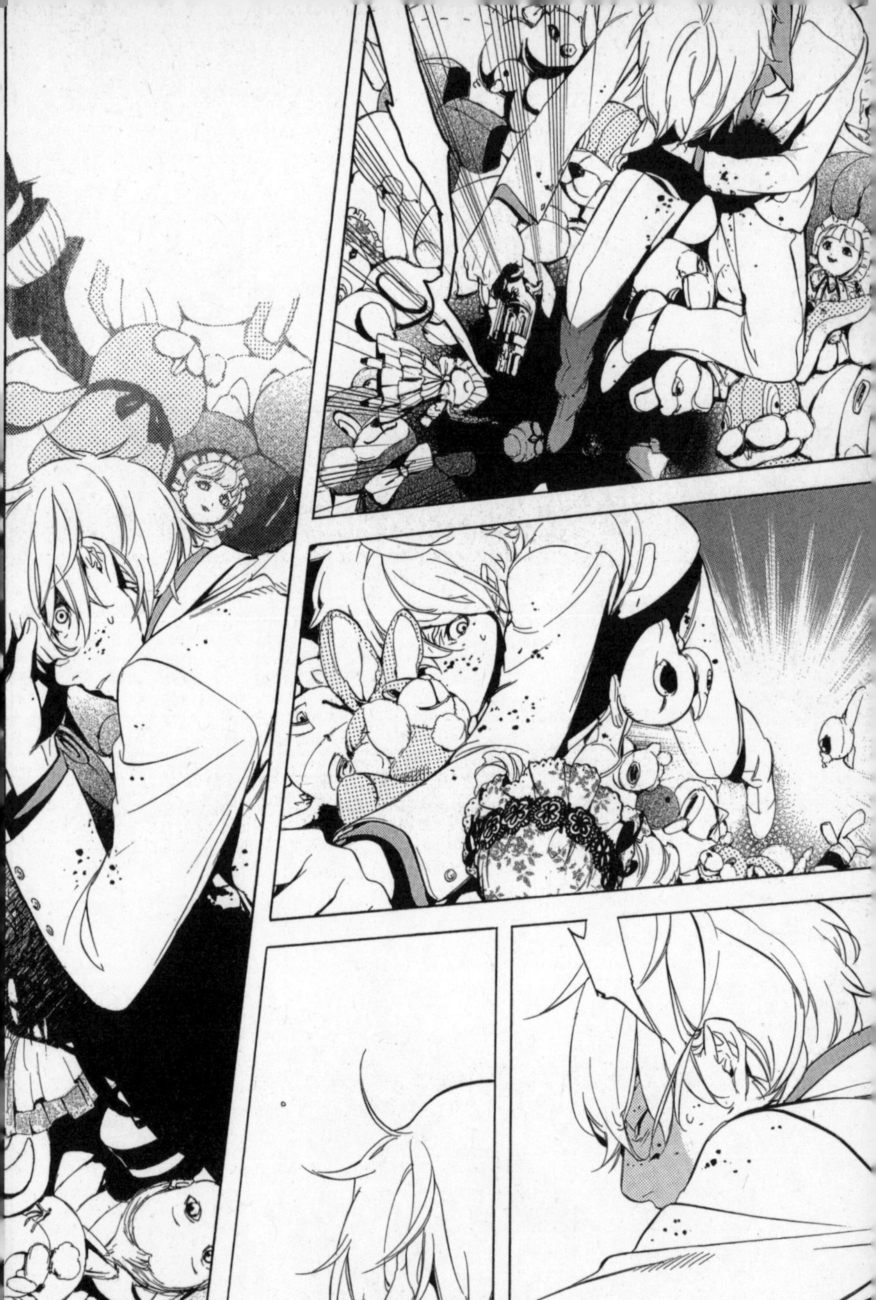

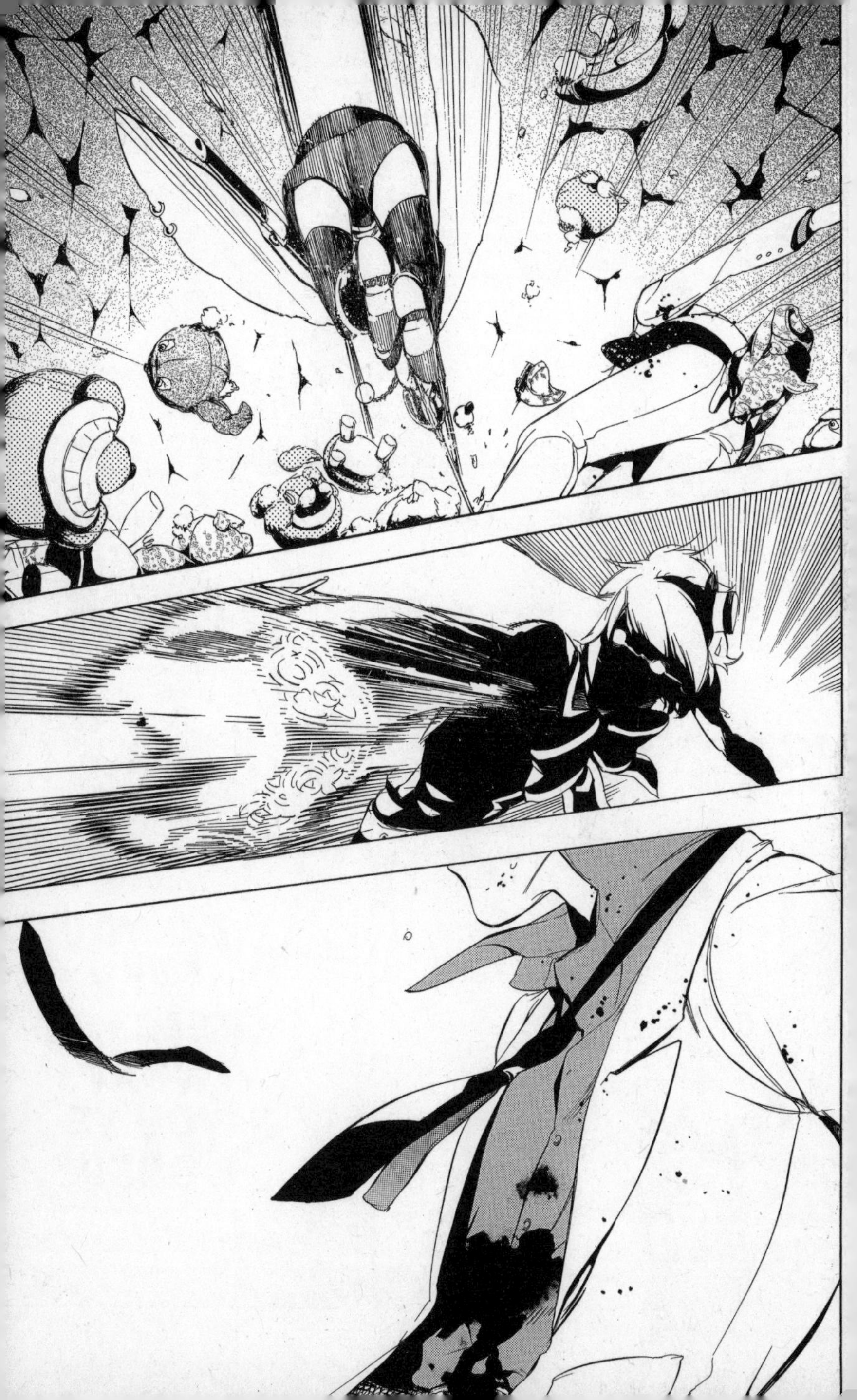

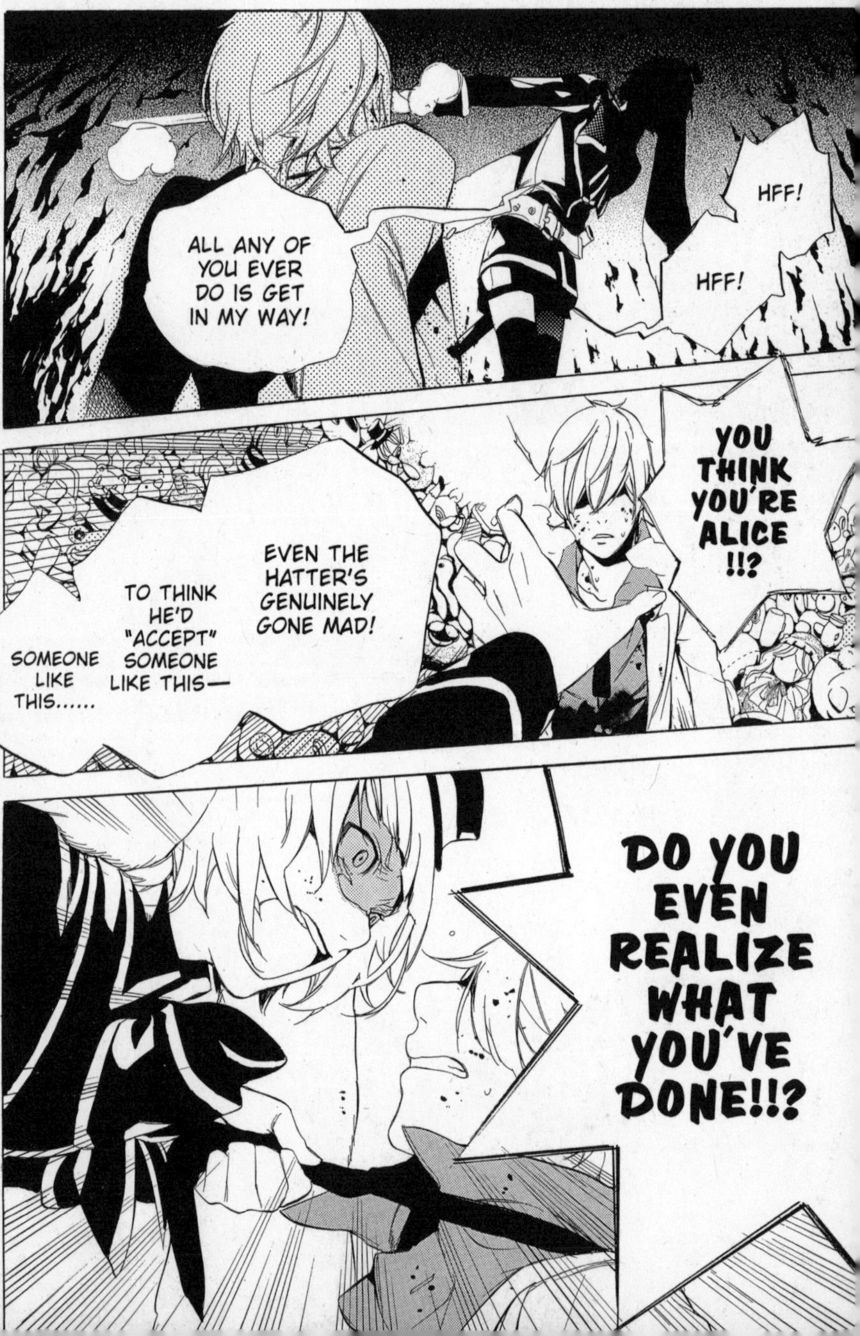
HFF!
HFF!
ALL ANY OF YOU EVER DO IS GET IN MY WAY!
YOU THINK YOU'RE ALICE !!?
EVEN THE HATTER'S GENUINELY GONE MAD!
TO THINK HE'D "ACCEPT" SOMEONE LIKE THIS—
SOMEONE LIKE THIS......
DO YOU EVEN REALIZE WHAT YOU'VE DONE!!?

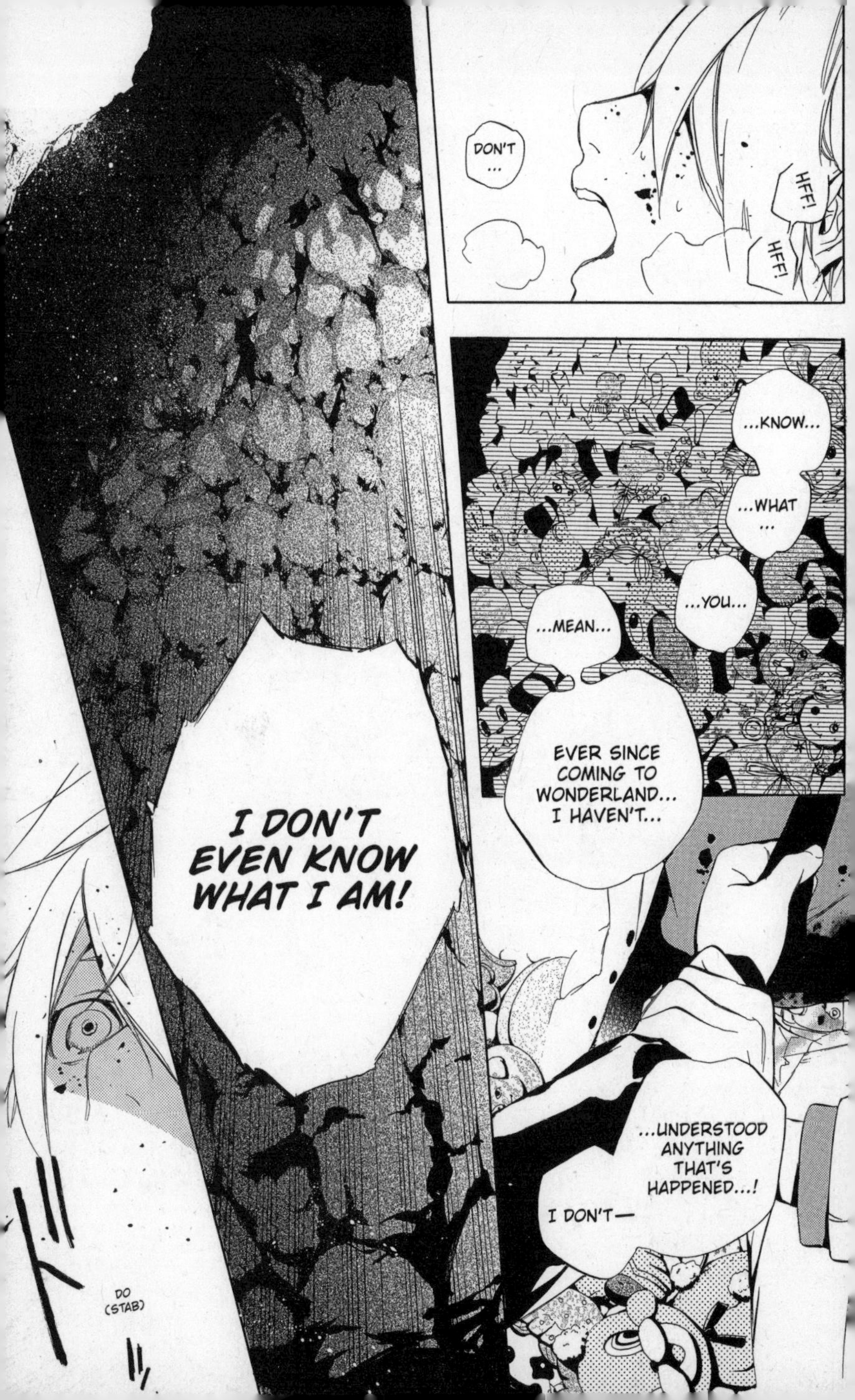
DON'T ...
HFF!
HFF!
...KNOW...
...WHAT ...
...YOU...
...MEAN...
EVER SINCE COMING TO WONDERLAND... I HAVEN'T...
...UNDERSTOOD ANYTHING THAT'S HAPPENED...!
I DON'T—
I DON'T EVEN KNOW WHAT I AM!
DO (STAB)

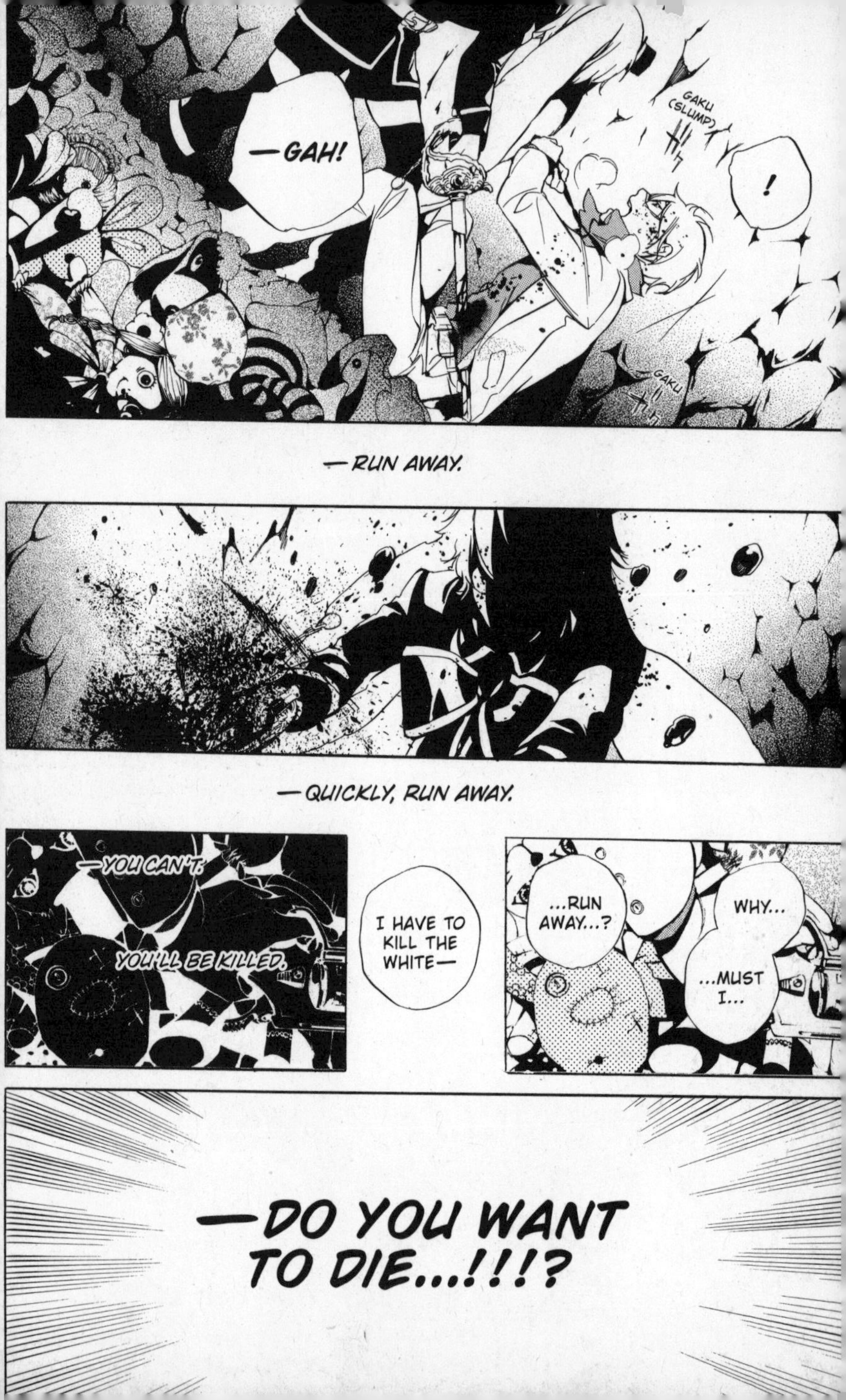
GAKU (SLUMP)
!
—GAH!
GAKU
—RUN AWAY.
—QUICKLY, RUN AWAY.
WHY...
...RUN AWAY...?
...MUST I...
I HAVE TO KILL THE WHITE—
—YOU CAN'T.
YOU'LL BE KILLED.
—DO YOU WANT TO DIE...!!!?

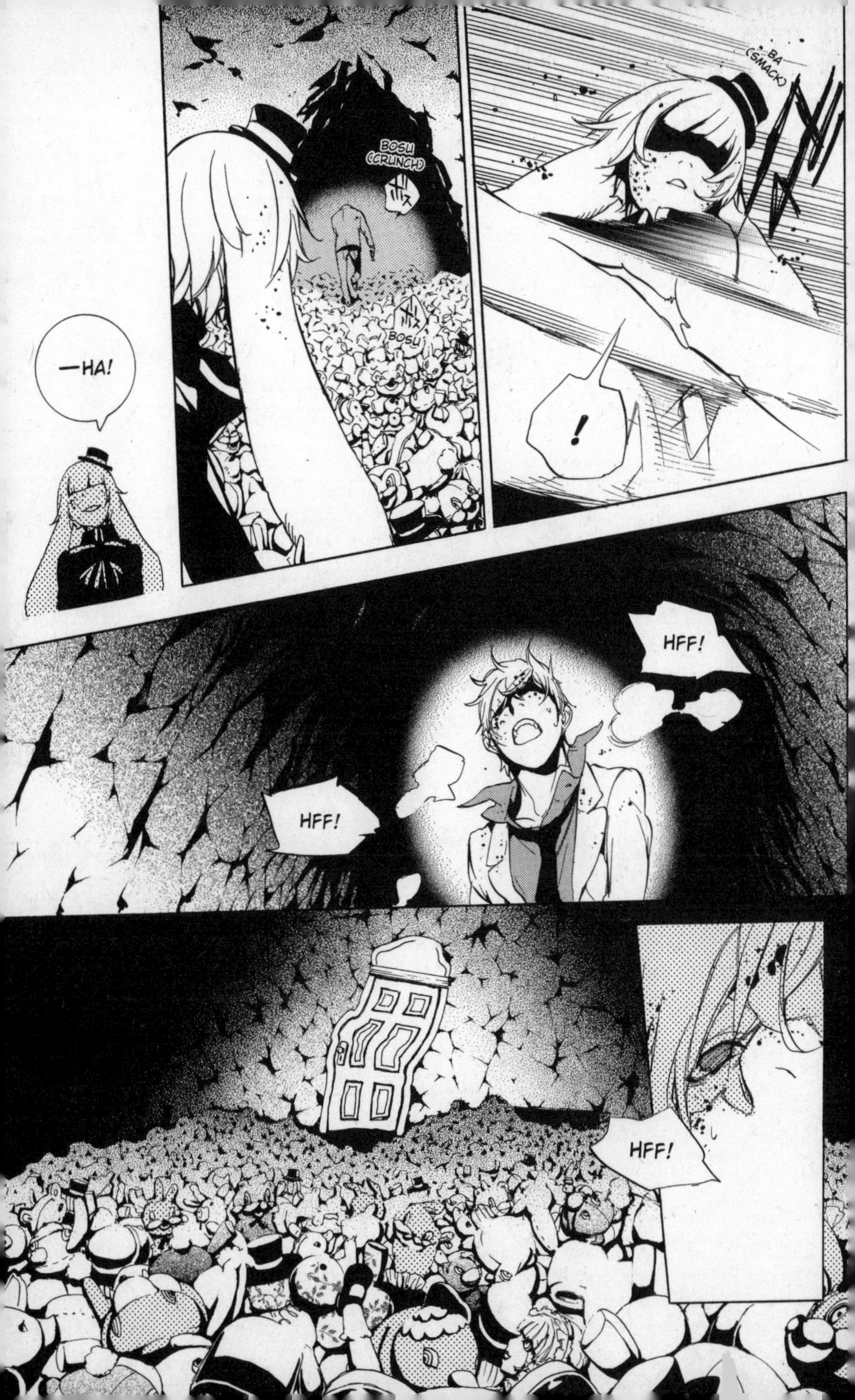
BA
(SMACK)
!
BOSU
(CRUNCH)
BOSU
—HA!
HFF!
HFF!
HFF!

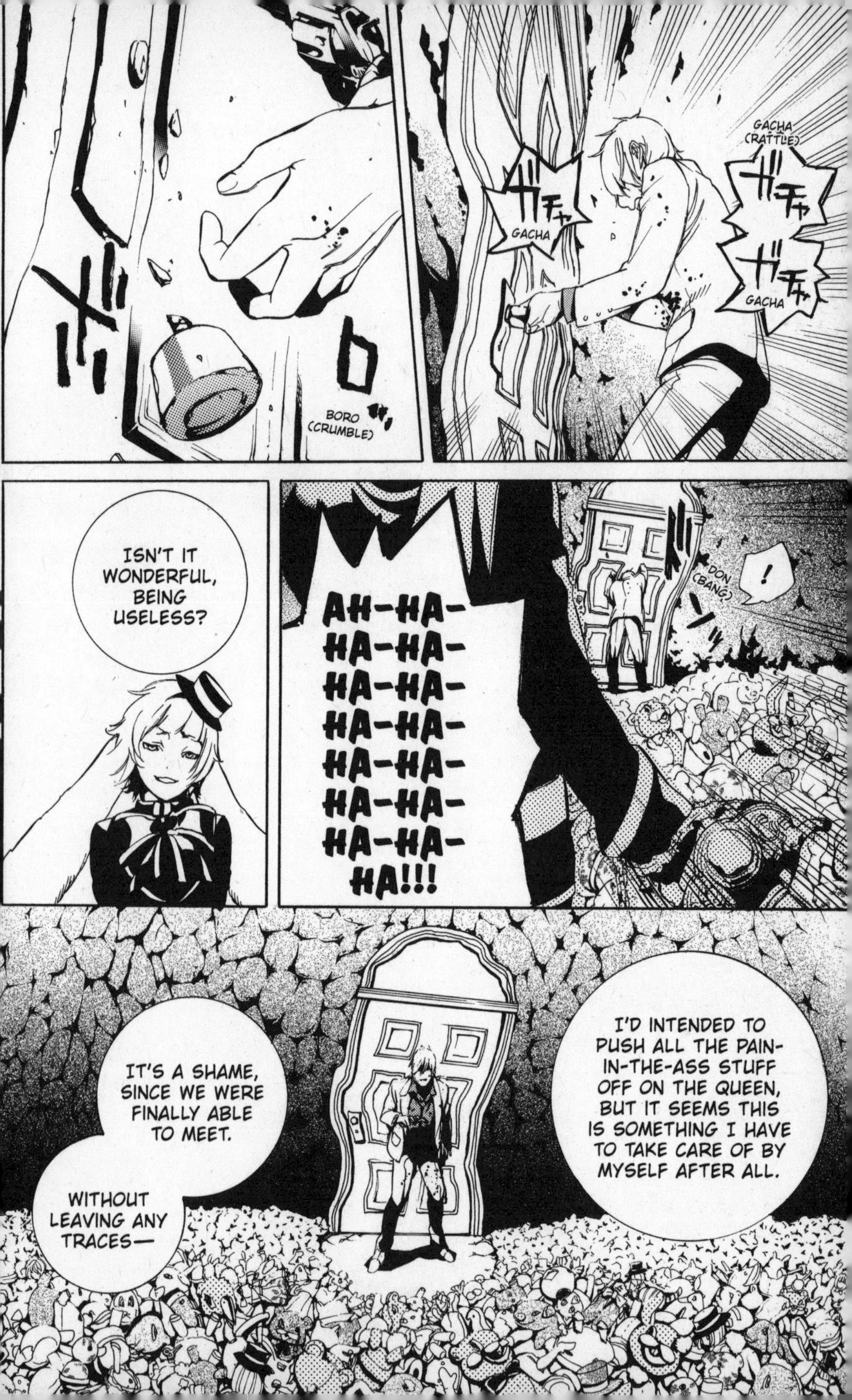
GACHA (RATTLE)
ガチャ
ガチャ
GACHA
ガチャ
GACHA
BORO (CRUMBLE)
!
DON (BANG)
AH-HA-HA-HA-HA-HA-HA-HA-HA-HA-HA-HA-HA-HA-HA!!!
ISN'T IT WONDERFUL, BEING USELESS?
I'D INTENDED TO PUSH ALL THE PAIN-IN-THE-ASS STUFF OFF ON THE QUEEN, BUT IT SEEMS THIS IS SOMETHING I HAVE TO TAKE CARE OF BY MYSELF AFTER ALL.
IT'S A SHAME, SINCE WE WERE FINALLY ABLE TO MEET.
WITHOUT LEAVING ANY TRACES—

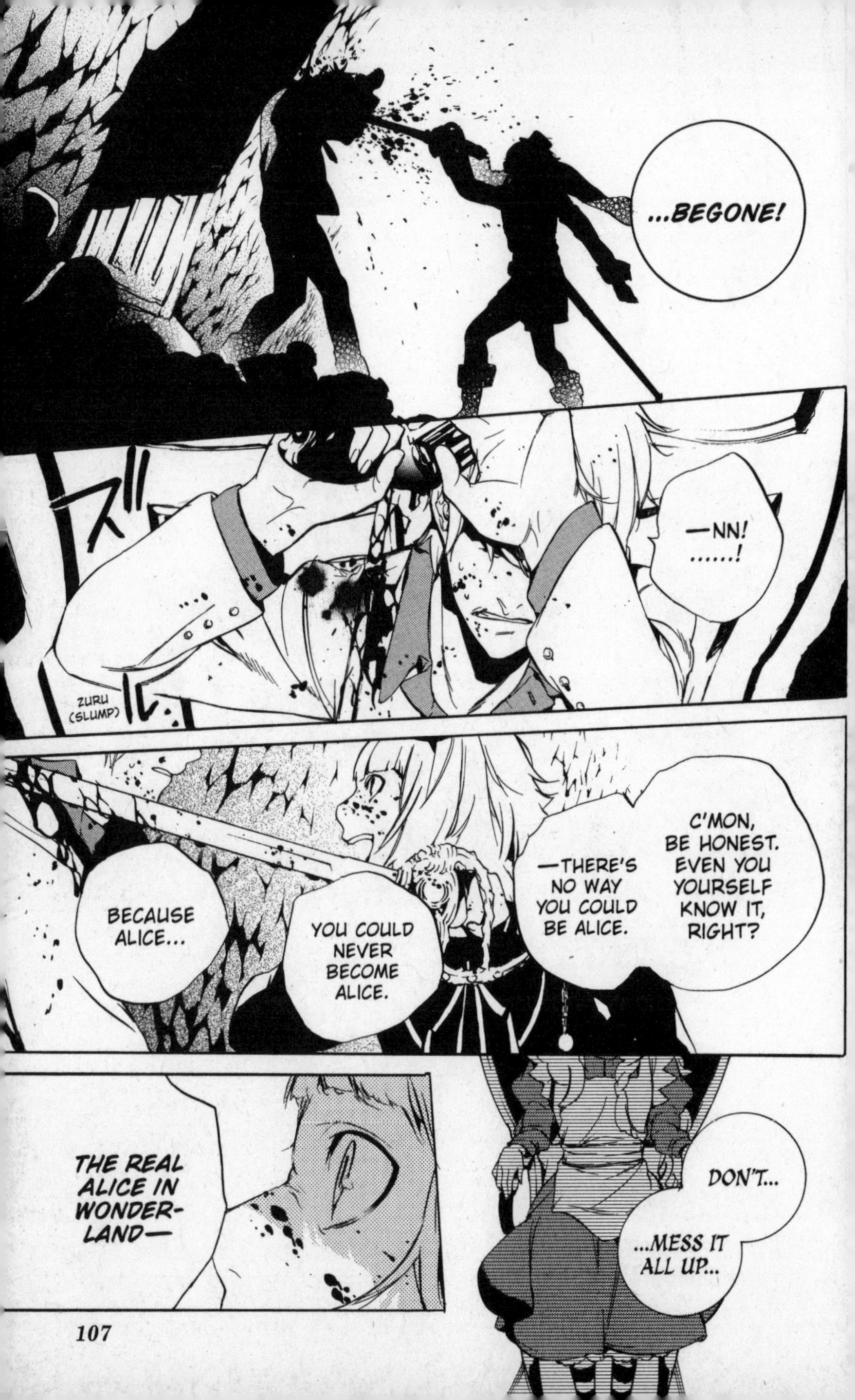
...BEGONE!
—NN! ......!
ZURU (SLUMP)
C'MON, BE HONEST. EVEN YOU YOURSELF KNOW IT, RIGHT?
—THERE'S NO WAY YOU COULD BE ALICE.
YOU COULD NEVER BECOME ALICE.
BECAUSE ALICE...
DON'T...
...MESS IT ALL UP...
THE REAL ALICE IN WONDER-LAND—

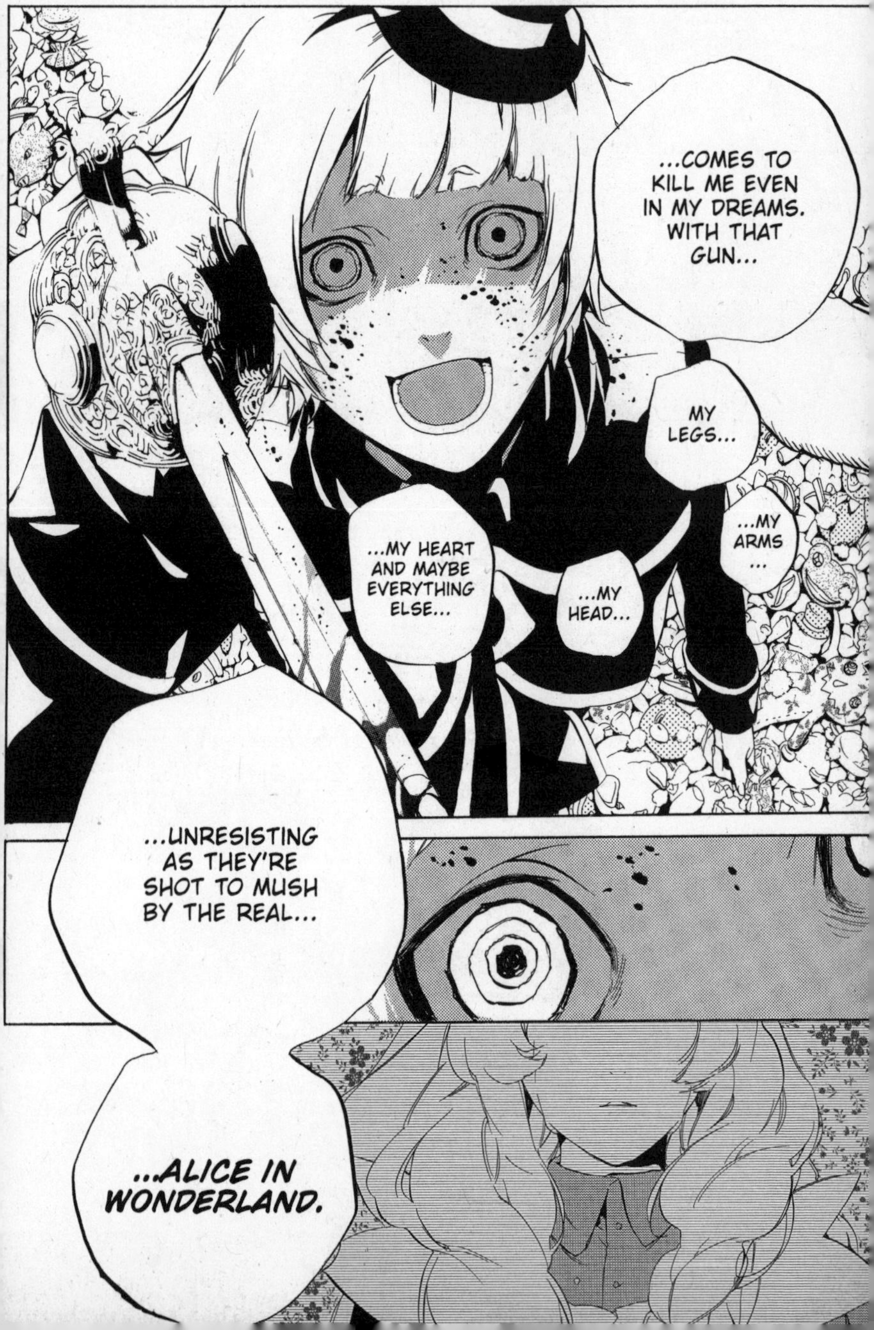
...COMES TO KILL ME EVEN IN MY DREAMS. WITH THAT GUN...
MY LEGS...
...MY ARMS...
...MY HEAD...
...MY HEART AND MAYBE EVERYTHING ELSE...
...UNRESISTING AS THEY'RE SHOT TO MUSH BY THE REAL...
...ALICE IN WONDERLAND.

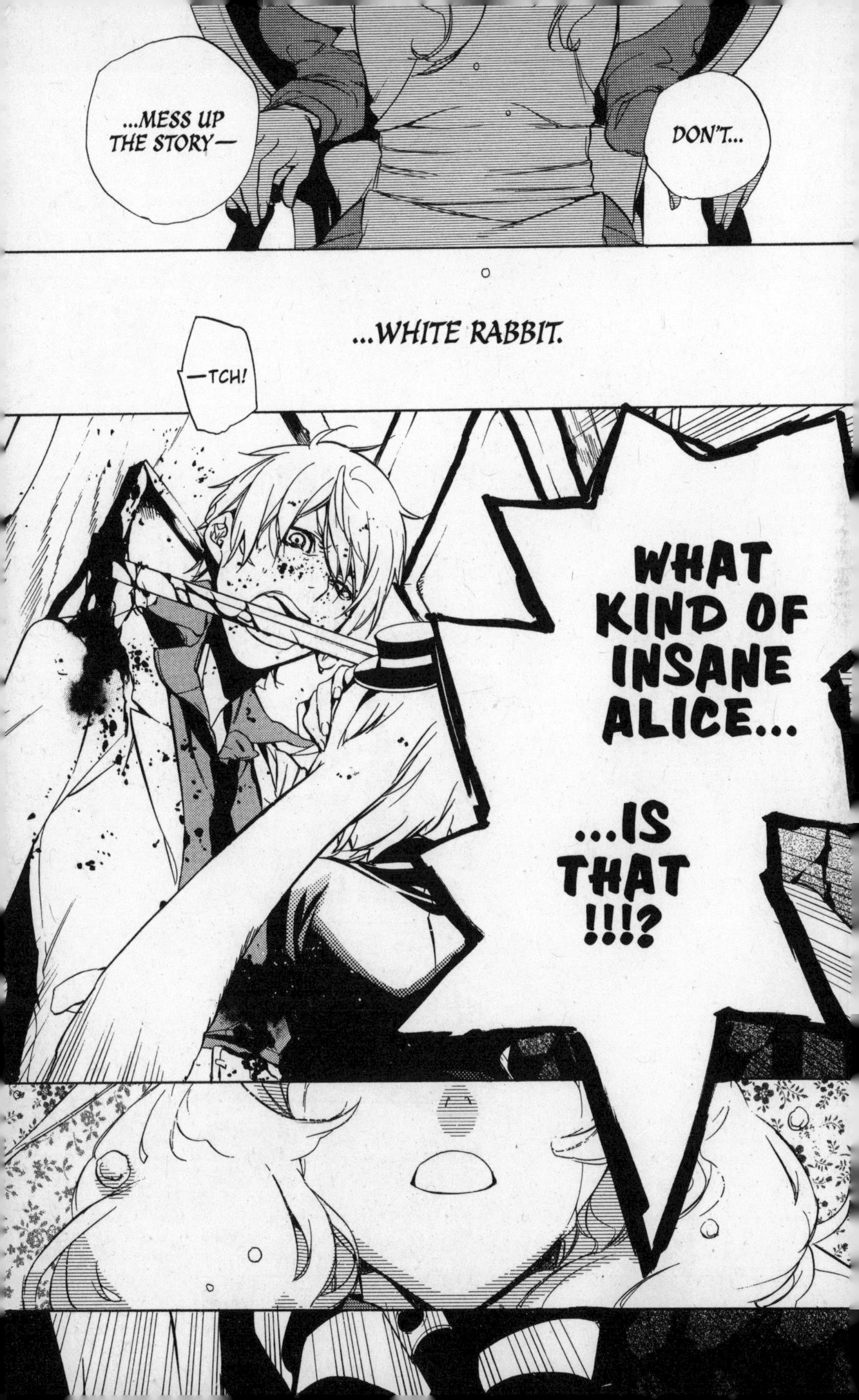
DON'T...
...MESS UP THE STORY—
...WHITE RABBIT.
—TCH!
WHAT KIND OF INSANE ALICE...
...IS THAT!!!?

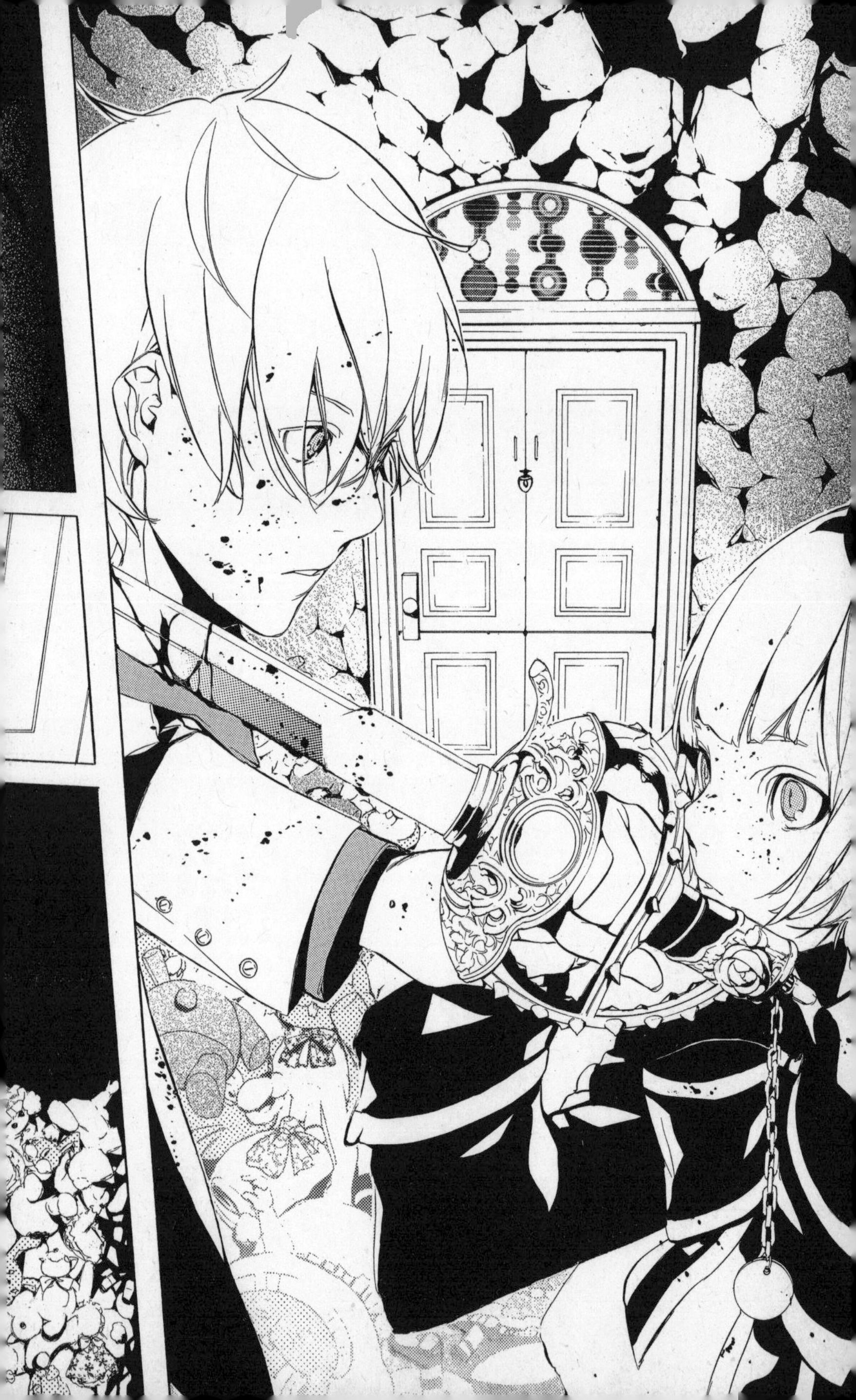

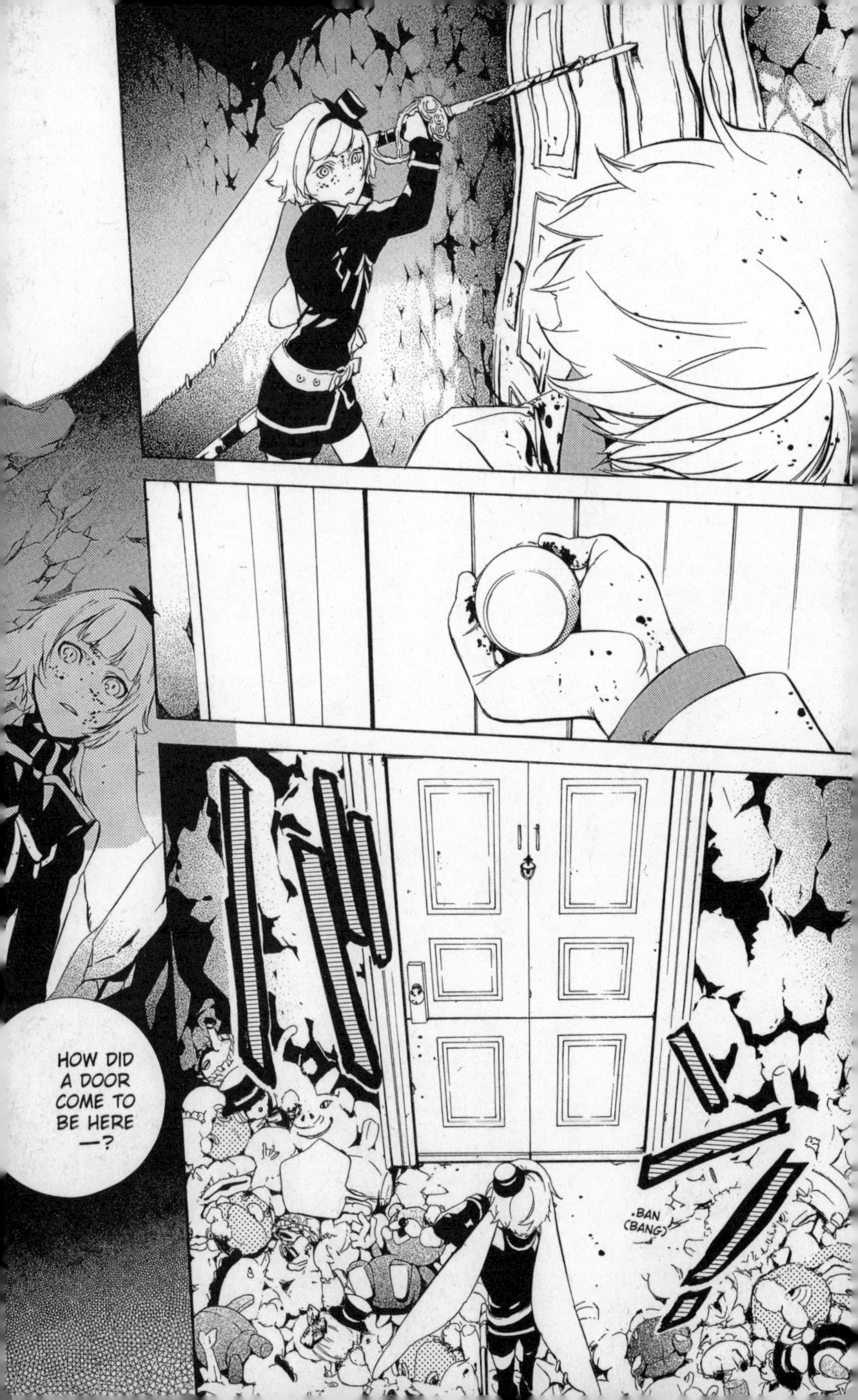
BAN (BANG)
HOW DID A DOOR COME TO BE HERE —?

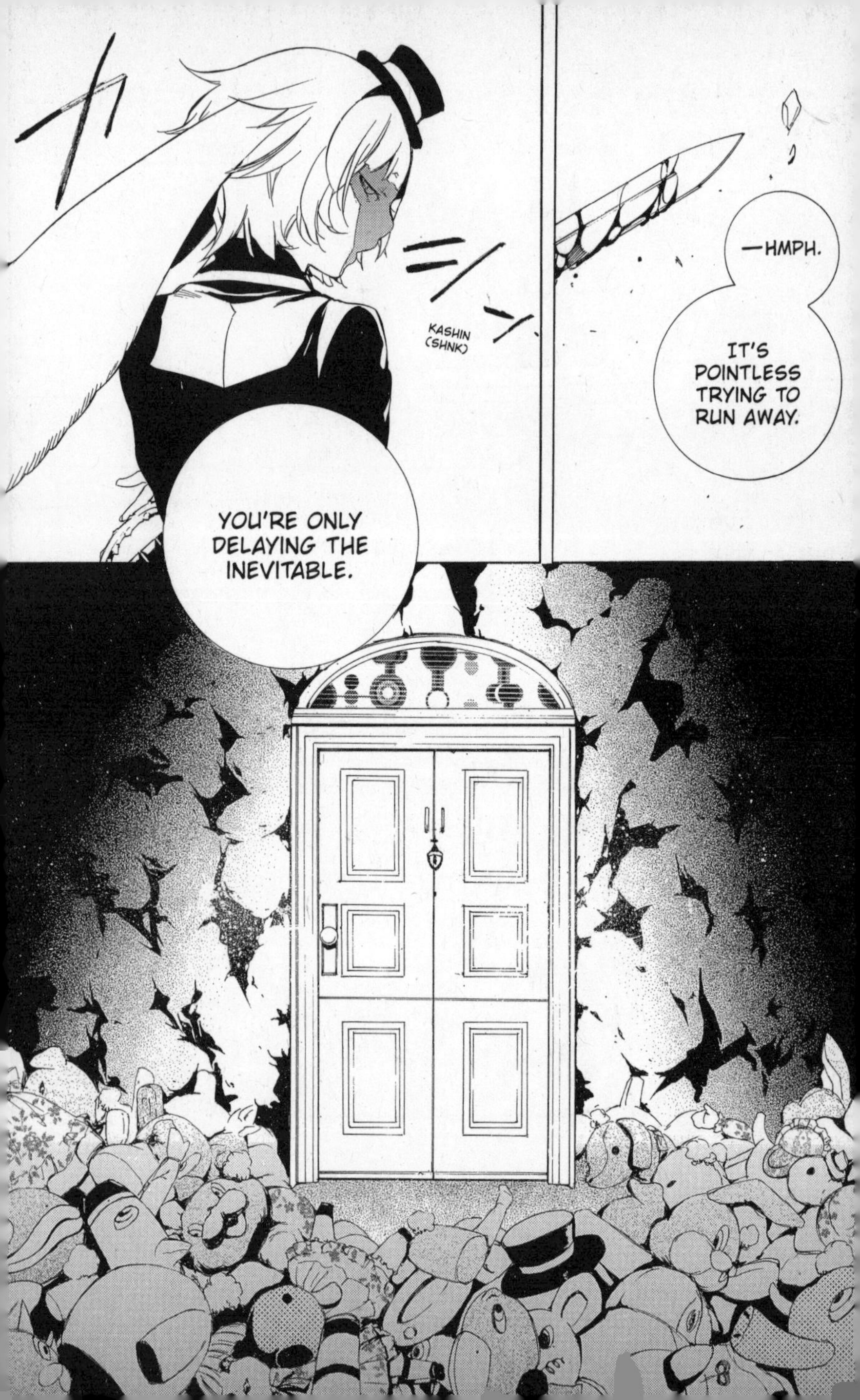
—HMPH.
IT'S POINTLESS TRYING TO RUN AWAY.
KASHIN (SHNK)
YOU'RE ONLY DELAYING THE INEVITABLE.

Chapter 28

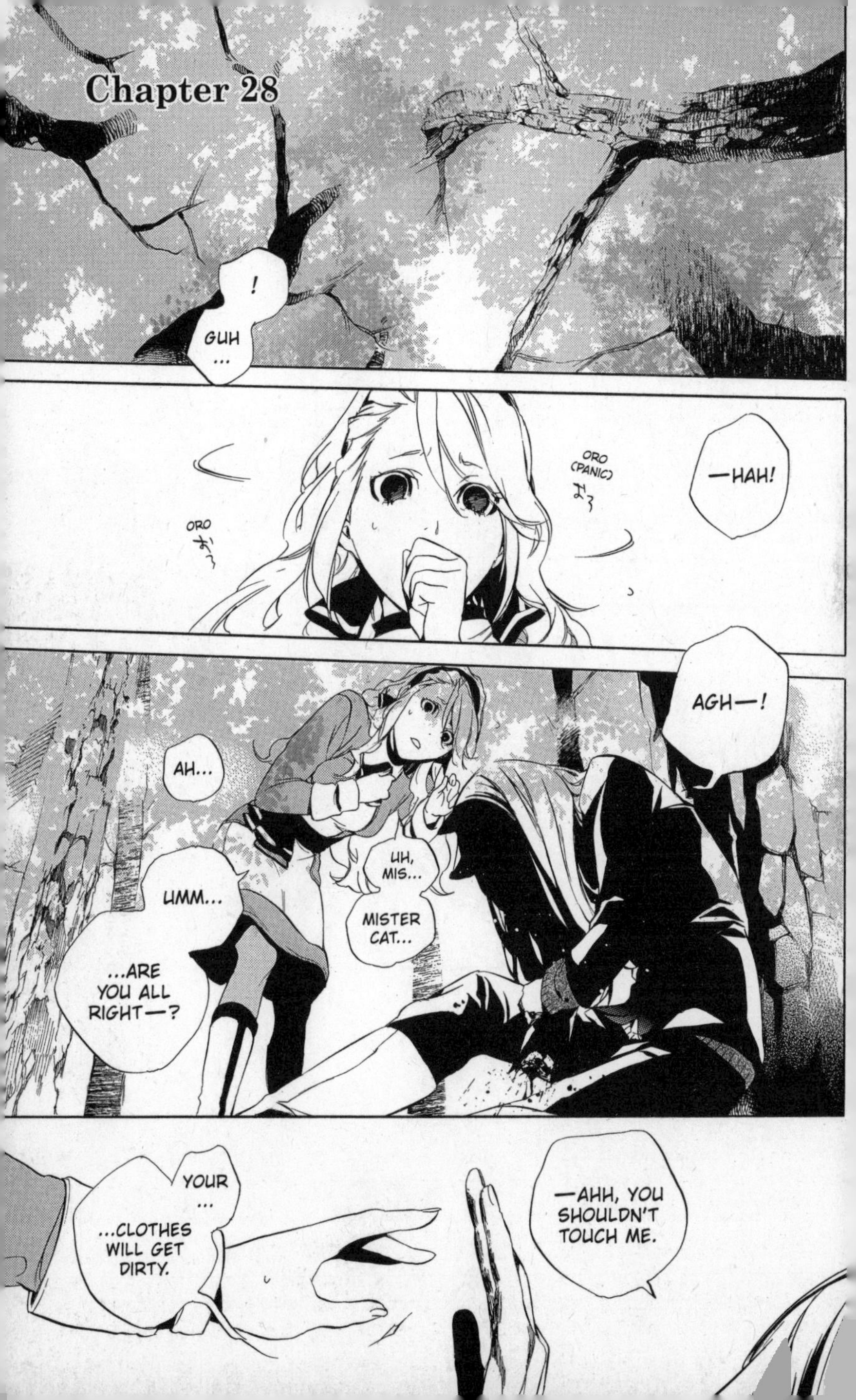

! GUH...
—HAH!
ORO (PANIC)
ORO
AGH—!
AH...
UH, MIS... MISTER CAT...
UMM... ...ARE YOU ALL RIGHT—?
—AHH, YOU SHOULDN'T TOUCH ME.
YOUR... ...CLOTHES WILL GET DIRTY.

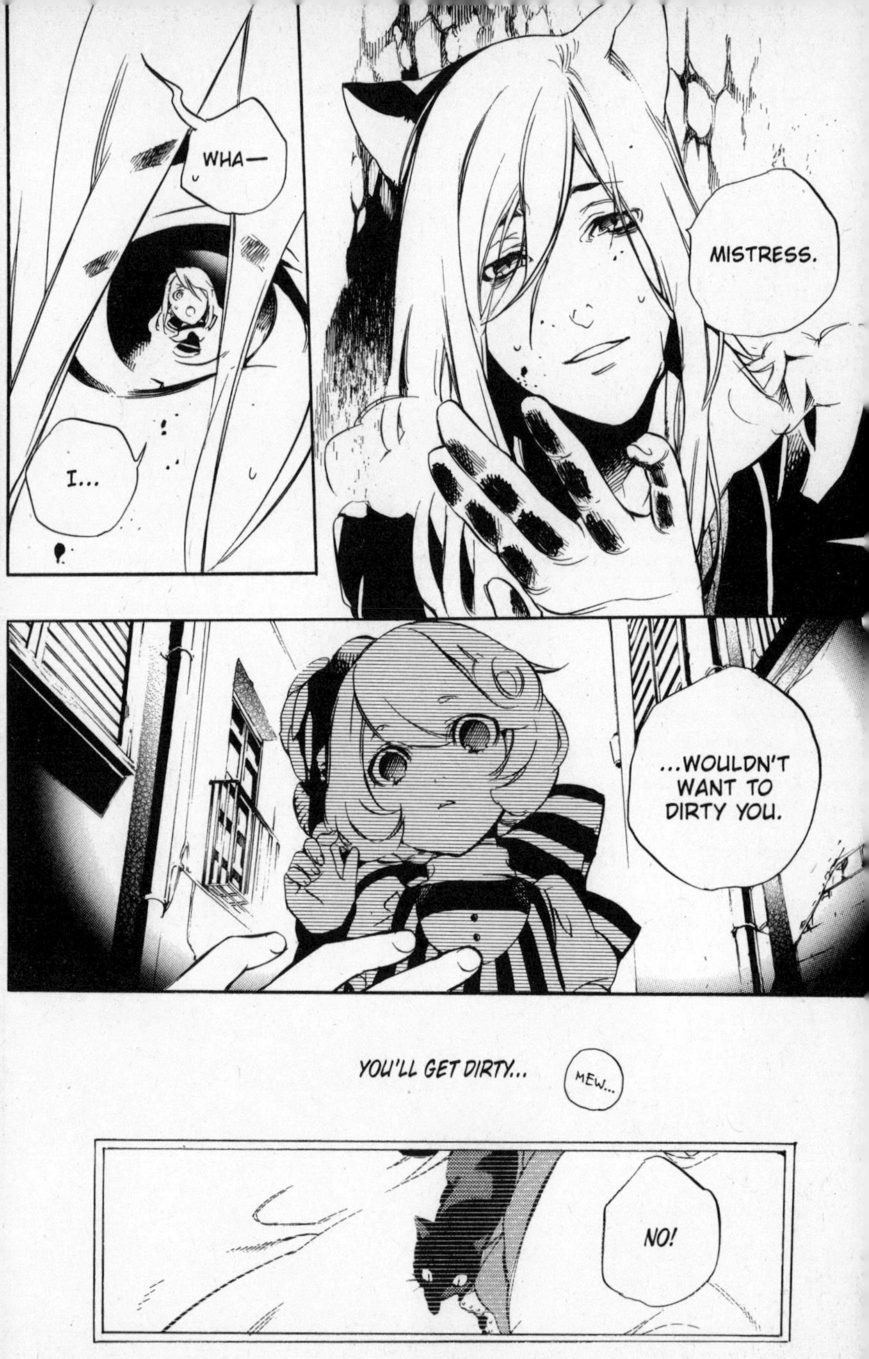
MISTRESS.
WHA—
I...
...WOULDN'T WANT TO DIRTY YOU.
MEW...
YOU'LL GET DIRTY...
NO!

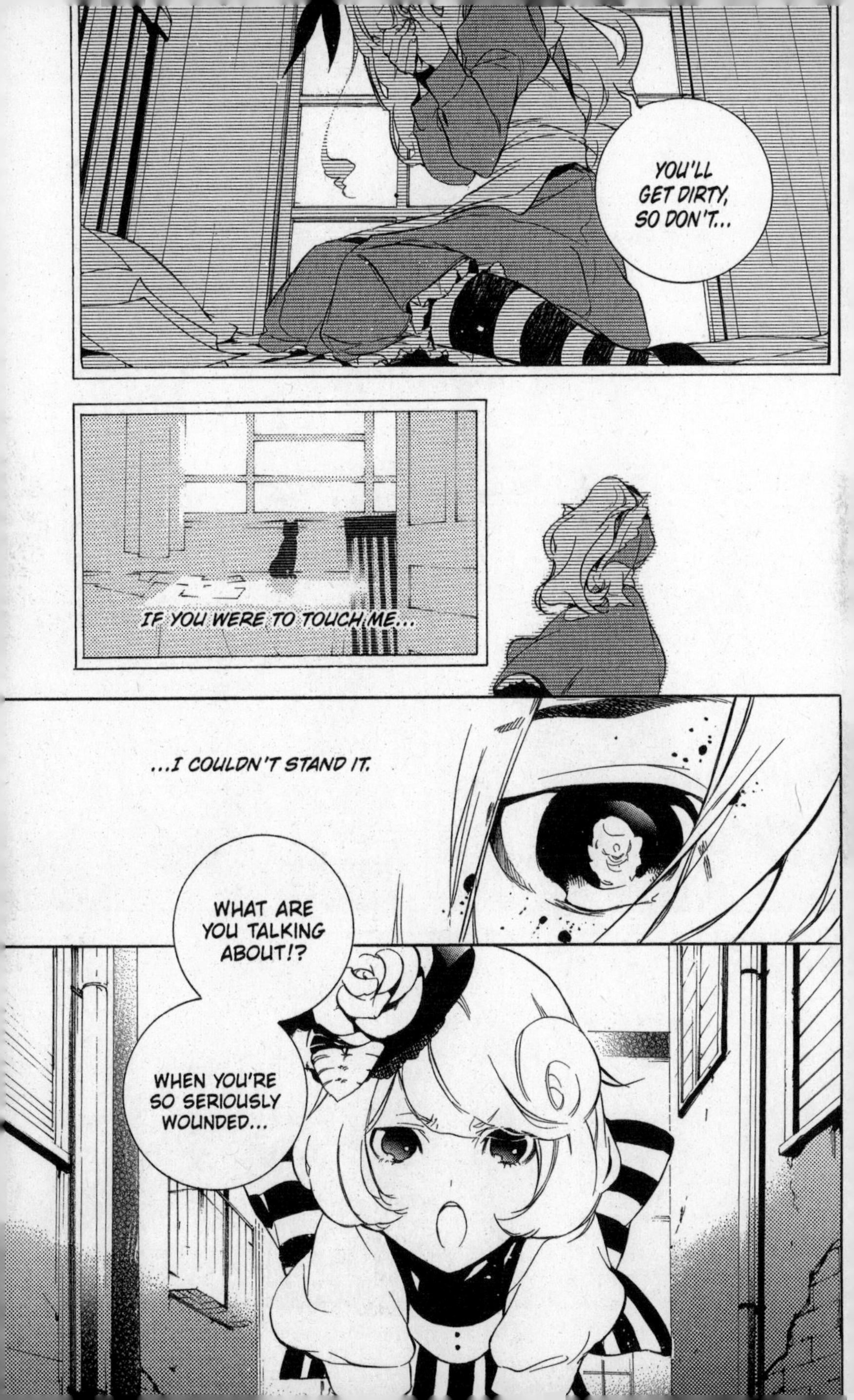
YOU'LL GET DIRTY, SO DON'T...
IF YOU WERE TO TOUCH ME...
...I COULDN'T STAND IT.
WHAT ARE YOU TALKING ABOUT!?
WHEN YOU'RE SO SERIOUSLY WOUNDED...

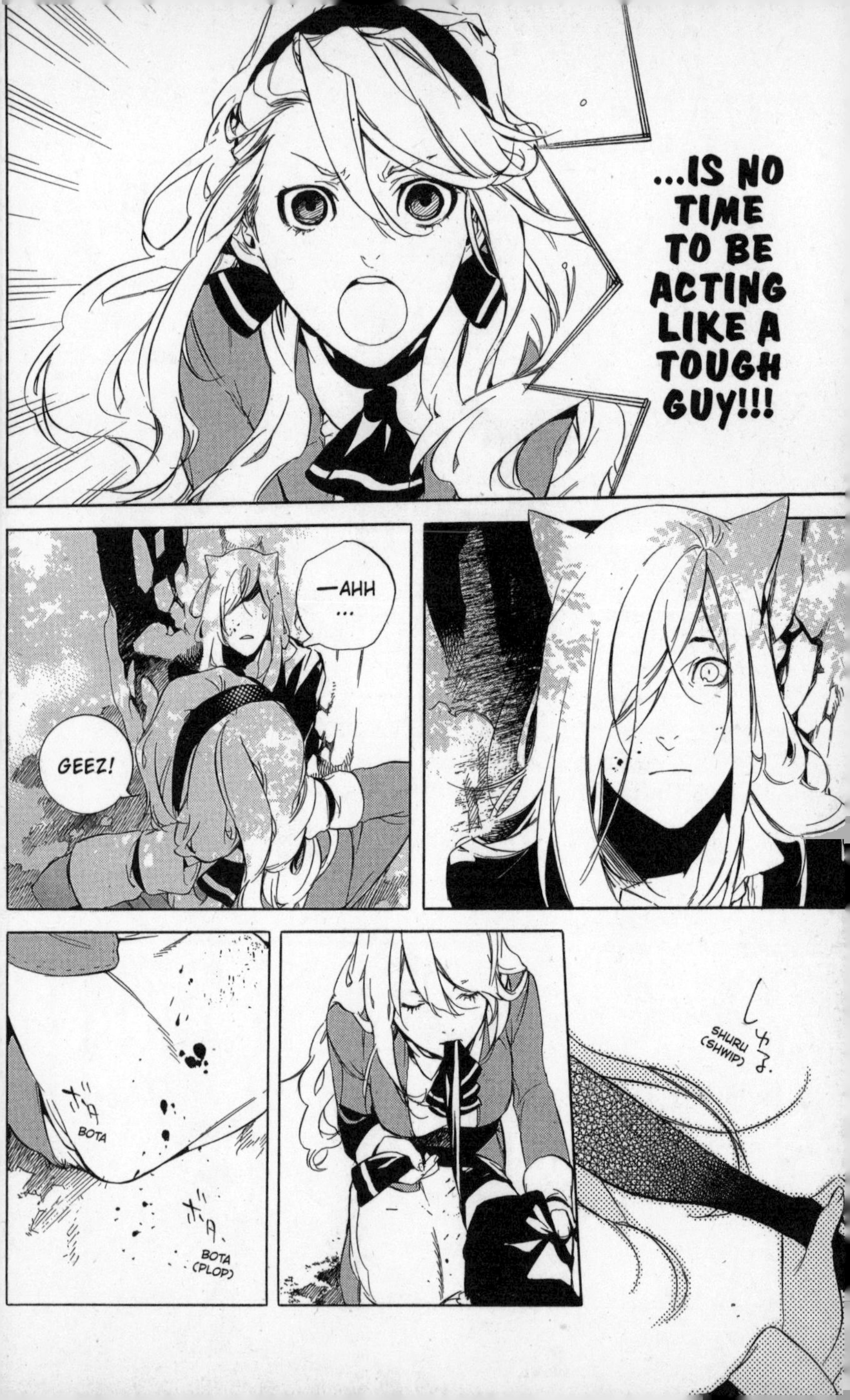
...IS NO TIME TO BE ACTING LIKE A TOUGH GUY!!!
—AHH ...
GEEZ!
しゅる
SHURU (SHWIP)
ボタ
BOTA
ボタ、
BOTA (PLOP)

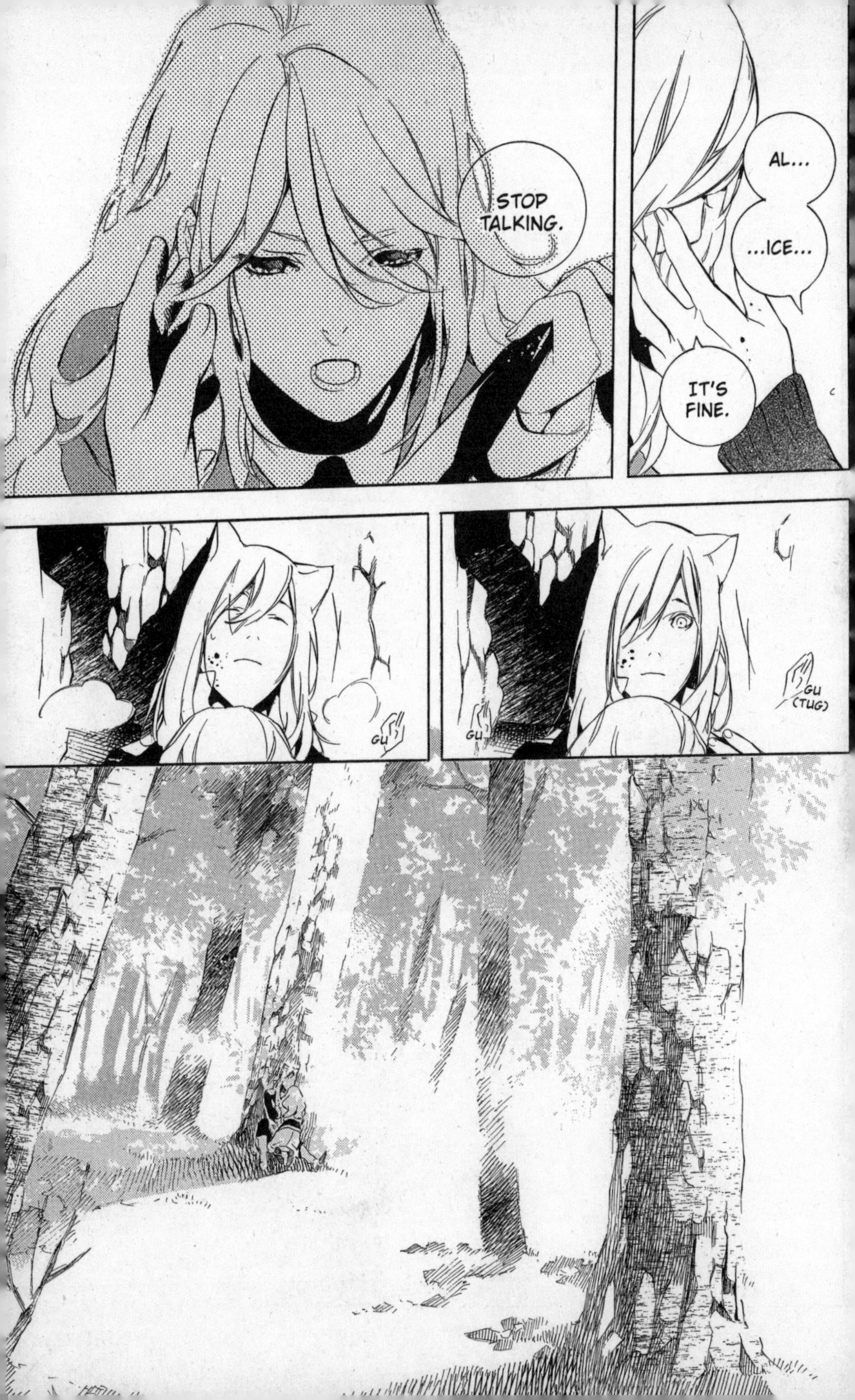
AL...
...ICE...
IT'S FINE.
STOP TALKING.
GU (TUG)
GU
GU

Chapter 28 Across.

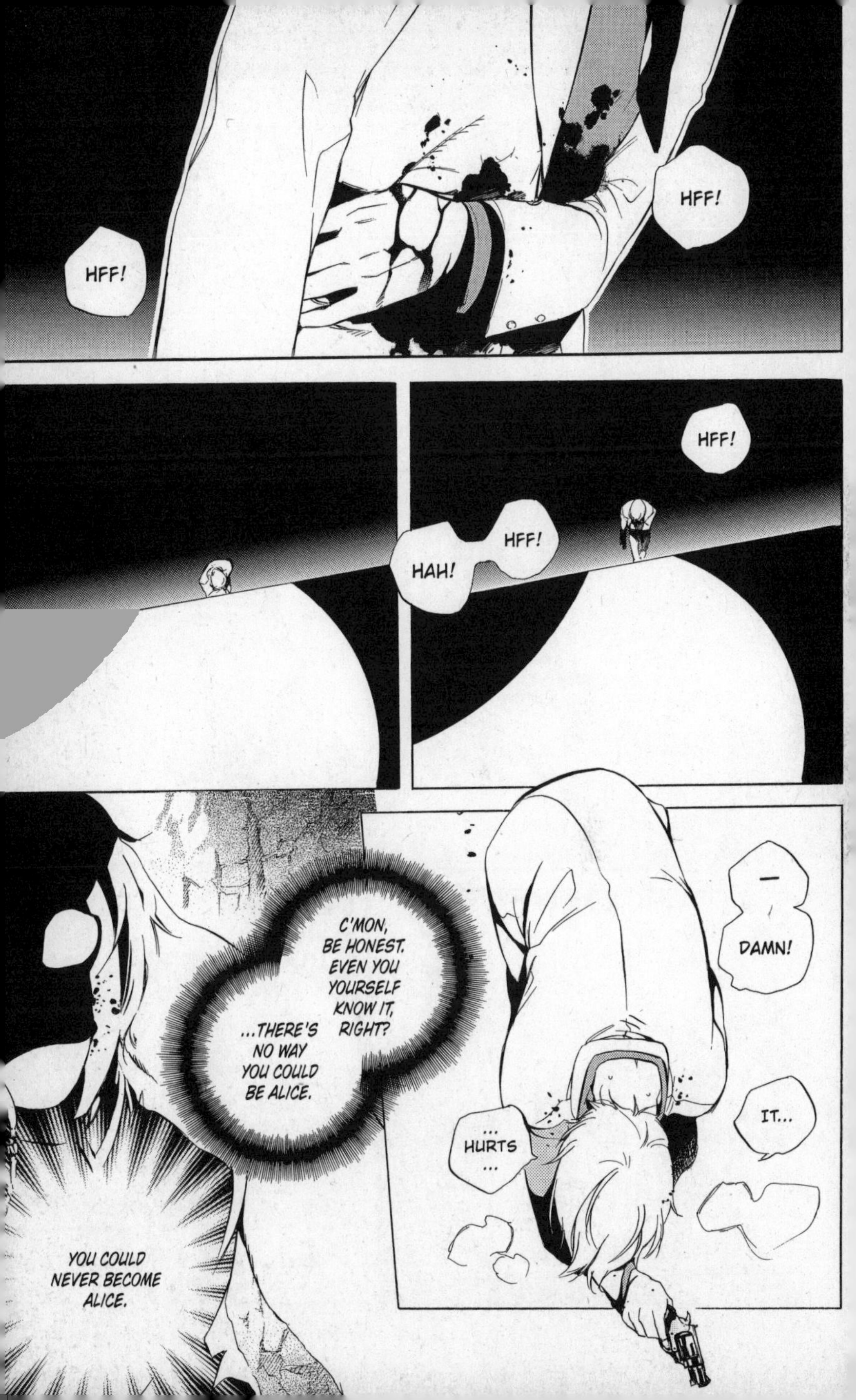
HFF!
HFF!
HFF!
HFF!
HAH!
— DAMN!
IT...
...HURTS...
C'MON, BE HONEST. EVEN YOU YOURSELF KNOW IT, RIGHT?
...THERE'S NO WAY YOU COULD BE ALICE.
YOU COULD NEVER BECOME ALICE.

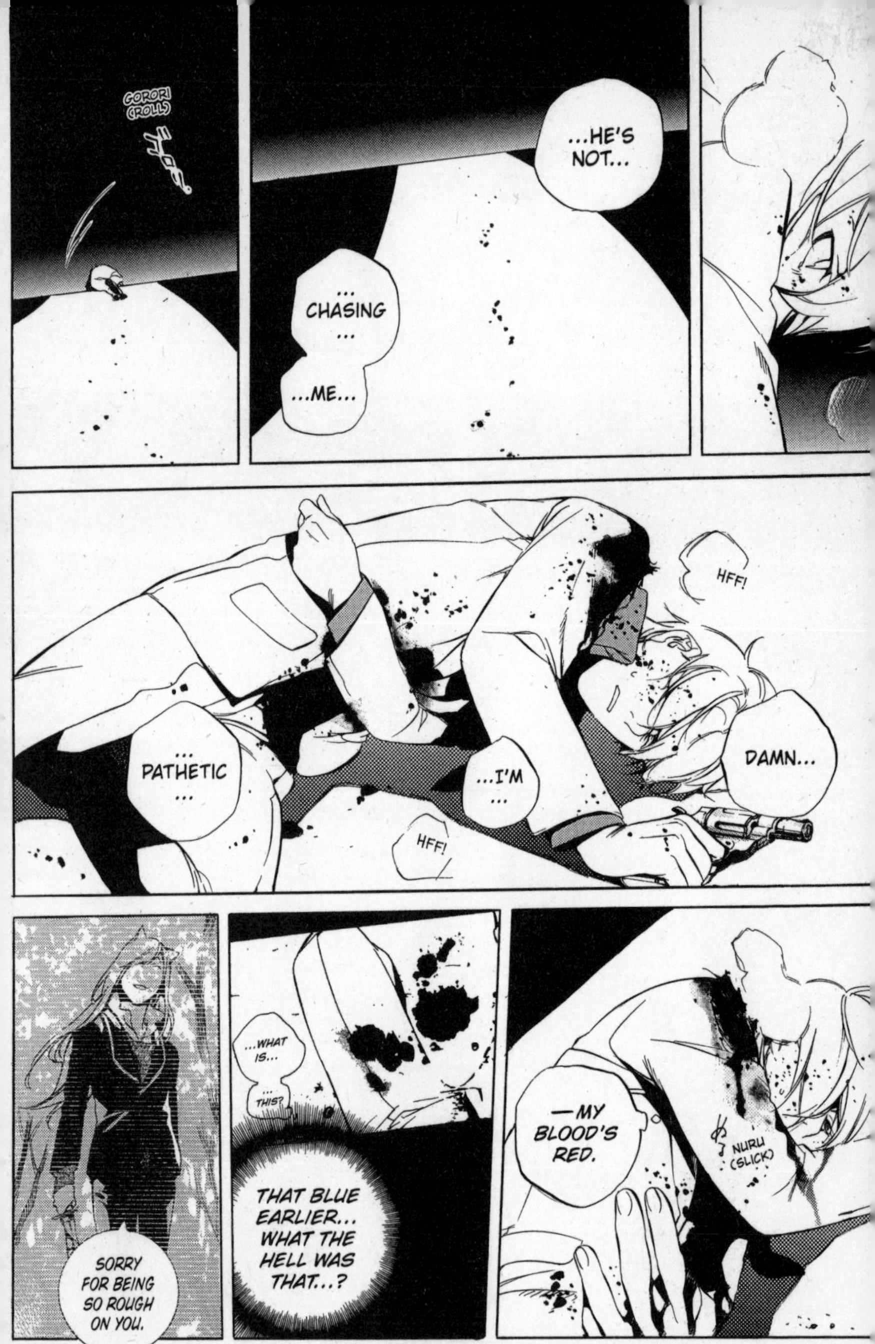
...HE'S NOT...
...CHASING... ...ME...
GORORI (ROLL)
HFF!
DAMN...
...I'M...
HFF!
...PATHETIC...
NURU (SLICK)
—MY BLOOD'S RED.
...WHAT IS... ...THIS?
THAT BLUE EARLIER... WHAT THE HELL WAS THAT...?
SORRY FOR BEING SO ROUGH ON YOU.

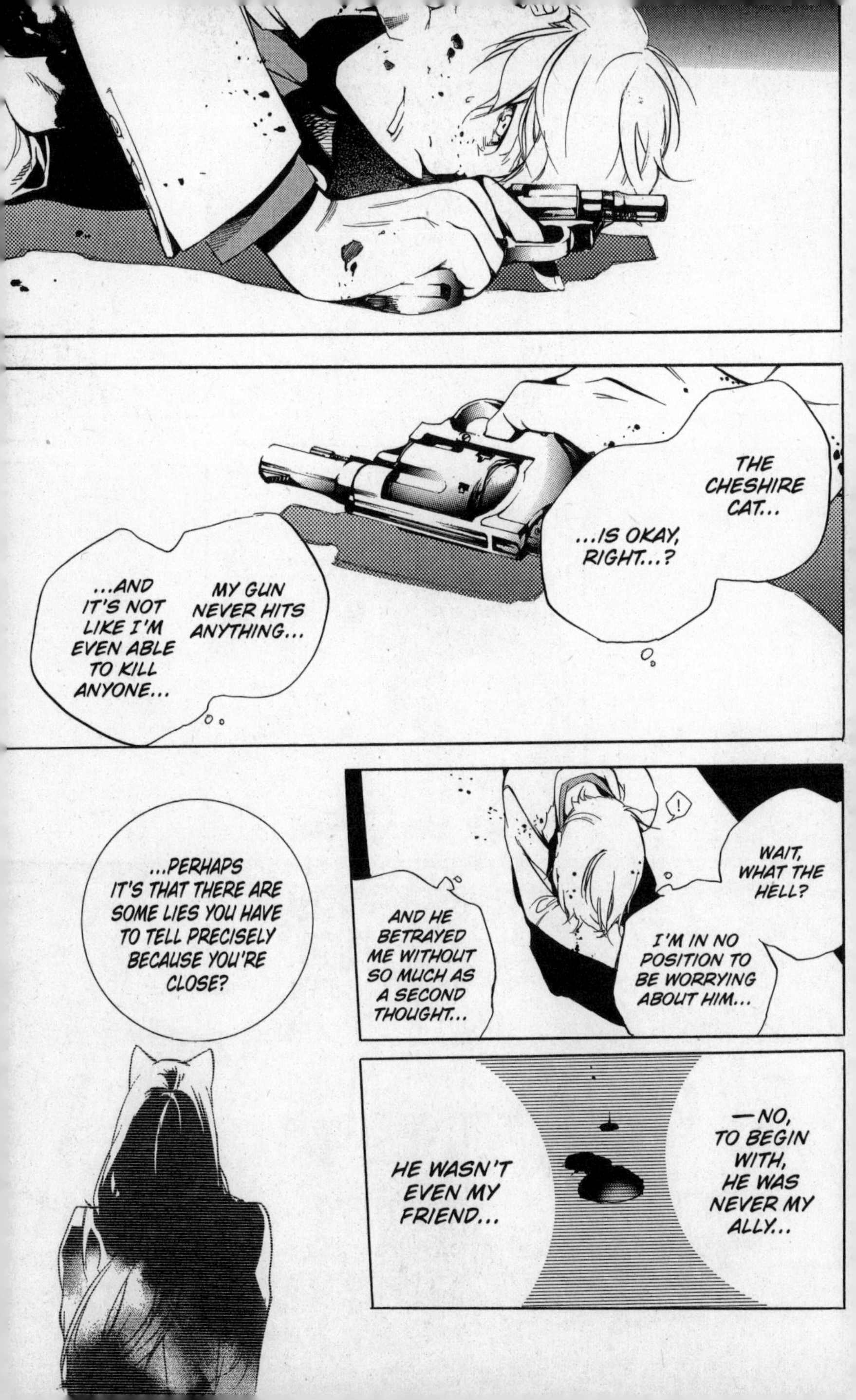
THE CHESHIRE CAT...
...IS OKAY, RIGHT...?
MY GUN NEVER HITS ANYTHING...
...AND IT'S NOT LIKE I'M EVEN ABLE TO KILL ANYONE...
!
WAIT, WHAT THE HELL?
I'M IN NO POSITION TO BE WORRYING ABOUT HIM...
AND HE BETRAYED ME WITHOUT SO MUCH AS A SECOND THOUGHT...
—NO, TO BEGIN WITH, HE WAS NEVER MY ALLY...
HE WASN'T EVEN MY FRIEND...
...PERHAPS IT'S THAT THERE ARE SOME LIES YOU HAVE TO TELL PRECISELY BECAUSE YOU'RE CLOSE?

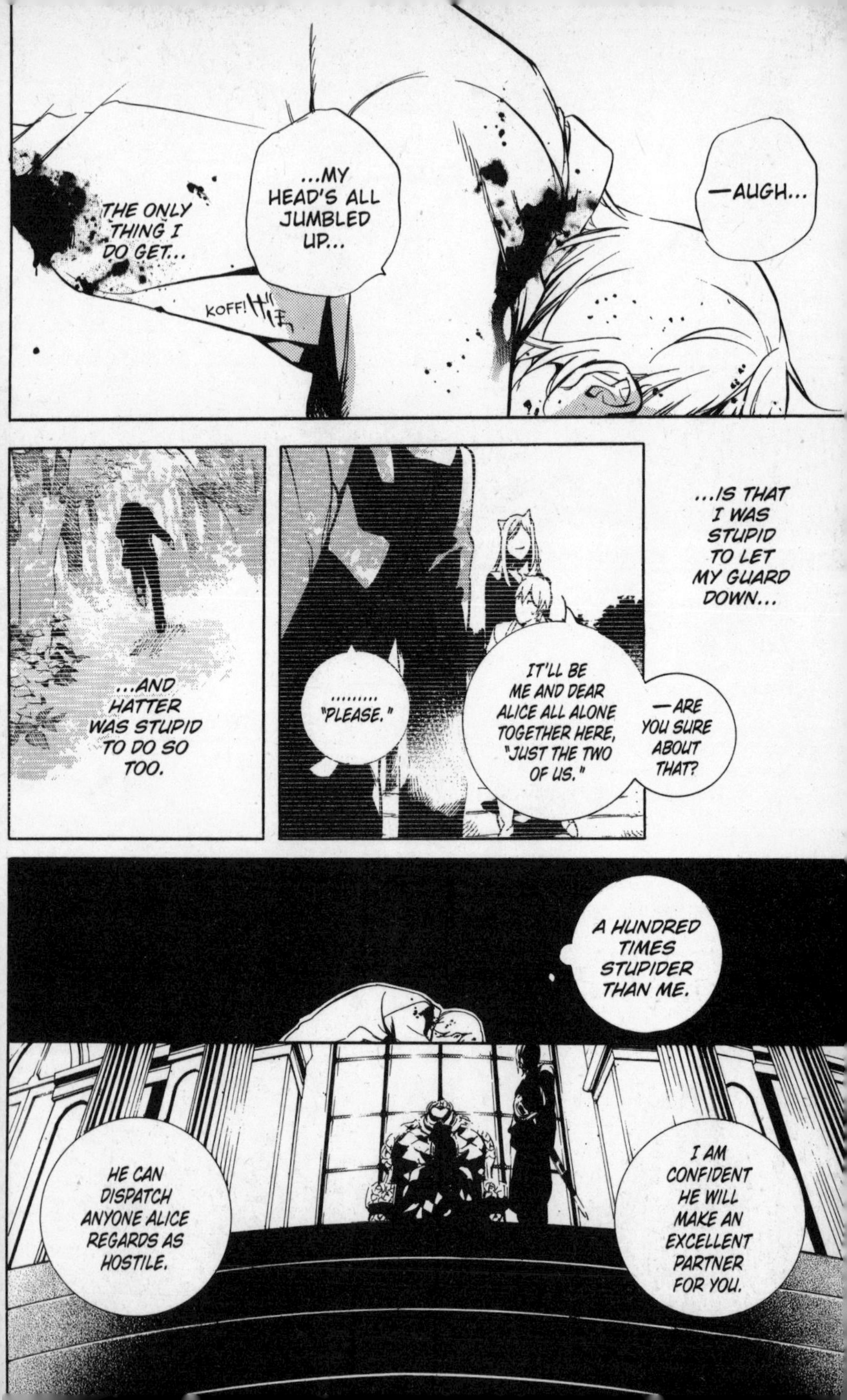
—AUGH...
...MY HEAD'S ALL JUMBLED UP...
THE ONLY THING I DO GET...
KOFF!
...IS THAT I WAS STUPID TO LET MY GUARD DOWN...
—ARE YOU SURE ABOUT THAT?
IT'LL BE ME AND DEAR ALICE ALL ALONE TOGETHER HERE, "JUST THE TWO OF US."
.... "PLEASE."
...AND HATTER WAS STUPID TO DO SO TOO.
A HUNDRED TIMES STUPIDER THAN ME.
I AM CONFIDENT HE WILL MAKE AN EXCELLENT PARTNER FOR YOU.
HE CAN DISPATCH ANYONE ALICE REGARDS AS HOSTILE.

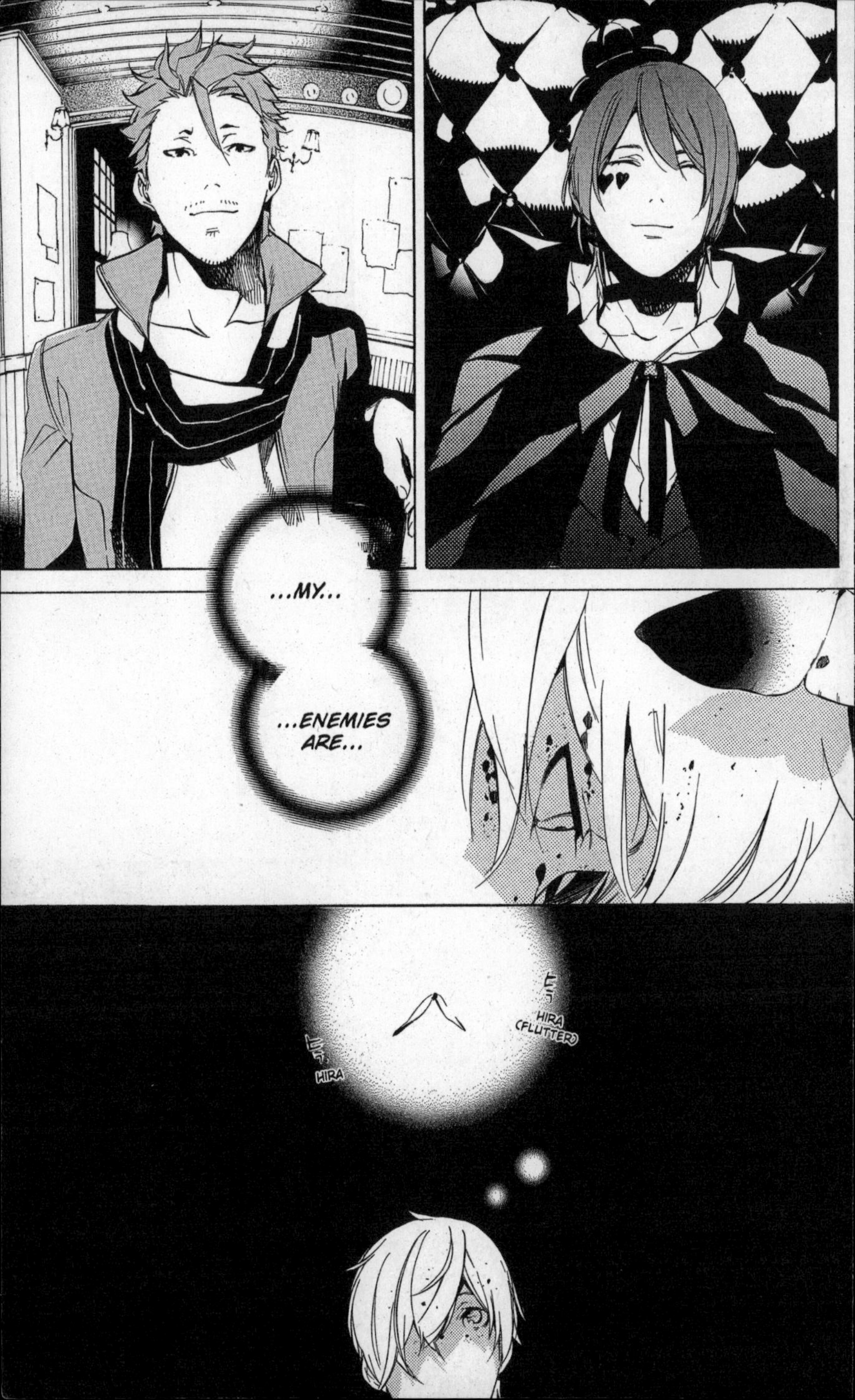
...MY...
...ENEMIES ARE...
HIRA (FLUTTER)
HIRA

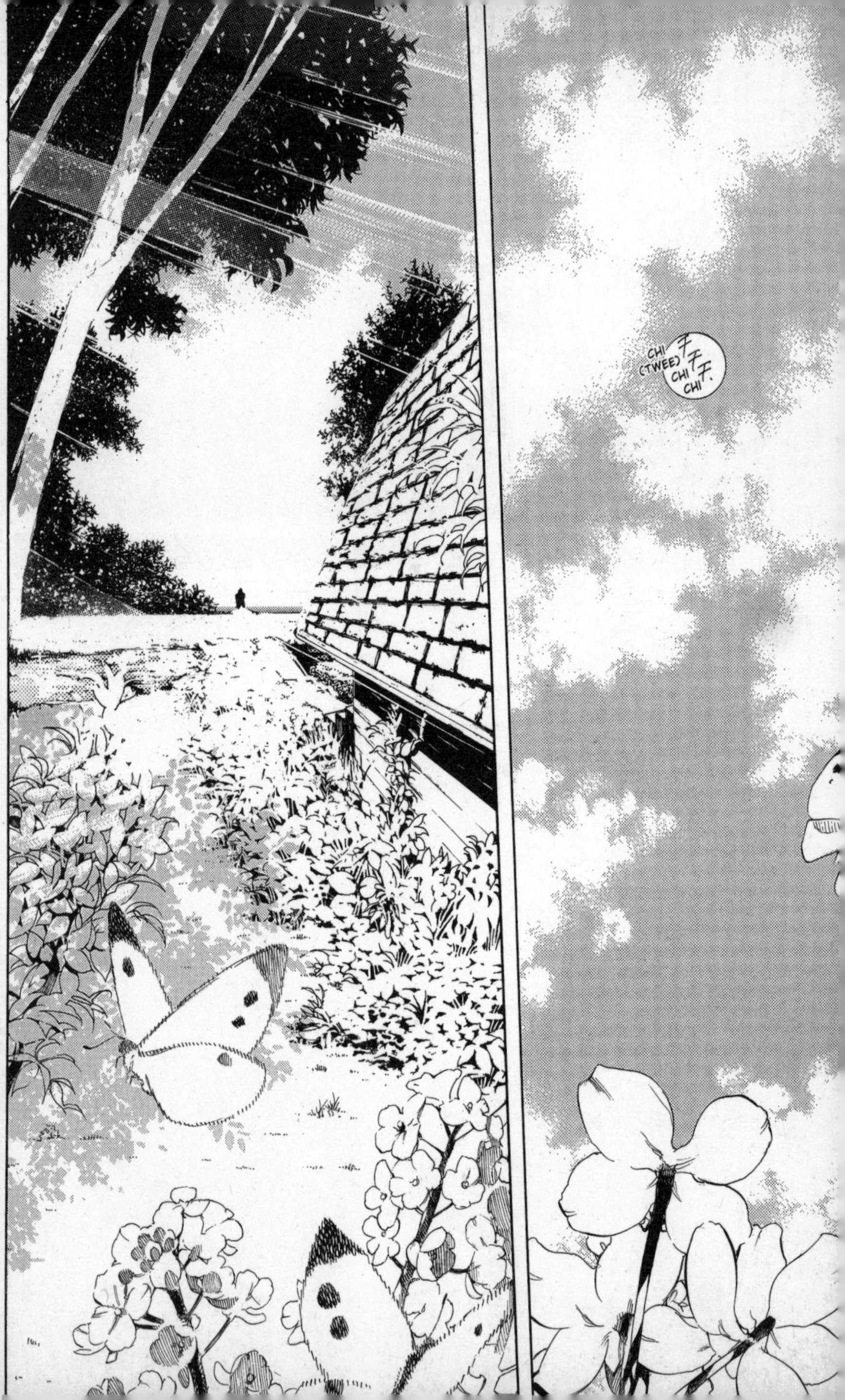
CHI
(TWEE)
CHI
CHI

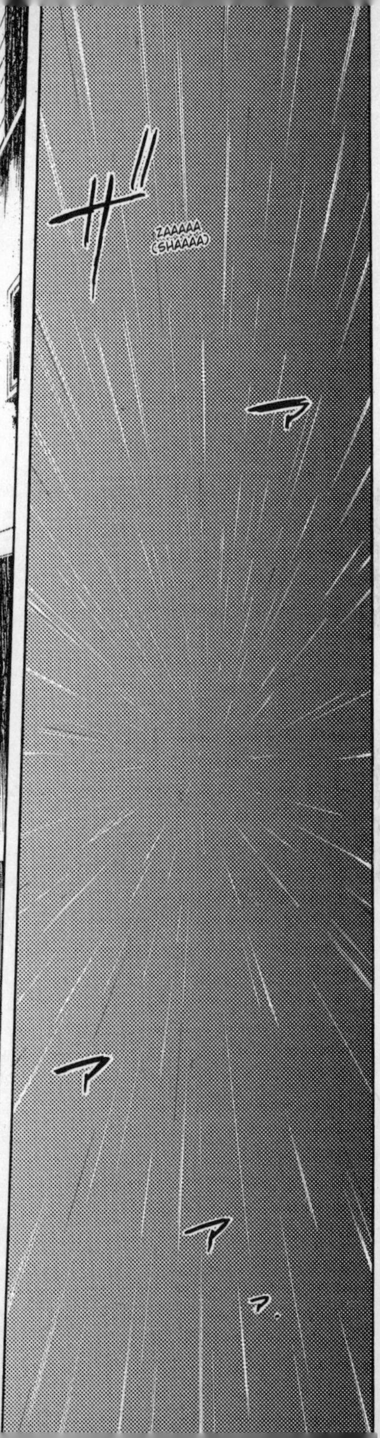
ザ!
ZAAAAA (SHAAAA)
ァ
ア
ア
ァ.
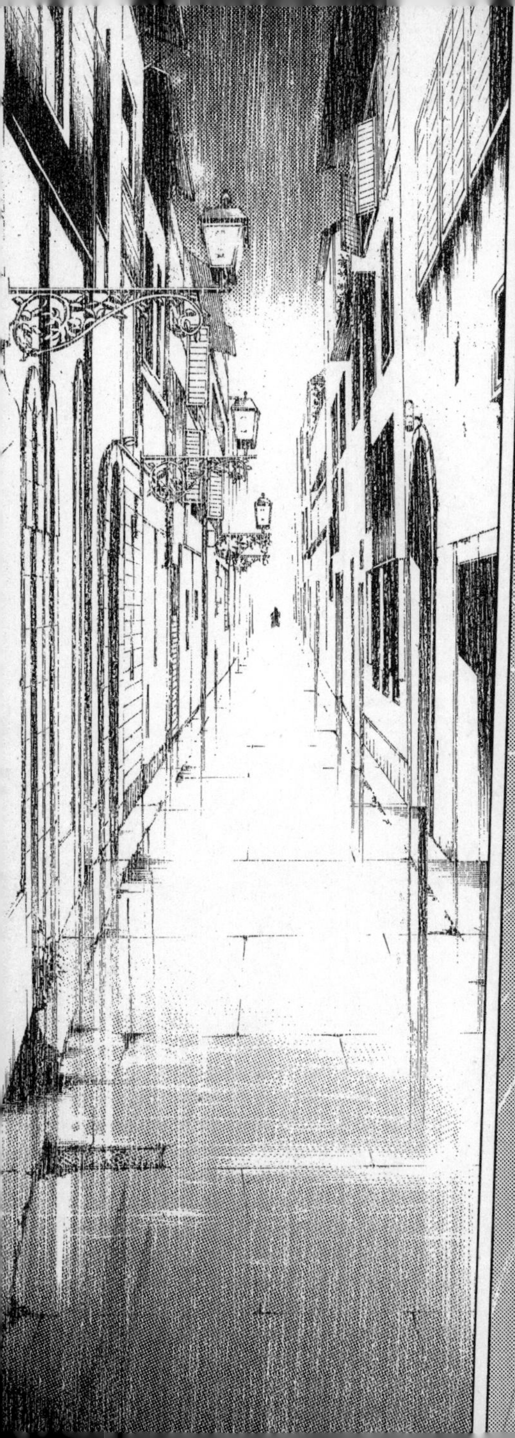

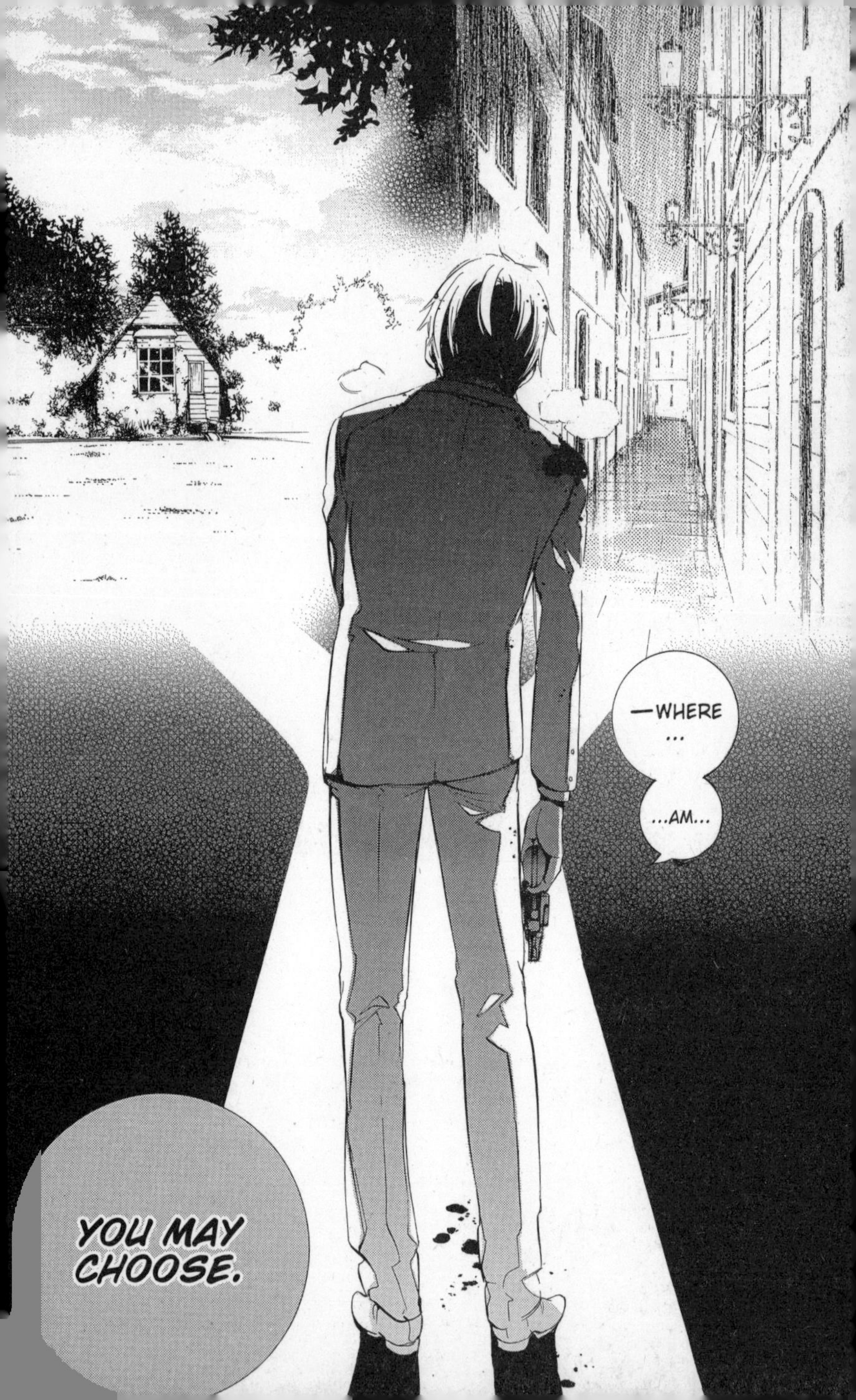
—WHERE ...
...AM...
YOU MAY CHOOSE.

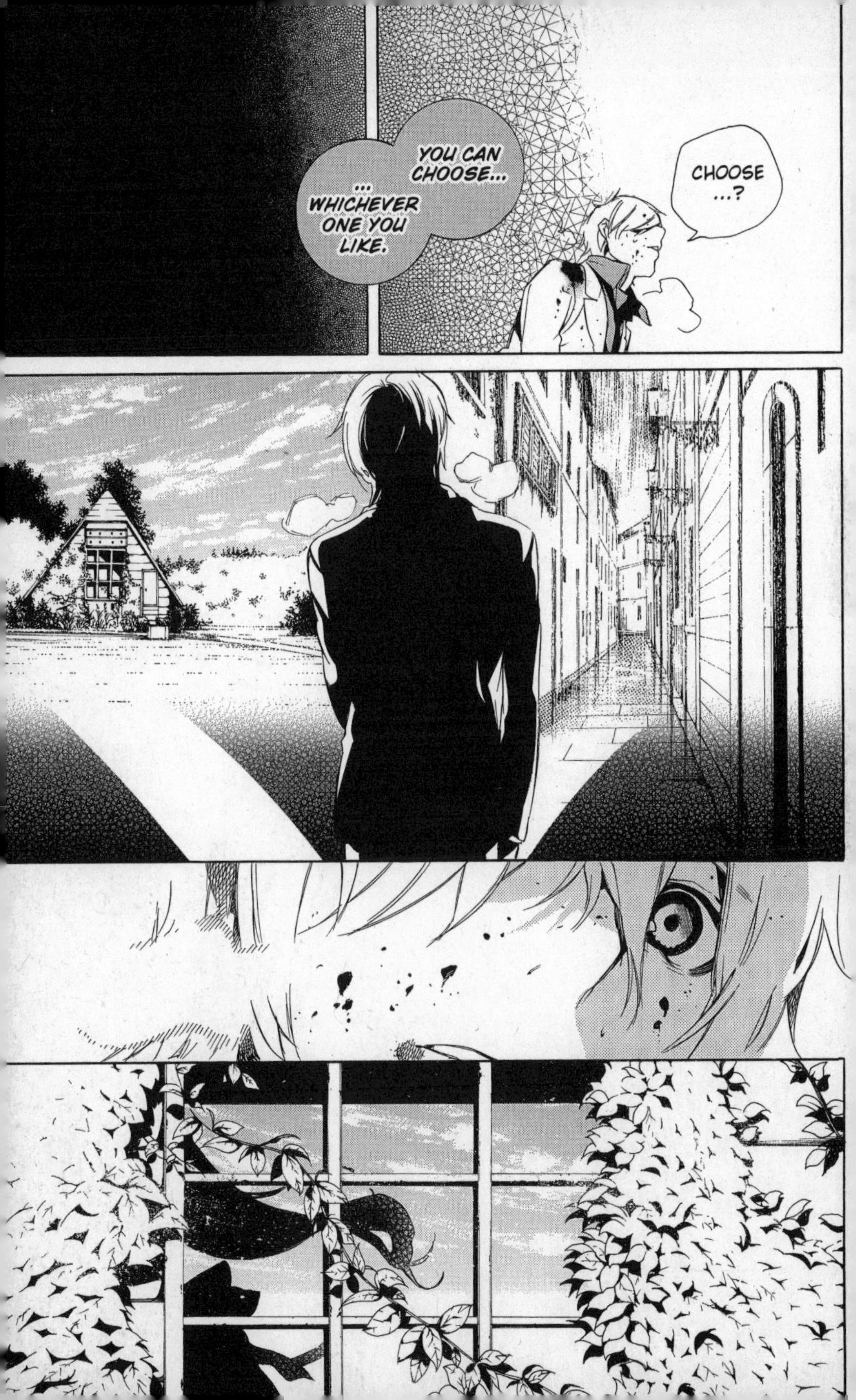
CHOOSE ...?
YOU CAN CHOOSE...
... WHICHEVER ONE YOU LIKE.

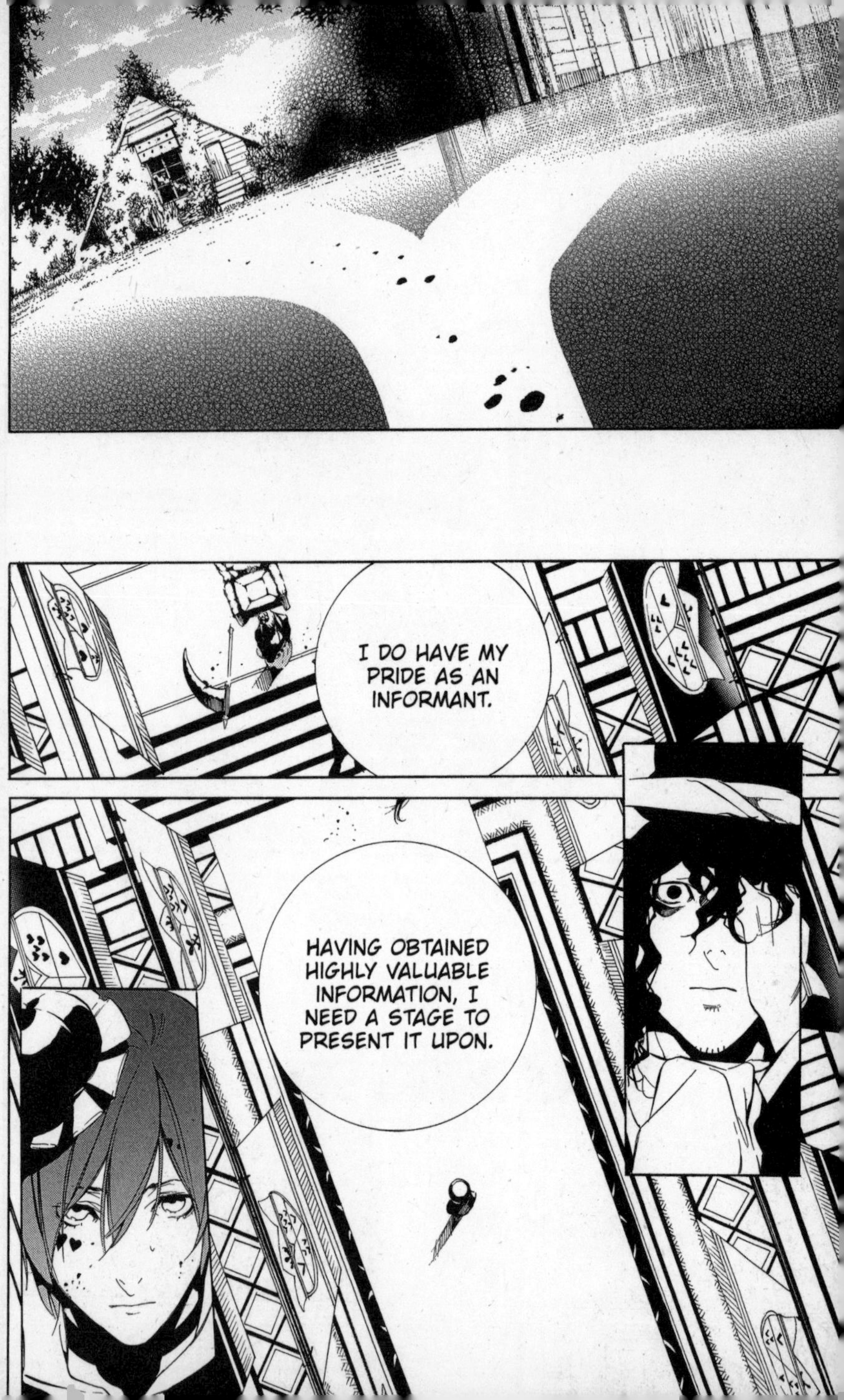
I DO HAVE MY PRIDE AS AN INFORMANT.
HAVING OBTAINED HIGHLY VALUABLE INFORMATION, I NEED A STAGE TO PRESENT IT UPON.

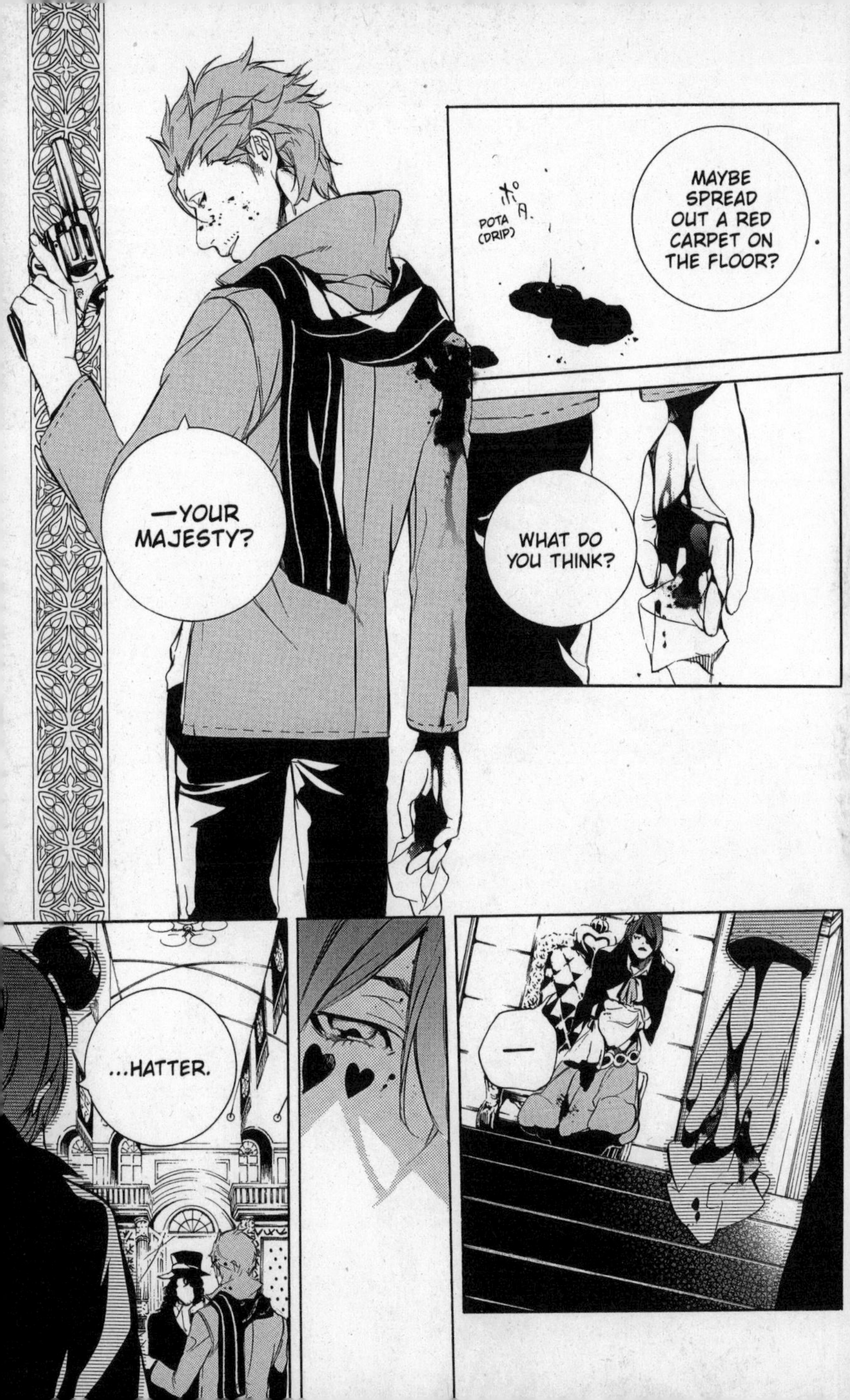
MAYBE SPREAD OUT A RED CARPET ON THE FLOOR?
ポタ
POTA (DRIP)
WHAT DO YOU THINK?
—YOUR MAJESTY?
—
...HATTER.

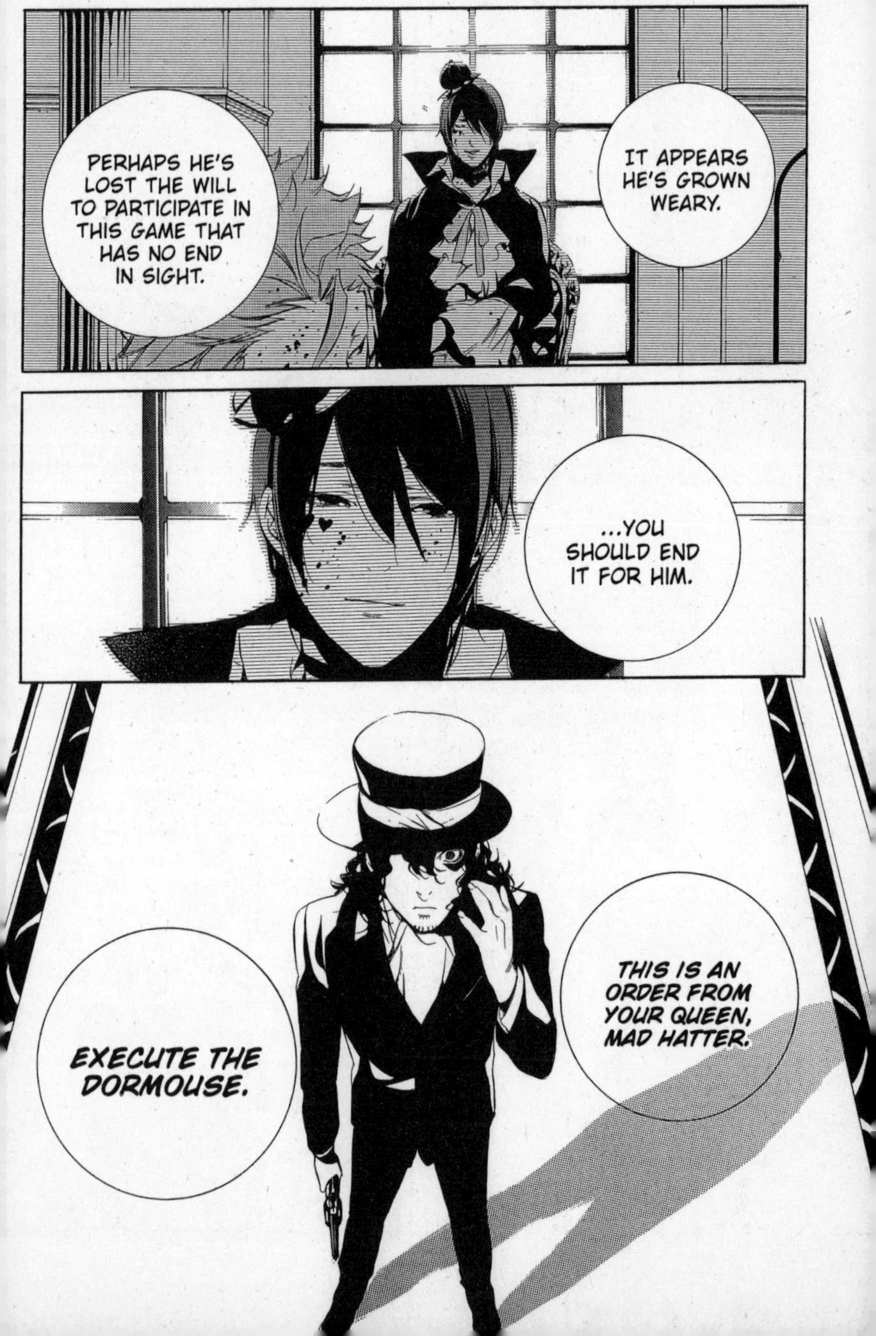
IT APPEARS HE'S GROWN WEARY.
PERHAPS HE'S LOST THE WILL TO PARTICIPATE IN THIS GAME THAT HAS NO END IN SIGHT.
...YOU SHOULD END IT FOR HIM.
THIS IS AN ORDER FROM YOUR QUEEN, MAD HATTER.
EXECUTE THE DORMOUSE.

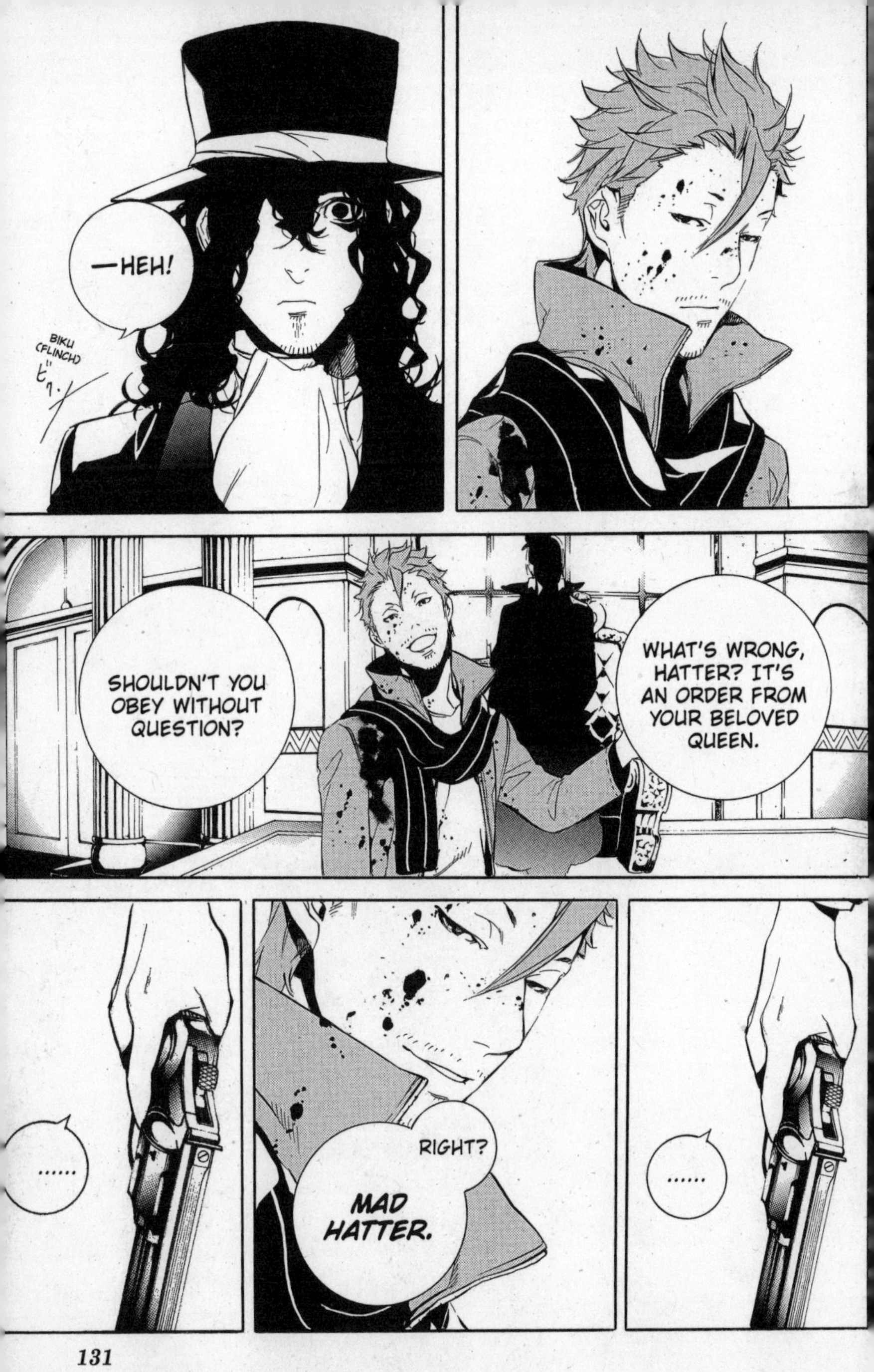
—HEH!
BIKU (FLINCH)
WHAT'S WRONG, HATTER? IT'S AN ORDER FROM YOUR BELOVED QUEEN.
SHOULDN'T YOU OBEY WITHOUT QUESTION?
......
RIGHT?
MAD HATTER.
......

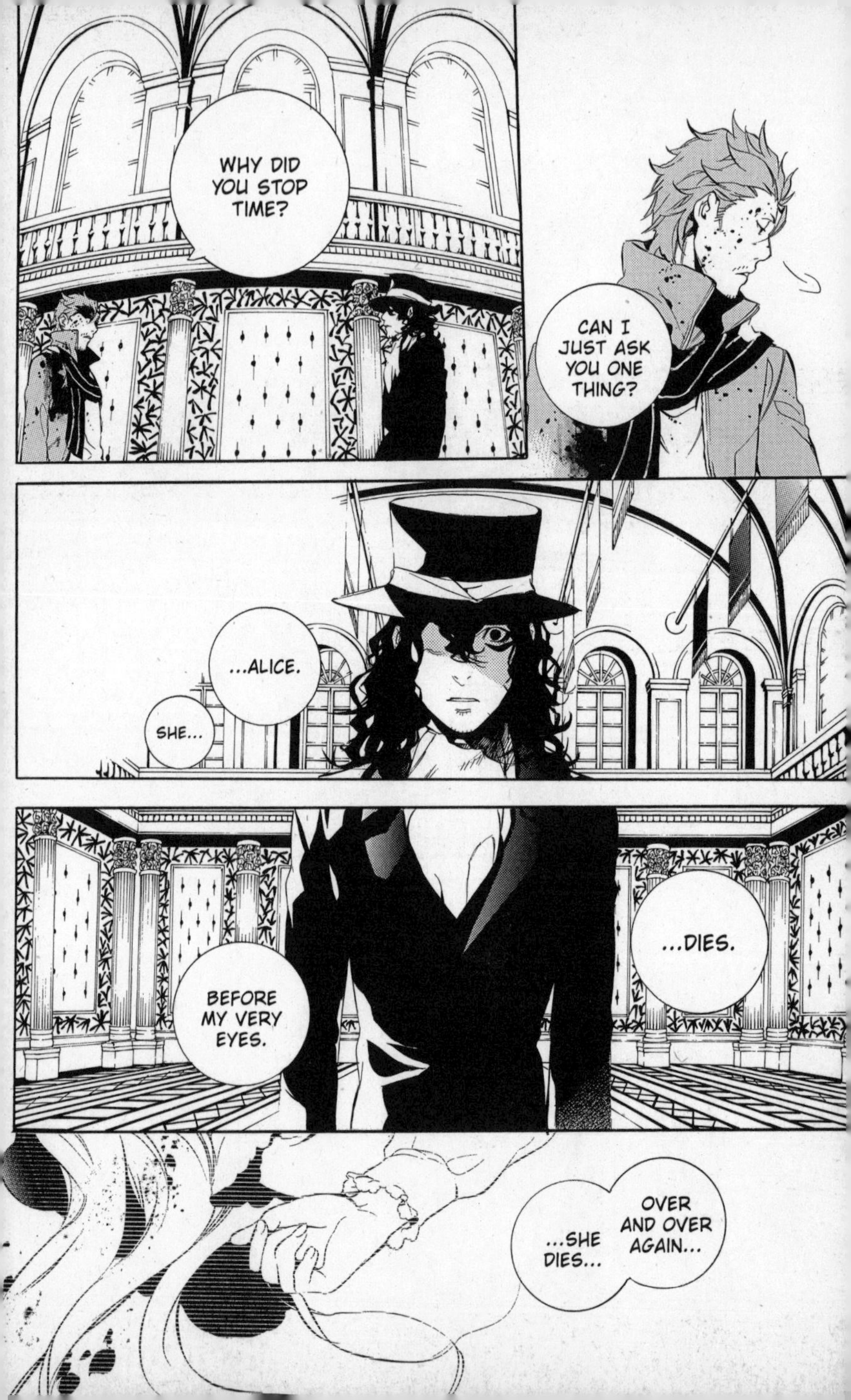
CAN I JUST ASK YOU ONE THING?
WHY DID YOU STOP TIME?
...ALICE.
SHE...
...DIES.
BEFORE MY VERY EYES.
OVER AND OVER AGAIN...
...SHE DIES...

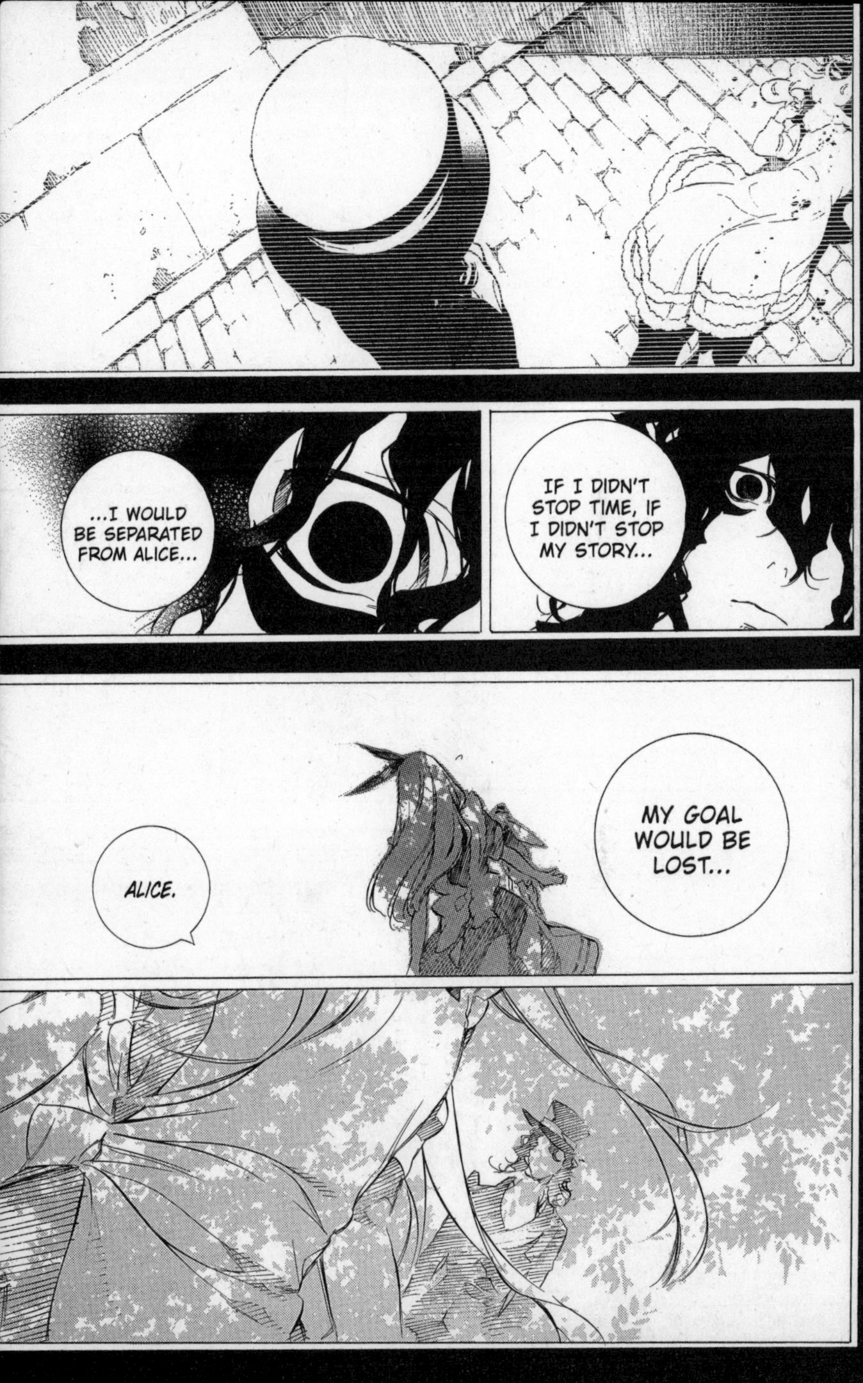
IF I DIDN'T STOP TIME, IF I DIDN'T STOP MY STORY...
...I WOULD BE SEPARATED FROM ALICE...
MY GOAL WOULD BE LOST...
ALICE.

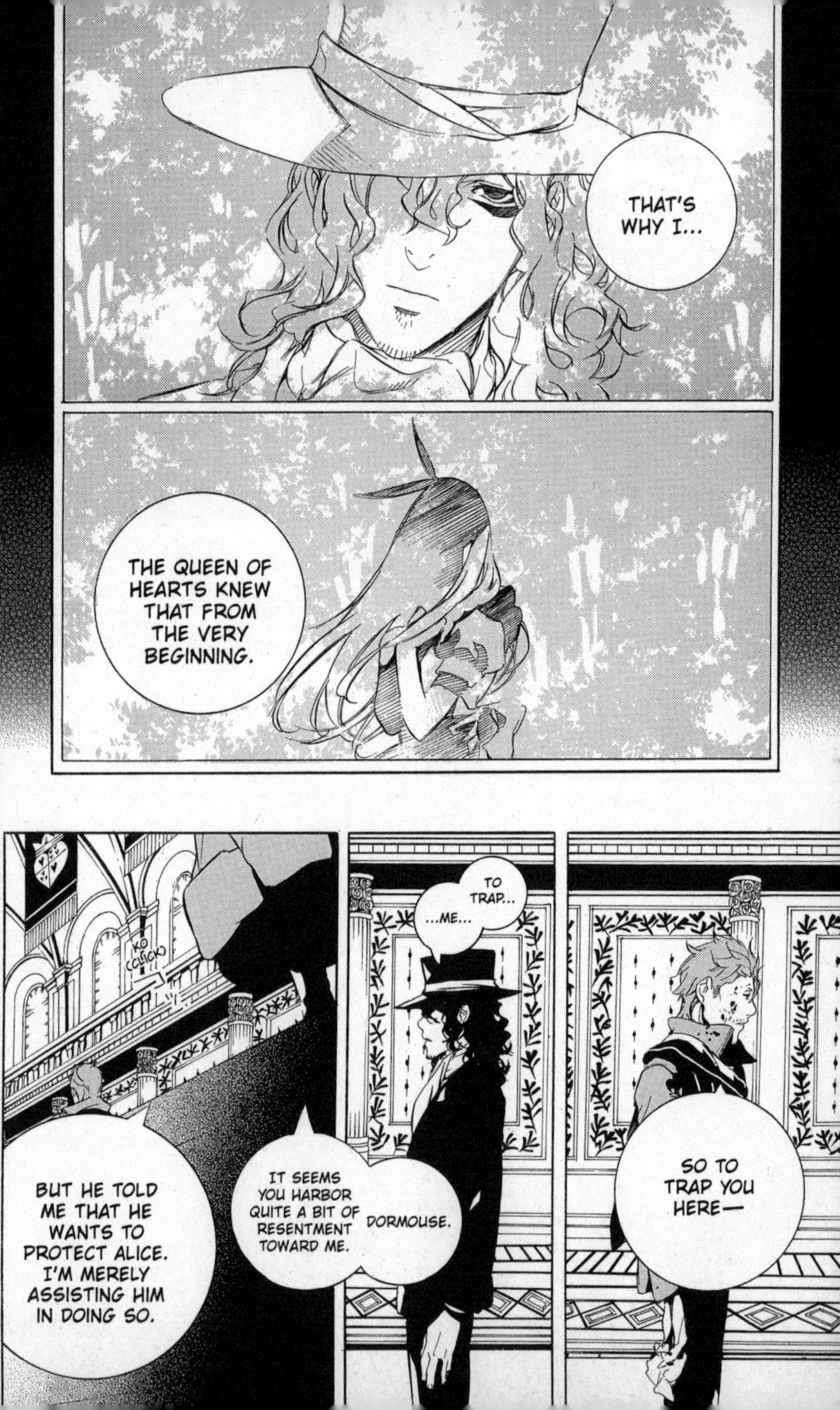
THAT'S WHY I...
THE QUEEN OF HEARTS KNEW THAT FROM THE VERY BEGINNING.
SO TO TRAP YOU HERE—
TO TRAP...
...ME...
KO (CLICK)
IT SEEMS YOU HARBOR QUITE A BIT OF RESENTMENT TOWARD ME.
DORMOUSE.
BUT HE TOLD ME THAT HE WANTS TO PROTECT ALICE. I'M MERELY ASSISTING HIM IN DOING SO.

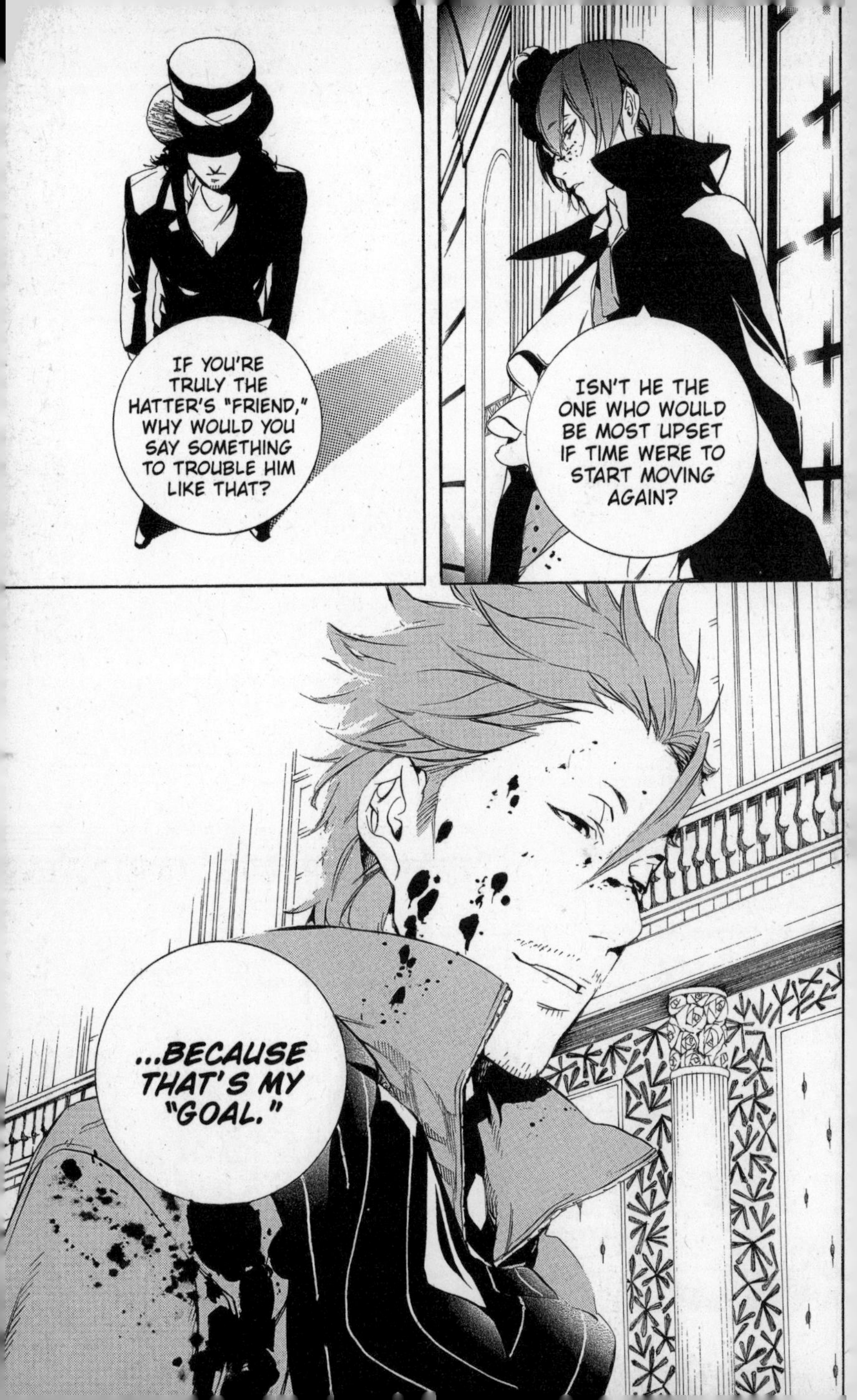
ISN'T HE THE ONE WHO WOULD BE MOST UPSET IF TIME WERE TO START MOVING AGAIN?
IF YOU'RE TRULY THE HATTER'S "FRIEND," WHY WOULD YOU SAY SOMETHING TO TROUBLE HIM LIKE THAT?
...BECAUSE THAT'S MY "GOAL."

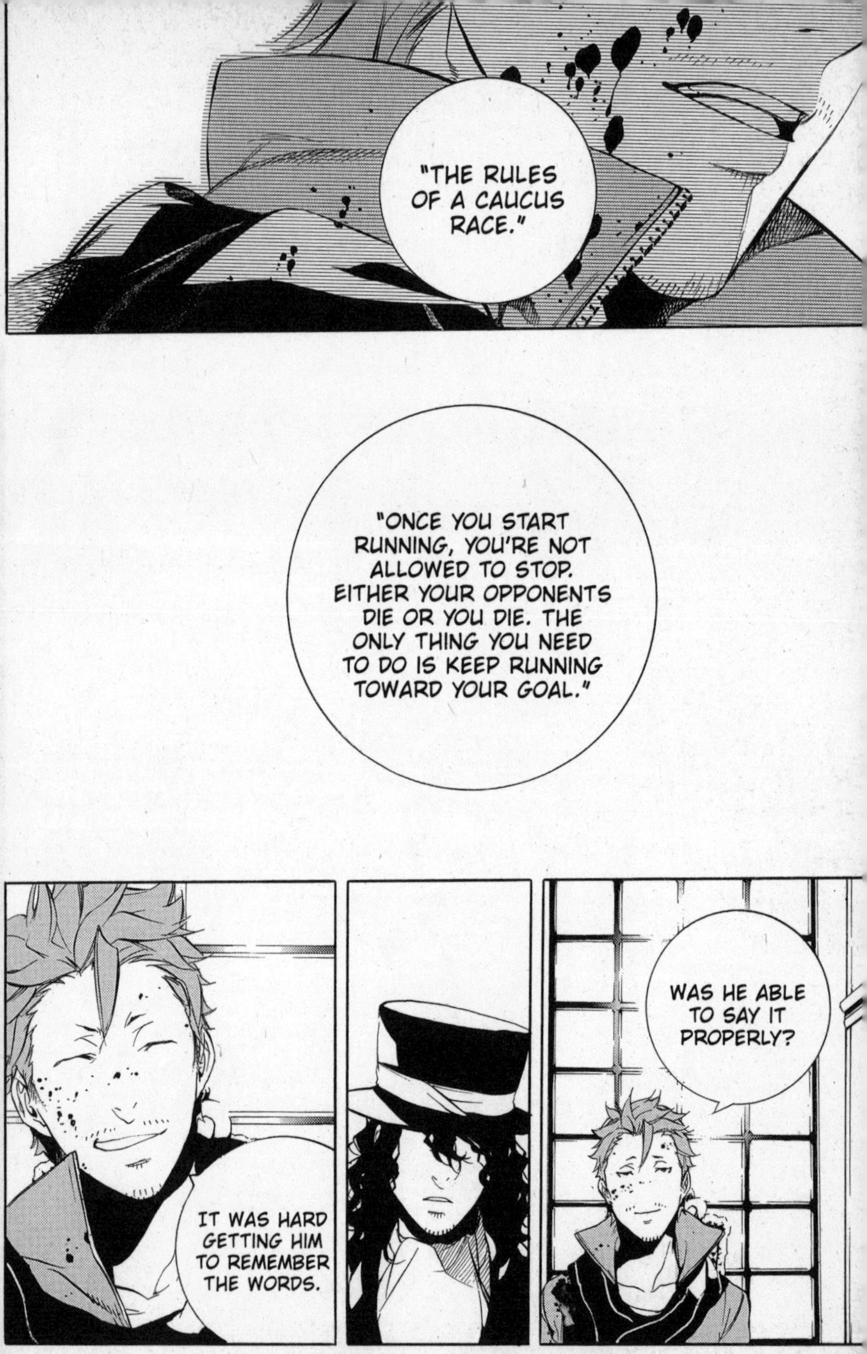
"THE RULES OF A CAUCUS RACE."
"ONCE YOU START RUNNING, YOU'RE NOT ALLOWED TO STOP. EITHER YOUR OPPONENTS DIE OR YOU DIE. THE ONLY THING YOU NEED TO DO IS KEEP RUNNING TOWARD YOUR GOAL."
WAS HE ABLE TO SAY IT PROPERLY?
IT WAS HARD GETTING HIM TO REMEMBER THE WORDS.

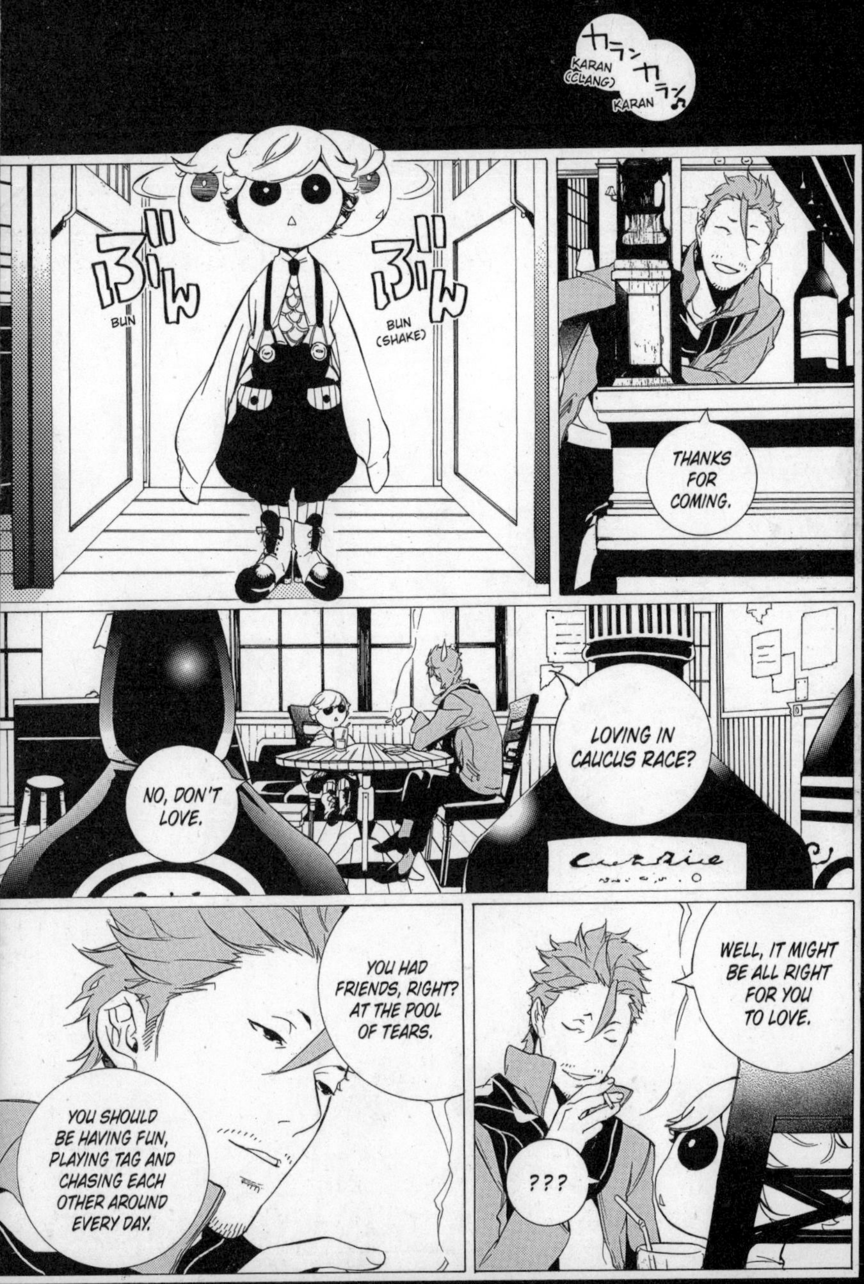
カランカラン♪
KARAN (CLANG) KARAN
THANKS FOR COMING.
ぶん
BUN (SHAKE)
ぶん
BUN
LOVING IN CAUCUS RACE?
NO, DON'T LOVE.
WELL, IT MIGHT BE ALL RIGHT FOR YOU TO LOVE.
???
YOU HAD FRIENDS, RIGHT? AT THE POOL OF TEARS.
YOU SHOULD BE HAVING FUN, PLAYING TAG AND CHASING EACH OTHER AROUND EVERY DAY.

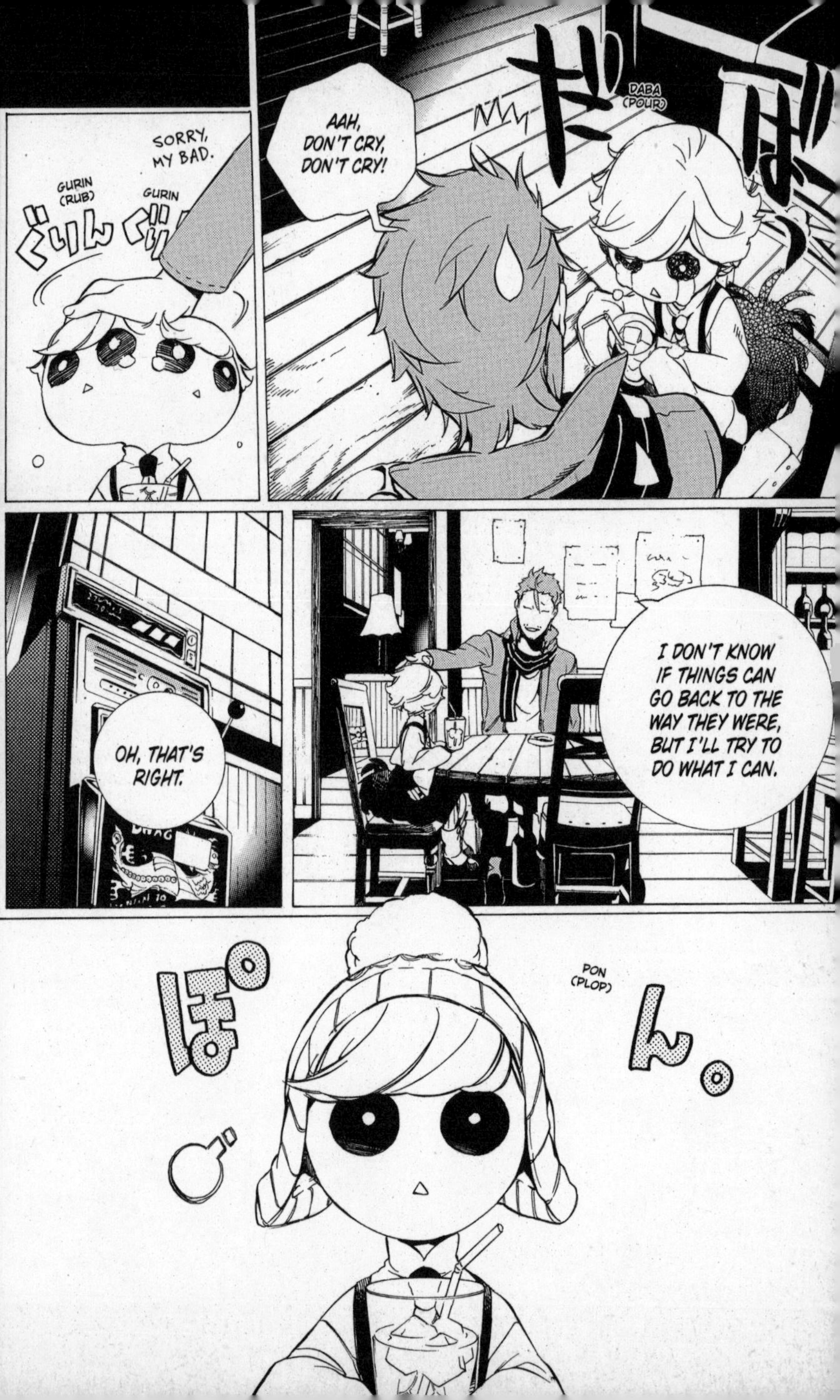
DABA (POUR)
AAH, DON'T CRY, DON'T CRY!
SORRY, MY BAD.
GURIN
GURIN (RUB)
I DON'T KNOW IF THINGS CAN GO BACK TO THE WAY THEY WERE, BUT I'LL TRY TO DO WHAT I CAN.
OH, THAT'S RIGHT.
PON (PLOP)

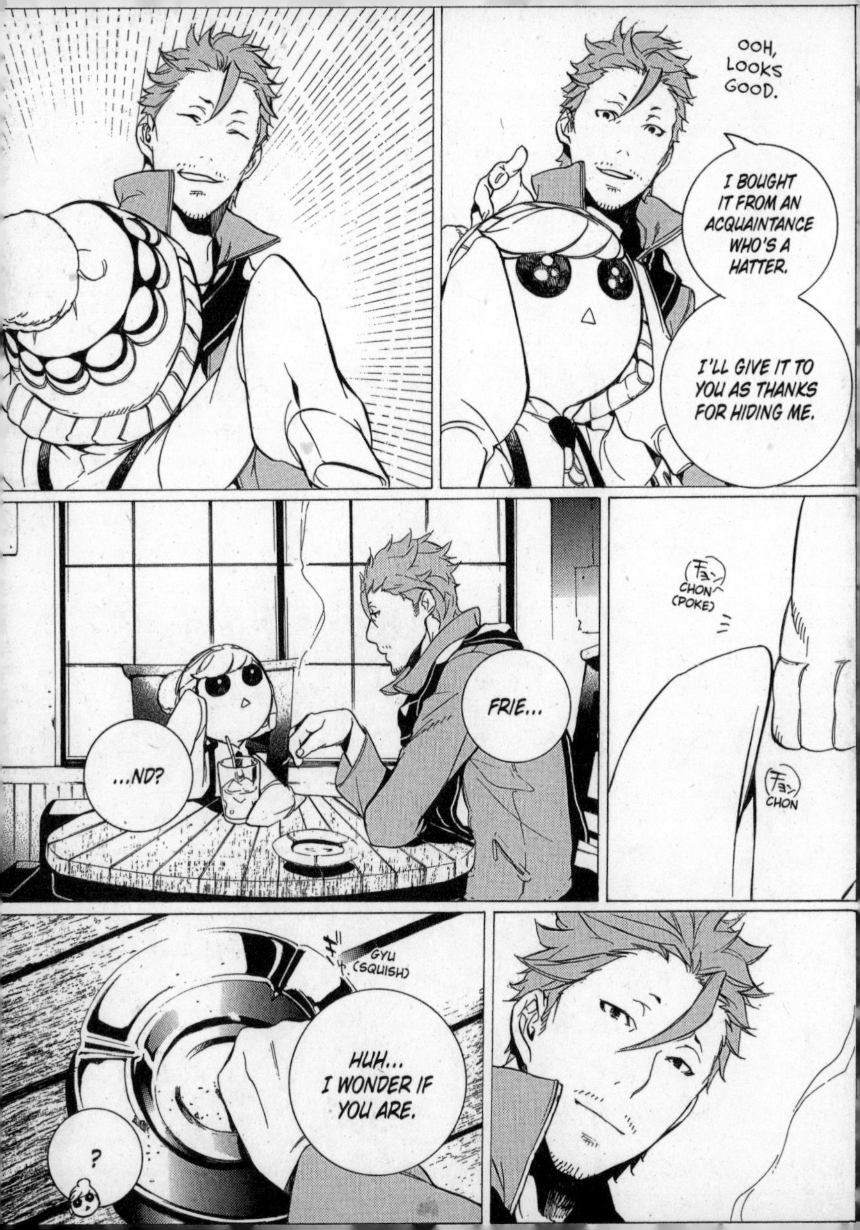

OOH, LOOKS GOOD.
I BOUGHT IT FROM AN ACQUAINTANCE WHO'S A HATTER.
I'LL GIVE IT TO YOU AS THANKS FOR HIDING ME.
CHON (POKE)
CHON
FRIE...
...ND?
GYU (SQUISH)
HUH... I WONDER IF YOU ARE.
?

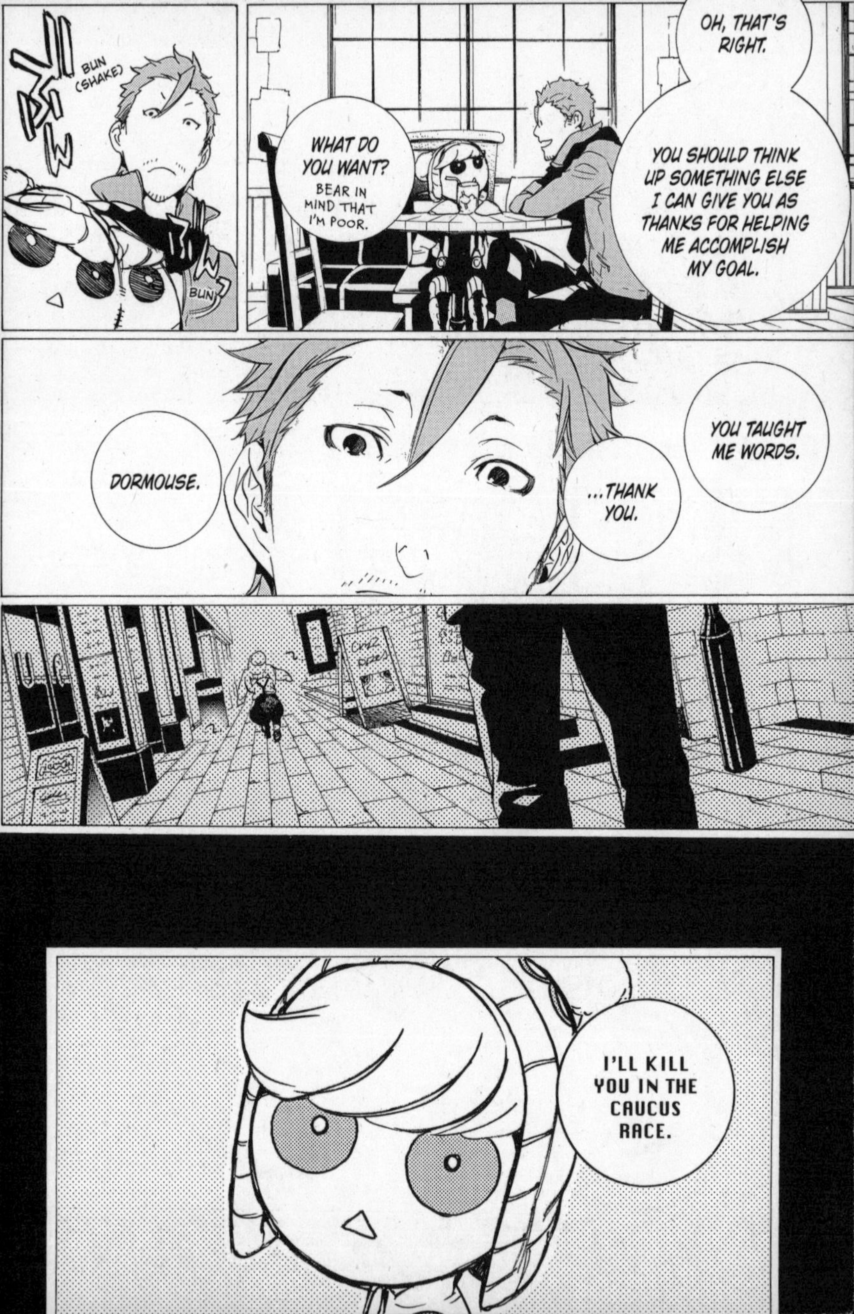
OH, THAT'S RIGHT.
YOU SHOULD THINK UP SOMETHING ELSE I CAN GIVE YOU AS THANKS FOR HELPING ME ACCOMPLISH MY GOAL.
WHAT DO YOU WANT?
BEAR IN MIND THAT I'M POOR.
BUN (SHAKE)
BUN
YOU TAUGHT ME WORDS.
...THANK YOU.
DORMOUSE.
I'LL KILL YOU IN THE CAUCUS RACE.

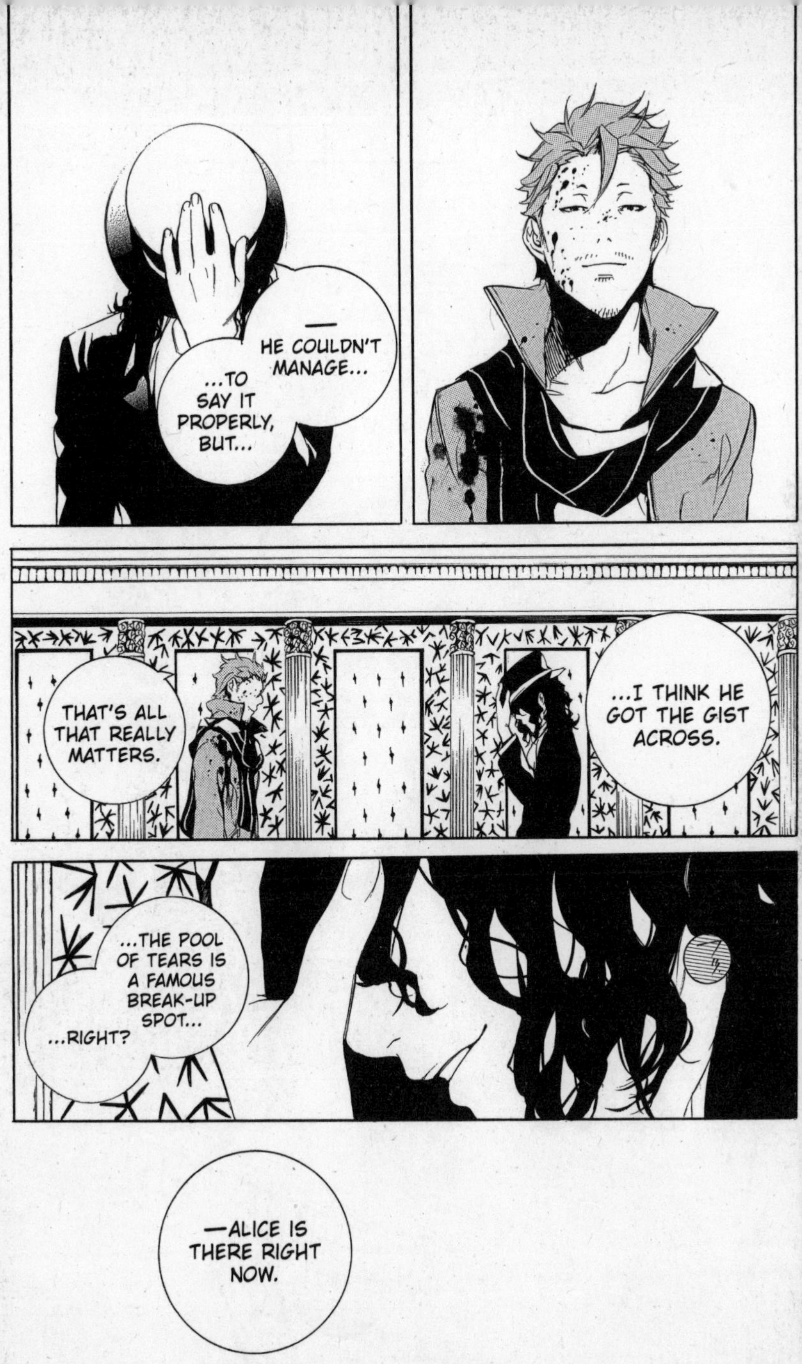
—HE COULDN'T MANAGE...
...TO SAY IT PROPERLY, BUT...
...I THINK HE GOT THE GIST ACROSS.
THAT'S ALL THAT REALLY MATTERS.
...THE POOL OF TEARS IS A FAMOUS BREAK-UP SPOT...
...RIGHT?
—ALICE IS THERE RIGHT NOW.

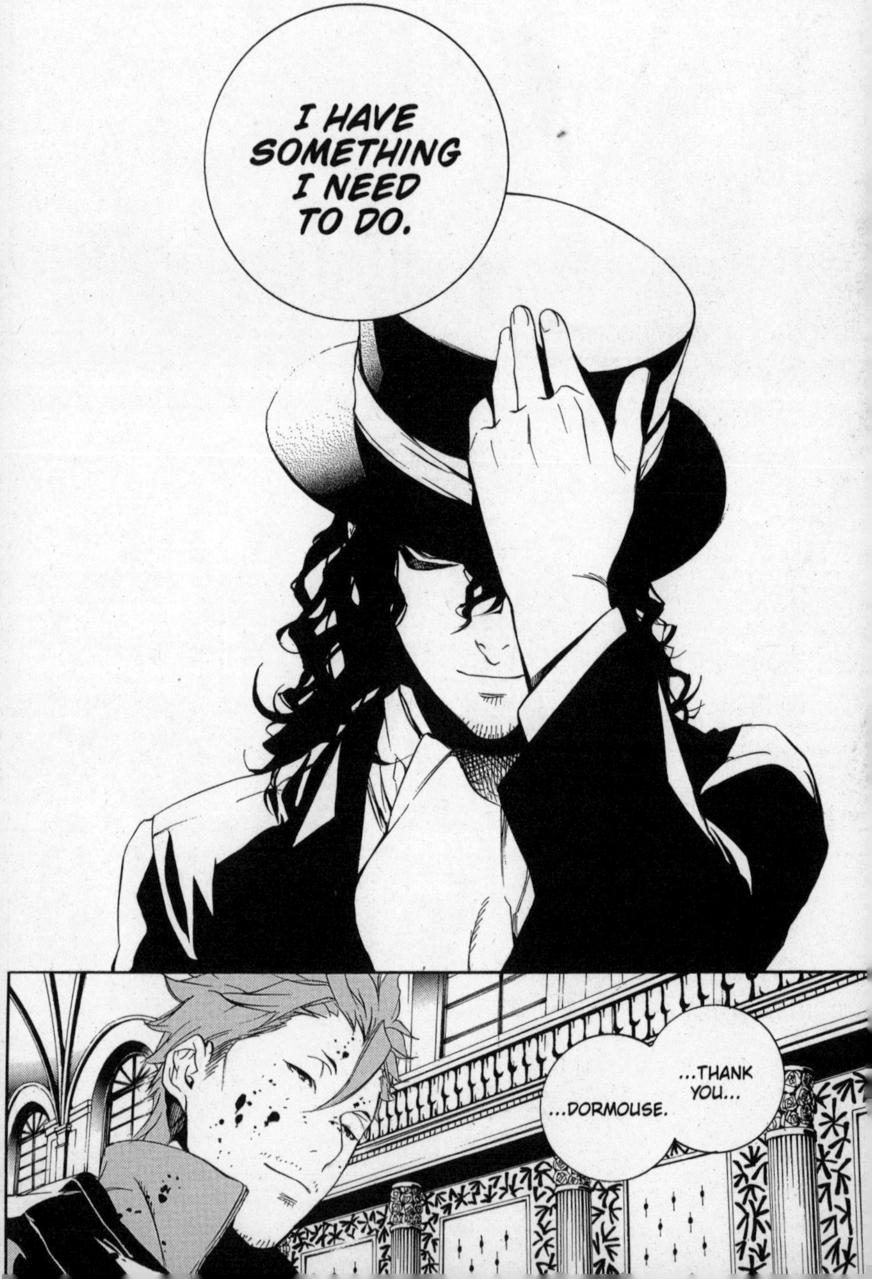
I HAVE SOMETHING I NEED TO DO.
...THANK YOU...
...DORMOUSE.

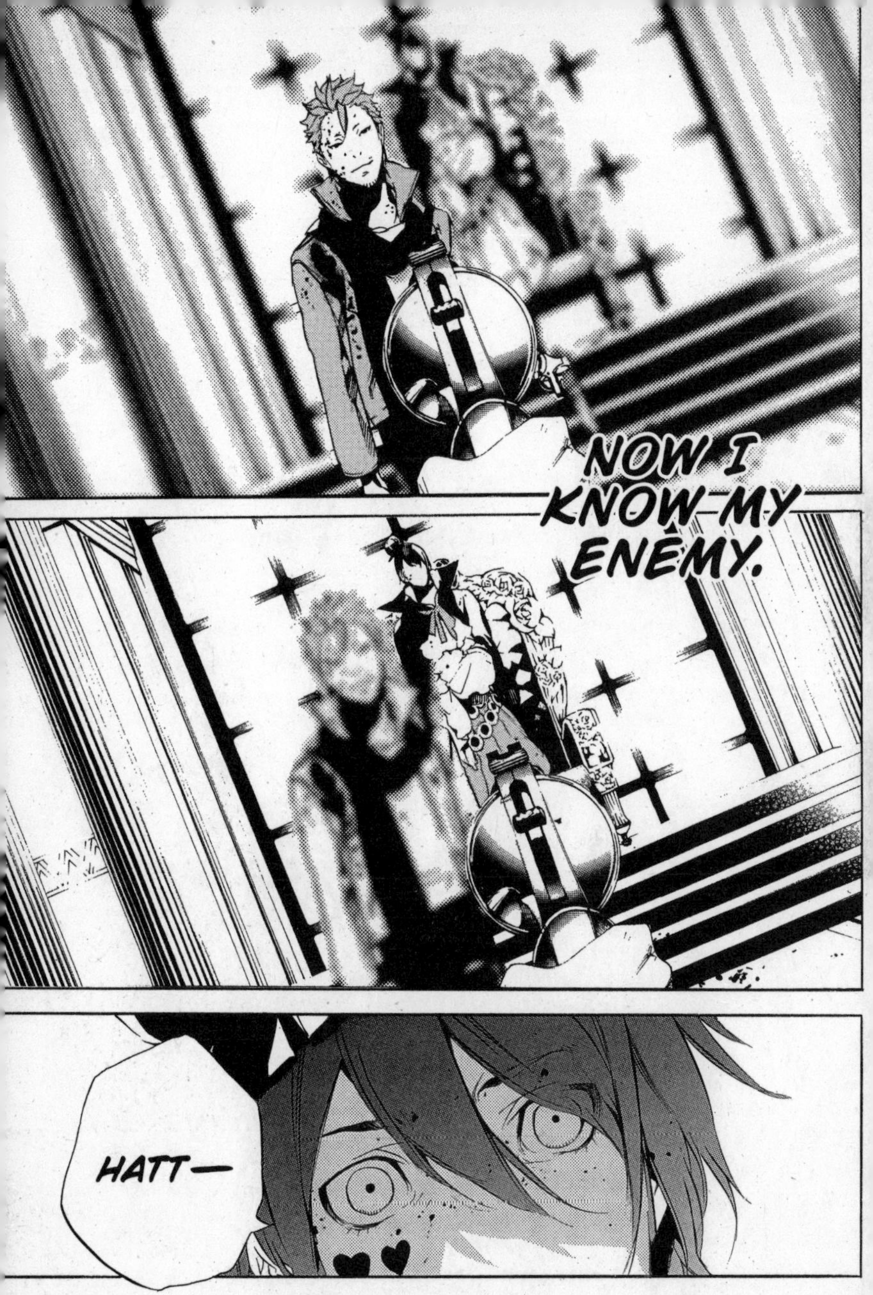
NOW I KNOW MY ENEMY.
HATT—

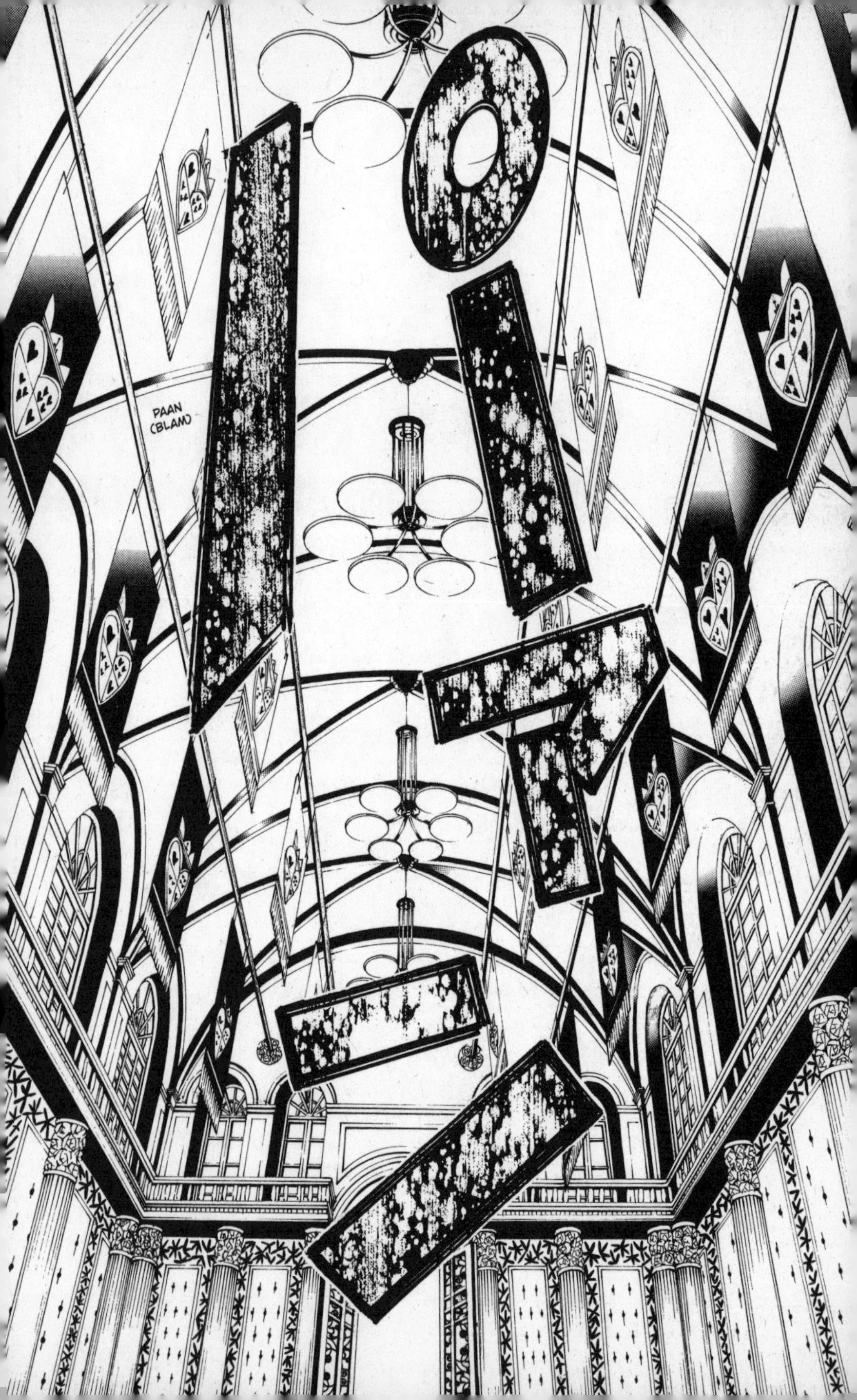
PAAN
(BLAM)

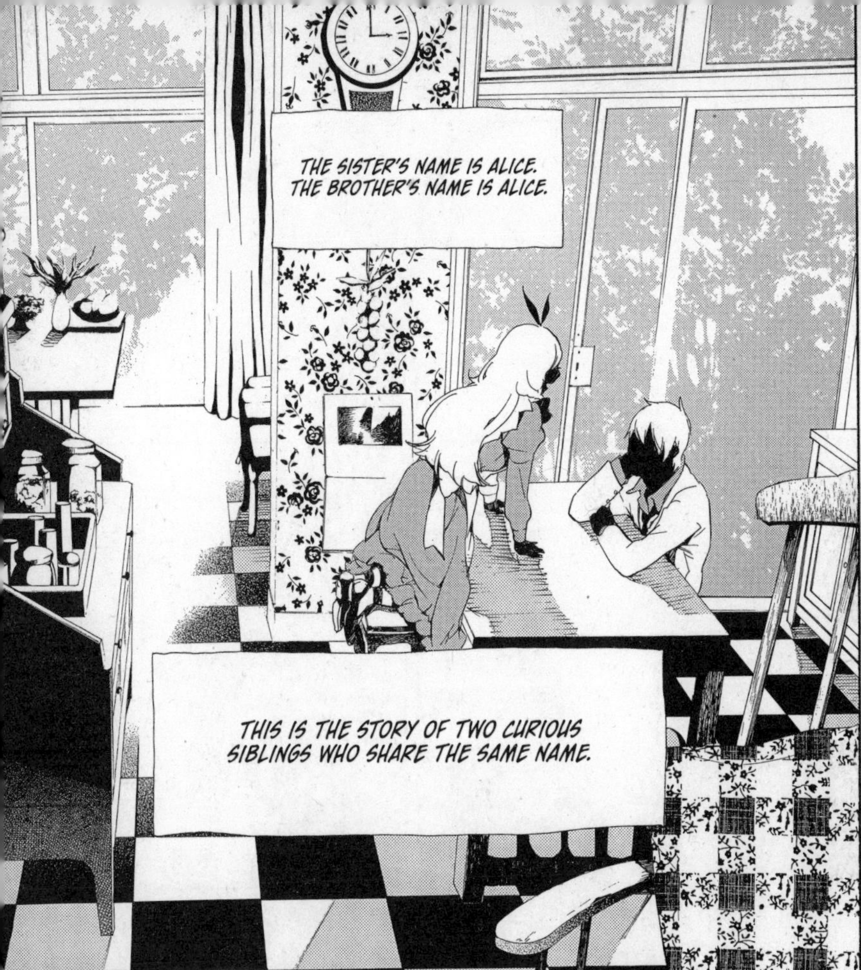
THE SISTER'S NAME IS ALICE. THE BROTHER'S NAME IS ALICE.
THIS IS THE STORY OF TWO CURIOUS SIBLINGS WHO SHARE THE SAME NAME.

"BECAUSE YOU WERE BORN TO BE HAPPY, AFTER ALL."

Chapter 29

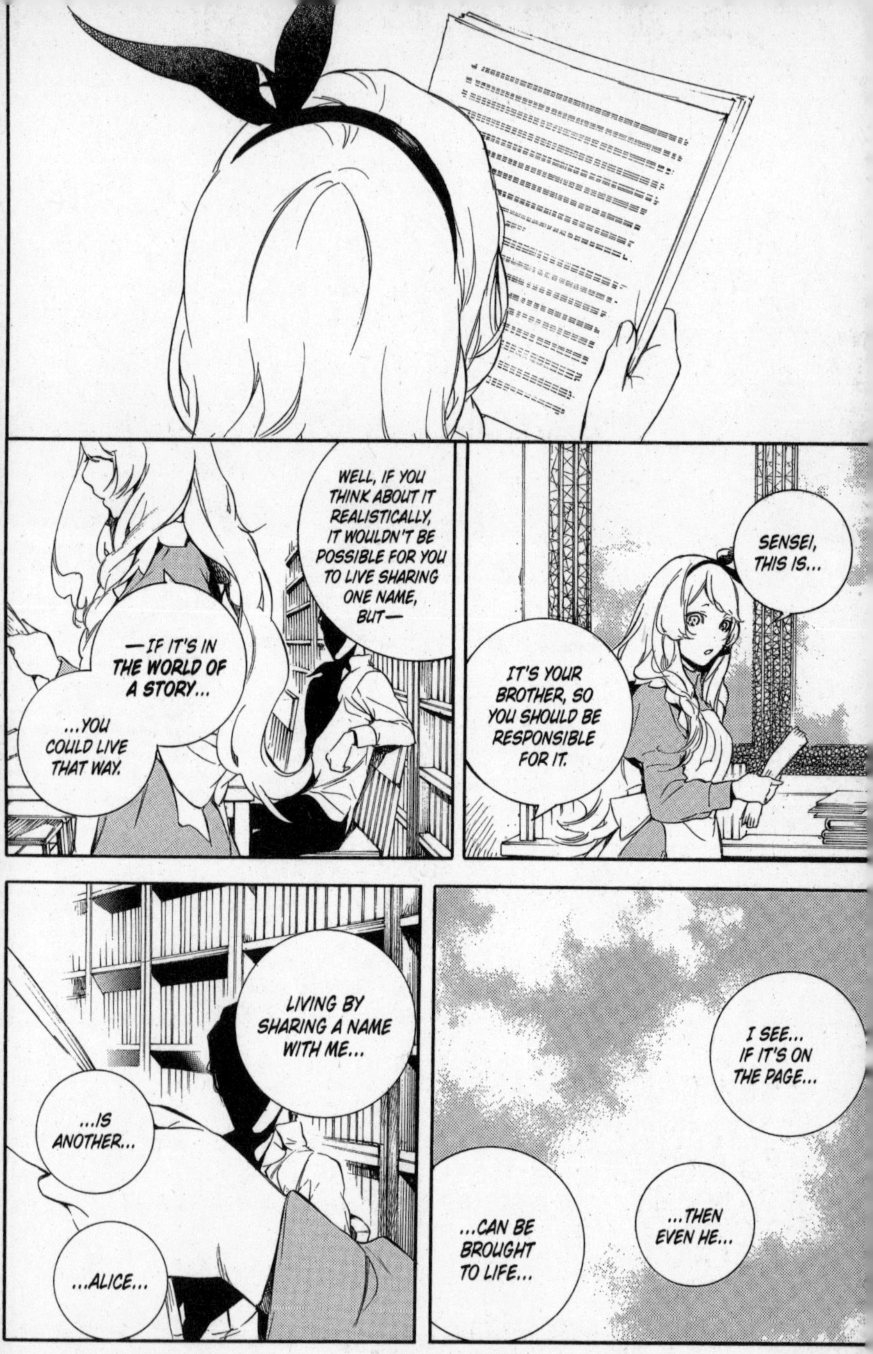
SENSEI, THIS IS...
IT'S YOUR BROTHER, SO YOU SHOULD BE RESPONSIBLE FOR IT.
WELL, IF YOU THINK ABOUT IT REALISTICALLY, IT WOULDN'T BE POSSIBLE FOR YOU TO LIVE SHARING ONE NAME, BUT—
—IF IT'S IN THE WORLD OF A STORY...
...YOU COULD LIVE THAT WAY.
I SEE... IF IT'S ON THE PAGE...
...THEN EVEN HE...
...CAN BE BROUGHT TO LIFE...
LIVING BY SHARING A NAME WITH ME...
...IS ANOTHER...
...ALICE...

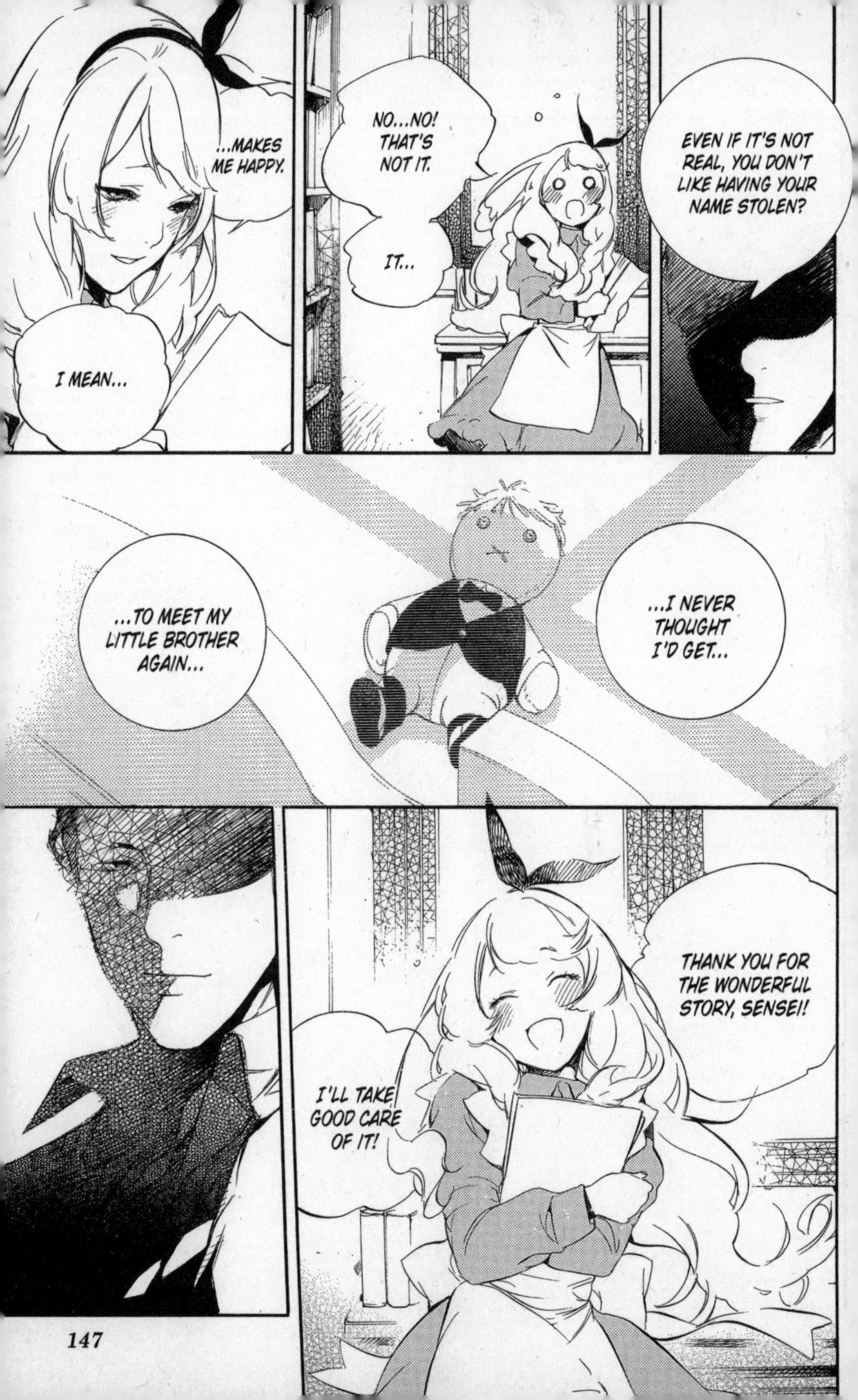
EVEN IF IT'S NOT REAL, YOU DON'T LIKE HAVING YOUR NAME STOLEN?
NO...NO! THAT'S NOT IT.
IT...
...MAKES ME HAPPY.
I MEAN...
...I NEVER THOUGHT I'D GET...
...TO MEET MY LITTLE BROTHER AGAIN...
THANK YOU FOR THE WONDERFUL STORY, SENSEI!
I'LL TAKE GOOD CARE OF IT!

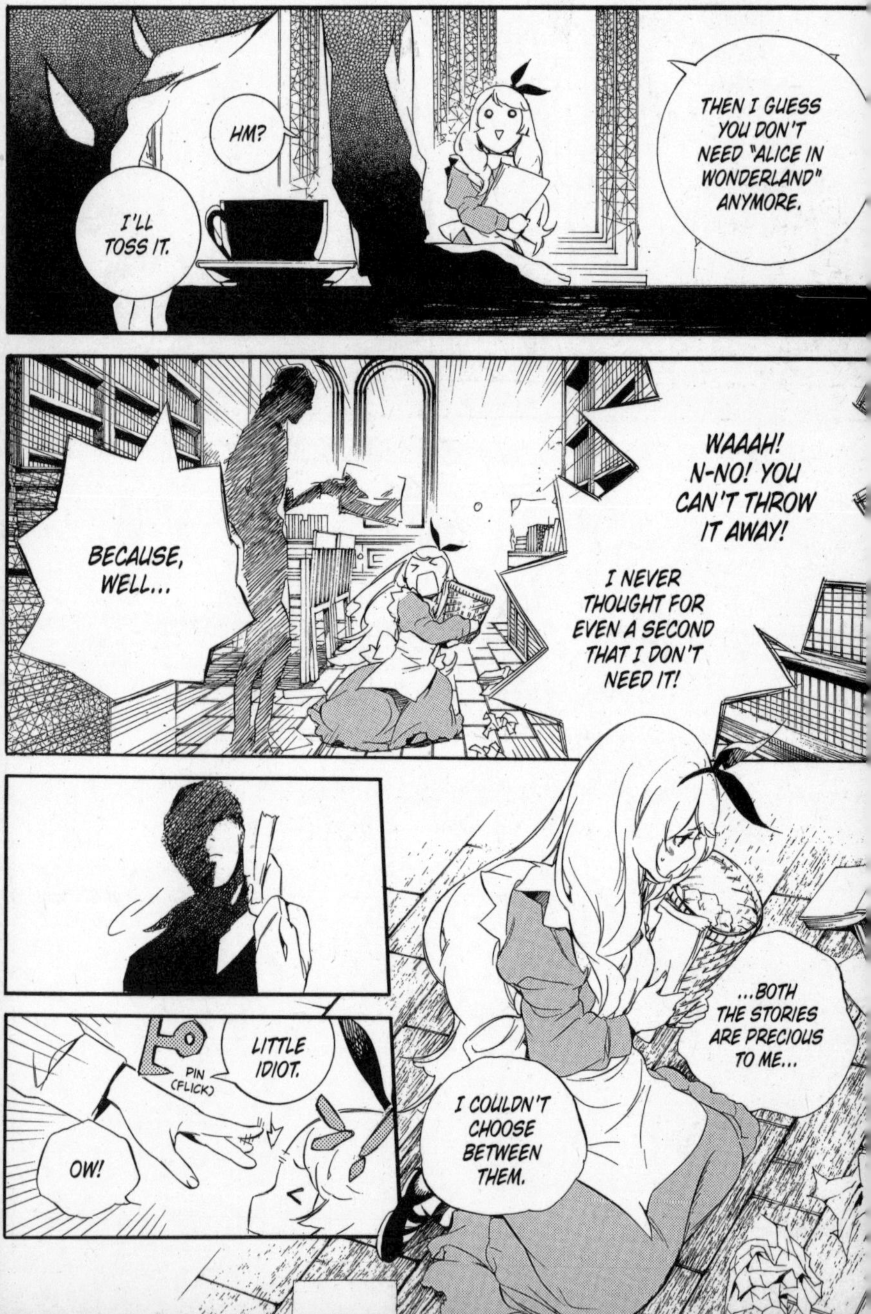
THEN I GUESS YOU DON'T NEED "ALICE IN WONDERLAND" ANYMORE.
HM?
I'LL TOSS IT.
WAAAH! N-NO! YOU CAN'T THROW IT AWAY!
I NEVER THOUGHT FOR EVEN A SECOND THAT I DON'T NEED IT!
BECAUSE, WELL...
...BOTH THE STORIES ARE PRECIOUS TO ME...
I COULDN'T CHOOSE BETWEEN THEM.
LITTLE IDIOT.
PIN (FLICK)
OW!

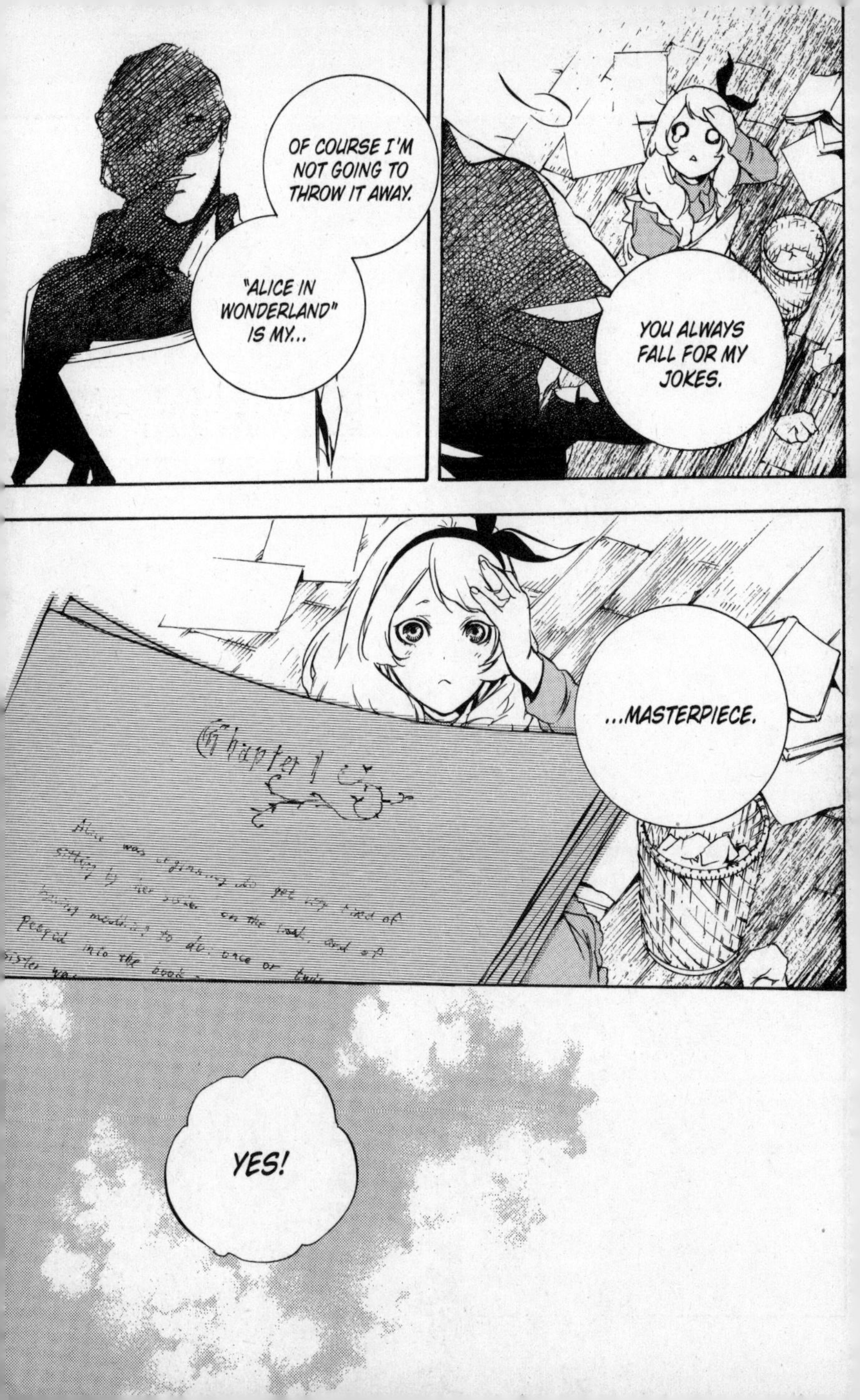
YOU ALWAYS FALL FOR MY JOKES.
OF COURSE I'M NOT GOING TO THROW IT AWAY.
"ALICE IN WONDERLAND" IS MY...
...MASTERPIECE.
Chapter I
YES!

Chapter 29 I Will Let You Decide.

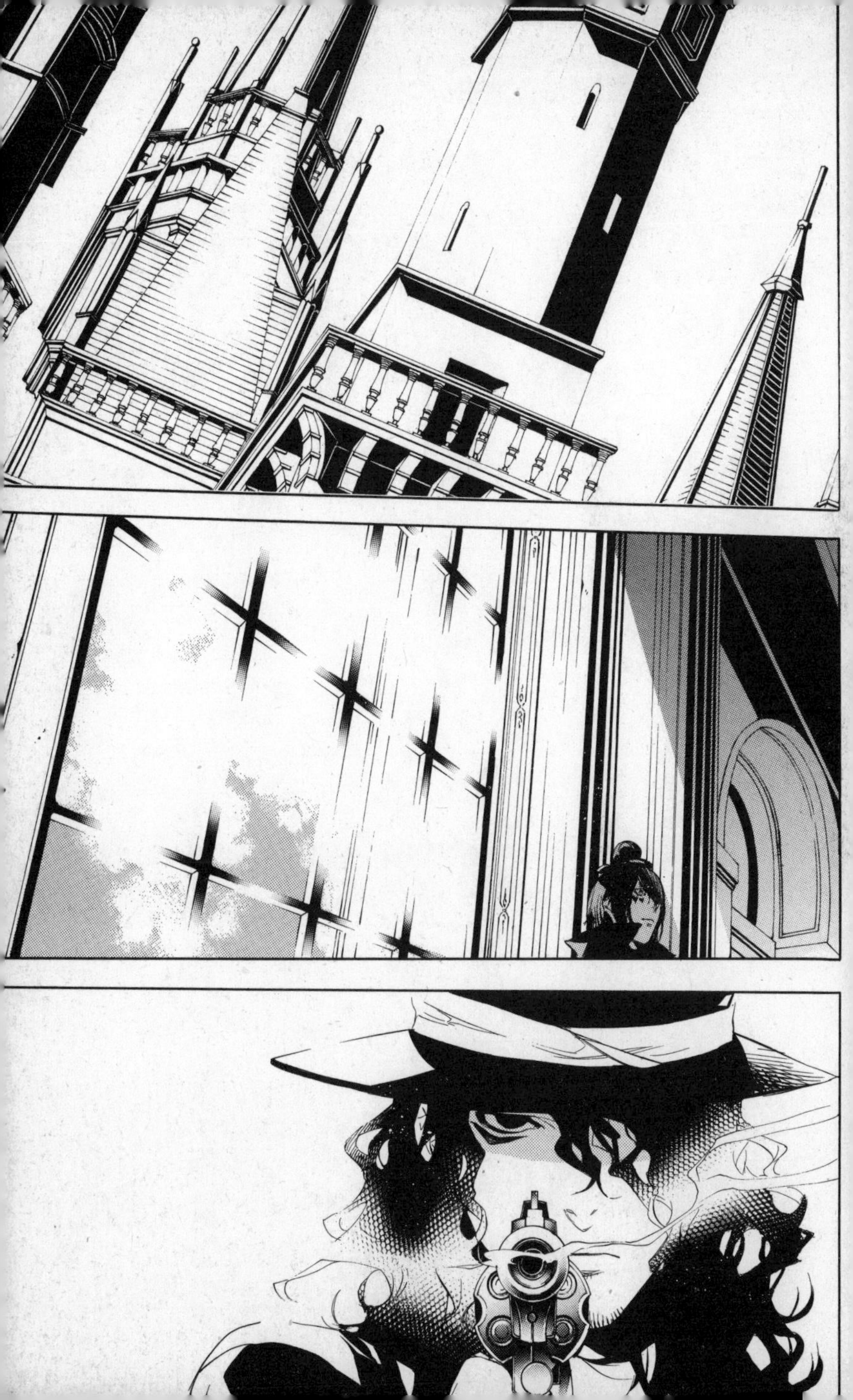

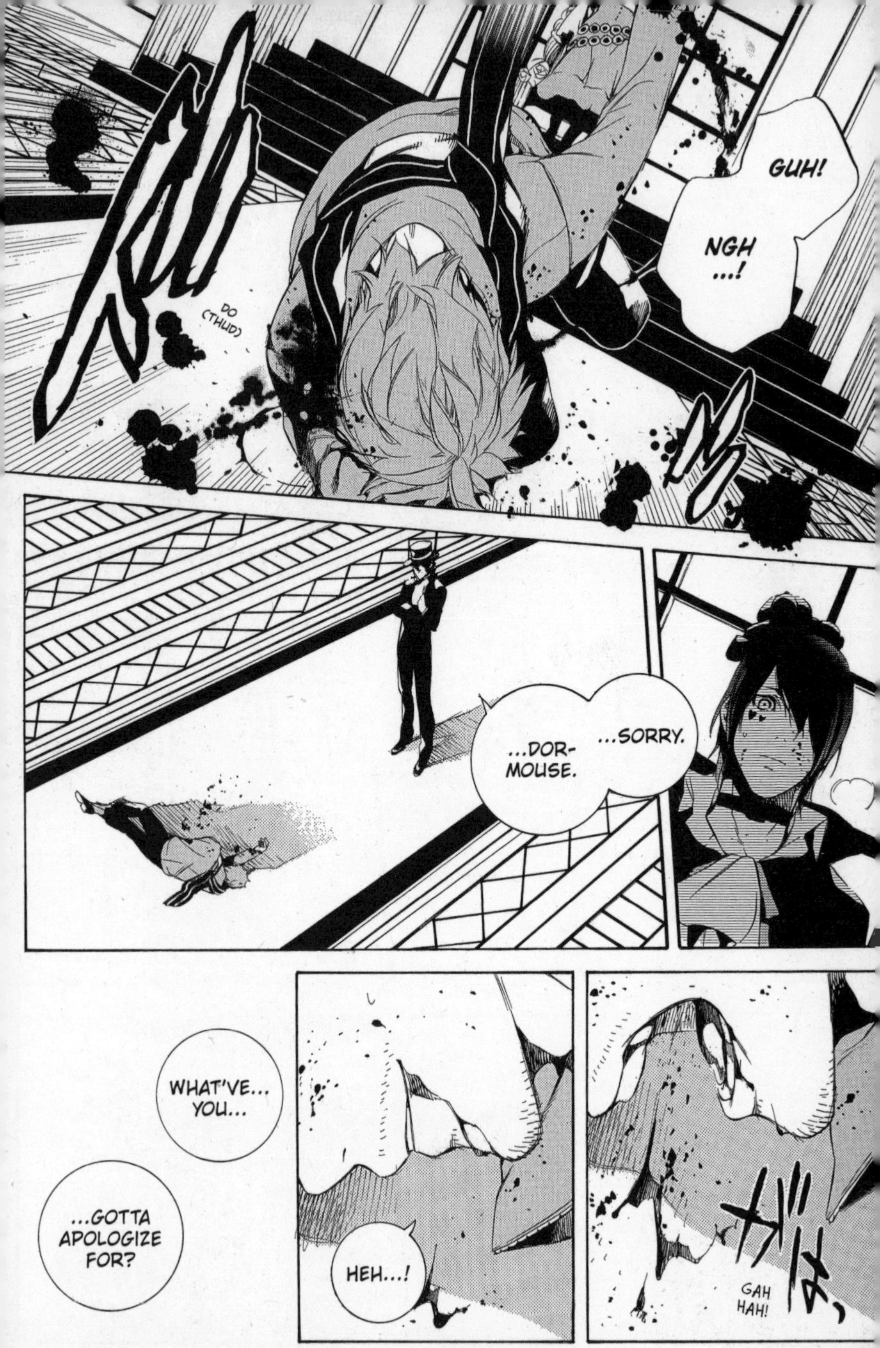
GUH!
NGH ...!
DO (THUD)
...SORRY.
...DOR-MOUSE.
GAH HAH!
HEH...!
WHAT'VE... YOU...
...GOTTA APOLOGIZE FOR?

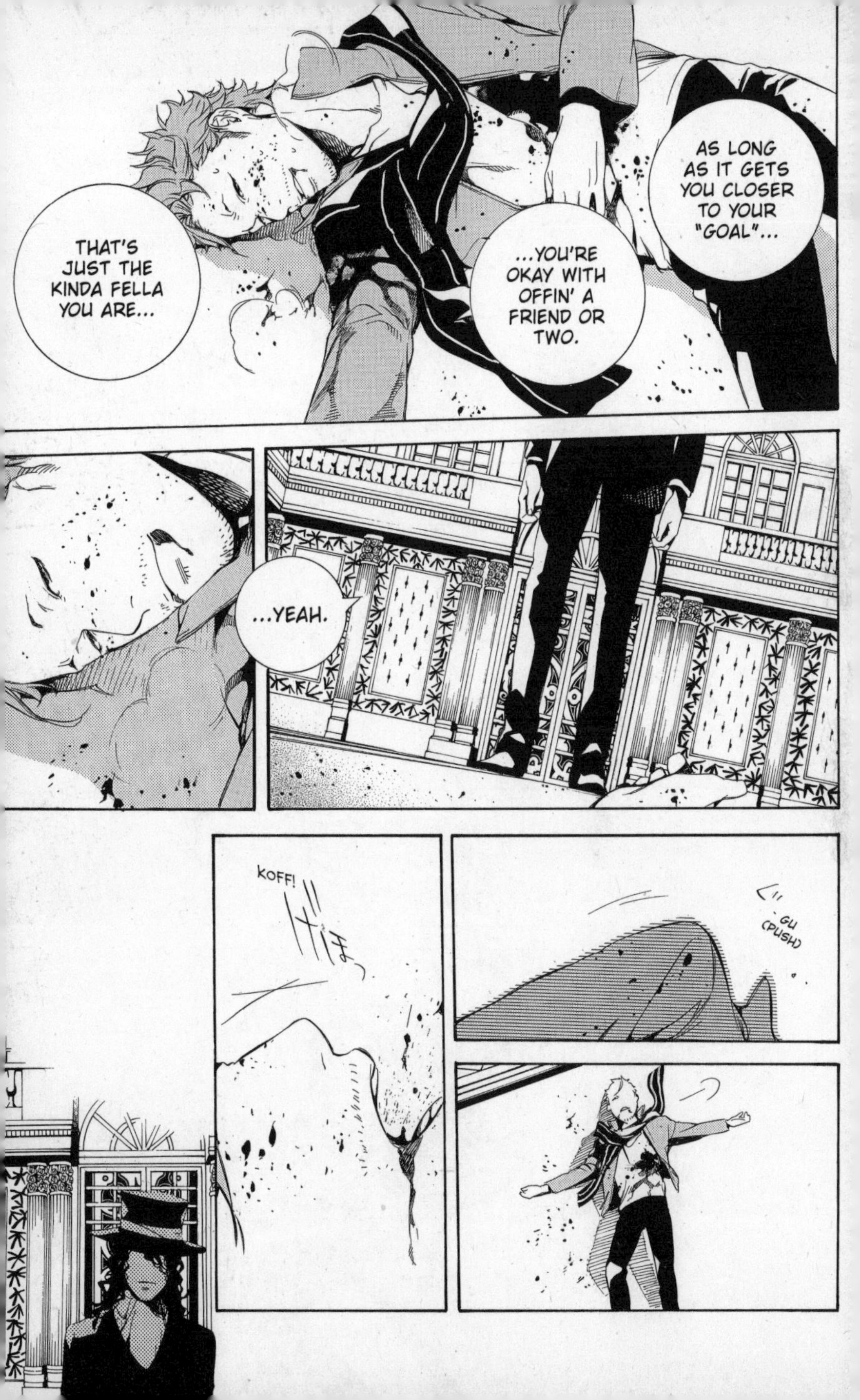
AS LONG AS IT GETS YOU CLOSER TO YOUR "GOAL"...
...YOU'RE OKAY WITH OFFIN' A FRIEND OR TWO.
THAT'S JUST THE KINDA FELLA YOU ARE...
...YEAH.
GU (PUSH)
KOFF!

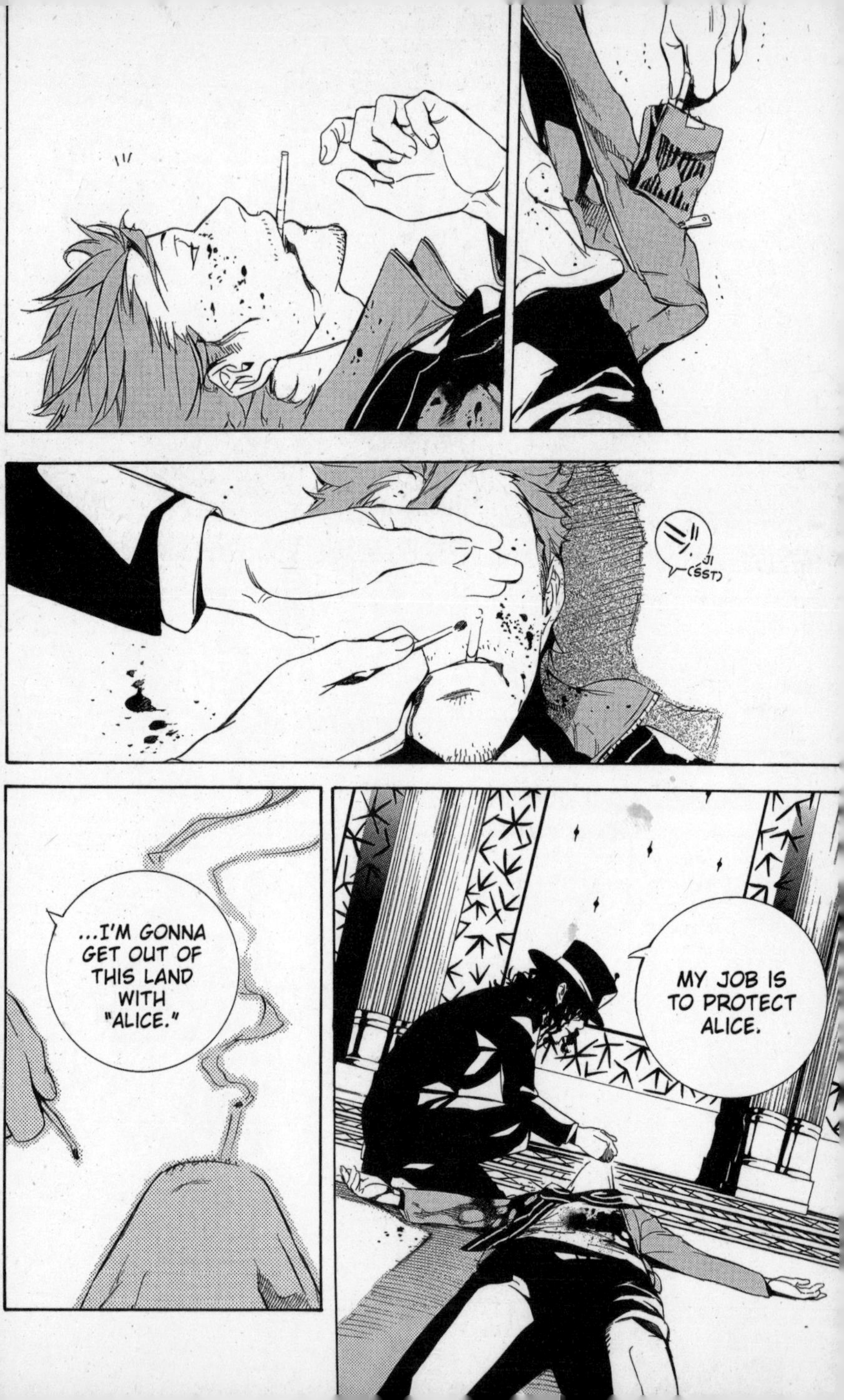
JI (SST)
MY JOB IS TO PROTECT ALICE.
...I'M GONNA GET OUT OF THIS LAND WITH "ALICE."

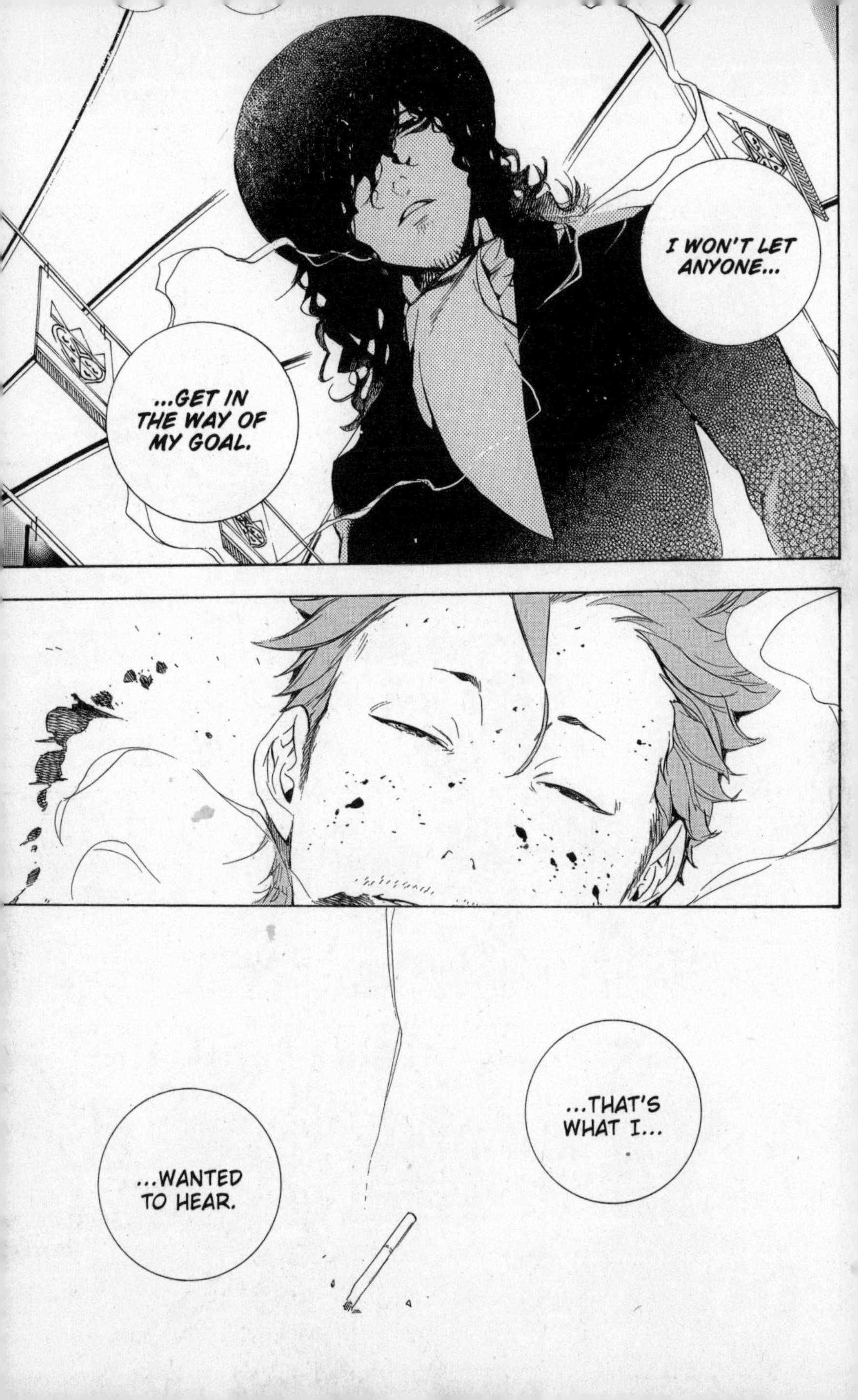
I WON'T LET ANYONE...
...GET IN THE WAY OF MY GOAL.
...THAT'S WHAT I...
...WANTED TO HEAR.

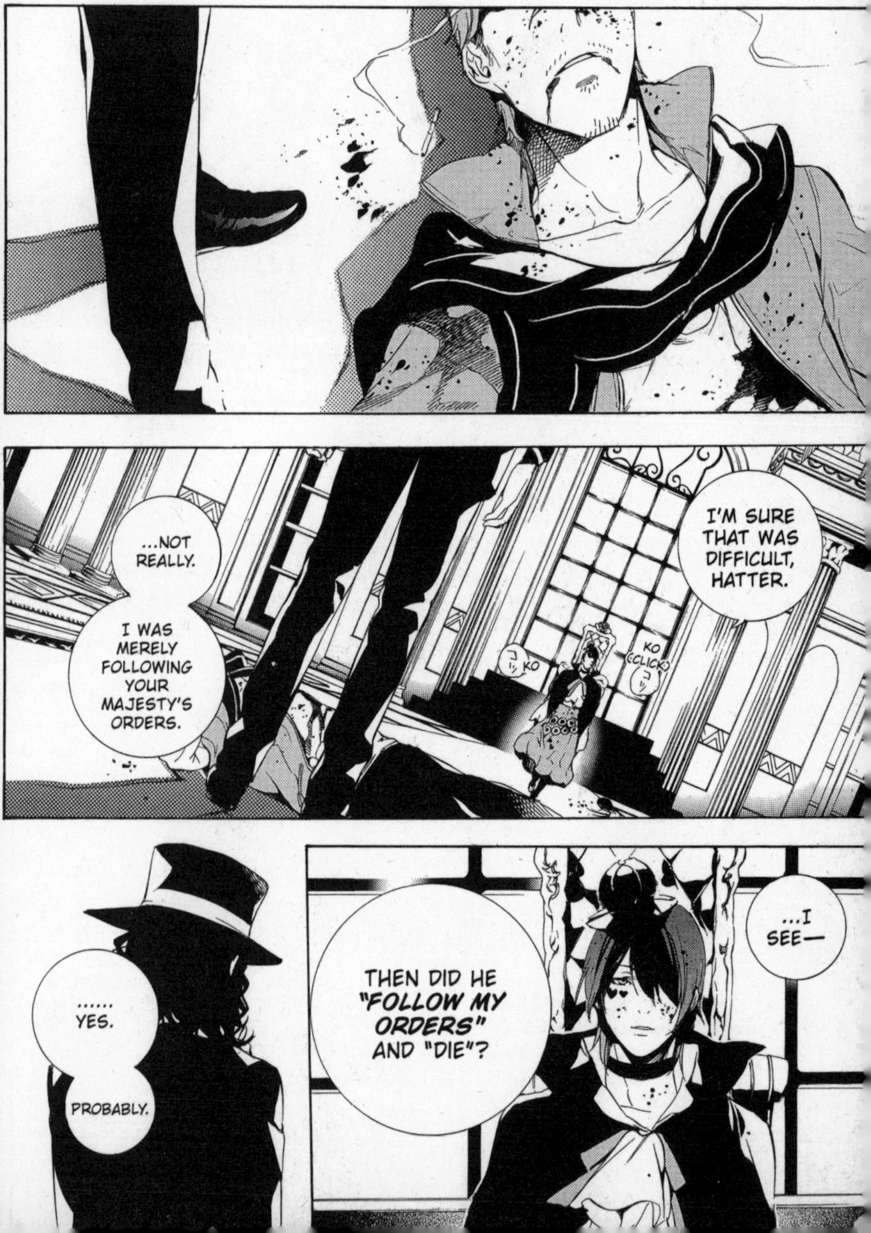
I'M SURE THAT WAS DIFFICULT, HATTER.
KO (CLICK)
KO
...NOT REALLY.
I WAS MERELY FOLLOWING YOUR MAJESTY'S ORDERS.
...I SEE—
THEN DID HE "FOLLOW MY ORDERS" AND "DIE"?
...... YES.
PROBABLY.

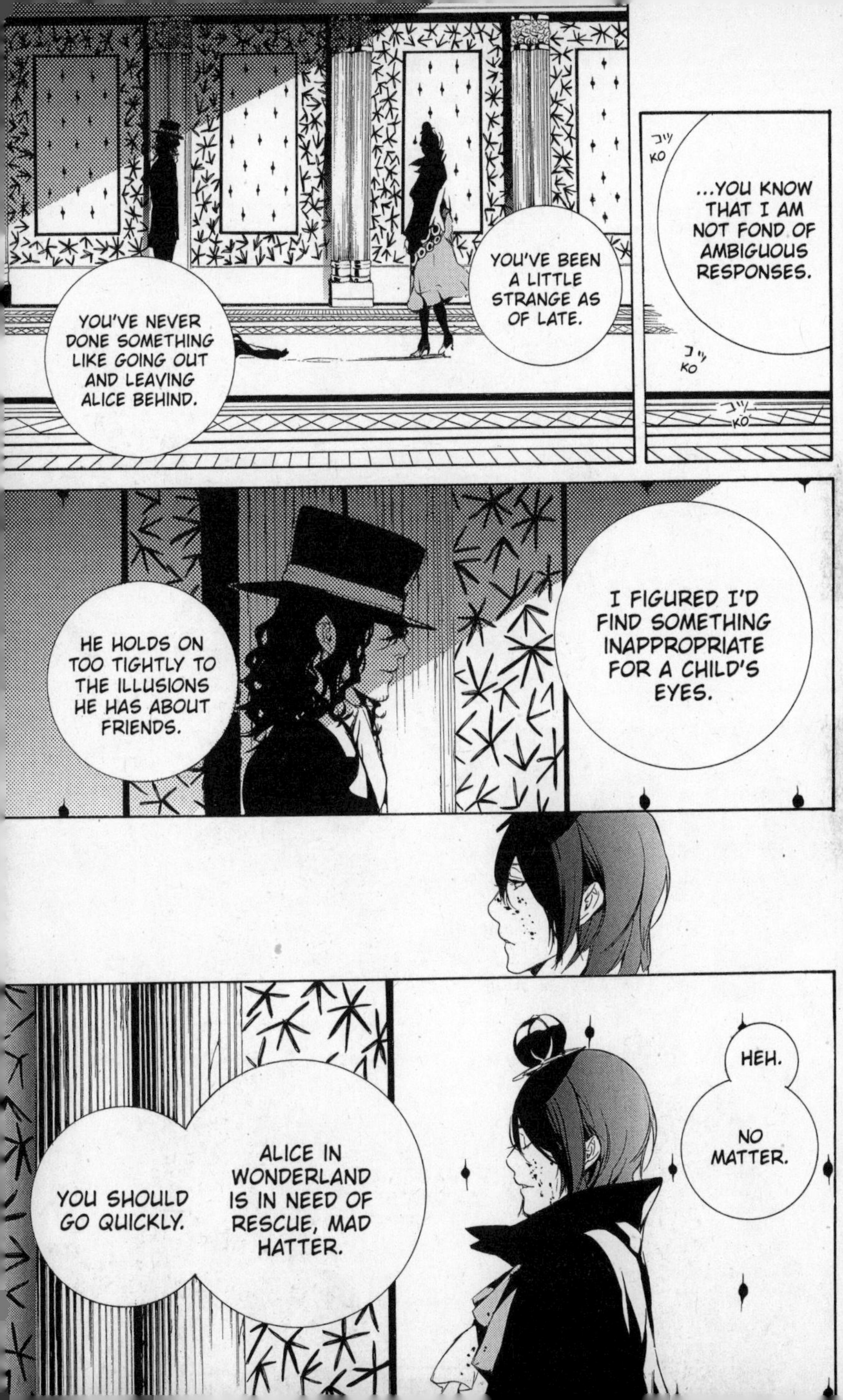

コッ KO
...YOU KNOW THAT I AM NOT FOND OF AMBIGUOUS RESPONSES.
コッ KO
コッ KO
YOU'VE BEEN A LITTLE STRANGE AS OF LATE.
YOU'VE NEVER DONE SOMETHING LIKE GOING OUT AND LEAVING ALICE BEHIND.
I FIGURED I'D FIND SOMETHING INAPPROPRIATE FOR A CHILD'S EYES.
HE HOLDS ON TOO TIGHTLY TO THE ILLUSIONS HE HAS ABOUT FRIENDS.
HEH.
NO MATTER.
ALICE IN WONDERLAND IS IN NEED OF RESCUE, MAD HATTER.
YOU SHOULD GO QUICKLY.

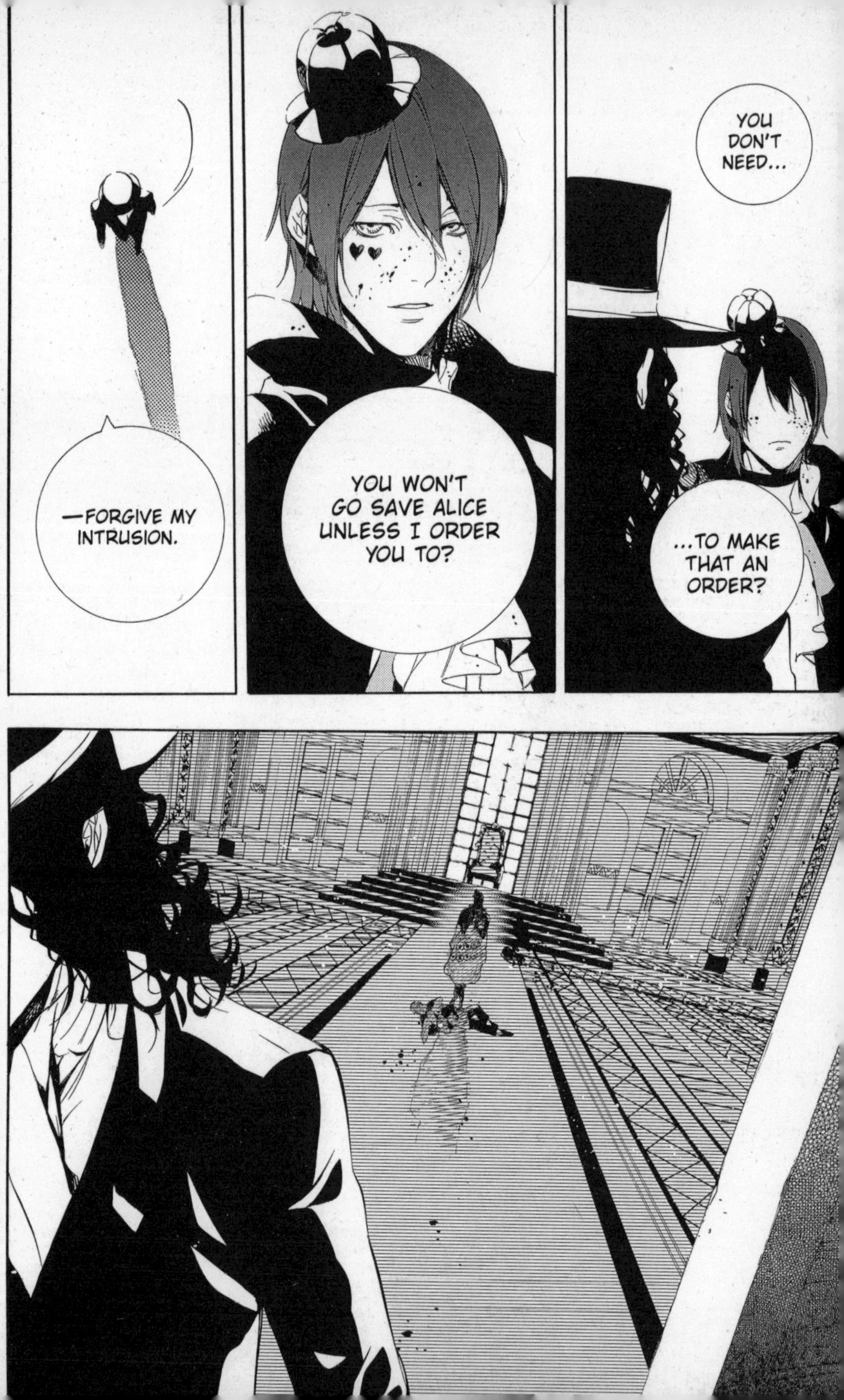
YOU DON'T NEED...
...TO MAKE THAT AN ORDER?
YOU WON'T GO SAVE ALICE UNLESS I ORDER YOU TO?
—FORGIVE MY INTRUSION.

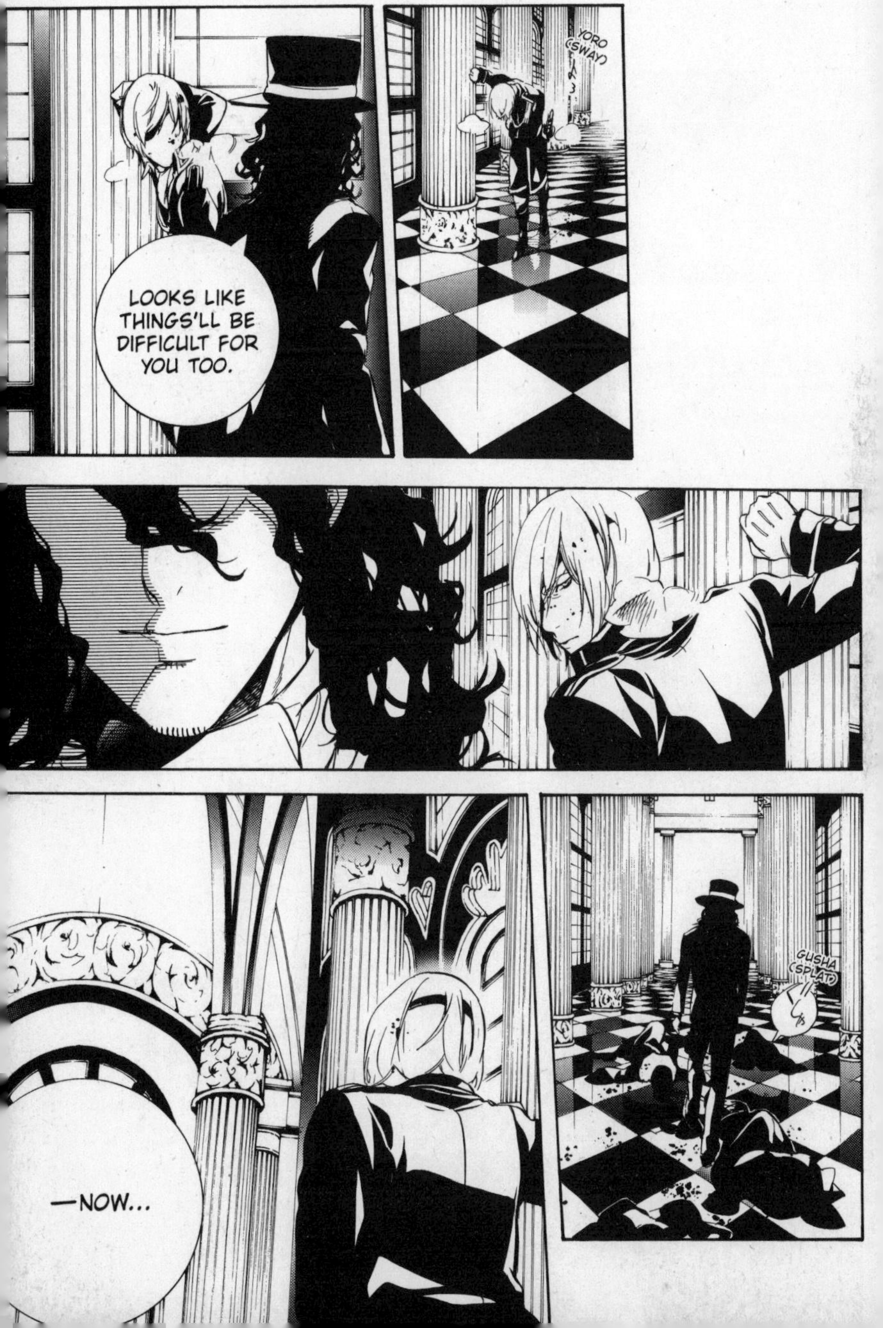
YORO (SWAY)
LOOKS LIKE THINGS'LL BE DIFFICULT FOR YOU TOO.
GUSHA (SPLAT)
—NOW...

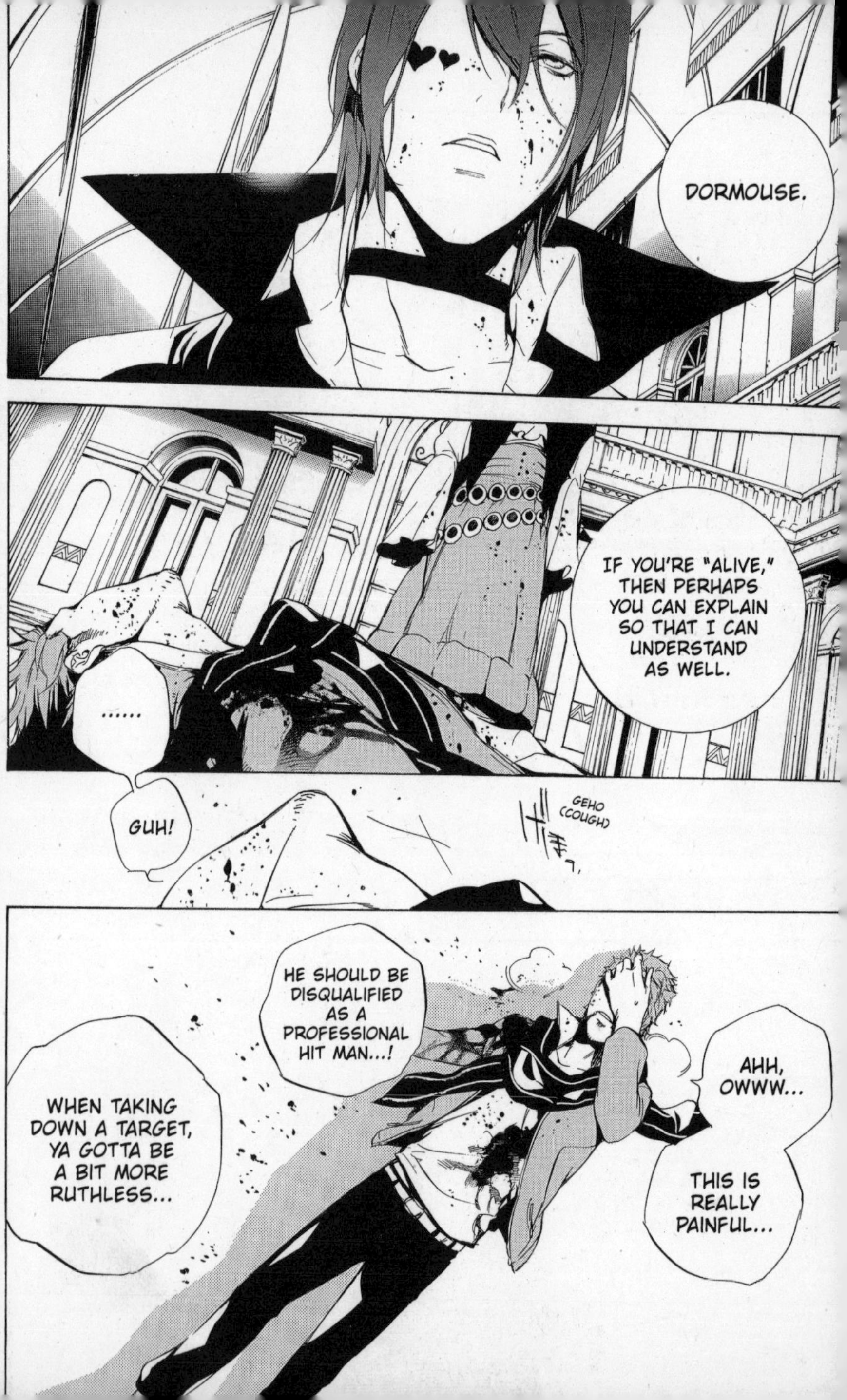
DORMOUSE.
IF YOU'RE "ALIVE," THEN PERHAPS YOU CAN EXPLAIN SO THAT I CAN UNDERSTAND AS WELL.
......
GEHO (COUGH)
GUH!
AHH, OWWW...
THIS IS REALLY PAINFUL...
HE SHOULD BE DISQUALIFIED AS A PROFESSIONAL HIT MAN...!
WHEN TAKING DOWN A TARGET, YA GOTTA BE A BIT MORE RUTHLESS...

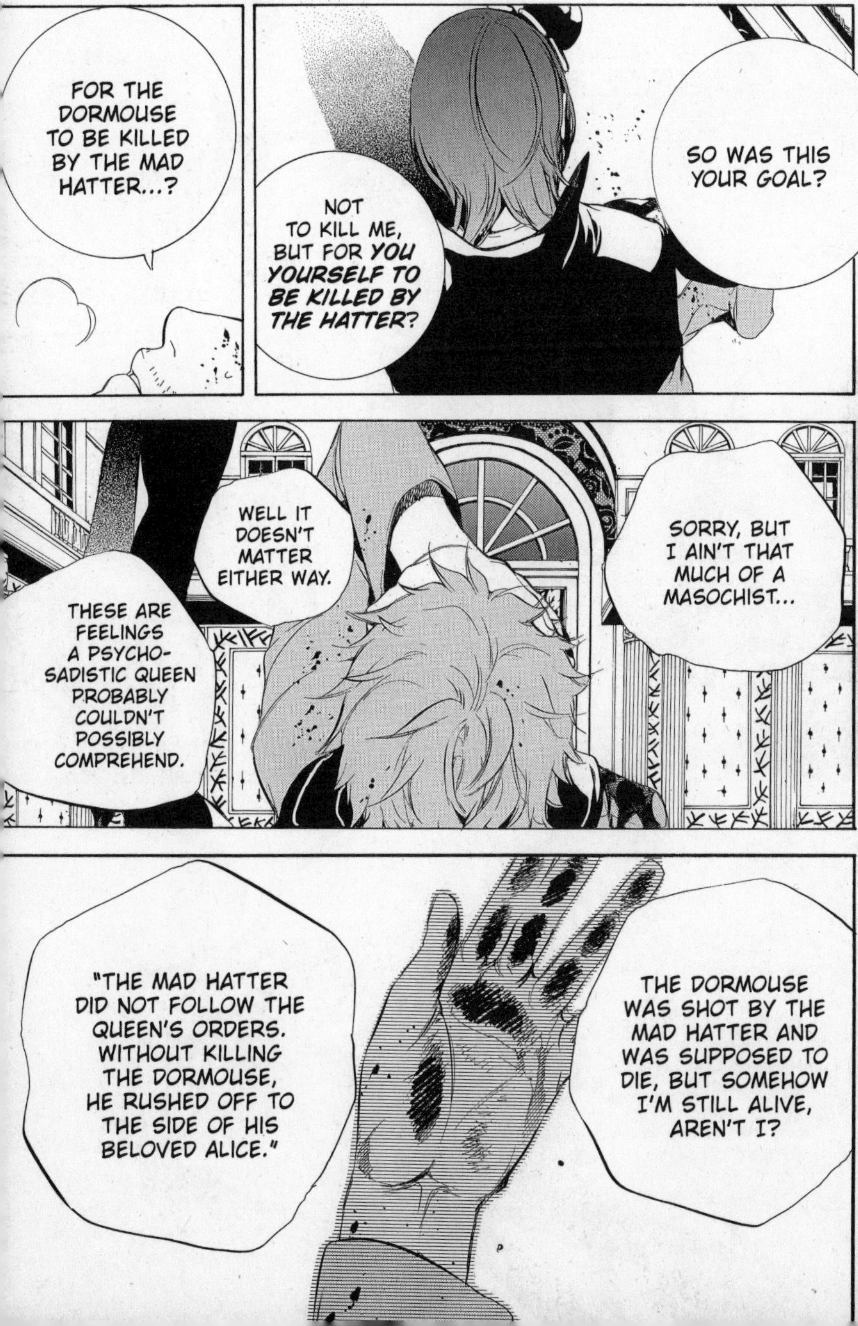
SO WAS THIS YOUR GOAL?
NOT TO KILL ME, BUT FOR *YOU YOURSELF TO BE KILLED BY THE HATTER?*
FOR THE DORMOUSE TO BE KILLED BY THE MAD HATTER...?
SORRY, BUT I AIN'T THAT MUCH OF A MASOCHIST...
WELL IT DOESN'T MATTER EITHER WAY.
THESE ARE FEELINGS A PSYCHO-SADISTIC QUEEN PROBABLY COULDN'T POSSIBLY COMPREHEND.
THE DORMOUSE WAS SHOT BY THE MAD HATTER AND WAS SUPPOSED TO DIE, BUT SOMEHOW I'M STILL ALIVE, AREN'T I?
"THE MAD HATTER DID NOT FOLLOW THE QUEEN'S ORDERS. WITHOUT KILLING THE DORMOUSE, HE RUSHED OFF TO THE SIDE OF HIS BELOVED ALICE."

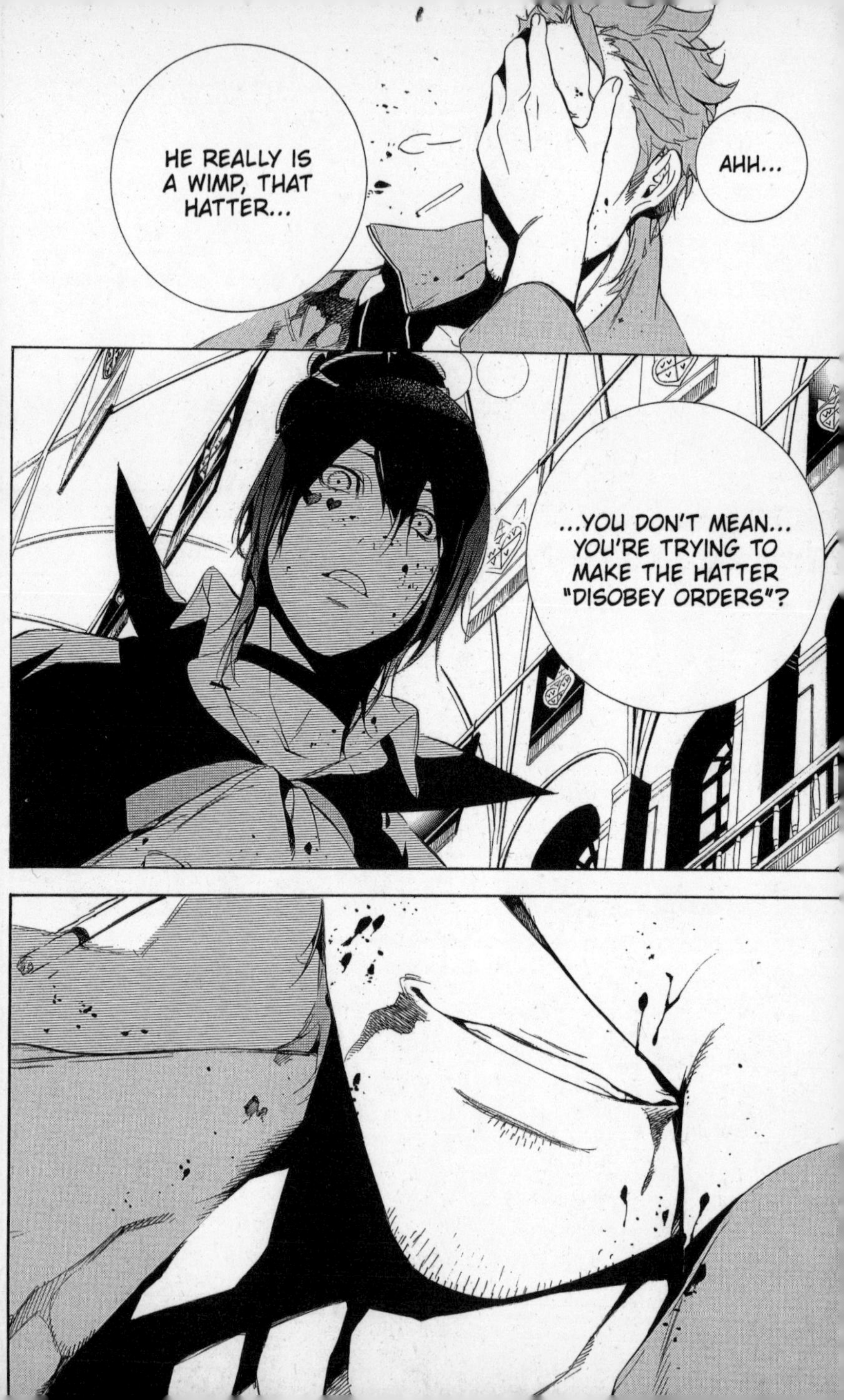
AHH...
HE REALLY IS A WIMP, THAT HATTER...
...YOU DON'T MEAN... YOU'RE TRYING TO MAKE THE HATTER "DISOBEY ORDERS"?

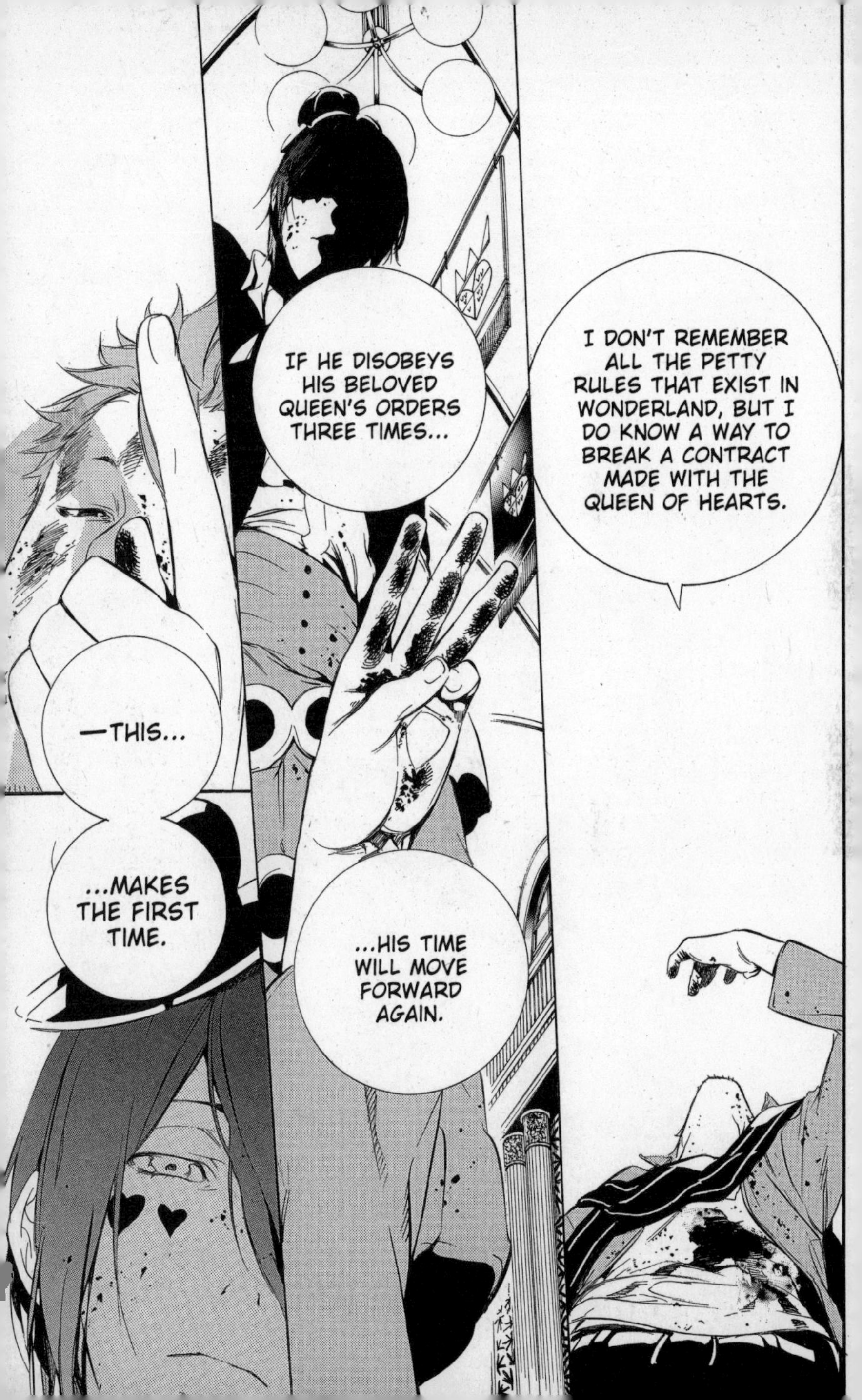
I DON'T REMEMBER ALL THE PETTY RULES THAT EXIST IN WONDERLAND, BUT I DO KNOW A WAY TO BREAK A CONTRACT MADE WITH THE QUEEN OF HEARTS.
IF HE DISOBEYS HIS BELOVED QUEEN'S ORDERS THREE TIMES...
...HIS TIME WILL MOVE FORWARD AGAIN.
—THIS...
...MAKES THE FIRST TIME.

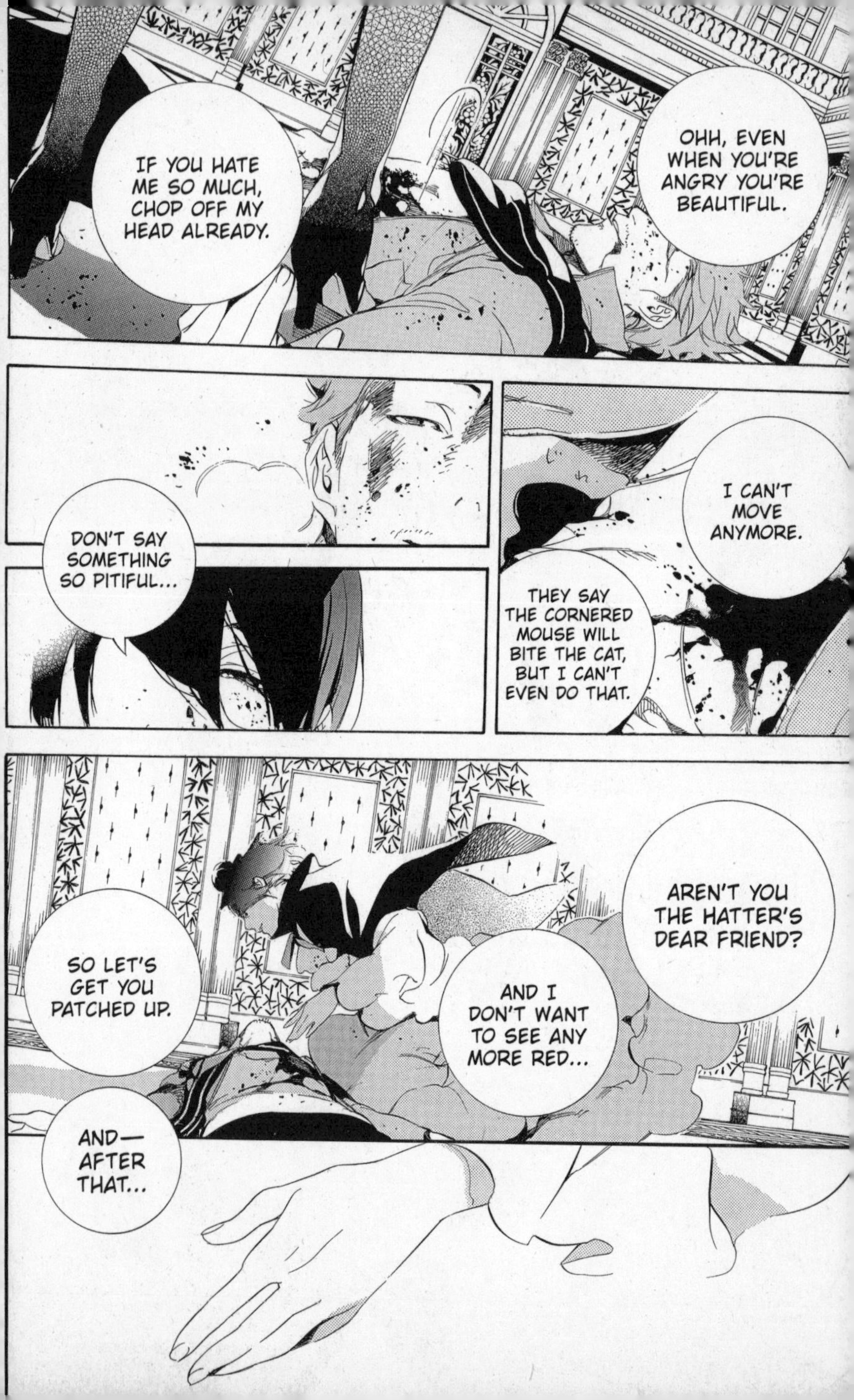
OHH, EVEN WHEN YOU'RE ANGRY YOU'RE BEAUTIFUL.
IF YOU HATE ME SO MUCH, CHOP OFF MY HEAD ALREADY.
I CAN'T MOVE ANYMORE.
THEY SAY THE CORNERED MOUSE WILL BITE THE CAT, BUT I CAN'T EVEN DO THAT.
DON'T SAY SOMETHING SO PITIFUL...
AREN'T YOU THE HATTER'S DEAR FRIEND?
AND I DON'T WANT TO SEE ANY MORE RED...
SO LET'S GET YOU PATCHED UP.
AND— AFTER THAT...

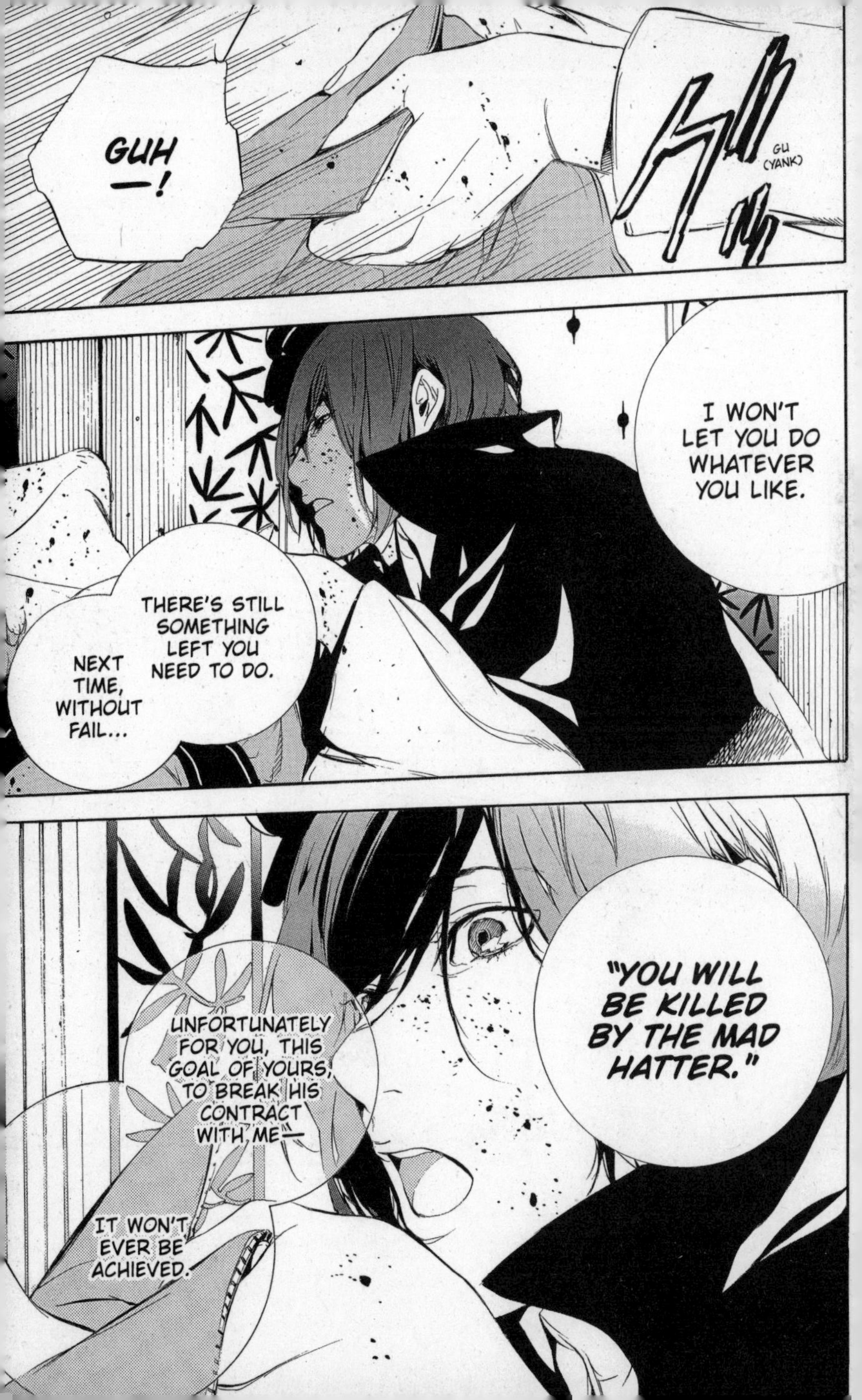
GU (YANK)
GUH—!
I WON'T LET YOU DO WHATEVER YOU LIKE.
THERE'S STILL SOMETHING LEFT YOU NEED TO DO.
NEXT TIME, WITHOUT FAIL...
"YOU WILL BE KILLED BY THE MAD HATTER."
UNFORTUNATELY FOR YOU, THIS GOAL OF YOURS, TO BREAK HIS CONTRACT WITH ME—
IT WON'T EVER BE ACHIEVED.

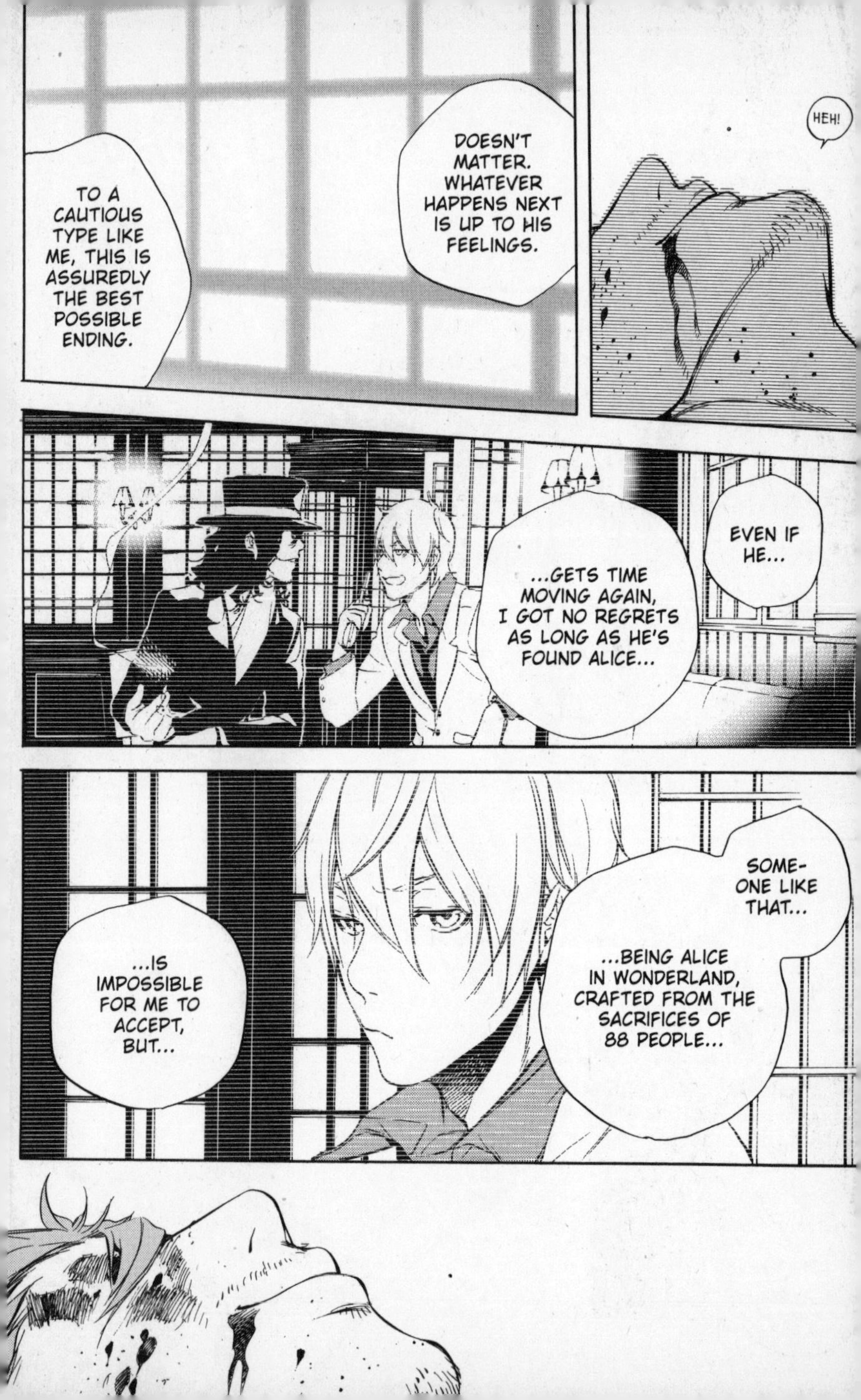
HEH!
DOESN'T MATTER. WHATEVER HAPPENS NEXT IS UP TO HIS FEELINGS.
TO A CAUTIOUS TYPE LIKE ME, THIS IS ASSUREDLY THE BEST POSSIBLE ENDING.
EVEN IF HE...
...GETS TIME MOVING AGAIN, I GOT NO REGRETS AS LONG AS HE'S FOUND ALICE...
SOME-ONE LIKE THAT...
...BEING ALICE IN WONDERLAND, CRAFTED FROM THE SACRIFICES OF 88 PEOPLE...
...IS IMPOSSIBLE FOR ME TO ACCEPT, BUT...

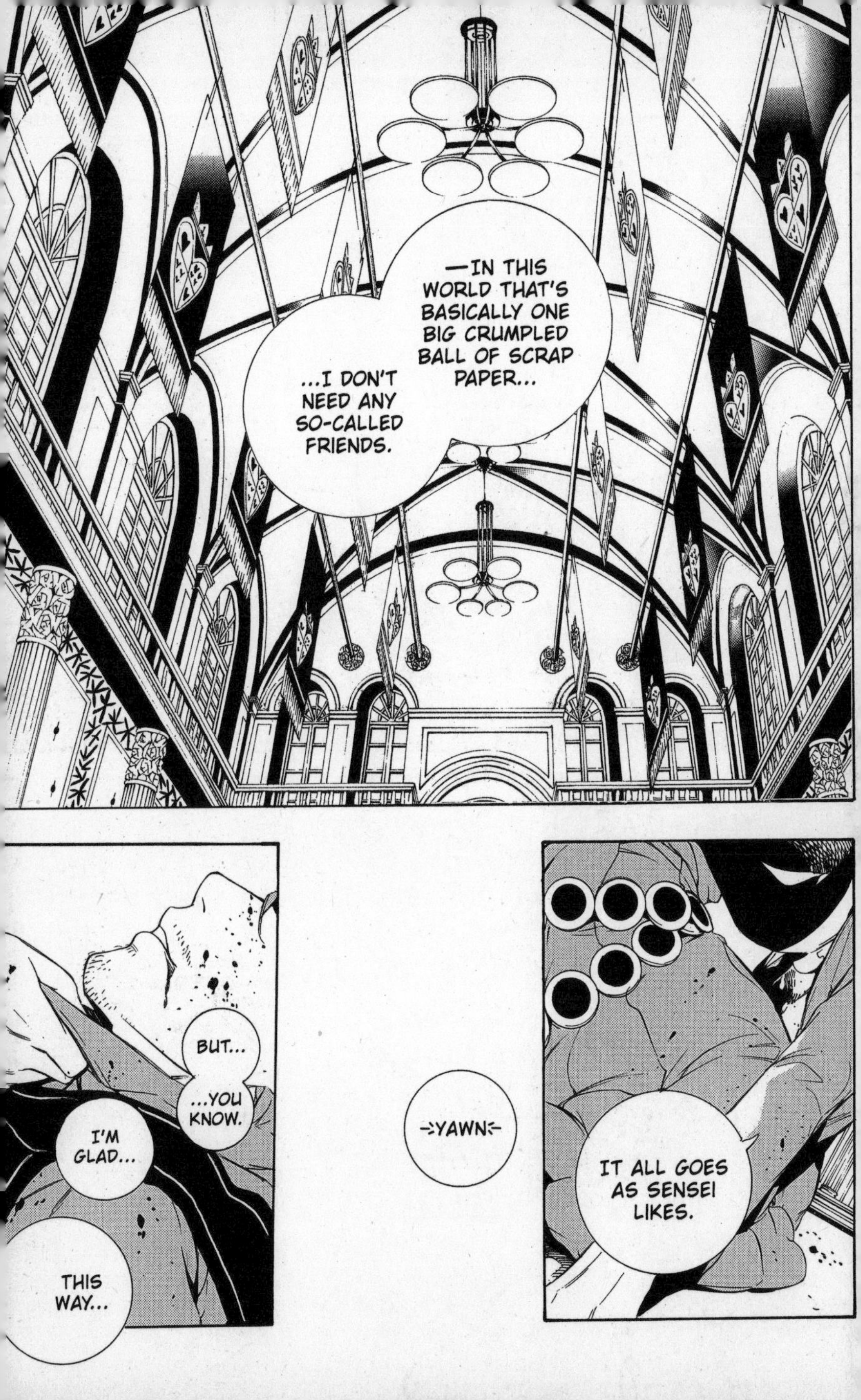
—IN THIS WORLD THAT'S BASICALLY ONE BIG CRUMPLED BALL OF SCRAP PAPER...
...I DON'T NEED ANY SO-CALLED FRIENDS.
IT ALL GOES AS SENSEI LIKES.
YAWN
BUT...
...YOU KNOW.
I'M GLAD...
THIS WAY...

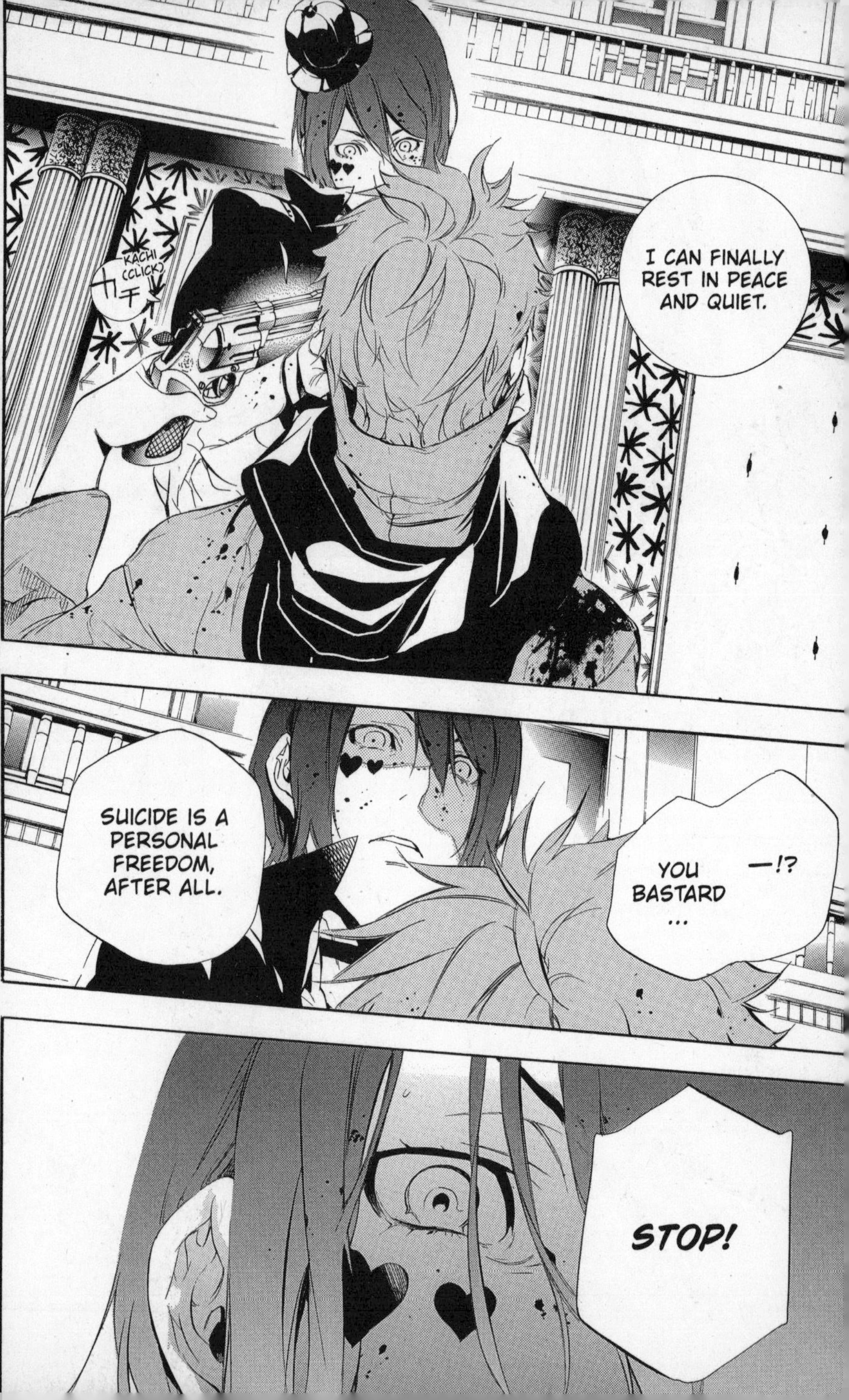
I CAN FINALLY REST IN PEACE AND QUIET.
KACHI (CLICK)
カチ
YOU BASTARD ... —!?
SUICIDE IS A PERSONAL FREEDOM, AFTER ALL.
STOP!

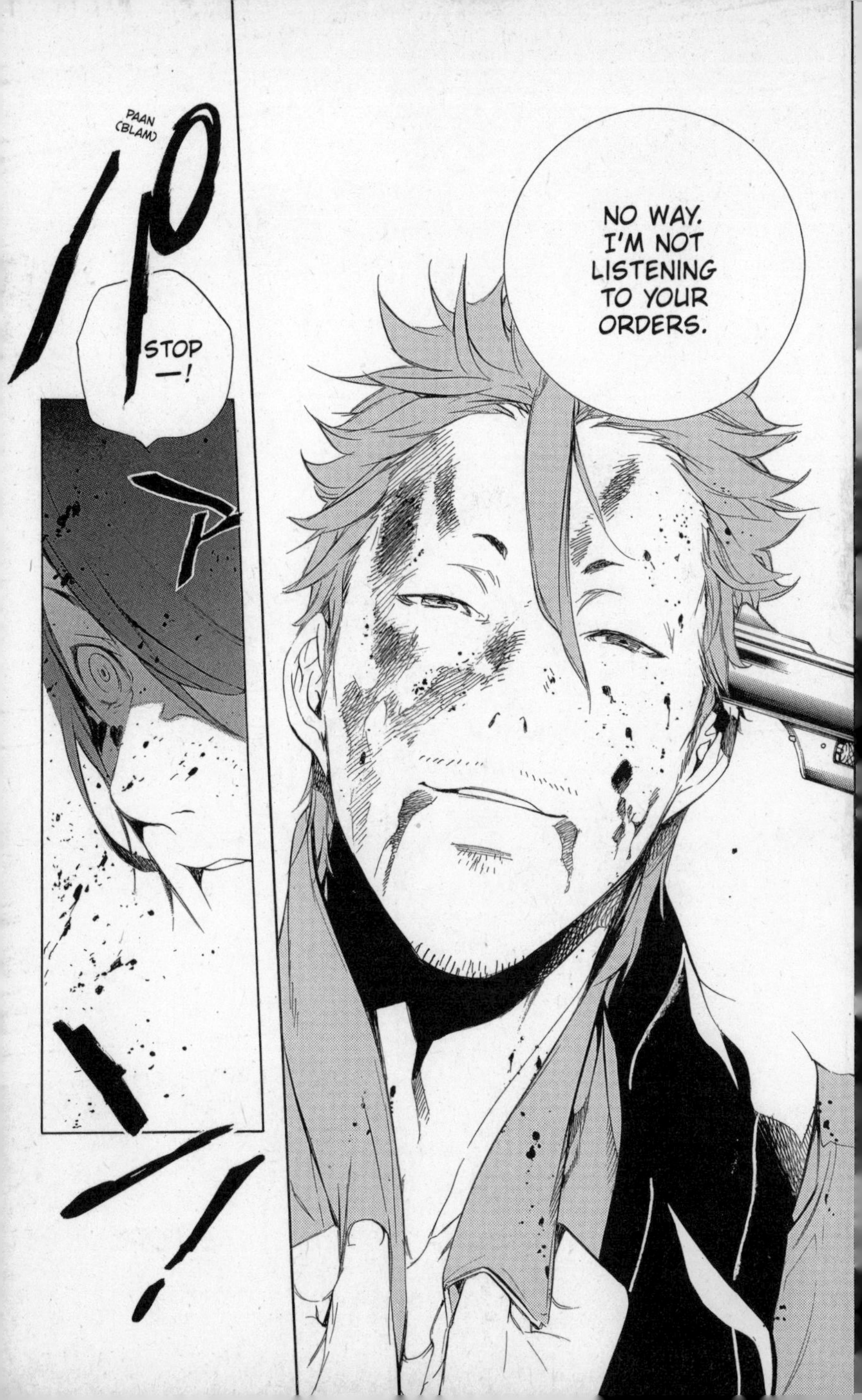
NO WAY. I'M NOT LISTENING TO YOUR ORDERS.
PAAN (BLAM)
STOP —!

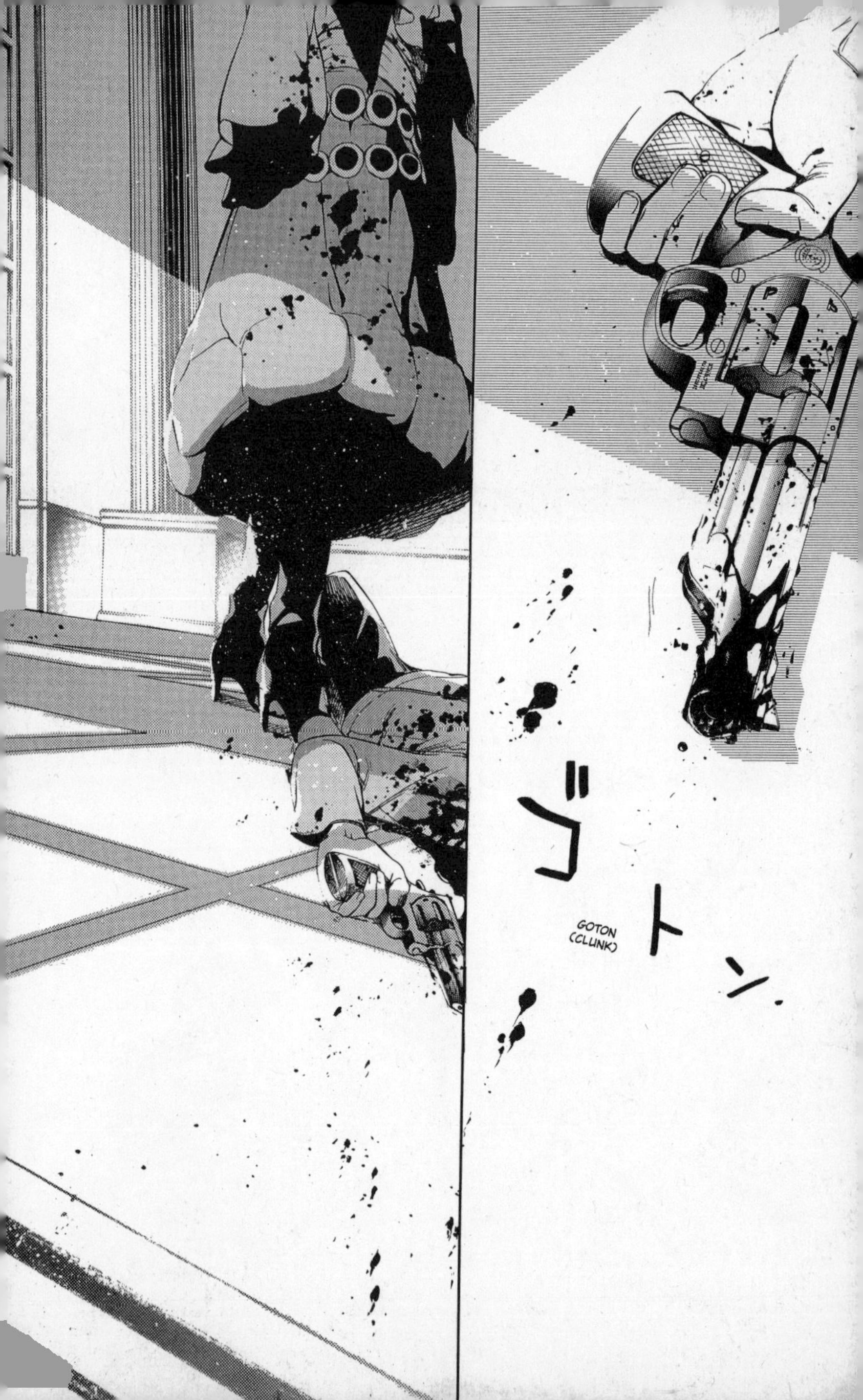
ゴトン
GOTON
(CLUNK)

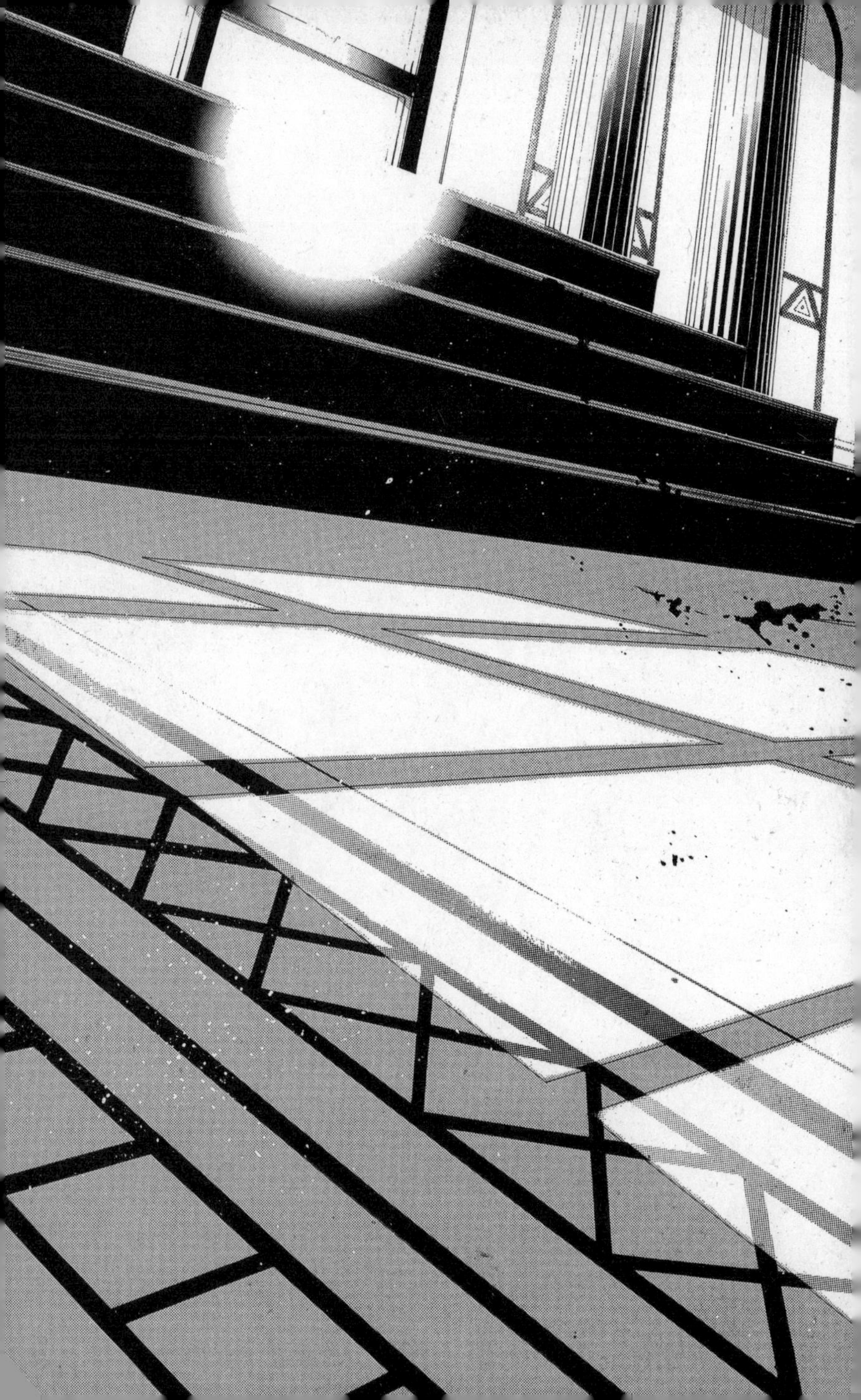

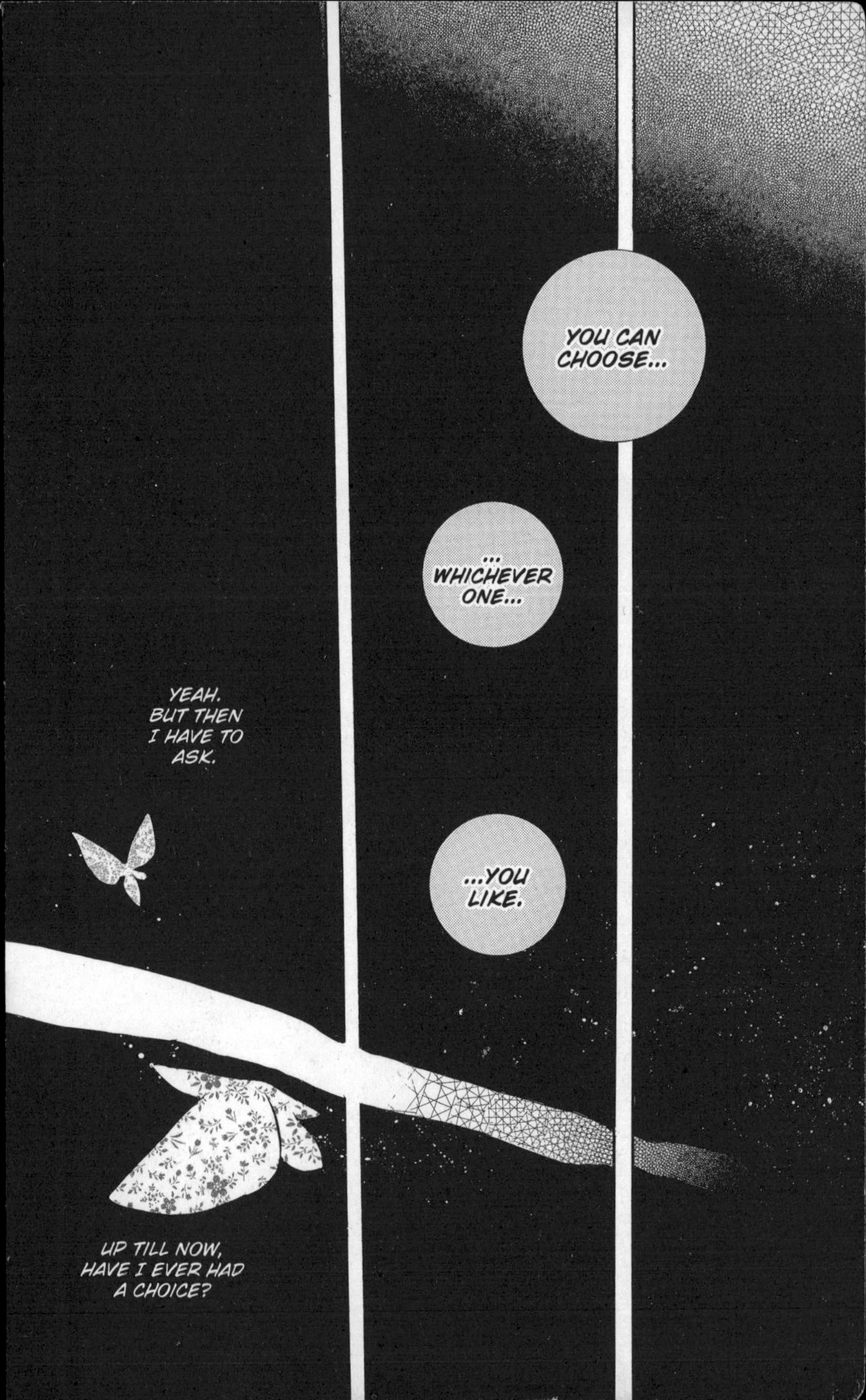
YOU CAN CHOOSE...
...WHICHEVER ONE...
...YOU LIKE.
YEAH. BUT THEN I HAVE TO ASK.
UP TILL NOW, HAVE I EVER HAD A CHOICE?

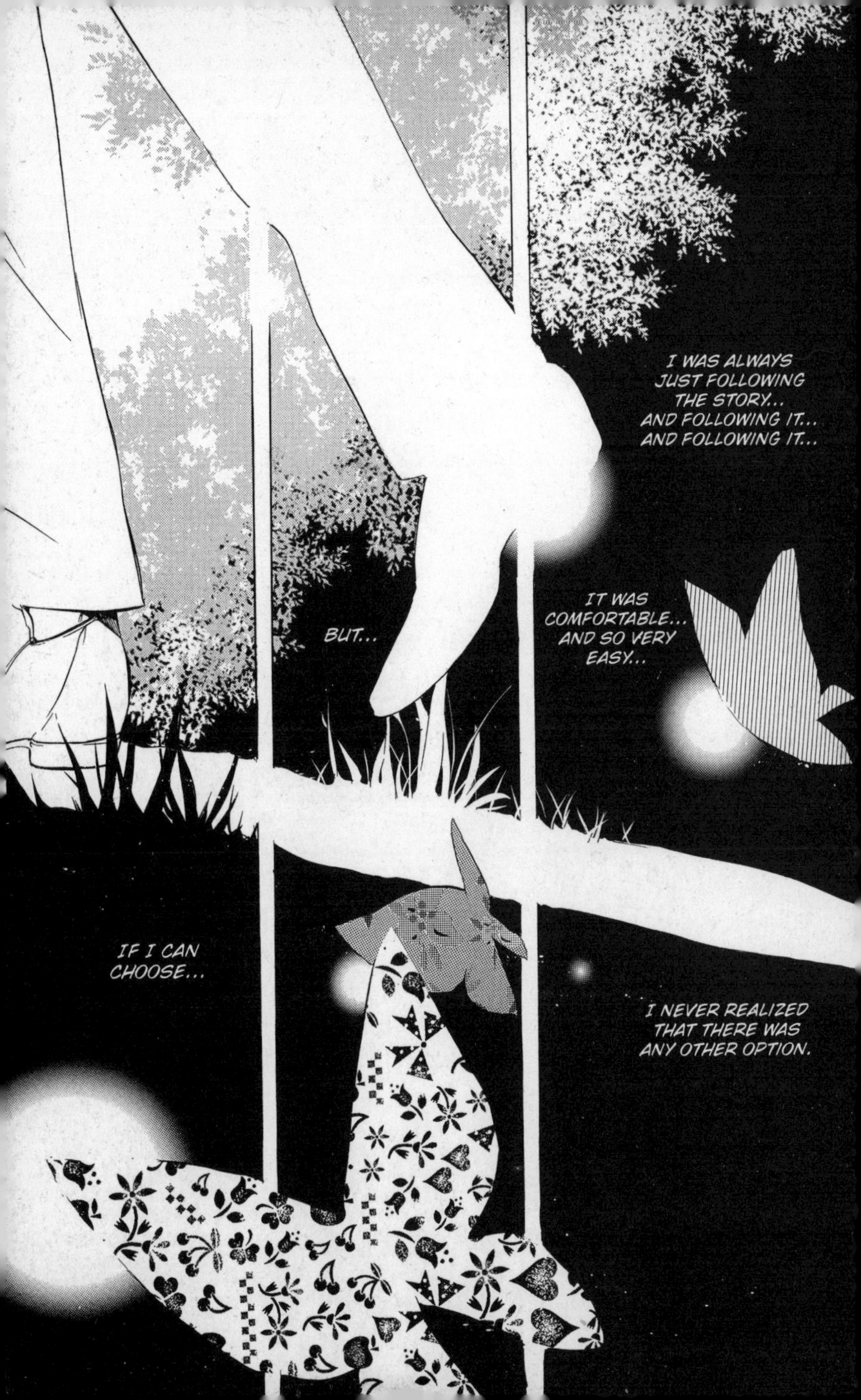
I WAS ALWAYS JUST FOLLOWING THE STORY... AND FOLLOWING IT... AND FOLLOWING IT...
IT WAS COMFORTABLE... AND SO VERY EASY...
I NEVER REALIZED THAT THERE WAS ANY OTHER OPTION.
BUT...
IF I CAN CHOOSE...

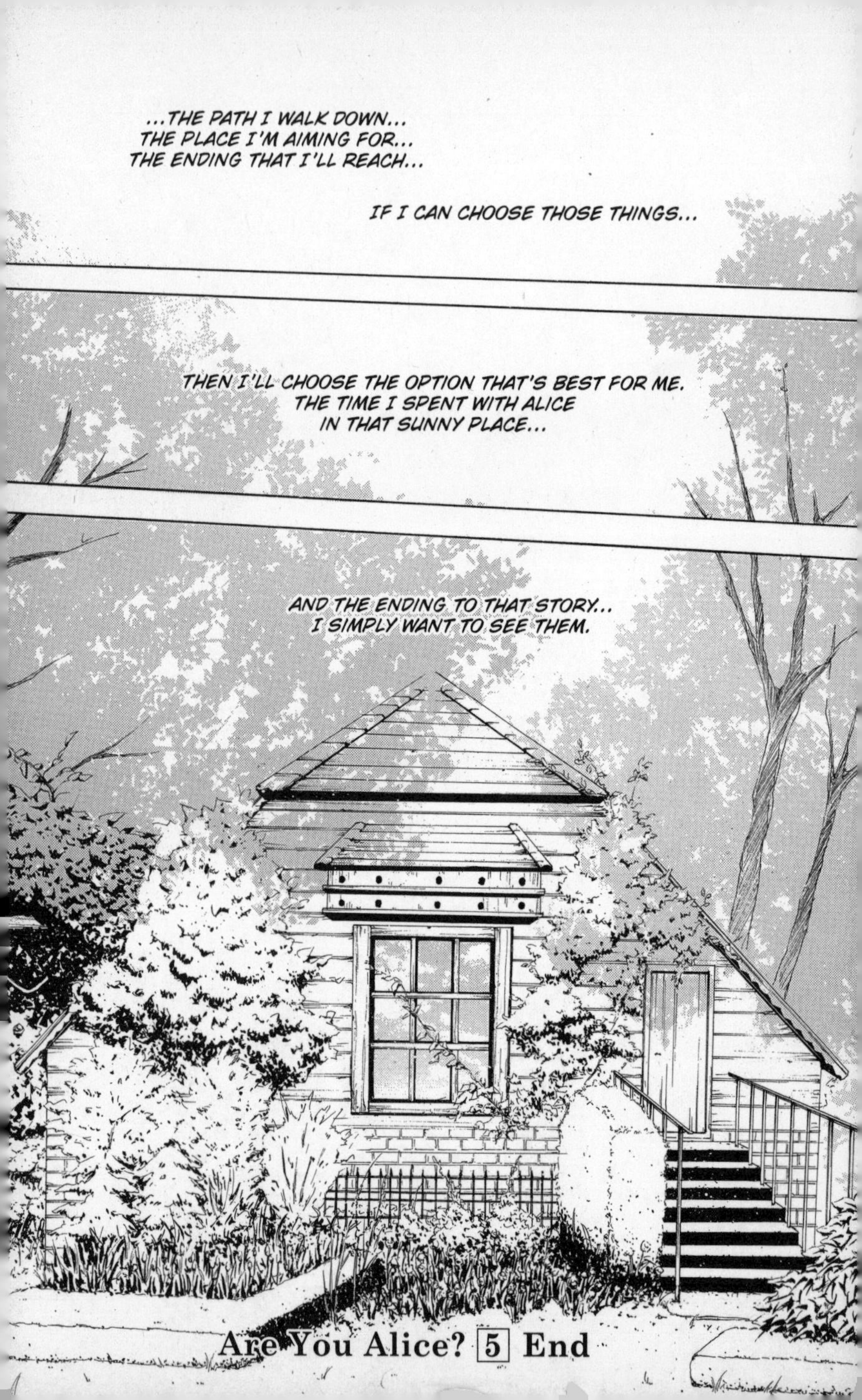
...THE PATH I WALK DOWN... THE PLACE I'M AIMING FOR... THE ENDING THAT I'LL REACH...
IF I CAN CHOOSE THOSE THINGS...
THEN I'LL CHOOSE THE OPTION THAT'S BEST FOR ME. THE TIME I SPENT WITH ALICE IN THAT SUNNY PLACE...
AND THE ENDING TO THAT STORY... I SIMPLY WANT TO SEE THEM.
Are You Alice? 5 End

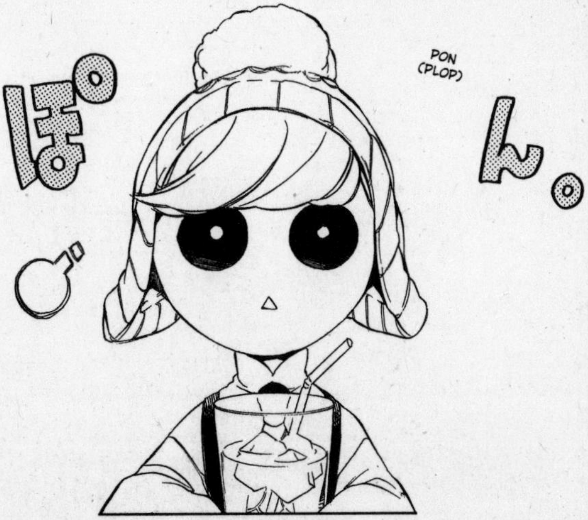
ぽ
ん。
PON
(PLOP)

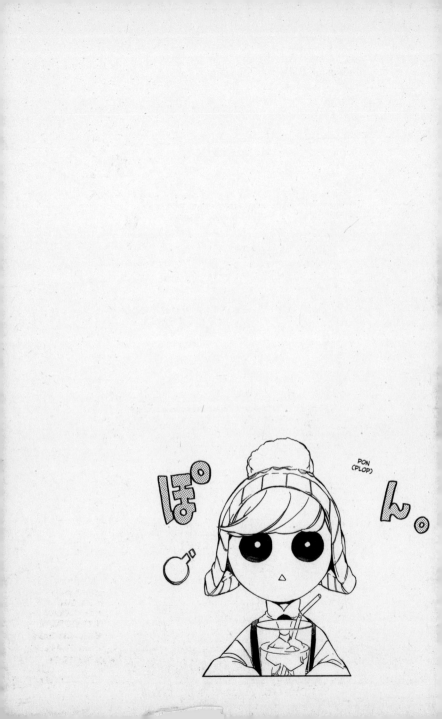

STAFF

✦ ORIGINAL WORKS
AI NINOMIYA

♣ ASSISTANT WORKS
**MIZUKI SAKAMAKI
REIN OFUJI
DATENSI
MARI**

IN WONDERLAND, YOU MAKE WHO FRIENDS?

HATTER

I WANNA MESS WITH HIM TO MY HEART'S CONTENT.

BY KATAGIRI

MOUSE

I WANNA BE FRIENDS WITH THE DODO.

BY DATENSHI

MARCH HARE

BECAUSE HE'S A MEDDLESOME BUT SWEET KID.

BY OFUJI

MISS CATERPILLAR

I WANNA HAVE "WONDERLAND STYLE" GIRL TALK WITH HER! ♪

SAKAMAKI

OHH MY!

and thanks! **SAKUMA**

The main characters of *Are You Alice?* are fundamentally inclined toward independent action, but Alice and Mister Hatter spending time together is rare lately, especially in this, the fifth volume I'm sending off!

Despite this, they're still merrily bickering with one another in the limited edition drama CD, so please check it out!

And with that, I hope to see you again in Volume 6!

Ai Ninomiya

ARE YOU ALICE? 5

IKUMI KATAGIRI
AI NINOMIYA

Translation and Lettering: Alexis Eckerman

Are you Alice? © 2012 by Ai Ninomiya / Ikumi Katagiri. © IM/Re;no, Inc. All rights reserved. First published in Japan in 2012 by ICHIJINSHA. English translation rights arranged with ICHIJINSHA through Tuttle-Mori Agency, Inc., Tokyo.

Translation © 2014 by Hachette Book Group, Inc.

Yen Press
Hachette Book Group
237 Park Avenue, New York, NY 10017

www.HachetteBookGroup.com
www.YenPress.com

Yen Press is an imprint of Hachette Book Group, Inc. The Yen Press name and logo are trademarks of Hachette Book Group, Inc.

First Yen Press Edition: June 2014

ISBN: 978-0-316-28618-3

10 9 8 7 6 5 4 3 2 1

BVG

Printed in the United States of America

Are You Alice?
5
CONTENTS!

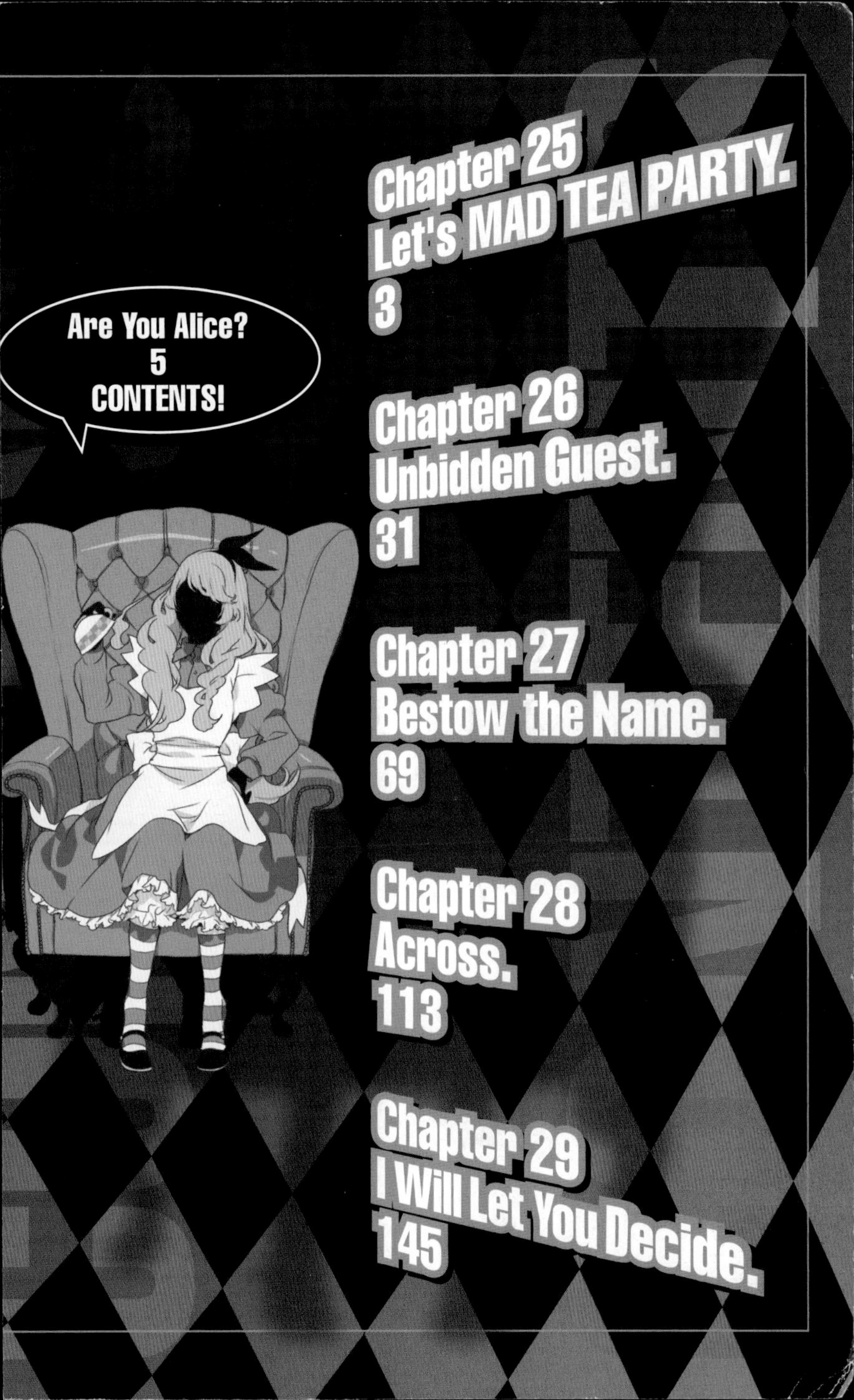

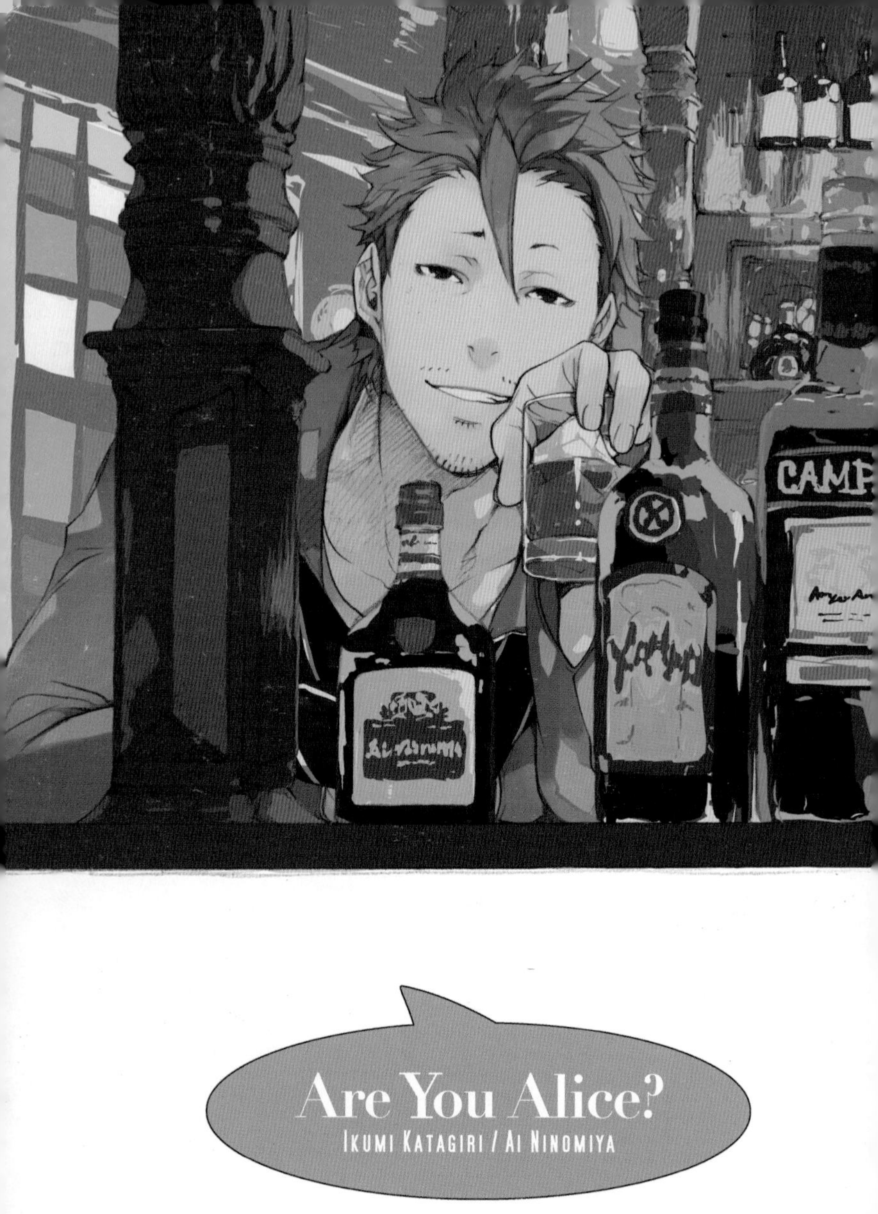
CAMP

Are You Alice?

IKUMI KATAGIRI / AI NINOMIYA